Frommer's

ATHENS
AND THE
GREEK ISLANDS

By Stephen Brewer

FROMMER'S STAR RATINGS SYSTEM

Every hotel, restaurant, and attraction listed in this guide has been ranked for quality and value. Here's what the stars mean:

★ Recommended
★★ Highly Recommended
★★★ A must! Don't miss!

AN IMPORTANT NOTE

A statue of Socrates, outside the University of Athens' neoclassical Academy building (p. 92).

CONTENTS

One of the famous Caryatid columns atop Athens' Acropolis (p. 74).

A LOOK AT ATHENS & THE GREEK ISLANDS

Ah, Greece. This Mediterranean country is one of the world's most seductive travel destinations, and there are so many ways to fall under its spell. Greece excels at ecstatic experiences—eternity viewed from the Acropolis heights, the stunning approach to Santorini's cliff-ringed harbor, the rugged walls of Crete's Samaria Gorge—but ultimately it wins your heart with more intimate moments: wildflowers blooming amid toppled marble columns, a Byzantine icon gleaming in a shadowy church, a donkey toiling up a steep hill, an elderly woman embroidering patterns that her village has stitched for centuries. Let our writer Stephen Brewer help you dig beneath the Zorba the Greek and Mamma Mia clichés, to explore Greece's cultural heritage in all its richness.

The clifftop village of Ia (also known as Oia, see p. 161), on the northwest edge of the island of Santorini, is a prime viewpoint for spectacular sunsets.

A sight for the ages: Athen's ancient "high city," the Acropolis (p. 74). The perfectly proportioned Parthenon, temple of the city's patron goddess Athena, is considered one of the planet's most important cultural monuments (which is why you may see renovation work going on when you visit).

While replica sculptures battle the elements on the Acropolis itself, their priceless originals are conserved and displayed downhill at the state-of-the-art Acropolis Museum (p. 78). Picture windows tie it all together with sweeping views of the sacred hilltop.

A traditional organ grinder plies his ages-old trade on an upscale shopping street in downtown Athens.

Outside Greece's Parliament (p. 84), soldiers of the elite Presidential Guard parade in colorful 19th-century uniforms.

Both Socrates and St. Paul discoursed atop the granite outcropping of the Areopagus Hill (p. 79); today, visitors and Athenians gather for stellar views across Athens in all directions.

Climbing the slopes of the Acropolis hill, the atmospheric Plaka neighborhood (p. 86) is a maze of medieval lanes lined with charming—if touristic—restaurants, shops, and cafes.

Trendy nightspots have revitalized the once-derelict Psyrri neighborhood (p. 90).

From much of Athens, you need only look up to spot the Acropolis, especially dramatic at night.

Completed in 1893, the ribbon-like Corinth Canal slices through high stone walls, dividing the Peloponnese from the rest of the Greek mainland.

Charioteer helmets are among the evocative relics displayed at Olympia (p. 123), where the first Olympic Games were held in 776 B.C.

The theater at Epidaurus (p. 123), from the 5th-century B.C. and still used for productions, has such perfect acoustics that a whisper on stage can be heard from the very top row of the tiered stone seating.

On see-and-be-seen Mykonos (p. 137), the most popular place for a pre-dinner drink is Little Venice, on the west side of the old town, where bars in old sea captains' mansions hang over the water's edge.

An essential day trip from Mykonos is the uninhabited isle of Delos (p. 149), legendary birthplace of Apollo. Among its haunting ruins, these marble lions spring from a terrace on the shores of the Sacred Lake.

Mykonos's adopted mascot, Petros the pelican, took shelter from a storm here in the 1950s and stayed for 30 years. His successors continue to charm visitors.

Sailing into Santorini's spectacular cliff-ringed bay (p. 152)—which is actually the flooded caldera of a collapsed volcano—is one of the great Greek experiences.

Donkeys gamely haul tourists up the steep path from the harbor to Fira (p. 160), Santorini's clifftop capital. To do as the locals do, take the cable car instead—the trip is quicker and the views just as amazing.

At Santorini's south end, beaches are carpeted with black and red volcanic sand. Red Beach is picturesquely snuggled below rugged lava cliffs near the millennia-old settlement of Akrotiri (p. 158).

A Byzantine icon from one of the many Orthodox churches on Paros (p. 181), with its rich Venetian-Ottoman heritage and world-famous marble.

The traditional craft of pottery is still alive on Naxos (p. 171), known for its golden beaches, verdant landscapes, and scenic villages, like quiet mountainside Apiranthos.

Dinner comes fresh from the sea in the old fishing harbor of Ammoudi (p. 161), just below Ia town on Santorini.

Tucked onto the narrow alleyways of Mykonos' Hora town—laid out in a maze to confuse long-ago pirates—casual bars and cafes lure vacationers.

CRETE

A port for a colorful fishing fleet, the Old Harbor in Iraklion (p. 189)—capital of Crete, and Greece's fifth-largest city—preserves a sense of the city's past, especially its 4 centuries under Venetian rule.

Thatched umbrellas shade sun-worshippers on the white sands at popular Vai beach (p. 224), at Crete's eastern tip, famous for its vast forest of Cretan date palms.

The ancient Cretan palace at Knossos (p. 196) was partly reconstructed and painted in vibrant colors in the early 20th century—a sacrilege to purists, but for many visitors a rich re-creation of Minoan life.

A popular day trip from Chania or Rethymnon is the trek through the Samaria Gorge (p. 219), where an incredibly scenic 15km (9-mile) trail leads through unspoiled landscapes to the sea.

Above low-key Matala beach (p. 200), on Crete's south coast, a seaside bluff is riddled with caves where Roman soldiers once encamped and 1960s hippies hung out.

Chania (p. 208), on the northwest coast of Crete, is one of Greece's most beautiful cities, with a colorful Venetian harbor, built to bolster Venice's power in the southern Mediterranean.

At the fish market in Iraklion, a vendor shows off spiny lobsters, a prized local delicacy.

Legend claims that the Psychro Cave (p. 199), a popular site on the Lasithi Plateau, was the birthplace of Zeus.

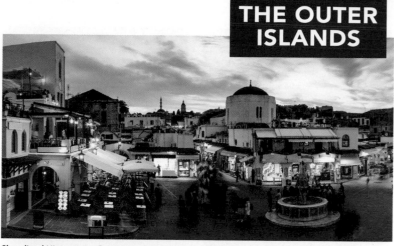

Shop-lined Hippocrates Square is a hive of activity in old Rhodes Town (p. 227). Once the stronghold of Crusader knights, the walled medieval quarter is the heart of the largest city in the Dodecanese islands.

A mosaic portrays Aesculapius, the god of medicine, greeting the great Greek physician Hippocrates, who founded the world's first medical school on his native Kos (p. 245). Today, visitors come to the island in search not of cures but of golden-sand beaches.

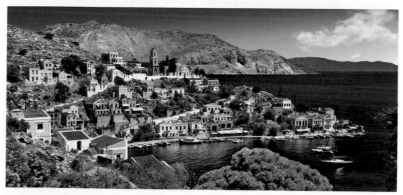

Pastel-colored houses line the horseshoe-shaped harbor of Yialos, the main town of the tiny, rugged island of Symi (p. 241), rightfully called "the jewel of the Dodecanese."

The endangered Mediterranean monk is protected in a National Marine Park, encompassing the pristine waters around the Sporades island of Alonissos (p. 270).

Beautiful pine-clad Skopelos (p. 265) has some 360 churches, many built by grateful islanders after surviving attacks by the Ottoman pirate Barbarossa.

Charming, unspoiled Skyros (p. 274) is a good place to buy local crafts, especially embroidery and ceramics, decorated with traditional folk designs.

An excursion boat ties up at scenic Lalaria Beach, one of more than 50 beaches ringing Skiathos (p. 257), the Sporades' most popular resort island.

THE BEST OF ATHENS & THE GREEK ISLANDS

The Acropolis, the theater at Epidaurus, the palace at Knossos—Greece's ancient wonders are legendary, enough in themselves to lure you to Athens and environs. Equally compelling is all that blue sky, that warm blue sea, and natural beauty that at times can seem almost mystical, as it does when looking into Santorini's caldera. But there's also so much else: The beaches, some of the world's most hedonistic places to stay, simple tavernas where a meal on the terrace can seem like the feast of a lifetime. Just the experience of sitting, watching, and taking it all in can be profound. To help you enjoy your time in Greece to the fullest, here's what we consider to be the best of the best.

THE best GREEK TRAVEL EXPERIENCES

- **Enjoy a taverna meal under the stars:** You can experience this pleasure anywhere in Greece, of course—maybe on an island with the sea in view, or in the countryside, with the scent of pine in the air, or even in busy, noisy Athens. The food is usually simple but fresh and delicious, the pace is almost always easygoing, and the spectacle of life buzzing around you is endlessly entertaining, like being in the theater. See "Where to Eat" sections throughout chapters 4 through 9.
- **Gasp at the Santorini caldera:** The cliffs glimmer in transcendent light, white villages look like a dusting of snow on the cliff tops, and boats sailing in and out of the harbor far below appear almost Homeric. Come sunset, one of Greece's most photogenic spectacles is a reliable show on this island where the sky is usually cloudless. See p. 154.
- **Gaze at the Acropolis, Athens:** You don't have to go out of your way to find a vantage point. The best approach is to let the sight take you unawares—let it catch you by surprise as you look up

from a narrow side street or traffic-choked square. In fact, the more mundane the surroundings from which you catch a glimpse of the timeless pediments and columns, the more remarkable this ancient wonder seems. One prime spot is the Grand Promenade; even Athenians get a thrill every time they follow this walkway around the base of the Acropolis Hill past some of the greatest monuments of antiquity. Think of the experience as time travel. See p. 74.

o **Get into the rhythms of Lalaria Beach, Skiathos:** Greece's beaches are among the most beautiful in the world, but nothing quite prepares you for the approach to this almost mystical cove in the Sporades archipelago. At first you won't quite know what that murmur is. Then you slowly become accustomed to the murmurous rumble of white marble stones rolling back and forth in the surf, amplified by sea cliffs dappled by the play of sun and turquoise water. See p. 264.

o **Descend onto the Lasithi Plateau, Crete:** First the road climbs and climbs; then suddenly you reach the summit of the pass and at your feet spreads a high haven of orchards and fields, studded with windmills and protected by a tidy ring of mountains. Your explorations can include a cave that's one of the alleged birthplaces of Zeus—it's not hard to believe a god would choose to be born up here, where the biggest pleasure is simply experiencing a slice of rural Cretan life. See p. 198.

o **Catch your first glimpse of Skyros Town, Skyros:** This hilltop *hora* appears to defy gravity—at first sight the white houses clinging to a rocky mount high above the coastal plain look like a mirage. Make the ascent to the upper town, where a walk along the steep, narrow lanes only heightens the illusion. See p. 274.

o **Succumb to the simple charms of Mykonos:** For all its glitz and glamour, worldly Mykonos shows off its best side in Hora, where wooden balconies hang from square white houses, outdoor staircases are lined with pots of geraniums, and oleander and hibiscus scent the air. Most picturesque of all is the Little Venice quarter, where the island's sea captains built their homes so close to the water's edge that waves wash against the lower floors. See p. 137.

best ENCOUNTERS WITH THE ANCIENT GREEKS

o **Envision life as it once was in the Agora:** Athens has no shortage of ancient ruins, but those of the Agora, the marketplace and social center of the ancient city, might be the most evocative. Even though most of the shops and stoas have been reduced to rubble, just enough remains (including the best-preserved Greek temple in the world and an ancient clock tower and weather station) to give you an idea of what the place must have been like when Socrates sat with his students on shady porticos and vendors hawked spices and oils. See p. 86.

o **Encounter the gods on Delos:** One of the most sacred places for ancient Greeks still inspires, even in jumbled ruin. As you walk among temples and skirt the shores of the sacred lake, you'll get a sense of what a trip to this island—the central point of the Cyclades—might have meant to a pilgrim of long ago. See p. 149.

o **Look out to sea from the Temple of Poseidon:** You only have to make the pleasant trip down the Attic coast to Sounion to appreciate how ancient Greeks understood the concept that location is everything. It's easy to imagine how the sight of the majestic temple warmed the hearts of sailors returning to Athens after months at sea; you can even recreate the experience with a swim from the rocks below the site. See p. 99.

o **Walk beneath the pines in Olympia:** The superheroes who bring most visitors to Olympia are not gods and artists but ancient athletes. Remnants of the city's games, inaugurated in 776 B.C., are copious; the stadium, gymnasium, training hall, and dormitories are scattered around the foot of the Kronion Hill. So vivid is the experience that you wouldn't be completely shocked to come upon a naked *pankration* competitor rubbing himself down with olive oil. See p. 123.

o **Gaze from the Acrocorinth:** Atop one of the world's most remarkable fortresses, high above the isthmus and the Corinth Plain, you seem to be sharing time and space with the Greek and Roman inhabitants of one of the most cosmopolitan cities in the ancient world. In those less polluted days, they had an even more far-reaching view—all the way to the gleaming columns of the Acropolis in Athens. See p. 115.

o **Consult the oracle at Delphi:** No other ancient site is quite as mysterious and alluring as this sanctuary to Apollo, nestled amid olive groves high above the Gulf of Corinth on the flanks of Mount Parnassus. It's easy to see why the spot was so transporting for the ancients, who flocked here to seek the enigmatic counsel of Apollo. See p. 127.

o **Take a bow in the theater at Epidaurus:** Even the inevitable crop of stage-struck wannabes belting out show tunes doesn't detract from the thrill of standing on the spot where ancient actors performed the Greek classics when they were new. The 55 tiers of limestone seats remain much as they were, and acoustics are so sharp that a stage whisper can be heard at the top of the house. See p. 122.

o **Admire ancient marbles on Paros:** Parian marble has a way of catching your gaze and not letting go. After all, the most famous statue in the world, the *Venus de Milo,* is sculpted from the translucently white and luminescent stone quarried on this island in the Cyclades. On the back lanes of Parikia you may also be intrigued by a much less formal display: Bits and pieces of columns and pediments, debris from ancient temples, are wedged willy-nilly into the walls of the 13th-century Venetian kastro, a head-spinning glimpse into civilizations past. See p. 178.

1

GREECE'S best MUSEUM MOMENTS

o **Become mesmerized in ancient storytelling in the Acropolis Museum:** More than any other ancient pieces, the Parthenon friezes' fragments of exquisitely carved marble capture snippets of good-natured divinity and humanity—in one, the goddess Athena Nike fastens her sandal (something you didn't think goddesses had to do). Priests, soldiers, and ordinary citizens parade across the marble strip, and you almost want to jump in and join the procession. See p. 78.

o **Lose track of time in Athens' National Archaeological Museum:** You don't have to be a classics scholar to realize you've stumbled into an embarrassment of riches here. There's no need to be methodical in your approach: Just wander and stop in front of the pieces that catch your eye—all those figures frozen in marble for eternity; all that gold, jewelry, and pottery. Irresistible favorites are the colorful frescoes that capture residents of the Minoan settlement of Akrotiri on Santorini going about everyday life as it was more than 3,500 years ago. See p. 93.

o **Regard the Minoan frescoes in the Archaeological Museum in Iraklion:** The athletes, dancers, and other subjects seem to reach across the millennia and touch us—so palpably you can understand why a modern French archaeologist looked at a 4,000-year-old scene of flounce-skirted court ladies and exclaimed, "Les Parisiennes!," giving the fresco its modern nickname. See p. 194.

o **Get ready for some frieze frenzy at the Archaeological Museum on Paros:** The carved Parthenon scenes in Athens aren't the only famous marble carvings in Greece. At the Archaeological Museum in Parikia, a fragment of the Parian Chronicle captures a march of Alexander the Great and other scenes from Greece's distant past. Another frieze nearby portrays the poet Archilochus, a 7th-century-B.C. master of the bon mot who famously sniped "'tis thy friends that make thee choke with rage." See p. 181.

o **Admire the figures in the Museum of Cycladic Art:** It's hard to distinguish the smooth, oblong, elongated figures from the modern pieces of Henry Moore, Picasso, and Modigliani they've inspired. More than 300 of these magnificent, 3,500-year-old masterworks are housed in this Athens museum's light-filled modern galleries. Their timelessness is haunting. See p. 95.

GREECE'S best TOWN & VILLAGE ADVENTURES

o **Meander into Anafiotika:** The most charming neighborhood in Athens is not posh or trendy. Charming, overused as the word is, really does apply here. The lower slopes of the Acropolis just above the Plaka were settled by craftsmen from the island of Anafi who came to Athens in the mid–19th century to work on the new buildings transforming the capital; they recreated their homeland with stepped streets and white cubical houses. Blue shutters, balconies with bougainvillea cascading over the railings, little blue domed chapels, the works—you'll feel like you've been whisked off to a Cycladic island. See p. 87.

o **Wander around Rhodes's Old Town:** Ancient, crusaders knights, Italian nobles, Ottoman lords, Italian aristocrats—who hasn't left their mark on what's arguably the most continuously inhabited medieval town in Europe? Behind the circuit of massive town walls is a maze of lanes that present a delight at every turn—beautiful mosques, fountains burbling in quiet squares, bright pink flowers spilling over balconies. See p. 227.

o **Take in the Venetian Harbor in Chania:** Find a spot on the western side of the harbor in this Cretan port city—maybe the terrace of the Firkas, the waterside fortress the Venetians built—and take in the view. The shimmering sea, a lighthouse, and waterside palaces are rendered even more exotic by the presence of mosques and minarets the Turks left behind. See p. 214.

o **Explore the Tragaea villages, Naxos:** Mazes of white houses interspersed with little chapels appear on pine-clad hillsides, Venetian towers cling to rocky spires, and boulders are strewn across green valleys carpeted with olive groves and lemon orchards. The highest and most noble village is Apiranthos, where streets are paved in marble and the houses are made of rough, gray stone hewn from the mountain. See p. 175.

GREECE'S best SEASIDE ESCAPES

o **Cruise along the southwestern coast of Crete:** Even on a public ferry, you will feel like Odysseus or another intrepid explorer as you chug past the mouths of mountain gorges, groves of cypress, hidden coves, and, every so often, a white-clad village tucked far away from the modern world. See p. 216.

o **Linger over lunch at Agios Sostis, Mykonos:** Paradise and Super Paradise are the island's famous beaches, but Agios Sostis's crescent of sand is much more paradisiacal—and coming upon such a tranquil spot on an island as famously boisterous as Mykonos is all the more satisfying. The water is warm, the sands are soft, and a lunch of grilled fish or pork is served beneath a flowering vine at a simple beachside taverna. See p. 142.

o **Soak in a hot spring at Bros Therma, Kos:** For one of Greece's most relaxing and memorable beach experiences, head to Bros Therma on the Dodecanese island of Kos, where sulfurous water bubbles to the surface of a natural, boulder-enclosed pool on the beach. Soak up therapeutic benefits—treatment of rheumatism and arthritis, among other ailments—then plunge into the cooler sea. See p. 251.

o **Feel the golden sands between your toes on Koukounaries Beach, Skiathos:** The perfect crescent backed by pines is a Greek-isle fantasy. Your surfside stroll will not be a solitary experience, but a short walk through shady, sandy-floored groves will deliver you to a string of quieter sands on the Mandraki Peninsula of this popular Sporades island. See p. 264.

o **Take a stroll on the Nafplion Promenade:** It's hard to believe that this beautiful, busy Peloponnesian town—a much fought-over prize for Turks and Venetians—is only a few steps behind you as you make your way along the Gulf of Argos, with the blue water shimmering and gentle waves crashing onto the rocks below you. At the end of the walk you can dip into the sea beneath the Acronafplia Fortress at Arvanitia—one of the most beautiful town beaches anywhere. See p. 119.

o **See the sea through the Portara, Naxos:** The great unfinished ancient temple doorway may lead to nowhere, but it beautifully frames the blue sea and the heights of Naxos Town's Venetian Kastro towering against the blue sky. You almost want to believe the legend that the massive marble portal was meant to be the entrance to the palace that the god Dionysus built for his lover, Ariadne. Taking a swim here is truly a divine experience. See p. 174.

o **Sail into Symi harbor:** A beautiful, broad, horseshoe-shaped expanse of blue sea is lined with pastel-colored houses and gracious neoclassical mansions from this Dodecanese island's shipbuilding and sponge-fishing heydays. The photogenic assemblage is all the more striking because the rest of the little island is rough and rugged, though with so many little chapels and remote monasteries that islanders claim you can worship in a different sanctuary every day of the year. See p. 241.

GREECE'S most FUN FAMILY OUTINGS

o **Browse the Central Market, Athens:** Big, noisy, smelly, and fragrant, this market's indoor and outdoor stalls bring together all the food of Greece, from exotic denizens of the deep to country cheeses and swinging meat carcasses. Just looking at all these riches is one of the city's top culinary experiences. Your kids might never settle again for that boring old stuff you pack in their school lunches. See p. 93.

o **Sail through the National Marine Park of Alonnisos Northern Sporades:** Dolphins will escort your cruise through pristine waters off an archipelago that is home to creatures as diverse as the shy Mediterranean monk seal and the mythical Cyclops—the cave where the one-eyed monster was blinded by Odysseus, according to Homer, is in the park. A swim in a secluded cove tops off the experience. See p. 270.

o **Romp in Syntagma Square, Nafplion:** No matter what's happening in the world, life seems pretty good from a table on this café-lined, tree-shaded expanse at the heart of the Old Town. Nafpliots and their visitors linger for hours, and kids have free rein to run and jump across the smooth marble paving stones. No one complains when it comes time to leave, because no matter where you're going, the only way out is along similarly enticing lanes. See p. 83.

o **Squeeze into Spilia Skotini (Dark Cave), Skiathos:** Even in the company of a boatload of camera-clicking fellow explorers, you and your young companions may feel an almost Robinson Crusoe-like sense of discovery as you float into this spectacular sea grotto. The splash of waves, the shimmer of the sea, and the luster of the light all conspire to transport everyone aboard into a watery fantasy world. See p. 264.

o **Hike the Samaria Gorge:** Yes, it will seem that you share the trail with just about every other traveler of all ages on the planet, but finding yourself in canyons only 3m (10 ft.) wide and 600m (1,969 ft.) deep is a profound experience nonetheless. It's all the more exhilarating when an eagle soars overhead and a kri-kri, the shy, endangered Cretan wild goat, makes a rare appearance. See p. 219.

o **See Athens from atop Mount Lycabettus:** Of the many heights in the capital, this craggy, pine-covered rise—Athens's highest hill—provides the best vantage point. You don't have to be a kid to think the ride up on the Teleferik (funicular) is a heck of a lot of fun, and the walk back down into Kolonaki is an invigorating adventure. You'll surely get a kick out of being so high above Athens, catching the breeze, and seeing the spectacle of the city spreading out at your feet and the Aegean glistening in the distance. See p. 96.

most TRANSPORTING RELIGIOUS MOMENTS IN GREECE

o **Walk down to the sea at Moni Gouverneto, Crete:** Greece's largest island is generously graced with beautiful monasteries, but this one on the Akrotiri Peninsula adds a bit of a thrill—a walk that begins in a tranquil courtyard and descends through a ravine etched with millennia-old hermitages to an isolated cove where a swim seems almost like a ritualistic plunge. See p. 215.

o **Climb Profitis Elias o Pilos, Sifnos:** It's quite a trek up the 850m-tall (2,789-ft.) mountain, the highest on this Cycladean island, to the isolated monastery at the summit. You'll understand the meaning of "Pilos," or "high one." A monk may be on hand to offer a glass of ice-cold water, and the views seem to extend across the entire Aegean Sea. See p. 162.

o **Savor the spiritual aura of the Cave of the Apocalypse, Patmos:** In the cave hermitage of St. John the Divine, you'll be surrounded by many icons, the very stone that served as the saintly pillow, and a sense of holiness. You might even hear "a great voice, as of a trumpet" that rang through a cleft in the overhang and delivered the Book of the Apocalypse, or Revelation. See p. 254.

○ **Count church domes from the Kastro in Skopelos Town, Skopelos:** In this Sporades island capital—one of the most appealing towns in Greece—123 churches punctuate the lanes that climb the hillside. The sight of so many blue domes will most likely inspire you to get to your feet and start exploring. See p. 263.

○ **Chance upon Kapnikarea Church, Athens:** This little Byzantine gem sits right in the middle of busy, shop-lined Ermou Street, on the site of an ancient temple to Athena and incorporating Roman columns from the Forum. Just setting eyes on the old stones and carvings immediately whisks you away from the contemporary buzz to a different time and place. See p. 87.

○ **Find all the doors to the Church of the Hundred Doors, Paros:** One of the oldest churches in the world is also, from the moment you step through the gates into the lemon-scented courtyard, one of the most other worldly, steeped in legend. Founded in the 4th century, the landmark is filled with frescoes, icons, and even reminders of a famous murder. See p. 181.

THE best LUXURY RETREATS IN GREECE

○ **Aqua Blu, Kos:** A sensational pool terrace merges seamlessly with handsome lounges, while guest rooms are design statements that combine contemporary chic with comfort, intimacy, and elegance. Guests are pampered with sea views, terraces, and such perks as fireplaces and private pools in some rooms and suites. Somehow the design-magazine-worthy surroundings don't dampen the staff's down-to-earth hospitality. See p. 247.

○ **Atrium Hotel, Skiathos:** Beautiful and comfortable accommodations that range from doubles to lavish maisonettes tumble down a pine-clad hillside above one of the island's nicest beaches, commanding endless sea views from multiple terraces and outdoor living spaces. Wood and warm stone are accented with antiques and island-style furnishings, all carefully chosen by the architect-family that built and still runs this stunning retreat. See p. 260.

○ **Cavo Tagoo, Mykonos:** Huge rooms and suites, set amid beautiful gardens, are filled with high-tech gadgetry, gorgeous handcrafted furnishings, sunken tubs, and other soothing comforts. Most rooms have sea-facing terraces, many with private pools and built-in divans and dining tables surrounded by exotic plantings. All in all, it provides a thoroughly decadent al fresco island experience. See p. 140.

○ **Elounda Mare, Crete:** At this low-key, intimate, and idyllic retreat—one of Europe's truly great getaways—swanky bungalows and other handsome guest quarters are tucked into verdant seaside gardens. All are furnished elegantly in traditional Cretan style, and expansive views extend over the Gulf of Elounda. A sandy beach and all sorts of shady seaside nooks are among many, many amenities. See p. 221.

○ **Esperas, Santorini:** You'll feel like a cliff dweller at this welcoming, intimate enclave of traditional houses teetering on the edge of the caldera in Ia. This enchanted perch seems like a world unto itself, soaking in stupendous views from the private terraces, beautiful pool and terrace, and comfortable and tasteful accommodations filled with traditional island furnishings. See p. 155.

o **Melenos Lindos Hotel, Lindos, Rhodes:** An authentically Lindian-style villa is a work of art, where hand-painted tiles, local antiques, handcrafted lamps, and weavings provide the backdrop for an almost otherworldly experience on a pine-scented hillside. Huge Lydian beds make anyone feel like a reclining pasha, while rooms open to large, nicely furnished, terraces that are embellished with statuary and architectural fragments and look out to an idyllic cove. See p. 234.

o **Petra Hotel and Apartments, Patmos:** The Stergiou family has created a luxurious haven on a hillside above Grikos Bay, lavishing personal attention to guests in spacious, beautifully appointed rooms and one- and two-bedroom suites that exude island style. Most quarters have balconies or open to lavish terraces furnished with pillowed divans for some Greek-island-style lounging. The main veranda is a gracious living space, a pool glistens off to one side, and sandy Grikos beach is just at the bottom of the lane. See p. 253.

o **St. George Lycabettus Hotel, Athens:** Large, nicely decorated guest rooms (each floor has a different theme, from art nouveau to minimalism) and a beautiful rooftop pool do justice to a wonderful location the pine-scented slopes of Lycabettus hill just above the designer-boutique-lined streets of Kolonaki. The choicest quarters have views of the Acropolis. See p. 68.

o **Spirit of the Knights, Rhodes City:** Five luxurious suites and a cozily medieval chamber are tucked away in a beautifully restored Ottoman house in the quietest part of Old Rhodes Town. Hand painted ceilings, original beams, Ottoman stained glass, marble baths, rich carpets and textiles, and other exquisite details embellish the exotic surroundings, while a beautiful courtyard is cooled by a splashing fountain. See p. 230.

o **Villa Marandi, Naxos:** A stone-and-stucco villa set in seaside gardens surrounding a large pool fulfills just about anyone's fantasy of a Greek-island getaway. Beautifully designed and maintained rooms are large, stylish, and supremely comfortable; all have large, well-furnished terraces, most with sea views. A private strip of beach lies at the end of the garden path, and an expert staff serves cocktails and inspired Mediterranean-style meals on a beautiful poolside terrace. See p. 172.

THE most affordable GREEK GETAWAYS

o **Carbonaki Hotel, Mykonos:** On Greece's most expensive island, there's no need to break the bank or sacrifice style and comfort. Just about all of these simply furnished but stylish rooms surround a beautiful, multilevel courtyard garden with a plunge pool, ensuring quiet (especially welcome at night, when late-night revelers make their way home along the little lane out front). See p. 141.

o **Fresh Hotel, Athens:** Soothing minimalist design, along with a rooftop pool, sun deck, and Zen-like spa, put a fresh face on the capital's gritty Omonia neighborhood. The youthful staff is helpful, and the laid-back ambiance is soothing. Among many modern amenities in the stylish, colorful rooms are window blinds that can be controlled from the beds—perfect for night owls not ready to face the morning sun. See p. 68.

o **Hotel Perivoli, Nafplion:** A hillside planted with citrus and olive groves is a magical setting for this smart, comfortable little Peloponnese resort where handsome rooms all open to terraces and balconies facing a pool and, glistening in the distance, the Gulf of Argos. See p. 111.

o **Kalimera Archanes Village, Crete:** Fresh whitewash and lots of blooming flowerboxes give Archanes' lively lanes and squares of neoclassical houses an usually tidy appearance. Tucked away among them in a lush walled garden are four 19th-century, meticulously restored stone houses, tastefully and traditionally furnished and accented with stone and beams. See p. 193.

o **Kapsaliana Village Hotel, Crete:** A rustic hamlet of honey-colored stone in hilly countryside above Rethymnon was once part the holdings of the Arkadi monastery; it has now been shaped into a distinctive and relaxing country getaway. Village houses along the old lanes have been redone with designer flair, with contemporary furnishings in terraced guest rooms offset by stone walls, arches, and wood beams. See p. 202.

o **Marco Polo Mansion, Rhodes City:** A 15th-century Ottoman mansion set in a lush garden is positively transcending. Each room is distinctive—one was a harem, another a hamam, another is lined with kilims—and all are decorated in deep hues that show off low-lying couches and stunning antiques. Excellent meals are served in the garden; non-guests are welcome to share in one of the island's nicest dining experiences. See p. 231.

o **Medieval Inn, Rhodes City:** No medieval gloom and doom here: This whitewashed old house surrounding a flower-filled courtyard is full of bright colors, while rooms are small and fairly basic but an excellent value given the comfort and ambiance and such amenities as a sunny roof terrace that invites long hours of lounging. See p. 232.

GREECE'S best PLACES TO EAT

o **Avli, Rethymnon, Crete:** This veritable temple to Cretan cuisine introduces diners to the freshest island ingredients. Fish and lamb, of course, appear in many different guises, as do mountain greens and other fresh vegetables, all served in a delightfully romantic garden, an arched dining room, and on a narrow lane out front. High-style accommodations, where Asian pieces and contemporary pieces are set against stone walls and wood beams, surround the restaurant garden and are tucked into nearby houses. See p. 203.

o **Benetos Restaurant, Patmos:** Benetos Matthaiou and his American wife, Susan, make it their business to deliver one of this Dodecanese island's nicest dining experiences, on the terrace of a Tuscan-style villa at the edge of the sea. Fresh ingredients come from gardens on the property and nearby waters and show up in dishes such as shrimp in phyllo and fresh fish baked in a citrus sauce or a simple arugula salad with shaved Parmesan. See p. 253.

o **Kronio, Lasithi Plateau:** This cozy and welcoming establishment serves the finest food on Crete's Lasithi Plateau, from thick lamb stews to homemade bread and cheese-stuffed pies. Service is so warm and welcoming that you may want to settle in for awhile—and you may, in nicely appointed rooms in the proprietors' countryside home, where a glistening swimming pool is among the comforts. See p. 193.

o **Lithos, Naxos:** A stylishly contemporary dining room tucked far away from the clamor of the waterfront beneath the walls of the Kastro is a quiet refuge of glistening white walls and floors accented with bright colors. These surroundings are as fresh as the kitchen's simple yet satisfying creations, a refreshing change from standard taverna fare. See p. 173.

o **Metaxy Mas, Santorini:** An out-of-the-way location in the countryside doesn't seem to deter eager diners, who pack into this stone-walled dining room and terrace from noon until the wee hours. The draws on this sophisticated island? Simple time-honored dishes made with the freshest ingredients. See p. 157.

o **Selene, Santorini:** This elegant retreat, occupying an old manor house in Pyrgos, consistently tops best-in-Greece lists and works its magic from the moment you step into the handsome dining room or onto the candlelit terrace overlooking vineyards and the distant sea. Dishes such as octopus with smoked eggplant, fava balls with capers, and herb-encrusted rabbit make creative use of local ingredients and are the favorites of haute-cuisine magazines. See p. 157.

o **Taverna Sklithiri, Skiathos:** If you're not swept away by the setting—a flowery terrace right on a golden beach with a turquoise sea almost lapping up against the tables—you really don't belong on a Greek island. Off the grill comes, of course, the freshest fish, along with simply prepared vegetables and manner of other seafood, including plump mussels roasted in white wine. See p. 262.

o **The Well of the Turk, Chania, Crete:** You will find your way to this all-but-hidden restaurant at the heart of the old Turkish quarter south of the Venetian Harbor by keeping your eye on the minaret, and asking for directions along the way. An enticing selection of Greek and Middle Eastern appetizers, juicy lamb dishes, meatballs mixed with eggplant, and other specialties are served on the ground floor of a Turkish house and in a lovely courtyard. See p. 211.

o **To Maereo, Mykonos:** You'll be remembering this delightful spot on a quiet lane when winter sets in back home—simple and atmospheric, serving good traditional fare at reasonable prices. Country sausage, meatballs, zucchini fritters, and other delicious fare fill the tempting, ever-changing menu, presented in a welcoming room and at a few tables in front. See p. 143.

GREECE IN CONTEXT

2

W hile most Greeks are besotted with all that is new—a common greeting is *Ti nea?* (What's new?)—most are also fiercely proud of those long-time attractions that enthrall visitors: Greece's mind-boggling physical beauty and its glorious past. Certainly, for most of us, to leave Greece without seeing Athens's Acropolis or Delphi, the most beautiful ancient site in all Greece, would be, as Aeschylus himself might have said, tragic. As for Greece's physical beauty, a trip into the Peloponnese or to Santorini or just about any other island will have you spouting clichés. Palamas, the poet who wrote the words to the Olympic Hymn, was reduced to saying of his homeland, "Here, sky is everywhere."

Of course, Palamas was right: The Greek sky, the Greek light, the Greek sea all deserve their fame. This is especially obvious on the islands. Greece has anywhere from 1,200 to about 6,000 islands (the count depends on what you call an island, an islet, or a large rock). In any event, almost all of the approximately 200 inhabited islands are ready and waiting to welcome visitors. On the islands and on the mainland, throughout the countryside, picture-postcard scenes are around every corner. Shepherds still urge flocks of goats and sheep along mountain slopes, and fishermen still mend nets by their caiques.

If this sounds romantic and enticing, it is. But remember that the Greek love of the new includes a startling ability to adjust to the unexpected. Everything—absolutely everything—in Greece is subject to change. It's not by accident that the most Greek of all remarks is, *"Etsi einai e zoe,"* which literally means "That's life," but might better be translated as "Whatchya gonna do?" With luck, you'll learn the Greek shrug, and come to accept—even enjoy—the unpredictable as an essential part of life in Greece.

Recently, the unpredictable has become almost the only thing that is predictable in Greece. Massive debts and the government's unpopular attempts to restructure the economy, involving tax hikes and salary and pension reductions, have led to strikes and demonstrations. Serious questions remain as to how Greece will solve its problems. Greeks suffer gravely, with runaway unemployment and the crushing burden of harsh austerity measures. Tourists are affected, too, though to a much lesser degree, as strikes continue to close museums and archaeological sites and disrupt travel. You will probably notice that most Greeks are deeply concerned about the future, yet they remain warm and hospitable to visitors—and convinced they will weather this storm as they have weathered so many others since the dawn of history.

A LOOK AT THE PAST

Greece has a long history, indeed. Here is a brief introduction to some of the main periods in Greek history—though the nationalistic terms "Greece" and "Greek" are fairly modern concepts. Still, for millennia, the people who lived here regarded themselves as unified by a common language and many shared traditions and beliefs.

Ancient History

The history of Greece and its willful people is longer and more absorbing than a cursory look can convey. The earliest continuously occupied site was discovered at the Franchthi Cave in southeast Argolid, Peloponnese; evidence suggests the cavern was inhabited as early as 20,000 B.C.

The Ancient Greeks settled and traveled throughout the Mediterranean and along the Black Sea coast. Some of the oldest and most important civilizations in Europe are considered to be those of the **Cycladic** cultures (3200–2000 B.C.) that flourished on Santorini (also known as Thera) and nearby islands, and the **Minoan** people (3000–1400 B.C.) of Crete. While Cycladic architectural remains are sparse, at the National Archaeological Museum (p. 93) and in other collections you can see elegant Cycladic figurines, fashioned from island marble, that are startlingly modern. Their culture was succeeded by the Minoans, the regional strongmen in seafaring and trade, who traded around the Mediterranean, selling timber, building ships, and possibly even sailing as far as England to obtain metal. Outstanding displays of Minoan culture can be viewed at the palace of Knossos (p. 196) near Iraklion, Crete, and the Iraklion Archaeological Museum (p. 194). Around 1627 B.C, however, a volcano on Thera erupted, perhaps triggering a tsunami that destroyed settlements on Minoan Crete, 63 nautical miles away, and contributed to the civilization's decline.

The **Mycenaeans** (1600–1100 B.C.) flourished on the southern mainland, in the present-day Peloponnese. The extensive remains of Mycenae (p. 117), with its defense walls, palace, and enormous beehive tombs, demonstrates the architectural skill and political power of these people, while the National Archaeological Museum in Athens (p. 93) is a showcase for their famous gold. In the *Iliad,* Homer commemorates the expedition led by Mycenae's best known king, Agamemnon, to recapture the beautiful Helen. The *Iliad* ends with the fall of Troy to the Greeks; Mycenae's own decline seems to have begun not long after, and is sometimes blamed on the mysterious invaders known as the Dorians.

Greece

BULGARIA

Drama Xanthi **THRACE**

Kavala Komotini

Alexandroupolis *Sea of Marmara*

Thasos

Samothraki

Mt. Athos

Limnos

AEGEAN SEA

EUROPE

Alonissos Lesvos
SPORADES (Mitilini) **GREECE**

Skyros **NORTHEASTERN** **TURKEY**
AEGEAN ISLANDS

Kimi

EVVIA

Izmir

Karystos Hios

Andros

Samos

Sounion
Kea Tinos Ikaria

Siros Mykonos
Delos Patmos

Serifos Paros Naxos
Antiparos Donoussa Kalimnos

Sifnos
CYCLADES Kos

Milos Ios Amorgos

Folegandros
Simi

Anafi
DODECANESE

To Crete Santorini Rhodes
(approx. 60 miles
from mainland) *Sea of Crete*

Karpathos

After the decline of the Mycenaeans in mainland Greece, it seems that people began to live in fiercely independent city states, often ruled by powerful tyrants. This period saw the spread of trade, the invention of coinage, and the emergence of writing, as the Greek alphabet replaced Linear A, the ancient Minoan script, and Linear B, created by the Mycenaeans. While each city state had its own calendar, system of weights and measures, and important deities, when the Persians from adjacent Asia Minor invaded Greece in 490 and 480 B.C., many of the Greeks—led by Athens and Sparta—stood together and turned back the Persians.

The Classical Era

Brief and glorious, the **Classical era** lasted from the 5th century B.C. to the rise of Philip of Macedon, in the mid–4th century B.C. This is when Pericles led Athens and when the Parthenon—and nearly every other ancient Greek monument, statue, and vase most of us are familiar with—was created. These ancient Greeks made advances in the arts, sciences, philosophy, and politics. Five of the seven Ancient Wonders were built during the Classical era: the statue of Zeus in Olympia (destroyed); the Colossus of Rhodes (destroyed); the Mausoleum at Halicarnassus, now Bodrum, Turkey (dismantled, some bas reliefs in the U.K.); the Temple of Artemis at Ephesus (destroyed); and the onetime tallest building, the Lighthouse in Alexandria (destroyed).

While the **Spartans** were known for their austere and militaristic form of governance, **Athens** took a different course with democracy. These city-states fought each other in the Peloponnesian War (431–404 B.C.), but soon thereafter they united against the massive invading force of the Persians. First the Greeks won, at the **Battle of Marathon** (p. 96) in 490 B.C. Ten years later, at Thermopylae, the Persians won against a small army led by King Leonidas of Sparta. Finally the Athenians defeated the Persians in 480 B.C. at the Battle of Salamis, led by Themistocles, who fought and won the battle decisively at sea.

The Hellenistic Era

The cities were weakened and unable to stop Philip of Macedon when he moved south to conquer Greece. His son, Alexander, became king of Macedon in 338 B.C., when he was only 23, and soon marched from his base camp at Dion all the way to India, conquering everything in his path. Alexander died under mysterious circumstances (poison? too much wine?) on the way home in 334 B.C., leaving behind the vast empire that he had conquered but had not had time to organize and administer. Alexander's leading generals divided up his empire, and declared themselves not just rulers but, in many cases, divine rulers.

Alexander's conquests, which included much of Asia Minor and Egypt, made the Greek language the administrative and spoken language of much of the world. Within Greece itself, powerful new cities, such as Thessaloniki, were founded. Old cities, such as Athens, were revivified and ornamented with magnificent new civic buildings, such as the 2nd-century-B.C. **Stoa of Attalos** (p. 86), which contained shops and offices.

The Roman Conquest

Along with most of Europe, North Africa, and Asia Minor, Greece was ruled by Rome from the 2nd century B.C. to the 3rd century A.D. The Romans honored the Greeks for their literature and art, and a tour of Greece and perhaps a year studying in Athens was common for many well-born Roman youths. The Greeks participated in what has become known as the Pax Romana, the several centuries of general peace and calm in the Roman Empire.

The Byzantine Empire & Beyond

In 324 B.C., the Roman emperor Constantine the Great took control of the Roman Empire, moving the capital from Rome to the Greek city of **Byzantium** on the Bosporus. He renamed his capital Constantinople (Constantine's City) and in a bold move, reversed the prosecutions of Diocletian, making Christianity the religion of his vast empire. After more than 1,000 years, Constantinople finally fell on May 29, 1453, to the **Ottoman Turks.**

In the following centuries, Greece was ruled by a bewildering and often overlapping series of foreign powers: Venetians and Franks from the West, and Turks from the East. Many Greeks left for western Europe and brought ancient Greek texts with them, influencing the Renaissance. Those who remained became a subject people. The phrase "under the Turkish yolk for 400 years" became a common refrain.

Independence & a United Greece

Greece's modern era follows its **War of Independence,** which began in 1821, when the bishop at the Monastery of Agia Lavra, Peloponnese, raised the flag of revolt and called for freedom or death. The ideals of Greece also captured the imagination of the Romantics in Western Europe; Lord George Gordon Byron (see box, p. 91) and others traveled to Greece to take up the fight. In 1827, combined forces of Britain, France, and Russia crushed the Ottoman and Egyptian naval forces at the **Battle of Navarino** in the Peloponnese and granted Greece autonomy under an appointed monarchy. Otto, the 17-year-old son of King Ludwig of Bavaria, became united Greece's first king.

By the end of the 19th century, Greece's capital was in Athens, but most of today's country was still held by the Turks and Italians. The great Greek leader from Crete, Eleftherios Venizelos (after whom Athens International Airport is named) led Greece in the **Balkan Wars** of 1912–1913. When the wars were done, Greece had increased its territory by two-thirds, incorporating much of Epirus, Macedonia, and Thrace in the north and the large islands of Samos, Chios, and Crete.

At the end of World War I, Greece invaded Turkey in an attempt to reclaim Constantinople and much of Aegean Turkey. Initially, the invasion went well, but the Turks, led by their future leader Mustafa Kemal (Atatürk), rallied and pushed the Greeks back to the sea. There, in 1922, in Smyrna (Izmir) and other seaside towns, the Greeks were slaughtered in what is still referred to in Greece as "The Catastrophe." In the **Treaty of Lausanne,** the boundaries of

Greece were fixed more or less as they are today, and Greece and Turkey agreed to an exchange of populations. Some 1.5 million Greeks who lived in Turkey were relocated to Greece, and about 500,000 Turks were sent from Greece to Turkey. Many spoke little or none of their ancestral language, and most were regarded with intense hostility in their new homelands.

Democracy, Prosperity & the Bailout

Whatever stability and prosperity Greece gained after the population exchange of the 1920s was seriously undercut by the harsh German and Italian occupations during **World War II.** The famines of 1941 and 1942 were particularly harsh; in Athens, carts went around the city each morning to collect the corpses of those who had died in the night. A bitter **civil war** (1944–49),

DATELINE

1627–00 B.C.	Eruption of volcano on Thera (Santorini); Akrotiri destroyed; the voyage of the Argonauts; exploits of Hercules.
1300–1200 B.C.	Mycenaean palace built atop Acropolis in Athinai (Athens)—a cultural, administrative, and military center.
800 B.C.	Formation of the Greek alphabet.
776 B.C.	First Olympic Games take place in Olympia.
600 B.C.	Coins first used as currency (Aegina's silver drachma).
508–07 B.C.	First Athenian democracy established.
480 B.C.	The Battle of Thermopylae. Greeks led by Sparta's King Leonidas fall to the Persians.
478 B.C.	Athens League forms and rules over Greek cities.
461 B.C.	First Peloponnesian War between Athens and Sparta.
447–38 B.C.	Parthenon built during Pericles's "Golden Age of Greece."
431 B.C.	Second Peloponnesian War.
336 B.C.	Alexander the Great succeeds Philip II and conquers Persia.
58 B.C.	Rome conquers Greece and adopts its gods.

A.D. 50	Apostle Paul preaches in Athens.
300s–400s	Athens is a philosophical and educational mecca; Hadrian's Library is rebuilt.
582	Slavs and Avars, from Central Asia, attack Athens.
1054	The Great Schism divides the east (Orthodox) and west (Roman) churches.
1100s–1400s	Greece conquered by Franks, Catalans, Venetians, and Ottomans.
1204	Frank Crusaders sack Constantinople.
1453	Constantinople is overrun by Turks.
1600s–1700s	Ottoman rule.
1801–03	Lord Elgin ships Parthenon sculptures to England.
1821	The War of Independence begins, lasting 9 years.
1827	In Battle of Navarino, Western powers crush Ottoman/Egyptian forces.
1829–33	Greece becomes a monarchy under 17-year-old Catholic Prince Frederick Otto of Wittelsbach, son of Bavaria's King Ludwig.

between pro- and anti-communist forces, further weakened Greece. Recovery began slowly—assisted by the Marshall Plan—and did not take hold until well into the 1960s. In 1967, a right-wing junta of army officers, nicknamed **the Colonels,** seized power, ended the monarchy, and were themselves toppled when democracy was restored in 1974.

In 1981, Greece was accepted into the **European Union** (Common Market) and began a period of initial prosperity (jump-started by EEC funding), followed by steady inflation. The euphoria of 2004 when Greece won the European soccer championship and hosted the wildly successful **Athens Olympics** soon fizzled. Greece, along with its EU neighbors, was trying to cope with the problems of illegal immigration, rising prices, an increasingly fragile ecosystem, and the economic recession that began to affect much of the world in 2008.

1834	Capital moved from Nafplion to Athens.
1843	Constitution demanded of King Otto in front of the palace (now Parliament, on Syntagma (Constitution) Square).
1896	First modern Olympic Games.
1922–23	Greece receives 1.1 million refugees from Asia Minor (Turkey); Athens's population doubles between 1920 and 1928.
1940–41	Italy and Germany occupy Greece in World War II.
1944	Churchill and Stalin agree on respective spheres of influence over Greece and Romania.
1946–49	Cold War hostilities fuel civil war.
1967	Martial law leads to a brutal 7-year dictatorship.
1973	Tanks invade Polytechnic campus, killing 34 students.
1981	Greece joins EEC (European Economic Community).
1996	Greece and Turkey come to brink of war over islet of Imia.
1999	Joint rescue efforts after earthquakes in Turkey and Greece thaw relations with Turkey.

2000	*Express Samina* ferry sinks near Paros, killing 80.
2001	John Paul II becomes first pope to visit Greece since 1054.
2002	Greece enters Eurozone.
2004	Greece soccer team wins European Championship; Olympic Games held in Athens.
2009	Triggered by massive debts, Greece is thrown into a financial crisis that shakes confidence in the euro and rattles world markets.
2009–present	Greece's debt crisis worsens; strikes, protests, and riots rock Athens and other cities. Unemployment soars, with joblessness among youth reaching 60%. New loans are issued and bailout packages put in place, along with new taxes and austerity measures.
2016	Immigrants, many from war-torn Syria, arrive in vast numbers, especially on Greek islands bordering Turkey. Macedonia closes its borders, stranding thousands of immigrants bound for Western Europe in northern Greece, where camps are opened.

Greece has since seen its finances crumble in a very public and, to many Greeks, a very humiliating way, leading the country to ask for help from the E.U. and subsequently the International Monetary Fund (IMF). Bailout packages have meant a slashing of government spending and extreme austerity measures. Many Greeks have had to accept these tough measures that have brought with them job losses and wage and pension cuts. Unemployment is high, jobs are scarce, wages shockingly low, and the cost of living is high. Meanwhile, the illegal migrant population has swelled, and younger people are looking for employment in other countries, much as the older generations before them had to do after World War II.

Many Greeks feel their country has been occupied once again, as it had been so many times during its turbulent history—this time by the E.U. and the IMF. Unable to devalue its currency, Greece has had to give up much of its sovereignty in order to accept bailouts, along with new even harsher austerity measures.

Yet there are reasons for optimism. Greece owns the largest maritime fleet in the world, and shipping and tourism account for the two biggest sectors of its economy (tourism has actually been up in recent years). Greece has untapped oil reserves in its sea and gold in its land and could become a major player in renewable energy in the near future. Meanwhile, much as they did in antiquity, all roads in Greece lead to Athens. With its enviable location, large port, and state-of-the-art infrastructure, the capital may well be the key to leading the country back into the light.

THE ARTS IN GREECE

Architecture

Many of the buildings we know best—from football stadiums to shopping malls—have Greek origins. The simple Greek *megaron* gave birth to both the temple and the basilica, the two building forms that many civic and religious shrines still embody. The Greek temple, with its pedimental facade, lives on in civic buildings, palaces, and ostentatious private homes throughout the world. Football and soccer are played in oval **stadiums,** the spectators now sitting on seats more comfortable than the stone slabs or dirt slopes they sat on in ancient Greek stadiums. Most **theaters** are now indoors, not outdoors, but the layout of stage, wings, and orchestra goes back to Greek theaters. The prototypes of shopping malls, with their side-by-side multiplicity of shops, can be found in almost every ancient Greek city. In fact, the mixture of shops and civic buildings, private homes, and public parks is one that most ancient Greeks knew very well. Many elegant homes still emulate the frescoed walls and pitched red-tile roofs of classical Greek antiquity.

In short, Greece was not just the "cradle of democracy," but the nursery of much of Western art and architecture. The portrait busts and statues of heroes that ornament almost every European city have their origins in ancient Greece. Both the elaborate vaulted funerary monuments and the simple stone grave markers of today can be found throughout ancient Greece.

Ancient Art

Ancient Greek art and sculpture have been major influences in the West and the East, shaping what is still considered the ideal. The gods themselves took on perfect human form in the marble **sculptures** created during the classical era, when Hellenic art reached its apex. Artists began carving and painting scenes on pediments and friezes as well, and sculpture flourished around the Mediterranean.

Athletic performance was exalted then as now, and perfection of the human form in motion was achieved in sculpture with Myron's *Discus Thrower* (surviving in copies). The greatest sculptor of classical Greece is said to be Phidias, who designed the **Parthenon friezes**—battles, legends, and processions, including serene-faced gods, representing order triumphing over chaos.

Rhodes, Corinth, and Athens all had their own styles of **pottery:** plants and animals, fantastical creatures, and humans, respectively. Black-figure pottery first appeared in the 7th century B.C. with humans as the subject, and Athens produced most of it. With the 530-B.C. invention of the red-figure technique (black background, red clay), attributed to an Andokides workshop vase painter, artists were able to paint in finer detail. Athens became a center of ceramic exports by the 4th century B.C., and quality suffered with mass-production, much as it has today.

Greece's artistic legacy didn't wither after the classical era. In medieval times, artists such as **Theophanes the Cretan** (died 1559) painted icons and frescoes; a number of good ones are in monasteries in Mount Athos and Meteora. **El Greco** (Kyriakos Theotokopoulos, 1541–1614), a student of Titian, was born in Crete, though he lived and died in Toledo, Spain.

Literature

The earliest known Greek writings are in Linear B, a Mycenaean script dating from 1500 to 1200 B.C. found on clay tablets, and refer to trade. The earliest literary works found are 8th- or 9th-century-B.C. epic poems by **Homer:** the *Iliad,* on the Trojan War; and the *Odyssey,* on the journeys of Odysseus (Ulysses). Both were written in ancient Greek, the oldest language in continuous use and the one on which the Latin alphabet is based. **Hesiod** (ca. 700 B.C.) wrote about his difficult rural life and a history of mankind, including the gods. Lyric poetry was sung in a chorus and accompanied by a lyre, also dating to about 700 B.C.

The ancient Greeks also invented drama, which told the stories of past heroes and legends in both tragedy and comedy. These performances were attended as religious festivals in honor of Dionysus. At the theater dedicated to him below the Acropolis, awards for best plays were bestowed and displayed on Tripodon Street in Plaka. **Aristophanes** wrote bold comedies that sometimes poked fun at democracy.

Herodotus first wrote literary prose, while **Thucydides** meticulously researched his account of the Peloponnesian War, influencing the scholarship of later historians. In the 4th century B.C., **Socrates, Plato,** and **Aristotle** (a student at Plato's Academy) wrote treatises on logic, science, politics, ethics, government, and dramatic interpretation that have been the centerpieces of learning for millennia.

The 20th century saw the international fame of two Greek masters. **Nikos Kazantzakis** (1883–1957) was born in Iraklion, Crete, when the island was still part of the Ottoman Empire. *Zorba the Greek* and other novels earned Kazantzakis nine Nobel Prize nominations and made him the most celebrated Greek writer of his time. *Zorba* and his novel *Last Temptation of Christ* were also made into internationally acclaimed films. **Constantine Cafavy** (1863–1933), born in Alexandria, Egypt, of Greek parents, is one of the most important figures in modern poetry. His most famous work is the beautiful "Ithaca," "When you depart for Ithaca, wish for the road to be long, full of adventure, full of knowledge." Anyone heading to Spetses, the Sarnoic Gulf island near Athens, might want to plunge into John Fowles' dark psychological novel *The Magus,* based partly on the author's experiences while teaching on the island in the 1950s. Travelers bound for the delightful little island of Patmos will want to read *The Summer of My Greek Taverna: A Memoir,* by Tom Stone, as much a cautionary tale as it is an evocation of island life.

Music

Greece has a long musical tradition, the word for "song" being related to ancient plays. The progression of Greek music took a different monophonic, rhythmic course than Western music, best represented in **Byzantine chant,** while folk and popular music has an Eastern character common to the Balkans and the former Ottoman Empire.

Popular music exploded in the cities after 1922, with musicians arriving from Asia Minor following the mass, religion-based population exchange. The hard-luck music of the refugees is called *rembetika* and has been likened to the blues, with a bouzouki player and usually a female vocalist in the ensemble, all seated in a row playing to small audiences.

Greek **folk music** is played during feasts on instruments such as the *bouzouki, oud, baglama, tambouras,* and *daouli.* Dancing is a big part of the event. There's even a type of rap (*mantinada*) on the islands of Crete and Amorgos in which performers make up the words as they sing. In towns, you might see and hear roaming street musicians, usually Gypsies, playing popular tunes on the accordion, guitar, violin, and sometimes a clarinet.

THE GODS & GODDESSES

For the ancient Greeks, the world was full of divine forces, most of which were thought to be immortal. Death, sleep, love, fate, memory, laughter, panic, rage, day, night, justice, victory—all of the timeless, elusive forces confronted by humans—were named and numbered among the gods and goddesses with whom the Greeks shared their universe. The most powerful of the gods lived with Zeus on Mount Olympos and were known as the Olympians. To make these forces more familiar and approachable, the Greeks imagined their gods to be somehow like themselves. They were male and female, young and old, beautiful and deformed, gracious and withholding, lustful and virginal, sweet and fierce.

As told by the ancient poets, the lives of the Olympians had elements of an eternal soap opera. Sometimes generous, courageous, insightful, the gods are also notoriously petty, quarrelsome, spiteful, vain, frivolous, and insensitive. And how could it be otherwise with the Olympians? Not made to pay the ultimate price of death, they need not know the ultimate cost of life. Fed on *ambrosia* ("not mortal") and *nektar* ("overcoming death"), they cannot go hungry, much less perish. When life is endless, everything is reversible.

Principal Olympian Gods & Goddesses

GREEK NAME	LATIN NAME	DESCRIPTION
Zeus	Jupiter	Son of Kronos and Rhea, high god, ruler of Olympus. Thunderous sky god, wielding bolts of lightning. Patron-enforcer of the rites and laws of hospitality.
Hera	Juno	Daughter of Kronos and Rhea, queen of the sky. Sister and wife of Zeus. Patroness of marriage.
Demeter	Ceres	Daughter of Kronos and Rhea, sister of Hera and Zeus. Giver of grain and fecundity. Goddess of the mysteries of Eleusis.
Poseidon	Neptune	Son of Kronos and Rhea, brother of Zeus and Hera. Ruler of the seas. Earth-shaking god of earthquakes.
Hestia	Vesta	Daughter of Kronos and Rhea, sister of Hera and Zeus. Guardian of the hearth fire and of the home.
Hephaestos	Vulcan	Son of Hera, produced by her parthenogenetically. Lord of volcanoes and of fire. Himself a smith, the patron of crafts employing fire (metalworking and pottery).
Ares	Mars	Son of Zeus and Hera. The most hated of the gods. God of war and strife.
Hermes	Mercury	Son of Zeus and an Arcadian mountain nymph. Protector of thresholds and crossroads. Messenger-god, patron of commerce and eloquence. Companion-guide of souls en route to the underworld.
Apollo	Phoebus	Son of Zeus and Leto. Patron-god of the light of day, and of the creative genius of poetry and music. The god of divination and prophecy.
Artemis	Diana	Daughter of Zeus and Leto. Mistress of animals and of the hunt. Chaste guardian of young girls.
Athena	Minerva	Daughter of Zeus and Metis, born in full armor from the head of Zeus. Patroness of wisdom and of war. Patron-goddess of the city-state of Athens.
Dionysos	Dionysus	Son of Zeus and Semele, born from the thigh of his father. God of revel, revelation, wine, and drama.
Aphrodite	Venus	Daughter of Zeus. Born from the bright sea foam off the coast of Cyprus. Fusion of Minoan tree goddess and Near Eastern goddess of love and war. Patroness of love.

GREEK FOOD & DRINK

Greeks take what they eat, and how it is prepared, very seriously. Whereas many non-Greeks go to a restaurant in the hopes of getting something different from home cooking, in Greece it is always high praise to say that a restaurant's food is *spitiko* (homemade). Here are some tips on places to eat in Greece and what to eat there.

Throughout the guide we try to tell you the best—and best value—inexpensive, moderate, and expensive restaurants and cafes in each "Where to Eat" section. Keep in mind that the prices at the most expensive place in a country hamlet could be an amazing bargain in Athens. As for prices on Mykonos and Santorini, if you sit down at a popular cafe and have a coffee or a glass of wine, you'll find out just how expensive even simple pleasures can be in Greece's most popular tourist destinations!

What & When to Eat

Greeks are more concerned with the quality and freshness of their food than they are with the place where it's served, which could literally be falling apart without anyone's minding, as long as the meal is good. Fruits and vegetables taste strong and fresh (you will likely remember the taste of a tomato long after returning home), and portions are generous. Other hallmarks of good Greek food are the generous use of pungent herbs for both flavoring food and making teas, and the generous use of olive oil.

For breakfast and as a snack, various savory pies are sold at countless holes-in-the-wall. *Tiropita* (cheese), *spanakopita* (spinach), and *bougasta* (cream/semolina) are the most common of these pies. *Koulouri* (round bread "sticks"), roasted chestnuts, and corn on the cob are sold on the street.

The midday meal is the biggest of the day, eaten at home around 2 or 3pm after being cooked in the morning by Mama or Grandma. Students are dismissed from school around 1pm, and shops and businesses close between 1:30 and 3pm. In the summer, when the heat of the day is unbearable, the midday meal is followed by a siesta. Then, depending on the day, it's back to work, out for the evening stroll, and then out for dinner at 10pm. Kids and all. If you want to eat where the locals do, look for restaurants that are full at 10pm—the Greek dinner hour. Dining in Greece is not a staid affair, and it'll be boisterous.

Note that restaurants that cater to tourists are open all day or at least earlier than the usual 7pm. You'll find these in tourist centers such as Plaka in Athens, and at beach resorts.

Countless neighborhood *tavernas* (square tables, paper tablecloths, woven-seat chairs) serve simple Greek food in big portions with barrel wine. There are many other kinds of restaurants, as well. There are also *psistaria* (grill restaurants) that serve up steaks and souvlaki (kebabs), and the *mageiria,* or cookhouses, serving buffet-style stews with rice, pasta, meat sauce, and fish. Generally, the mageireia is the Greek equivalent of the fast-food joint, except the food is slow-cooked and kept warm; it's ready to serve when you walk in—the kind of place where you can sit down for lunch and eat by yourself. Almost every village has at least one **kafeneion** (coffeehouse), and usually two. Families, and women on their own, usually sit at tables outside. Indoors, the kafeneion is still an almost exclusively male establishment and often functions as a clubhouse. Men stop by, play a hand of cards or *tabli* (backgammon), and nurse a coffee or an ouzo for hours. **Ouzeries** specialize in starters, traditionally washed down with the anise-flavored liqueur ouzo. While an *ouzeri* is usually similar to a *kafeneion* (but with the emphasis more on ouzo), the food often a bit heartier, often including grilled sausage or octopus.

Greeks almost never drink without eating something, if only some chunks of feta cheese, a few olives, and perhaps some cucumber and tomato slices. This is an especially wise custom, especially when drinking fiery and potent ouzo, which turns a deceptively milky hue when diluted with water.

Menus in tourist-oriented restaurants are usually in Greek and English, but if not, just ask for help from your waiter, who is probably fluent in restaurant English. He may even take you into the kitchen to eye what's available. Often, the printed menu has little bearing on what is available, and it never hurts to ask what's special that day. If you want tap water, not bottled, ask for it from the *vrisi* (tap). If you want the house wine, ask what their own wine is (*to diko sas krasi*), lest you be guided to much more expensive bottled wine. Increasingly, however, the house wine is not local, but just a cheap, mass-produced wine, perhaps "decanted" surreptitiously from a large cardboard container hidden away in the kitchen.

Service is included in the bill, but it is customary to leave your waiter another 5% to 10% at a simple place, more at a fancier establishment with noteworthy service. Some Greeks do and some do not tip in family-owned and -operated places, but the wait staff, counting on seasonal earnings, often expect a tip from foreign tourists. As anywhere, feel no obligation to tip when service is poor or indifferent, but service in Greece is usually so friendly and personal that you'll want to leave something.

If you go out with Greek friends, prepare to go late and stay late and to put up a losing fight for the bill. Greeks frown on bill splitting; usually, one person is host, and that is that. And, if you are invited to a Greek home for a meal, assume that everything will run hours late and that you will be offered an unimaginable amount of food. This is especially true on holidays—it's for a good reason that the week after Easter, most newspapers carry supplements on "How to Lose the Weight You Gained at Easter."

The Basics

Greeks consume more **olive oil** than any other nation (some 30 liters per person per year) and they want that oil to be not just Greek, but from specific regions, preferably from specific groves. The olives of the Peloponnese are especially admired, with Kalamata olives prized both for oil and eating. **Cheese** is the other staple of the Greek diet. Some visitors to Greece leave thinking that feta is the only Greek cheese. They are wrong. Although a slab of feta, usually sprinkled with oregano, tops most Greek salads, there's a wide variety of cheeses. Most Greek cheeses, like feta, are made from sheep or goat's milk. Creamy *mizithra* is more delicate than feta, best when eaten fresh and soft, but useful when cured and grated on pasta. *Kefalotyri* and *graviera* are popular favorites, slightly bland, but with enough tang to be interesting. A standard Greek snack consist of olives, a chunk of bread, and a slab of cheese. Fresh Greek fruit and vegetables in season are top notch and still make up a major part of the Greek diet.

Meze

Greeks eat a lot of starters, called *mezedes* or *meze,* which include dips and salads, before the main course or on their own. There's always a bowl of salad, usually Greek horiatiki, or village salad. A taverna meal usually starts with meze, whereas they're the main course at *ouzeries,* late-evening joints where you wash down the snacks with ouzo, an anise-flavored liqueur. Of the dips, *tzatziki* with yogurt, garlic, and cucumber is popular, as is fava, a bean purée. Sample a selection of *kroketes* (croquettes) made with potato, cheese, zucchini, or tomato if they're on the menu, or seafood dishes such as marinated or grilled *ochtapodi* (octopus) or *melitzanosalata* (eggplant salad).

Meat & Fish

Greeks say "Get to the roast" when they mean "Get to the point." Meat is popular even in this nation surrounded by the sea, whether it's a *brizola* (plain cut steak) or chop, *stifado* (rabbit stew), or *lemonato* (lemon-flavored roast).

Kebabs—better known here as **souvlaki** (small spit) or **gyro** (meat shaved off a vertical rotisserie)—are usually served with different kinds of pitas and sauces to slather and wrap around the pieces of chicken or pork.

Moschari yiouvetsi is chunks of beef baked with orzo pasta, onion, tomato, and wine in individual clay pots. Another baked dish is *arni kleftiko:* lamb usually cooked with cheese and herbs in a packet of wax paper. More lamb dishes are *arni psito* or *arni tou fournou,* roasted with garlic and herbs. *Katsika* (goat) is cooked in a similar way.

You can also get beef *stifado,* a stew made with copious amounts of wine, rosemary, tomato, and baby onions. You've likely never seen a slab of *brizola hirini* (pork) like those you'll get here, which have no resemblance to the small North American chops. Get it as a cheaper but filling and tasty substitute for *brizola moscharisia* (beef steak). *Avgolemono* (egg-and-lemon sauce) also goes with pork, lamb or *pastitsio,* a lasagna made with ground beef and macaroni. Layered with potatoes, eggplant, and béchamel, it becomes moussaka.

Ground beef is also the main ingredient for **keftedes,** a meat patty that can stand alone, "beefed up" with egg, grated onion, bread crumbs, and spices, then coated in flour before being fried. Mixed with rice and dropped in water with an avgolemono sauce, it becomes *giouvarlakia. Biftekia* is a meat patty, not beef steak. You can also find *gemista* (ground beef mixed with rice and stuffed in large tomatoes or green peppers), cabbage, vine leaves, *kolokithakia gemista* (zucchini/courgettes), and *papoutsakia* (eggplant/aubergines, meaning little shoes).

As for the bounty of the sea: a *psarotaverna* is a restaurant that serves mainly fish. The fresh catch will often will displayed on ice, or the waiter will bring around a fish to show it off and display its freshness, then often fillet it at the table. A good restaurant will also explain exactly how your choice will be prepared—most fish are best when grilled and sprinkled with mountain herbs. Fish is usually sold by the kilo, not the serving, so be sure to clarify the cost before ordering.

Dessert

Many Greek restaurants do not serve dessert, and Greeks often troop off after a meal to a pastry shop (the tongue-twisting *zacharopolasteion*). In recent years, many tavernas have started to serve a free dessert, ranging from simple apple slices with honey and cinnamon to ice-cream confections topped with sparklers. Yogurt (*yiaourti*) is best when served from a traditional clay container and drizzled with honey (*meli*). *Mustalevra,* grape must and flour, is dark, wobbly, and sweet. Baklava is flaky, thin phyllo pastry layered with walnuts and pistachios and soaked in honey syrup; variations include a candied fruit or chocolate center. *Dandourma* is an ice cream concoction mixed with milk and cherry syrup, and *kaimaki* is a uniquely flavored ice cream (literally frozen cream).

Wine

Harsh-tasting *retsina,* the strong pine-resin wine that actually accompanies some Greek foods quite nicely, is a small part of the story of Greek wine, which extends back some 6,500 years and even has a hero, Dionysus, the god of wine. In antiquity, it's believed that Greeks didn't drink wine with their dinner but paired it with fruit, nuts, and desserts. It was also watered down by the host, as it still is in some restaurants, especially at the height of summer.

In tavernas, you may or may not shun barrel wine (*krasi*), ordered by the kilo (not liter), and brought to the table in distinctive tin jugs. The better grapes are normally reserved for bottles, but if you can lower your nose, so to speak, this is all part of the taverna experience. Most of the time, it'll be pretty good.

Rosés also shouldn't be ignored, as these are produced mainly in the mountainous regions and go well with a mix of dishes such as meze. In rural areas and on the islands, wine is produced (and if not bottled, then barreled) on the family plot, alongside the cans of olive oil and jars of honey. It may not be great, but families have had the opportunity to perfect their techniques over the years, and some have turned into well-respected wine estates.

There's also a huge selection to choose from, from regions and domaines all over the country. We have our favorites (Amethystos is consistently good), but we aren't above buying the local *hima*—barrel wine sold at the corner store in 1.5-liter water bottles. Some wines can be excellent one year and less good the next, so ask at the neighborhood cava (wine shop/off-license/liquor store) for a recommendation.

Ouzo

Although most Greeks now prefer whiskey, the national distilled drink is still this clear, licorice-flavored liqueur that turns cloudy when you add water, though you can also drink it neat. It is said to be called "uso" from the phrase "Anis Uso Per Marsilia" stamped on sacks of anise imported from Sicily but meant for Marseilles. Ouzo is made from fermented grape skins, mixed with star anise and other herbs, boiled in a still, and stored for a few months before being diluted to 80 proof/40% alcohol. Drink too much and you'll get a killer headache; one or two glasses is enough. It's usually consumed with appetizers and seafood (hence *ouzeries*), on islands and by the seaside. It was traditionally the drink of fishermen and at *kafenia* (coffee shops), where you still find older men sitting around drinking ouzo as they talk and play cards or backgammon.

Crete's version, *raki* (lion's milk), also Turkey's national drink, isn't flavored with anise and is more like Italian grappa. It's called *tsipouro* in other regions of the country. You can get smooth *rako-melo* (raki and honey) on some of the Cyclades islands.

WHEN TO GO

Just about everyone agrees that the best time to visit is Greece is spring and early summer (mid-Apr to mid-June) or autumn (Sept to mid-Oct). At these times you'll avoid the summer high season, with its high heat, high prices, and big crowds. These drawbacks loom especially large if you plan on visiting some of the more popular islands, Mykonos and Santorini first and foremost among them. In the spring, you'll see more wildflowers than you could have imagined—and swim in a sea that's a bit cool but more pleasant than you had hoped for. In the autumn, you will enjoy golden days with still-warm waters.

Of course, there are a few considerations to keep in mind outside of high season, especially if you plan to travel to any of the islands. Off-season there are fewer boats and flights to the islands, and several island shops, hotels, and restaurants do not open until June and then close in October. During the off-season life comes to a standstill on many islands, or at least turns its back to tourism, and wintertime rains can dampen any romantic notions of lonely wandering in empty landscapes.

During **Easter week,** nearly every hotel room outside of Athens is booked well in advance by city Greeks who head to the country to celebrate Greece's most important holiday. Many sites and museums are closed Good Friday, Easter Saturday, and Easter Sunday, while many shops close on Good Friday and Easter Saturday. (See "Holidays," p. 29).

Weather

Greek weather is getting less predictable every year, but some things everyone agrees on: the winters can be chilly (sometimes with unusual bursts of warm weather, then again, sometimes it even snows in Athens). It can go from warm to downright numbing. Many buildings are not insulated, and the centrally controlled heating is often intermittent, making the cold season seem very long indeed. Summers are just plain hot (and usually dry), sometimes reaching 110°F (43°C). As the saying goes, only mad dogs and Englishmen would venture out in the midday sun, hence the siesta between 3 and 6pm. The seasonal north (Etesian) winds blow mid-July to mid-August, but it can get very windy anytime, stopping ferry transport. Even though our temperature chart for Athens reflects some sound statistics (note that this is the *average* daily temperature, not the daytime high), don't be surprised if you find deviations from it when you visit Greece. Our figures for Crete are based on Iraklion's temperature/precipitation.

Average Monthly Temperatures & Precipitation

		JAN	FEB	MAR	APR	MAY	JUNE	JULY	AUG	SEPT	OCT	NOV	DEC
Athens	Temp °F	50	50	54	59	67	75	81	81	75	67	59	53
	Temp °C	10	10	12	15	19	23	27	27	23	19	15	11
	Precip. (in.)	1.9	1.6	1.6	.9	.7	.3	.2	.3	.4	2.1	2.2	2.4
Crete	Temp °F	54	55	57	61	68	73	79	77	73	68	63	57
	Temp °C	12	13	14	16	20	23	26	25	23	20	17	14
	Precip. (in.)	3.5	2.7	2.3	1.1	.6	.1	.1	0	.7	2.6	2.3	3.1

Holidays

In addition to the following holidays, every day in Greece is sacred to one or more saints. That means that every day, at least one saint (and everyone named for that saint) is being celebrated. Many towns and villages also celebrate the feast days of their patron saints. Tiny chapels that are used only once a year are opened for a church service followed by all-day wining and dining. If you're lucky, you'll stumble on one of these celebrations.

JANUARY

Feast of St. Basil (Ayios Vassilios). St. Basil is the Greek equivalent of Santa Claus. The holiday is marked by the exchange of gifts and a special cake, *vassilopita*, made with a coin in it; the person who gets the piece with the coin will have good luck. January 1.

Epiphany (Baptism of Christ). Baptismal fonts and water are blessed. A priest may throw a cross into the harbor and young men will try to recover it; the finder wins a special blessing. Children, who have been kept good during Christmas with threats of the *kalikantzari* (goblins), are allowed on the 12th day to help chase them away. January 6.

FEBRUARY

Carnival (Karnavali). Be ready for parades, marching bands, costumes, drinking, dancing, and general loosening of inhibitions, depending on the locale. Some scholars say

the name comes from the Latin for "farewell meat," while others hold that it comes from "car naval," the chariots celebrating the ancient sea god Poseidon (Saturn, to the Romans). On the island of Skyros, the pagan "goat dance" is performed, reminding us of the primitive Dionysiac nature of the festivities. Crete has its own colorful versions, whereas in Athens, people bop each other on their heads with plastic hammers. Celebrations last the 3 weeks before the beginning of Lent.

MARCH

Independence Day and the Feast of the Annunciation. The two holidays are celebrated simultaneously with military parades, especially in Athens. The religious celebration is particularly important on the island of Hydra and in churches or monasteries named Evangelismos (Bringer of Good News) or Evangelistria (the feminine form of the name). March 25.

APRIL

Sound-and-Light Performances. These begin on the Acropolis in Athens and in the Old Town on Rhodes. Nightly through October.

Feast of St. George (Ayios Yioryios). The feast day of the patron saint of shepherds is an important rural celebration with dancing and feasting. Arachova, near Delphi, is famous for its festivities. The island of Skyros also gives its patron saint a big party on April 23. (If the 23rd comes before Easter, the celebration is postponed until the Mon after Easter.)

MAY

May Day. On this urban holiday, families have picnics in the country and pick wildflowers, which are woven into wreaths and hung from balconies and over doorways. May Day is still celebrated by Greek communists and socialists as a working-class holiday. May 1.

Hippocratic Oath. Ritual recitations of the oath by the citizens of Kos honor their favorite son, Hippocrates. Young girls in ancient dress, playing flutes, accompany a young boy in procession until he stops and recites in Greek the timeless oath of physicians everywhere. May through September.

Feast of St. Constantine (Ayios Konstandinos). The first Orthodox emperor, Constantine, and his mother, **St. Helen (Ayia Eleni),** are honored. It's a big party night for everyone named Costa and Eleni. (Name days, rather than birthdays, are celebrated in Greece.)

JUNE

Athens Festival. Featured are superb productions of ancient drama, opera, orchestra performances, ballet, modern dance, and popular entertainers. The festival takes place in the handsome Odeum of Herodes Atticus, on the southwest side of the Acropolis. June to early October.

Folk-Dance Performances. The site of these performances is the theater in the Old Town of Rhodes.

Lycabettus Theater. A variety of performances are presented at the amphitheater on Mount Likavitos (Lycabettus) overlooking Athens. Mid-June to late August.

Miaoulia. This celebration on Hydra honors Hydriot Admiral Miaoulis, who set much of the Turkish fleet on fire by ramming it with explosives-filled fireboats. Weekend in mid-June.

Aegean Festival. In the harbor of Skiathos town, the Bourtzi Cultural Center presents ancient drama, modern dance, folk music and folk dance, concerts, and art exhibits. June through September.

International Classical Musical Festival. This annual festival takes place at Nafplion, in the Peloponnese. One week in June or July.

Midsummer Eve. The now-dried wreaths of flowers picked on May Day are burned to drive away witches, in a version of pagan ceremonies now associated with the birth of John the Baptist on June 24, Midsummer Day. June 23 to June 24.

Navy Week. The celebration takes place throughout Greece. In Volos, the voyage of the Argonauts is reenacted. On Hydra, the exploits of Adm. Andreas Miaoulis, naval hero of the War of Independence, are celebrated.

JULY

Puppet Festival. Hydra's annual festival has drawn puppeteers from countries as far away as Togo and Brazil. Early July.

Epidaurus Festival. Performances of classical Greek drama take place in the famous amphitheater. July to early September.

Hippokrateia Festival. Art, music, and theater come to the medieval castle of the Knights of St. John, in the main harbor of Kos. July and August.

Dionysia Wine Festival. This is not a major event, but it's fun if you happen to find yourself on the island of Naxos.

Wine Festival at Rethymnon, Crete. Rethymnon hosts a wine festival as well as a **Renaissance Festival.** Sample the wines, then enjoy the Renaissance theatrical and musical performances. Mid-July to early September.

ORTHODOX EASTER & holy week

The Greek calendar revolves around religious holidays. **Orthodox Easter** (*Pascha*)—usually a week later than Western Easter, and the only holiday calculated according to the Julian calendar—is the nation's biggest. Most of the native population—97% of whom are Greek Orthodox—observe the traditions. Most people who did not fast for the 40 days of Lent begin fasting during Holy Week, which starts on the Monday before Easter. On **Holy Tuesday,** devotees whitewash their houses and walkways. On **Wednesday,** they bring holy oil home from church and use it, along with sprigs of basil, to bless the households. On **Holy Thursday,** they receive Communion, and priests in special dress read biblical accounts of the Last Supper during an all-night vigil. At home, followers boil eggs and dye them red to symbolize the blood of Christ and rebirth. Many also bake Easter bread (*tsoureki*) and biscuits (*koulourakia*). Church bells solemnly toll on **Good Friday,** and at around 8pm, a candlelit procession through the parish accompanies a decorated funeral bier (*epitaphios*) of Christ. On **Saturday,** they attempt to scare away any remaining bad spirits that might hinder the Resurrection (*Anastasi*). Most people go to their neighborhood church just before midnight with candles (*lambades*); the children carry lavishly decorated ones, often received as traditional gifts from their godparents. The lights of the church are dimmed at midnight, symbolizing Christ's death. The priest then brings out the holy flame, brought from Jerusalem for the occasion, and passes it to church members, who light one another's candles while saying "*Christos anesti*" ("Christ is risen"). Youths light fireworks, and congregants return home with their lit candles and bless their homes by "drawing" a cross on the doorframe with the candle's smoke. On **Easter Sunday,** they break the Lenten fast by cracking the eggs and eating *mageritsa* soup, made with dill, rice, and *avgolemono* (egg-lemon) sauce, and the innards of Sunday's roast lamb. Easter Sunday brings much feasting, drinking, and dancing, as the smell of lamb permeates the air from roof-terrace spit-roasts. At church, passages on the Resurrection are read in many languages, symbolizing world unity. **Easter Monday** is a national holiday.

Feast of Ayia Marina. The feast of the protector of crops is widely celebrated in rural areas. July 17.

Feast of the Prophet Elijah (*Profitis Elias*). The prophet's feast day is celebrated in the hilltop shrines formerly sacred to the sun god Helios.

AUGUST

Feast of the Transfiguration (*Metamorphosis*). This feast day is observed in the numerous churches and monasteries of that name, though they aren't much for parties. August 6.

Aeschylia Festival of Ancient Drama. Classical dramas are staged at the archaeological site of Eleusis, home of the ancient Mysteries and birthplace of Aeschylus, west of Athens. August to mid-September.

The Aegina Music Festival takes place across the island in August; information from www.aeginagreece.com; ✆ **698/131-9332.**

SEPTEMBER

On Spetses, the anniversary of the **Battle of the Straits of Spetses** is celebrated on the weekend closest to September 8 with a reenactment in the harbor, fireworks, and an all-night bash.

Aegina honors its famous nut, the pistachio, with the **Pistachio Festival** every September (**www.aeginagistikifest.gr**).

OCTOBER

Ochi Day. General Metaxa's negative reply (*ochi* is Greek for no) to Mussolini's demands in 1940 conveniently extends the feast-day party with patriotic outpourings, including parades, folk music and folk dancing, and general festivity. October 28.

NOVEMBER

Feast of the Archangels Gabriel and Michael *(Gavriel and Mihail).* Ceremonies are held in the many churches named for the two archangels. November 8.

DECEMBER

Feast of St. Nikolaos *(Ayios Nikolaos).* This St. Nick is the patron saint of sailors. Numerous processions head down to the sea and to the many chapels dedicated to him. December 6.

Christmas. The day after Christmas honors the Gathering Around the Holy Family *(Synaksis tis Panayias).* December 25 and 26.

New Year's Eve. Children sing Christmas carols *(kalanda)* outdoors while their elders play cards, talk, smoke, eat, and imbibe. December 31.

SUGGESTED GREECE ITINERARIES

Traveling in Greece is ever so enjoyable, but even the most ardent Hellenophile will admit that the experience can be unpredictable at times. Weather, strikes, inconvenient schedules—the best-laid plans can easily go astray. But with some advance planning, good luck, and a willingness to be flexible, you can see what you set out to visit in Greece, and unexpected sights and unanticipated delights will most likely be part of the package, too. So, that said, here are some ideal ways to see the best of Athens and the islands. These routes rely on buses, cars, ships, and planes, and they are geared to summer travel, when it's much easier to move from island to island than it is off season. And now, as you set off for Greece, *Kalo taxidi!* (Have a good trip!)

ATHENS & THE ISLANDS IN 1 WEEK

One week? That's almost a sacrilege in this country where *siga, siga* (slowly, slowly) is a well-meaning mantra to enjoy life at a reasonable pace. So, even though you have only a week to explore one of the richest, most intriguing places on earth, do slow down a bit when you can and appreciate everything that's unfolding around you.

Day 1: Athens & the Acropolis ★★★

Arrive in Athens and get settled in your hotel. Yes, even though there's so much to see, you deserve a nap, maybe a refreshing swim if you're fortunate enough to be staying in a hotel with a pool. Relax a bit—you have time. Summer hours keep most monuments and museum open late, plus sights in the sprawling capital are fairly concentrated and you needn't venture much beyond the **Acropolis** (p. 74) this first day. This ancient marvel is probably within walking distance of your hotel, maybe even within sight of it. The ascent through the **Beule Gate** and up a well-worn path is stirring, and what lies beyond is even more so: The ruins of the perfectly proportioned Parthenon and surrounding temples, summoning up the glory of classical Greece. Continue the spell with a walk through the **Acropolis Museum** (p. 78), where the sculptures and statuary that once adorned the Acropolis temples are on display, including the magnificent Parthenon Frieze. Then stroll along the **Grand Promenade** (p. 80), a cobblestone-and-marble, pedestrian-only boulevard that skirts the Acropolis Hill. You'll get a glimpse of the **Theater of Dionysus** (p. 82), where the newest dramas of Aeschylus, Sophocles, and Euripides once delighted audiences. Plunge back into the present day, by following Adrianou (Hadrian) Street through the colorful **Plaka** neighborhood (p. 86). End your day by strolling around the evocative ruins of the **Ancient Agora** (p. 86), once the business and political hub of ancient Athens. Then it's time for dinner, maybe beneath a shady plane tree at a long-time favorite, the **Platanos Taverna** (p. 72).

Day 2: Athens & Santorini

No need to rush out of the hotel at the crack of dawn. You can probably get a mid- to late-afternoon boat to Santorini, your next stop, leaving time for a mid-morning visit to Athens' **National Archaeological Museum** (p. 93), with the world's finest collection of Greek antiquities. (Depending on where you're staying, you may want to walk at least part of the way there, best up Athinas Street for a stop at the lively, colorful **Central Market**; see p. 93.) Essential galleries are the Mycenaean Collection, with gold death masks and many other magnificent treasures of the civilization whose king, Agamemnon, launched the Trojan War; the Cycladic Collection's enigmatic marble figures; and the colorful and charming frescoes of the Thira Collection—from Santorini, where you're heading next.

Now it's time to take the Metro to **Piraeus** and board the Santorini-bound boat. You could also fly to Santorini, but boat is by far the best way to get to a Greek island. There's nothing like appreciating the passing view while you talk or read a book. Although it takes longer to travel this way than by plane (the trip to Santorini is about 5 hours by fast ferry, as long as 9 hours by slow boat) it beats sitting in coach any day. You'll want to be on deck as the boat sails into the Santorini's caldera, one of the great Greek experiences. Cliffs rise glimmering even in the moonlight, while the lights of the white villages atop the rim twinkle high above you. In fact, some of the best hotels on Santorini are perched on the side of the cliffs—two of our favorites, ensured to make a stay on the island a special occasion, are **Esperas** in Ia (p. 155) and **Astra Apartments** in Imerovigli (p. 155).

Day 3: Santorini ★★★

You probably won't want to venture too far away from the **caldera** (p. 154) in the morning. If you aren't lucky enough to be spending the morning on your private terrace overlooking the spectacle, walk at least

Athens & the Islands in 1 Week

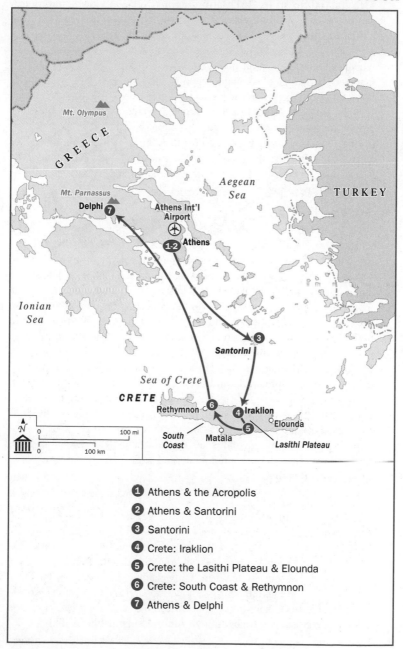

1 Athens & the Acropolis

2 Athens & Santorini

3 Santorini

4 Crete: Iraklion

5 Crete: the Lasithi Plateau & Elounda

6 Crete: South Coast & Rethymnon

7 Athens & Delphi

a portion of the 10km (6-mile) path that follows the top of the cliff from **Fira** (p. 160) to **Ia** (p. 161), affording a bird's-eye view of the outrageously blue waters and clusters of white houses perched on top of the cliffs like a dusting of snow. From stops along the caldera you can catch the bus to the southern end of the island and **Ancient Akrotiri** (p. 158), which is Greece's version of Pompeii—a prosperous Minoan-era town that was buried in a volcanic eruption around 1500 B.C., leaving its houses and warehouses remarkably well-preserved. Adjoining the site is **Paralia Kokkini (Red Beach),** carpeted in red volcanic pebbles and perfect for an afternoon swim and nap. Come evening, take the bus back up the island to Ia, where watching the sunset is a celebratory event accompanied with a glass of wine. Then head down to **Ammoudi,** the little fishing port below Ia, for a seafood dinner at **Katina's** (p. 157) or another waterside taverna.

Day 4: Iraklion ★★★

High-speed ferries make the crossing from Santorini to Crete in under 2 hours. But as you'll discover in Greece, schedules don't always cooperate with your plans. So if there's not a morning boat, fly to Iraklion. (You should have a choice of several morning flights in high season.) Your first stop on the island is the palace of **Knossos** (p. 196), the dramatic ruins that about 3 millennia ago made up the center of Minoan culture. Then it's on to the center of town and late lunch at the **Pantheon** (p. 192) in the market (actually, it's in an arcade known as Dirty Alley, but don't let that put you off the excellent food). Spend the rest of the afternoon in Iraklion's **Archaeological Museum** (p. 194) for a look at beautiful frescoes portraying Minoan life and other exuberant artifacts of this sophisticated culture. As a cooling breeze picks up in the evening, it's time to get back into the swing of modern life, but gently so, by joining Irakliots for a stroll around the old city. A mandatory stop at some point in your ramblings is one of the cafes at **Ta Liontaria (the Lions) square** (p. 197), overlooking the fountain adorned with four leonine symbols of the Venetian Republic.

Day 5: The Lasithi Plateau ★★★ & Elounda ★

Since you have only two more days on this large, diverse, and fascinating island, rent a car to see as much of the beautiful landscapes as you can. That said, don't overdo it—Crete's pleasures are meant to be savored. On Day 5 make the short but scenic drive up to the **Lasithi Plateau** (p. 198), a glorious slice of rural Crete where a tidy patchwork of orchards and fields spreads out to the encircling hills. Enjoy a long lunch up here at the **Kronio** restaurant (p. 193), then drop back down to the coast for a late afternoon swim in the crystalline waters off the **Elounda peninsula** (p. 220).

Day 6: Crete's South Coast & Rethymnon ★★

Begin Day 6 by heading south from Iraklion to the coast around **Matala** (p. 200), a little over an hour away. This pleasant beach resort is famous for its cliffs riddled with caves that have housed everyone from Roman soldiers to 1960s hippies. The real draw here are the beaches—the best are **Kommos,** a long stretch of sand just north of Matala, and isolated **Red Beach,** reached by a 20-minute hike over a headland on the south side of town. By early afternoon, be on the road again for the hour drive back north to **Rethymnon** (p. 201), an inviting and exotic maze of Venetian and Turkish houses and mosques, crowded onto a sea-girt peninsula with and a massive seaside fortress. Treat yourself to an early meal in the romantic garden of **Avli** (p. 203), famous for its innovative preparations of Cretan cuisine. Allow time to get back to Iraklion (an hour's drive east) for the 9pm sailing to Piraeus. Treat yourself to a cabin or berth so you can sleep through the overnight crossing.

Day 7: Delphi ★★★

You'll arrive in Athens early, all too early, about 6 or 7am. But you should be well rested, and you have an entire day ahead of you—and still so much to see. A day trip to **Delphi** (p. 127) shows off the **Temple of Apollo,** Greece's most mysterious and alluring ancient site, a memorable place to spend your last day in Greece. Even the bus trip is a thrill, through glorious mountain scenery with vistas off to the Gulf of Corinth. CHAT tours (p. 285) is one of several companies running day trips that leave Athens around 8:30 or so and have you back in the city by 7pm, time for one last dinner and glimpse of the floodlit Acropolis.

ATHENS & THE ISLANDS IN 2 WEEKS

Two weeks allows time to take in the must-see ancient monuments in Athens and also get a good taste of island life. Though touring the islands can be require a bit of work and some logistics, we've tried to minimize the wear and tear.

Day 1: Athens ★★★

Start your first day in Greece with the landmark you can't go home without seeing: The **Acropolis** (p. 74). The ascent through the **Beule Gate** and up a well-worn path is stirring, and what lies beyond is even more so: The ruins of the perfectly proportioned Parthenon and surrounding temples, summoning up the glory of classical Greece. Continue the spell with a walk through the **Acropolis Museum** (p. 78), where the sculptures and statuary that once adorned the Acropolis temples are on display, including the magnificent Parthenon Frieze. Then stroll along the **Grand Promenade** (p. 80), a cobblestone-and-marble, pedestrian-only boulevard that skirts the Acropolis Hill. You'll pass the **Theater of Dionysus** (p. 82), where the newest dramas of Aeschylus, Sophocles, and Euripides once delighted audiences. Following Adrianou (Hadrian) Street through the colorful **Plaka** neighborhood (p. 86), then end your sightseeing by strolling around the evocative ruins of the **Ancient Agora** (p. 86), once the business and political hub of ancient Athens. After that, it's time for dinner, maybe beneath a shady plane tree at a long-time favorite, the **Platanos Taverna** (p. 72).

Day 2: Athens

Begin the day with a visit to Athens' **National Archaeological Museum** (p. 93), with the world's finest collection of Greek antiquities. (Depending on where you're staying, you may want to walk at least part of the way there, best up Athinas Street for a stop at the lively, colorful **Central Market; see p. 93.**) Essential galleries are the Mycenaean Collection, with gold death masks and many other magnificent treasures of the civilization whose king, Agamemnon, launched the Trojan War; the Cycladic Collection's enigmatic marble figures; and the Thira Collection's colorful and charming frescoes from Santorini. Find a spot for lunch in the atmospheric neighborhoods of **Plaka** (p. 86) or **Monastiraki** (p. 86). Then make your way along Aiolou Street for a look at the **Roman Forum** (p. 89) and the adjacent **Tower of the Winds** (p. 89), probably the city's most unusual landmark from the ancient world. Turn off Aiolou into **Pandrossou,** a pedestrian alley that was the Turkish bazaar during Athens' 400 years of Ottoman rule; the narrow lane lined with stalls is still souk-like. Continue west through the Plaka to Syntagma Square, stopping for a coffee and pastry at **Oraia Ellada** (entrances on both 36 Pandrossou and 59 Mitropoleos). Relax for a spell and soak in the spectacular view of the Acropolis. A walk across **Syntagma Square** (p. 83) puts you figuratively and literally in the center of Athens, with the formidable **Parliament Building** (p. 84) rising to one side. Follow tree-lined Vasillis Sofias, the city's Museum Row, east to the **Museum of Cycladic Art** (p. 95) for a look at the elegantly simple and symmetrical marble figures created more than 3,000 years ago. Walk north through Kolonaki—a neighborhood favored by well-heeled Athenians—to the funicular that climbs **Lycabettus Hill** (p. 96). From the breezy summit, there are mesmerizing views of the Acropolis and across the city to the sea. The spectacle is a good send-off, as it's now time to collect your bags at your hotel, take the Metro to Piraeus, and board the Crete-bound ferry. Boats to the island, equipped with cabins and berths for a good night's sleep, sail from Piraeus at about 9pm.

Day 3: Crete ★★★

You'll dock in Iraklion early in the morning—too early to do much but enjoy a coffee. So, after stashing your bags at your hotel (you probably won't be able to check in yet) join the other early risers at **Kir-Kor,** a venerable old pastry shop overlooking the fountains in **Ta Liontaria (the**

Athens & the Islands in 2 Weeks

SUGGESTED GREECE ITINERARIES

Athens & the Islands in 2 Weeks

1 Athens & the Acropolis
2 Athens Museums & Sights
3 Crete: Iraklion
4 Crete: South Coast & Rethymnon
5 Crete: Chania
6 Crete: Samaria Gorge
7 Crete: Moni Preveli & Iraklion
8 Santorini
9 Naxos
10 Naxos: Tragaea Valley & Beaches
11 Mykonos
12 Day Trip to Delos
13-14 Hydra

Lions) square (p. 197). The treat here is *bougasta,* a flaky, light-as-a-feather cheese-filled pastry. Since you have a whole day to work off the calories, also try the gloriously thick Cretan yoghurt with a generous drizzle of island honey. Next, head for the palace of **Knossos** (p. 196), the dramatic ruins that about 3 millennia ago made up the center of Minoan culture. Then it's on to the center of town and late lunch at the **Pantheon** (p. 192) in the market (actually, it's in an arcade known as Dirty Alley, but don't let that put you off the excellent food). Spend the rest of the afternoon in Iraklion's **Archaeological Museum** (p. 194) for a look at beautiful frescoes portraying Minoan life and other exuberant artifacts of this sophisticated culture. As a cooling breeze picks up in the evening, it's time to get back into the swing of modern life, but gently so, by joining Irakliots for a stroll around the old city.

Day 4: The South Coast of Crete & Rethymnon ★★

On Day 4, you'll head west to Rethymnon, but rather than taking the speedy National Road along the north coast of the island, go off the beaten path and head south across the mountains to the **Messara Plain,** some of the most fertile agricultural land in Greece. Set your sights on one of two beaches near the resort town of Matala—**Red Beach,** reached by a 20-minute hike south over a headland from Matala, and **Kommos,** a long stretch of sand just north of town. After a swim, head north and west again, with a leisurely amble through the scenic **Amari Valley** (p. 206), a panorama of vineyard- and orchard-covered mountain slopes beneath the snow-capped peak of Mount Ida. On a high plateau just to the north of the valley, the ornate **Arkadi Monastery** (p. 206) is a patriotic landmark for Greece, the scene of a bloody fight against the Turks in the 1860s. Then make the half-hour drive down to the coast and **Rethymnon** (p. 201), an inviting place to dine and spend the night amid an exotic maze of Venetian and Turkish houses, mosques, and a massive seaside fortress.

Day 5: Chania ★★★

It's a short drive west from Rethymnon to Chania, only 72km (45 miles), but there's no hurry—you've got time to make a detour onto the **Akrotiri Peninsula,** jutting into the Cretan Sea just east of Chania. The lands at the northern tip of the peninsula are the holdings of three adjacent monasteries. The most remarkable is the 11th-century **Monastery of Katholiko** (p. 215), where St. John the Hermit and his followers lived in caves. A steep path leads past the hermitages and ends at the sea, where you can end your pilgrimage with a swim in a paradisiacal little cove. Then it's on to **Chania** (p. 208), one of the most beautiful cities in Greece. Settle in for 2 nights—we recommend **Doma** (p. 210), an outpost of traditional Cretan hospitality, and the **Porto Veneziano** (p. 210), so close to the water that you'll feel like you're on a ship. Then find a spot on the western side of the harbor, maybe the terrace of the Firkas, the waterside fortress the Venetians built—and take in the view of shimmering sea and waterside palaces. A good place for dinner is the **Well of the Turk** (p. 211), tucked away beneath an exotic minaret.

Day 6: Samaria Gorge ★★★

The longest gorge in Europe, the **Samaria Gorge** (p. 219) is one of the most traveled places in Crete, but crowds of eager hikers don't detract from the spectacle of its narrow passageways and sheer steep walls. Copses of pine and cedar and a profusion of springtime wildflowers carpet the canyon floor, where a river courses through a rocky bed. The hike ends with a well-deserved swim in the Libyan Sea. The easiest way to visit the gorge is on an organized tour. Chania's **Diktynna Travel** (p. 208) is notable for its small groups and knowledgeable and personable guides. Trips leave Chania early, around 8am, and return at 6 or 7pm.

Day 7: Moni Prevli ★★★ & Iraklion ★

You'll be heading east again today, to Iraklion to spend the night before boarding a morning boat to Santorini. Take the day slow and easy. First stop along the north coast is the pretty town of **Vrisses** (p. 216), which rests its fame on thick, creamy yogurt, topped with local honey and savored at a well-shaded cafe table alongside a rushing stream. Just outside of the town in the village of Alikambos, the **Church of the Panagia** (p. 237) houses some of the finest fresco cycles in Crete. Continue on the north coast highway, then detour south through the mountains to the isolated monastery of **Moni Preveli** (p. 207), a beautiful place with a bloody past: its monks led rebellions against the Turks in the 1820s and during World War II hid Allied soldiers from the Germans. Palm Beach reached by a steep path from the monastery grounds, is one of the most lovely stretches of sand on Crete. You'll be in **Iraklion** in time for an evening walk along the ramparts of the **Koules** (p. 195), the mighty, wave-lapped fortress built by 16th-century Venetians.

Day 8: Santorini ★★★

Take an early boat to **Santorini** (p. 152). You'll probably be leaving around 9am and traveling by a high-speed hydrofoil. Though the airplane-like cabin is enclosed, try to wedge your way onto deck as the boat sails into the deep harbor with its high lava-streaked cliffs, created by a volcanic eruption around 1500 B.C. Sailing into Santorini is one of the world's great travel experiences. Once you've checked into your hotel (or, if it's too early to do do, at least leave your bags there), walk a portion of the 10km (6-mile) path that follows the top of the cliff from **Fira** (p. 160) to **Ia** (p. 161), affording a bird's-eye view of the outrageously blue waters and clusters of white houses perched on top of the cliffs like a dusting of snow. From stops along the caldera you can catch the bus to the southern end of the island and **Ancient Akrotiri** (p. 158), Greece's version of Pompeii—a well-preserved Minoan-era town that was buried in that same 1500 B.C. eruption that shaped modern Santorini. Adjoining the site is **Paralia Kokkini (Red Beach),** carpeted in red volcanic pebbles and perfect for an afternoon swim and nap. Come evening, take the bus back up the island to Ia, where watching the sunset is a celebratory event accompanied with a glass of wine. Then head down to **Ammoudi,** the little fishing port below Ia, for a seafood dinner at **Katina's** (p. 157) or another waterside taverna.

Day 9: Naxos ★★

A morning or early afternoon departure will give you the nice part of a day on **Naxos** (p. 171), the largest, greenest, and most scenic island in the Cyclades. (The boat trip from Mykonos takes about 1½ hr.) For a close-to-perfect island retreat settle into **Villa Marandi** (p. 172), set in seaside gardens a couple of miles outside Naxos Town. **Studios Kalergis** (p. 172) is another nice choice, with attractive units hanging over Agios Yeoryios (St. George) beach at the edge of Naxos Town. Spend some hours relaxing before setting out for an evening walk out to the Portara, an unfinished ancient doorway above the harbor. Then follow the steep lanes into the hilltop Kastro, the Venetian fortress and the neighborhood of tall houses that surround the walls. It's an atmospheric setting for a meal at **Lithos** or **Taverna to Kastro** (p. 173).

Day 10: The Tragaea Valley ★★★ & Naxian Beaches

Rent a car for a day to explore Naxos, with its appealing mountain valleys and long stretches of sand. In the garden of an estate in **Melanes** (p. 176) outside Naxos Town, you'll find a 6th-century B.C. *kouros,* a huge marble statue of a beautiful youth. Villages on the lower slopes of **Mount Zas,** the highest mountain in the Cyclades, preserve the rhythms of agrarian life. **Apiranthos** (p. 176), with marble streets, is especially pretty, and **Taverna Lefteris** (p. 173) is a good stop for lunch. To the south, near Sangri, some columns and walls of a **Temple of Demeter** (p. 177), goddess of grain, still stand amid fertile fields. Just to the east is a string of sandy beaches that bring many northern Europeans to Naxos. Skirt the sands on small roads to find the most appealing spot; your best chance for finding a cove to yourself is at Pyrgaki, the southernmost beach on this stretch of coast but only 21km (13 miles) from Naxos Town.

Day 11: Mykonos ★★

You're island hopping in earnest now. In season you have a good choice of morning boats from Naxos to **Mykonos** (p. 137), where you'll arrive just after noon. Check into your hotel—our top choices would be in or just outside **Mykonos Town** (p. 143), because this old Cycladic port is so beautiful and so convenient to the rest of the island. For hedonistic and stylish luxury, it's hard to beat **Cavo Tagoo** (p. 140), while the in-town

Carbonaki (p. 141) gets high marks for good-value comfort and lots of charm. Now it's time to hit the beach (aside from partying, this is the island's favorite pastime). To see the most of the island in your short time here, rent a car—you'll only need it for 24 hours. Paradise and Super Paradise are the island's legendary beaches, but Agios Sostis on the north coast is much less crowded and just as beautiful, with warm, crystal-clear water washing the soft sands. You can get a late lunch at **Kiki's** (p. 142), a simple beachside taverna. In the evening, succumb to the Cycladic charms of Mykonos Town (better known as Hora), with its wooden balconies hanging from white cubical houses and outdoor staircases lined with pots of geraniums. A drink on a seaside terrace in **Little Venice** (p. 145) shows off the island's worldly appeal.

Day 12: Delos ★★★

Begin the day with another swim at one or two of the Mykonos beaches that help put this all-too-popular island on the map (see p. 151 for beaches on Mykonos). You might want to drop by **Paradise** and **Super Paradise** just to see the scene, but for some quieter beach time drive out to **Kalo Livadi (Good Pasture),** a beautiful stretch of sand at the end of a farming valley, or **Panormos,** a dune-backed crescent edging a bay on the north coast. Whichever you choose to go, be back in Mykonos Town in early afternoon to return the car and catch a boat for the short crossing to nearby **Delos** (p. 149). In ancient times this little outcropping was the most famous island in Greece—birthplace of Apollo, a sacred religious sanctuary, a flourishing trade center, and headquarters of the Delian League, the confederation of Greek city-states. As you step ashore and see such famed antiquities as the **Terrace of the Lions,** it soon becomes clear what all the fuss was about. The last boat heads back to Mykonos about 4pm, so plan your trip to allow 2 hours or so on the island—and remember to bring sunscreen and a wide-brimmed hat.

Days 13 & 14: Hydra ★★★

A morning boat from Mykonos will have you back in Athens by midafternoon. But don't pack your island togs away just yet. For one last fling, turn right around and board a hydrofoil at Piraeus for the idyllic Saronic Gulf island of **Hydra** (p. 129), about 2 hours away. You'll arrive in plenty of time to check into your hotel and then have dinner near the harbor, maybe at **To Steki** (p. 132). The next morning, you'll have one more carefree island day to hike, swim, and roam through Hydra Town. A trip by water taxi to the beach at Ayios Nikolaos nicely shows off the rugged shoreline. Boats to Piraeus run frequently, from around 7am to 8pm, so you can time your return to Athens in the evening of Day 14 or morning of Day 15 accordingly.

ATHENS & THE ISLANDS FOR FAMILIES

Yes, we know what kids want—a swimming pool! But you've come all the way to Greece, so here we show off the best of Athens and the islands while trying to balance the needs of young travelers, too.

Day 1: Athens ★★★

Need to work off some fidgets after a long plane ride? Start your first day in Greece with the landmark you can't go home without seeing: The **Acropolis** (p. 74). True, there's a lot of climbing as you ascend through the **Beule Gate** up a well-worn path, but what lies at the top makes the hike all worthwhile: The ruins of the perfectly proportioned Parthenon and surrounding temples. Find a spot to sit and just gaze at those massive columns, summoning up the glory of classical Greece. Then help the kids put it all together with a visit to the **Acropolis Museum** (p. 78), at the base of the hill, where the original sculptures and statuary from the site are on display. If their legs are up to it, you can then stroll along the **Grand Promenade** (p. 80), a cobblestone-and-marble, pedestrian-only boulevard that skirts the Acropolis Hill, and end your sightseeing by strolling around the evocative ruins of the **Ancient Agora** (p. 86), where Socrates once conducted open-air seminars and St. Paul sought converts for the new religion of Christianity. After that, it's time for dinner, maybe beneath a shady plane tree at a long-time favorite, the **Platanos Taverna** (p. 72).

Day 2: Athens

Begin the day with a visit to Athens' **National Archaeological Museum** (p. 93), with the world's finest collection of Greek antiquities. Youngsters will be intrigued by the gold death masks in the Mycenaean Collection, with its Trojan War connections; the Thira Collection's colorful and charming frescoes from Santorini are as fascinating as an ancient comic strip. Then walk south down through Omonia Square to the lively, color-ful **Central Market** (p. 93). The sheeps' heads and live chickens may gross them out, but there's also tasty picnic fare to be picked up. Make your way down Aiolou Street for a look at the **Roman Forum** (p. 89) and the adjacent **Tower of the Winds** (p. 89), then swing west through the Plaka to **Syntagma Square** (p. 83). Enjoy your picnic in the **National Gardens** (p. 84), where the kids can let off some steam. End your picnic in time to see the **Changing of the Guard** (p. 84), every hour on the hour at the nearby Parliament Building. Walk northwest through Kolonaki—a neighborhood favored by well-heeled Athenians—to the funicular that climbs **Lycabettus Hill** (p. 96). The kids will love the ride, and at the top, you'll all be mesmerized by the views of the Acropolis and across the city to the sea. Return to your hotel in time for an late afternoon swim in the pool; if your hotel doesn't have a pool, the **Athens Hilton,** in Kolonaki

Athens & the Islands for Families

1. Athens & the Acropolis
2. Athens Museums & Sights
3. Corinth & Nafplion
4. Nafplion & Epidaurus
5. Olympia
6. Delphi – Athens – Crete
7. Crete: Chania
8. Crete: Samaria Gorge
9-10. Rhodes: Rhodes Town
11. Rhodes: Lindos
12. Symi
13. Symi: Taxixarchis Mihailis Panormitis Monastery
14. Back to Athens

at 46 Vassilissis Sofias Avenue, will let you use theirs, 5€ a person on weekdays, 10€ on weekends.

Day 3: Corinth ★★★

Pile the family into a rental car. (For ease of getting out of Athens, you might want to zip out to the Athens airport on the Metro and get the car from a rental office out there.) No one's going to get too squirmy, as there's not too much driving to do today. First stop is the **Isthmus of Corinth** (p. 114), the narrow neck of land, only 6.3km (4 miles) wide, that connects the Peloponnese to the rest of mainland Greece. Before the Corinth Canal was dug in the 1890s, ships had to sail an extra 400km (240 miles) around the Peloponnese to reach Athens. You can observe the canal, the ship traffic—and, most impressively, the 86m-high (282-ft.) walls of rock through which the canal was cut—from a well-marked overlook off the highway. You might also see some daredevils bungee-jumping off the railroad bridge across the canal.

Just beyond the Isthmus, the **Acrocorinth** (p. 115), one of the world's most remarkable fortresses, looms into view, looking as if it's still there to defend the city of **Corinth** (p. 115) below. Signs point to the temples, agora, fountains, and other sprawling ruins of the Greek and Roman city, where kids will get a good sense of this ancient powerhouse that once rivaled Athens in wealth. (See if they can spot examples of Corinthian columns, with their ornately decorated tops.) End the visit with a drive up to the Acrocorinth, with its three rings of massive fortifications, and mountaintop views that sweep across the sea to the east and west.

It's just another 55km (33 miles) on to **Nafplion,** where you'll settle in for the next 2 nights. A good choice for families is the **Hotel Perivoli** (p. 111), on a hillside outside town with large family units and a sparkling pool. If you stay in a hotel without a pool, make your first stop Arvanitia, the town beach at the end of a pine-scented promenade.

Day 4: Nafplion ★★★ & Epidaurus ★★★

Nafplion's **Old Town** (p. 119), crowded onto a narrow peninsula that juts into the Bay of Argos, is decidedly family friendly, almost entirely closed to car traffic in the area surrounding marble-paved **Syntagma Square.** The first thing young explorers will probably want to do is climb up (part of the way via 999 steps cut into the cliff face) to the fortifications of the **Acronafplia** (p. 119), the southeastern heights which have defended the city for some 5,000 years. Here, the massive walls of the **Palamidi Fortress** (p. 120) ramble across a bluff above the sea and the city. Once back down, an ice cream from the venerable **Antica Gelateria di Roma** (p. 110), at 3 Pharmakopoulou, is in order after all that climbing.

In the afternoon, drive out to **Epidarus** (p. 122), one of the best-preserved classical Greek theaters in the world. The acoustics are so perfect that a whisper onstage can be heard at the top of the 55 tiers—plant the kids at the top of the house then step on stage to demonstrate. The adjoining **Sanctuary of Asklepius at Epidaurus** was one of the most famous healing centers in the Greek world, dedicated to Asklepius, son of Apollo and god of medicine. Tell the kids that one of the sanctuary's favorite treatments involved serpents flicking their tongues over an afflicted body part—they may never complain again about a visit to the pediatrician.

Day 5: Olympia ★★★

Pack up the car and set off for **Olympia** (p. 123), site of the original Olympic Games. The drive is less than 3 hours, leaving time to visit the ruins and museums in the afternoon and early evening. Remains of the stadium, gymnasium, training hall, and dormitories richly evoke the city's famous ancient games, inaugurated in 776 B.C. You can pique their interest by explaining certain gee-whizz aspects of the ancient games— such as the fact that strangulation and metal knuckles were considered perfectly acceptable tactics. Young athletes can stretch their legs with a lap or two around training fields still lined with columns. The **Hotel Europa** (p. 111) is a good choice for a night's stay because it has a big pool; guests at the smaller but delightful **Hotel Pelops** (p. 114) may use the Europa pool as well.

Day 6: Delphi & the Sanctuary of Apollo ★★★

You're in for a bit of driving today. It's about 3½ hours from Olympia to Delphi, but for much of the way the scenery is spectacular—you'll follow the highway around the northern coast to Patras and then Rio, where a dramatic bridge crosses the Gulf of Corinth; that's followed by more scenic coastline as you head east to Delphi. No other ancient site is quite as mysterious and alluring as the **Sanctuary of Apollo** (p. 129). Even youngsters can sense the awe as they climb the Sacred Way to the Temple of Apollo, where priestesses once received cryptic messages from the god. Views over the cliffs and crags of Mt. Parnassus are pretty spectacular, too. Plan to be back in the car about 4pm or so. That allows 5 hours to make the drive to Athens (a little over 2 hr.), drop off the car, and get to Piraeus to board the 9pm boat to Chania, on Crete. (To save time and hassle, see if your car rental company will allow you to drop off in Piraeus.) One you've settled into the cabin for the night crossing, head to the dining room for a meal.

Day 7: Chania

You'll arrive in Chania early, so settle in for a full day of relaxing in one of the most beautiful cities in Greece. An especially welcoming base for families is the **Villa Andromeda** (p. 208), a former seaside estate that housed the German High Command during World War II and has a shady garden and swimming pool. When it's time to explore the city, you won't need to wander too far away from the city's colorful **Venetian Harbor**

(p. 214), with its lighthouse, palaces, and massive *arsenali* (warehouses), one of which houses a replica of a Minoan ship.

Day 8: Samaria Gorge ★★★

Any travel agency in town can arrange the 18km (11-mile) excursion through the **Samaria Gorge** (p. 219), the longest gorge in Europe. Make sure your kids are up for a long though relatively easy hike. You know their limits, but keep in mind that once into the canyon—only 3m (10 ft.) wide in places with walls that can be up to 600m (1,969 ft.) high—there's no turning back. Equip your clan with hats and sunscreen and carry snacks and bathing suits, for a refreshing dip in the Libyan Sea at the end of the hike. Don't load yourself down with too much water; you'll come upon several freshwater springs along the way. Your tour organizer will have you back in Chania in time for dinner.

Days 9 & 10: Rhodes City ★★★

If you're up for a long sea voyage, take the bus to Heraklion and board a boat to Rhodes. It's a 14-hour cruise (great for reading and sea-gazing) but if a day of enforced R&R doesn't appeal to your traveling companions, fly instead. However you get to Rhodes, make **Old Town** (p. 234) your base. If the children are tired of togas and dusty columns, this medieval enclave is the perfect antidote—one of Europe's great historic quarters, with all the storybook atmosphere a young traveler could desire. Many hotels have pleasant gardens, and the **Spirit of the Knights** (p. 230) has a little plunge pool. Two landmarks will fire up youngsters' imaginations. The **City Walls** (p. 235), 4km (2½ miles) in length and 12m thick (40 ft.) in places, are complete with fortified gates and bastions. You can walk around the walls in their entirety, either in the dry moat between the inner and outer walls, or along the ramparts on top. The **Street of the Knights** (p. 236) is one of the best-preserved and most evocative medieval relics in the world, a 600m-long (1,968-ft.) stretch of cobbles where crusader knights of various nations maintained their towered, crenellated inns. For a quick dip, join the locals at **Elli beach** (p. 239), where the waves almost lap up against the walls surrounding the Old Town.

Day 11: Lindos ★★

Frequent buses make the trip to the most picturesque town on the island outside of Rhodes Old Town, a collection of white-stucco houses tucked between the sea and a towering **ancient acropolis** (p. 237). Kids will probably want to board a donkey (also known as a "Lindian taxi") for a slow plod all the way to the top. There, atop a flight of stone steps, are a medieval castle and an ancient Greek terrace littered with the remains of a great assembly hall with a grand columned portico. Way down below is a beach that is just too tempting to resist.

Day 12: Symi ★★

Take a morning ferry to **Symi** (p. 241), where even cranky young travelers will be impressed as the boat sails into beautiful, mansion-lined **Yialos harbor.** One of the pleasures of this rugged little island is the slow pace. You'll want to climb the 375 or so wide stone steps, known as the Kali Strata (the Good Steps), to picturesque **Horio** (p. 244), the old island capital. There the **Archaeological and Folklore Museum** (p. 244) shows off a replica of an old island house. The beaches on Symi aren't spectacular, but there's good swimming from the shoreline right around Yialos.

Day 13: Taxixarchis Mihailis Panormitis Monastery ★★★

A favorite outing from Yialos is this unexpectedly grand, white-washed **monastery** (p. 244) dedicated to the patron saint of seafaring Greeks, tucked away on Symi's hilly, green southwestern corner. A charming museum is filled with wooden ship models, and a heavily frescoed church and chapels open off a courtyard. The most exciting way to reach the monastery, especially with kids, is by boat; there is also twice-a-day bus service from Yialos and Horio. However you get there, count on a refreshing swim in Panormitis Bay.

Day 14: Back to Athens

Now it's time to head back to Athens. No better way to end a vacation in Greece than with a sea voyage, and, depending on timing, you can catch the once-a-week boat from Symi to Piraeus or return to Rhodes and take one of the overnight ferries than run a bit more frequently from there. Then, of course, there's plan B—a quick flight from Rhodes to Athens.

ISLAND HOPPING IN 2 WEEKS

What could be more essentially Greek than sailing from one idyllic island to another? Even the experience of getting from island to island, with your feet propped against the deck railing as the blue Aegean slips by, can seem like a dream come true. Okay, a reality check: You might soon learn that the term "you can't get there from here" originated in the Greek islands, and even the best-laid plans often fall victim to weather, mechanical breakdowns, or last-minute schedule changes. Here, though, is a plan that, provided all goes well, might fulfill any island-hopper's dreams. If you don't have a full 2 weeks to spend, you can lift out any portion of this tour.

Day 1: Athens & the Acropolis ★★★

Arrive in Athens and get settled in a hotel. You can't come to Greece without getting at least a glimpse of some of the ancient marvels of Western Civilization. Relax a bit first, though: Summer hours keep most monuments and museum open late, plus sights in the sprawling capital are fairly concentrated. The **Acropolis** (p. 74) is probably within walking distance of your hotel, maybe even within sight. The ascent through the **Beule Gate** and up a well-worn path is stirring, and what lies beyond is even more so: The ruins of the perfectly proportioned Parthenon and surrounding temples, summoning up the glory of classical Greece. Continue with a walk through the **Acropolis Museum** (p. 78), where the sculptures and statuary that once adorned the Acropolis temples are on display, including a section of the magnificent Parthenon Frieze. Then stroll along the **Grand Promenade** (p. 80), a cobblestone-and-marble, pedestrian-only boulevard that skirts the Acropolis Hill. You'll get a glimpse of the **Theater of Dionysus** (p. 82), where the newest dramas of Aeschylus, Sophocles, and Euripides once delighted audiences. Plunge back into the present day, by following Adrianou (Hadrian) Street through the colorful **Plaka** neighborhood (p. 86). End your day by strolling around the evocative ruins of the **Ancient Agora** (p. 86), once the business and political hub of ancient Athens. Then it's time for dinner, maybe beneath a shady plane tree at a long-time favorite, the **Platanos Taverna** (p. 72).

Day 2: Athens to Alonissos ★★

You'll spend the day on the move, first traveling from Athens by morning bus to—depending on boat schedules—either Ayios Konstantinos or Volos, two mainland ports each 3 to 4 hours north of Athens. Boats depart from both for **Alonissos** (p. 270), 2 hours off the mainland by hydrofoil, 4½ hours by ferry. Any good travel agency in Athens can help you make arrangements for the combined bus and boat trip. You'll probably settle onto the island in time for a sunset cocktail on the terrace of your hotel—a good choice is the **Paradise** (p. 272), nestled above Parikia, the port, amid pines with outlooks over a serene bay that's one of the best spots on the island for a refreshing swim. Enjoy a seafood dinner at **Archipelagos** (p. 271), on the Parikia waterfront.

Day 3: Hora & Kokkinokastro

You'll quickly learn that the life on Alonissos is pretty slow-paced, and you might be tempted to spend the day in a lounger and soak up some sun, as many northern European visitors do. If you feel like being a bit more active, however, hike from Parikia up to **Hora,** the old hilltop capital, in less than an hour along an old, stepped mule track—do this in the morning, though, before the heat of the day. In summer, a bus makes the trip, and also goes out to the beach at **Kokkinokastro** (p. 273), about 3km (2 miles) north of Patitiri, where the walls of the ancient city of Ikos are visible beneath the waves. Snorkelers and divers might want to stop in at **Alonissos Triton Dive Center,** in Patitiri (p. 274) and arrange an excursion to one of the outlying shipwrecks.

Island Hopping in 2 Weeks

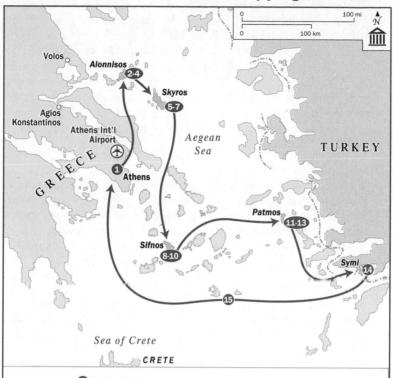

1. Athens & the Acropolis
2. Alonissos
3. Alonissos: Hora & Kokkinokastro
4. Alonissos: National Marine Park of the Northern Sporades
5. Skyros
6. Skyros: Skyros Town
7. Skyros: North and South
8. Sifnos
9. Sifnos: Apollonia Villages & Kastro
10. Sifnos: Profitis Elias o Pilos & Vathy
11. Patmos
12. Patmos: Holy Sights
13. Patmos: Psili Ammos Beach
14. Symi
15. Back to Athens

Day 4: National Marine Park ★★★

Alonissos is surrounded by the waters of the 2,200 sq. km (849 sq. miles) **National Marine Park of Alonissos Northern Sporades** (p. 273), the largest marine protected area in the Mediterranean, encompassing eight islands (of which only Alonissos is inhabited), 22 rocky outcroppings, and the waters that surround them. The park is home to the highly endangered Mediterranean monk seal, as well as falcons, dolphins, and wild goats. Excursion boats from the dock in Patitiri make day-long outings through the scattered island refuges, stopping for lunch, swimming, snorkeling, and a walk to the island's one outpost of civilization, the all-but-abandoned **Megistis Lavras** monastery.

Day 5: Alonissos to Skyros ★★

It's time to move on to another Sporades, adrift by itself in the Aegean. You'll appreciate just how remote **Skyros** (p. 274) is when you try to get there. Check boat schedules with one of the agencies on the Parikia waterfront. In the summer, a few boats a week travel directly from Alonissos to Skyros; otherwise you'll need to sail from Alonissos to Kymi, on the island of Evvia, where you can get a ferry to Skyros. With a day of travel you'll probably arrive before sundown, in time to see the spectacle of mirage-like **Skyros Town** (p. 274), with its white, flat-roofed houses clinging to a high rocky bluff. That's where you'll want to settle in for 2 nights, either in the heights of Skyros Town at the **Nefeli** (p. 276) or another hotel within walking distance of Skyros Town.

Day 6: Skyros Town

You can divide the day between sightseeing in Skyros Town and spending some time on the beach without traveling very far. Do your exploring of Skyros Town in the morning, to spare yourself the uphill climbs in the heat of the day. A mandatory stop is the **Manos Faltaits Historical and Folklore Museum** (p. 277), where you'll see examples of the local plates, embroidery, weaving, carved furniture, and clothing that are still a part of everyday life on the island. A sandy beach stretches just beneath Skyros Town at **Magazia** (p. 278), at the bottom of a stairway from Plateia Rupert Brooke. That's Rupert Brooke as in the famous British World War I poet, who died on Skyros in 1915. A huge statue in the square commemorates him.

Day 7: North & South

Skyros is an island divided, between the fertile, forested north and the arid, rugged south. You can see easily see both is a day of exploring by rental car. First set your sights on **Palamari** (p. 278), at the northern tip of the island, where behind the sandy beach are remnants of walls built by ancient settlers. The island's best beach is here in the north, on the west coast at **Agios Fokas** (p. 278), where little bays are edged with white pebbles. A single road leads south through a desolate, rocky landscape and ends at **Tris Boukes Bay** (p. 278), where Rupert Brooke is buried in a simple grave.

Day 8: Skyros to Sifnos ★★★

This is another day full of travel, with an early start on the 7 or 8am ferry from Skyros to Kymi; the crossing takes a little less than 2 hours. Once in Kymi, you'll board a bus for the 2½-hour trip down to Athens, and from there take the metro to Piraeus. If all goes well, you'll be in Piraeus with plenty of time to spare for 3 or 4pm (depending on the day) sailings to **Sifnos.** That will put you in Sifnos around 9pm, in time for a late dinner—actually, an early dinner by Greek standards. If you stay at the delightful hilltop **Petali** (p. 167), dine on the terrace there, looking out over the Apollonia villages.

Day 9: The Apollonia Villages ★★ & Kastro ★★

Spend the morning rambling through the island's capital, **Apollonia** (p. 168), really a cluster of six villages (or five or seven, depending on whom you ask) that tumble across the inland hills in haphazard fashion. Flagstone footpaths wind down to the town's main square, **Plateia Iroon** (Hero's Square), where the **Popular and Folk Art Museum** (p. 168) is a showplace for island embroidery, weaving, and traditional Sifnian earthenware pots and jars. Relax over a light meal on the terrace of the **Gerontopoulos Café,** just off the square in the Hotel Anthousa, then catch a bus or follow the well-marked footpath down to **Kastro** (p. 169), a somberly medieval fortress town where tall Venetian-era houses line a maze of little lanes. In one of them, an archaeological museum shows off bits of pottery and friezes from the Greek and Roman city that occupied these heights 3,000 years ago. The prettiest sight in town is the **Church of the Eftamartyres (Seven Martyrs),** atop a sea-girt promontory far beneath a clifftop promenade that skirts the town's outer flanks. Get on the bus for the trip out to another incredibly picturesque spot, **Chrysopigi** (p. 167), a beloved monastery on a rocky islet. You'll want to step into the tranquil courtyard and simple church if they're open, but the real reason to come here is to swim at sandy **Apokofto** beach, nestled alongside an adjacent cove.

Day 10: Profitis Elias o Pilos ★★ & Vathy ★★

Put on some sturdy walking shoes and set out early in the cool of the morning for the hour-long hike up to the island's most famous monastery, **Profitis Elias o Pilos** (p. 170). The path is fairly easy, but steep; O Pilos means "high one," and the monastery sits atop a 850m (2,789-ft.) summit. At the top, one of the few monks in residence will probably offer you a glass of cool water. The descent is easier, naturally, and you can spend the rest of the day beneath a pine tree along the beach at **Vathy** (p. 170). Buses serve this serene village, where **Monastery of the Taxiarchis**

Evangelistrias (Archangel of the Annunciation) seems to rise right out of the surf.

Day 11: Sifnos to Patmos ★★★

The beautiful monasteries on Sifnos should have whetted your appetite for your next destination: Patmos, one of Greece's holiest islands, where St. John the Apostle supposedly received his divine revelations. First, though, you'll have to get there, and the logistics will make you wish for some divine intervention, or a private yacht. The easiest way is to take a morning boat from Sifnos to Piraeus, where you can immediately hop on the afternoon boat to Patmos, arriving in the late evening. To enjoy the island in style—and you deserve some spoiling after all that travel—settle into the **Petra Hotel and Apartments** (p. 253) or **Porto Scoutari** (p. 254).

Day 12: Patmos & the Holy Sights

First stops on Patmos (well, after a morning swim) are the island's two famous religious sights: the **Cave of the Apocalypse** (p. 254), perched on a hillside above Skala, the port; and atop the hill, the fortress-like **Monastery of St. John** (p. 255), with its treasure-filled frescoed chapels, surrounded by medieval **Hora.** Buses from Skala serve both. Begin by exploring Hora, a labyrinth of whitewashed stone homes, shops, and churches. After a visit to the monastery, walk down the well-marked path to the famous cave where St. John the Divine (aka the Apostle) allegedly received the word of God. From there, it's an easy descent back down to Skala.

Day 13: Psili Ammos ★★★

Time out for a beach day. Set your sights on **Psili Ammos** (p. 255), an isolated fine-sand cove bordered by cliffs. It's possible to walk to Psili Ammos from the little settlement of Diakofti, about a 30-minute trek on goat paths (wear real shoes) but most sunseekers arrive by one of the caiques leaving Skala harbor in the morning and returning around 4 to 5pm. Groves of pine trees provide plenty of shade, and a simple taverna sells snacks. End the visit on a romantic note, with an excellent dinner on the seaside terrace at **Benetos** (p. 253), just outside Skala in Grikos.

Day 14: Symi ★★

Take a morning ferry from Patmos to **Symi** (p. 241), where you'll pull into beautiful, mansion-lined **Yialos harbor.** You'll want to climb the 375 or so wide stone steps, known as the Kali Strata (the Good Steps), to picturesque **Horio** (p. 244), the old island capital. There the **Archaeological and Folklore Museum** (p. 244) shows off a replica of an old island house. You'll still have time for an excursion out to **Taxixarchis Mihailis Panormitis,** an unexpectedly grand white-washed **monastery** (p. 244) dedicated to the patron saint of seafaring Greeks, tucked away on Symi's hilly, green southwestern corner. A charming museum is filled with wooden ship models, and a heavily frescoed church and chapels open off a courtyard. The best way to reach the monastery is by boat, although there is also twice-a-day bus from Yialos and Horio. While there, count on a refreshing swim in Panormitis Bay.

Day 15: Back to Athens

Now it's time to head back to Athens. Depending on timing, you can catch the once-a-week boat from Symi to Piraeus or sail to **Rhodes** and take one of the overnight ferries than run a bit more frequently from there. Then, of course, there's plan B—a quick flight from Rhodes to Athens where you can get ready for your flight home.

ATHENS

This is Athens: Exciting, exasperating, worldly, and oh so hot. Home to gods, goddesses, and some of the history's greatest philosophers and athletes, Athens is an ancient city with a modern edge. Glorious ancient monuments are a backdrop for the city's greatest resource, 4 million Athenians—cosmopolitan, hedonistic, and forward-thinking, despite their nation's gravely uncertain economic future.

As you explore Athens, try to make the city your own. See the Acropolis, explore the Agora, visit ancient temples and Byzantine churches. Most of all, take a *siga, siga* (slowly, slowly) approach. Walk streets lined with neoclassical mansions; take in the scents; linger in courtyard gardens and on rooftop terraces. For cool respite head to the National Gardens, and for gorgeous sunsets perch on the peak of Lycabettus hill. Check out stalls laden with fresh fruit, nuts, and mounds of Aegean seafood in the 19th-century glass-and-steel Central Market. Discover the urban chic of Gazi, Pyssri, and other once-neglected downtown neighborhoods. You'll find that Athens is beautiful and gritty, ancient and modern, sultry and restless, frustrating yet seductive, and most of all—like the sight of the Acropolis looming above it all—rather unforgettable.

ESSENTIALS

Arriving

BY PLANE The **Athens International Airport Eleftherios Venizelos** (www.aia.gr; © **210/353-0000**), 27km (17 miles) northeast of Athens, is usually called "Venizelos," or "Spata" after the nearest town. Venizelos is a large, modern facility, with plenty to keep you busy, including a small museum with rotating art exhibits and ruins found during the airport's construction. An Athens Info-Point offers excellent city brochures and guides, plus digital tours of the city. The **Greek National Tourism Organization** (abbreviated GNTO in English-speaking countries, EOT in Greece) has an information desk in the arrivals hall. The Pacific baggage storage (left luggage) facility in the main terminal arrivals area is officially open 24 hours a day and charges 2€ per piece per day.

The **Metro** (www.amel.gr) is the most convenient, least expensive, and fastest way to get from the airport to downtown or vice versa. The trip takes roughly 40 minutes, and trains run every half-hour from 6:30am to 11:30pm. (Trains from the city to the airport run 5:50am–10:50pm.) Cost is 10€ one way, 18€ for a round-trip within 48 hours; one-way fare for two people is 18€, and for three people, 24€. **Buses** (www.oasa.gr), which run 24 hours a day, depart from outside the arrivals hall of the main terminal building (doors 4 and 5). Bus service from the airport to Syntagma Square (X95) or to Piraeus (X96) costs 6€. The X95 runs every 10 minutes from 7am to 10pm and every half-hour from 10pm to 7am. The X96 runs every 20 minutes from 7am to 10pm and every 40 minutes from 10pm to 7am. You can buy a ticket from a booth beside the bus stop or on the bus; you must validate your ticket by punching it in the machine within the bus. For more information on public transport, see p. 284.

Taxis from the airport to downtown Athens charge a flat rate which includes tolls and luggage. Once you are in the taxi, make sure the meter is set on the correct tariff (tariff 1 is charged 5am–midnight; tariff 2 midnight–5am). If you're going to Omonia Square, the price is 32€ (late-night rate 42€); for the Plaka/Makrigianni districts (at Hadrian's Gate), the rate is 35€ (nighttime 50€). Depending on traffic, the drive can take under 30 minutes or well over an hour—something to remember when you return to the airport. Hertz, Avis, and Alamo **rental cars** are also available at the airport.

BY CAR If you arrive by car from **Corinth** (to the southwest), the signs into Athens will direct you fairly clearly to Omonia Square, which you will enter from the west along Ayiou Konstantinou. In Omonia, signs *should* direct you on toward Syntagma Square and other points in central Athens (signs in Omonia disappear mysteriously). If you arrive from **Thessaloniki** (to the north), the signs pointing you into central Athens are few and far between. It is not a good idea to attempt this for the first time after dark. Your best bet is to look for the Acropolis and head toward it until you see signs for Omonia or Syntagma squares.

BY BUS There are two main stations for **KTEL** (www.ktel.org), the national bus company, near each other in the northwestern part of the city. **Terminal A,** 100 Kifissou (℃ **210/512-9233**), handles buses to and from the Peloponnese and parts of Northern Greece; this terminal is often referred to as Kifissou, or Kifissou Terminal A. **Terminal B** (260 Liossion St.; ℃ **210/831-7096**) handles buses to and from Central Greece (including Delphi, Thebes, Evvia, and Meteora) and some destinations to the north and east of Athens; this terminal is often referred to simply as Liossion or Liossion Terminal B. Public bus no. 051 (1.20€) runs to both terminals. A taxi from either to Syntagma Square should cost 8€ to 18€; if traffic is light, the ride is less than 20 minutes, but it can take an hour.

A third station, the **Mavromateon terminal** (www.ktelattikis.gr; ℃ **210/880-8080;** Metro: Victoria Square) is at the entrance to Areos Park at Patission and Alexandras, just north of Omonia Square near the Archaeological Museum. Also known as the Areos Park Terminal, it handles buses for most destinations in Attica, including Sounion. The closest metro station, Victoria Square, is 2 blocks away.

BY TRAIN   Trains from the south and west arrive at the **Peloponnese station** (Stathmos Peloponnisou; ✆ **210/513-1601**), about a mile northwest of Omonia Square on Sidirodromeon. Trains from the north arrive at **Larissa station** (Stathmos Larissis; ✆ **210/529-8837**), just across the tracks from the Peloponnese station on Deligianni. From the Larissa Metro station near both train stations you can easily reach Omonia, Syntagma, and other central points on line 2 (Larissa). A taxi to the center of town should cost about 10€.

BY BOAT   Most boats arrive at and depart from **Piraeus,** the main harbor of Athens's main seaport, 11km (7 miles) southwest of central Athens. It's a 15-minute Metro ride (fare 1.40€) from Monastiraki, Omonia, and Thissio Metro stations. The far slower bus no. 040 (fare 1.40€) runs from Piraeus to central Athens (with a stop at Filellinon, off Syntagma Square) every 15 minutes between 5am and 1am and hourly from 1am to 5am. To get to Athens International Airport, you can take the X96 bus (6€) or the metro (10€; change at Monastiraki station). You may prefer to take a taxi to avoid the hike from your boat to the bus stop or subway terminal, but be prepared for serious bargaining. The normal fare on the meter from Piraeus to Syntagma should be 15€ to 20€, but many drivers offer a flat fare, which can be as much as 30€.

If you arrive at Piraeus by hydrofoil (Flying Dolphin), you'll probably arrive at **Zea Marina** harbor, about a dozen blocks south across the peninsula from the main harbor. Getting a taxi from Zea Marina into Athens can involve a wait of an hour or more—and cab drivers usually drive hard bargains. To avoid both the wait and big fare, walk up the hill from the hydrofoil station to catch bus no. 905 (fare 1.40€), which connects Zea to the Piraeus Metro station, where you can continue on into Athens. You must buy a ticket at a newsstand or at the small stand near the bus stop before boarding the bus. If you arrive late at night, however, you may be out of luck, as both the newsstand and the ticket stand may be closed.

If you disembark at the port of **Rafina** (about an hour's bus ride east of Athens), you'll see a bus stop up the hill from the ferryboat pier. Inquire about the bus to Athens; it runs often and will take you to the Mavromateon/Areos Park bus terminal, near the junction of Leoforos Alexandras and Patission. The terminal is 1 block from the Victoria Square Metro stop and about 25 minutes by trolley from Syntagma Square. From the bus terminal, there are buses to Rafina every half-hour. As confusing as the multiple terminals can be, the staff at the visitor information office in Athens and at the airport (see below) are extremely helpful in telling you which bus leaves from where and how to get to the right terminal.

Visitor Information

The **Greek National Tourism Organization (EOT or GNTO)** is at 7 Tsoha St., Ambelokipi (www.visitgreece.gr; ✆ **210/870-0000;** Metro: Ambelokipi). The office is officially open Monday through Friday, 8am to 3pm, and is closed on weekends. The GNTO information desk office is at 18–20 Dionissiou Aeropagitou St. (✆ **210/331-0392;** Metro: Acropolis; Mon–Fri 9am–7pm;

Sat–Sun 10am–4pm). An information desk (© **210/345-0445**) and an Info-Point (© **210/325-3123;** www.atedco.gr) are also located at the airport. Two Info-Points are in the city in the Makrigianni district on the corner of Amalias Avenue and Dionisiou Aeropagitou Street (near the Acropolis metro station and the Acropolis Museum) and in the port of Piraeus. They have excellent brochures and city maps, plus digital tours of the city, and staff is generally eager to help you navigate the city. Info-Points operate daily from 9am to 9pm. Information about Athens, free city maps, transportation schedules, hotel lists, Available 24 hours a day, the **tourist police** (© **210/171**) speak English as well as other languages, and will help you with problems or emergencies.

City Layout

To get your bearings as you explore Athens, you may find it helpful to look up to the **Acropolis,** west of Syntagma Square, and to **Mount Likavitos (Lycabettus),** to the northeast. From most parts of the city, you can see both.

Think of central Athens as an almost perfect equilateral triangle, with its points at **Syntagma (Constitution) Square, Omonia (Harmony) Square,** and **Monastiraki (Little Monastery) Square,** near the Acropolis. The area bounded by Syntagma, Omonia, and Monastiraki squares is defined as the commercial center, from which cars are banned except for several cross streets.

At one time **Omonia Square**—Athens's commercial hub—was considered the city center, but nowadays, most Greeks think of **Syntagma Square,** site of the House of Parliament, as ground zero. The two squares are connected by parallel streets, **Stadiou** and **Panepistimiou.**

West of Syntagma Square, **Ermou** and **Mitropoleos** lead slightly downhill to **Monastiraki Square.** From Monastiraki Square, **Athinas** leads north back to Omonia past the Central Market. The old warehouse district of **Psyrri,** now a hip enclave, is between Athinas and Ermou.

If you stand in Monastiraki Square and look south, you'll see the Acropolis. At its foot are the **Ancient Agora** (p. 86) and the **Plaka,** Athens's oldest neighborhood. The Plaka's twisting labyrinth of streets can challenge even the best navigators, but the district is small enough that you can't go far astray, and it's a pleasant place in which to wander aimlessly. Many Athenians speak some English, and almost all are helpful to direction-seeking strangers.

Neighborhoods in Brief

Athens is a collection of many different neighborhoods, each with its own distinctive flair. Take time simply to stroll around the central city from one neighborhood into another. Part of the walk should be along the **Grand Promenade,** the walkway that stretches from Hadrian's Gate past the Acropolis to the Ancient Agora, past Thissio and on to the Kerameikos cemetery.

Around the Acropolis At the base of the Acropolis and the pine-clad slopes of Lofos Filopappou (Filopappos Hill) and Lofos Mousson (Hill of the Muses) are elegant residential enclaves. The **Grand Promenade** leads to the Acropolis Museum, the Theater of Dionysus, and other sights.

Syntagma (Constitution) Square The heart of Athens is the focal point of the city's political and civic life, from protest rallies to New Year's celebrations. Syntagma is the home of much of governmental Athens: The handsome neoclassical building at the head of the square is the **Greek Parliament**

building, formerly the Royal Palace, where you'll see the Changing of the Guard several times a day. Adjacent to Parliament are the **National** (p. 84) **and Zappeion** (p. 85) **Gardens.**

Plaka Spreading below the Acropolis, Plaka is the most touristic neighborhood in the city. Its maze of narrow medieval streets—many named after Greek heroes from either classical antiquity or the Greek War of Independence—twist their way past ancient sites, Byzantine churches, offbeat museums, and 19th-century homes. Restaurants and cafes line many lanes of this pedestrian neighborhood. It's atmospheric, romantic, and nostalgia-inducing. **Anafiotika** (p. 87), a Cycladic-style town at the base of the Acropolis, is a tiny village within a village.

Monastiraki This neighborhood on the fringe of the Agora and the Roman Forum is best known for its flea markets. They're open every day but are usually best—and most crowded—on Sunday. Many tavernas, cafes, and shops line the streets. The most appealing street by far is **Adrianou,** with restored houses now occupied by restaurants and cafes on one side and the Agora on the other—and Acropolis views to boot.

Psyrri Between Athinas and Ermou streets, Psyrri was once derelict and forgotten; now warehouses have been converted and neoclassical houses restored. Trendy bars, restaurants, clubs, cafes, tavernas, galleries, and *mezedopoleia* (establishments offering "small plates") are side by side with some still-remaining workshops. This area comes alive in the late afternoon until the early morning hours. Its outer pockets remain a bit gritty.

Gazi West of Psyrri is this bohemian enclave where Athens's modern heart beats to its own rhythm. **Gazi Square,** surrounded by some of the city's coolest bars and eateries, is where locals socialize (drink in hand) when the bars are full, creating a scene that can only be found in the most popular Greek islands at the height of summer. Between Psyrri and Gazi is **Kerameikos** (p. 90), the little-visited ancient cemetery with many stunningly beautiful classical sculptures and part of the city's ancient walls. Gazi was once an industrial wasteland where a foundry spewed black gas fumes (thus the name Gazi, which means gas) from smokestacks. The cavernous spaces have been converted to an arts complex known as Technopolis (p. 91).

Omonia and Exarchia Time was, Omonia was a grand *plateia* (square), surrounded by neoclassical buildings and a place for couples to stroll. Today it's gritty, encircled by an endless swirl of traffic, and frequented by some decidedly shady denizens. To the east of Omonia Square, the bohemian student neighborhood **Exarchia** covers 50 city blocks, crisscrossed with buzzing squares and pedestrian streets. The **National Archaeological Museum** (p. 93) is at the edge of Exarchia, north of Omonia Square.

Kolonaki and Lycabettus The elegant neighborhood tucked beneath the slopes of Lycabettus hill has long been the favorite address of well-to-do Athenians. The streets (many for pedestrians only) are packed with designer houses, art galleries, and night and day gathering spots. **Leof Vasiliss Sofias,** one of the most imposing streets in Athens, is lined with neoclassical mansions, many of which now house museums (among them the **Benaki;** see p. 95), earning the nickname the Museum Mile. A funicular ride leaves all the urban chic behind for the top of **Lycabettus hill** (p. 96) and the spectacle of Athens laid out under your feet like a sparkling map.

Getting Around
BY PUBLIC TRANSPORTATION

You can use the same tickets anywhere on Athens' Metro, bus, trolley, and tram system (except for bus E22, which heads to the coast and costs 1.60€ more, and the metro to the airport, which costs 10€ one way). The best online source for information, with a trip planner that allows you to map out a route, is Transport for Athens (www.oasa.gr). Tickets are sold at Metro stations or at *periptera* (ticket kiosks) scattered throughout the city; you can buy them individually or in packets of 10. **Fares** are 1.40€ for a single ride, 4.50€ for a day pass; a ticket covers all travel for a 90-minute period, even if you switch from a bus to a Metro train or vice versa. **Be certain to validate** your ticket in the machine when you enter the Metro platform or get on a bus or tram, and *hold on to your ticket.* Uniformed and plainclothes inspectors periodically check tickets and can levy a fine of anywhere from 5€ to 60€ on the spot.

The **Metro** runs from 5:30am to midnight Sunday through Thursday; on Friday and Saturday, trains run until 2am. All stations are wheelchair accessible. Stop at the Syntagma station or go to the GNTO (p. 208) for a system map. Even if you do not use the Metro to get around Athens, you may want to take it from Omonia, Monastiraki, or Thissio to Piraeus to catch a boat to the islands. (Don't miss the spectacular view of the Acropolis as the subway goes above ground by the Agora.) Three stations—Syntagma Square, Monastiraki, and Acropolis—handsomely display finds from the subway excavations. The system is continually being expanded, so expect occasional construction delays.

You can also get almost everywhere you want in central Athens and the suburbs by **bus** or **trolley,** which run 24 hours a day. It can be confusing, however, to figure out which bus to take, especially now, as many bus routes change when new Metro stations open. Even if you know which bus to take, you may have to wait a long time until the bus appears—usually stuffed with passengers. Check out the **Athens Urban Transport Organisation** (www.oasa.gr; © **185**) for directions, timetables, route details, and maps.

Athens's **tram** (www.tramsa.gr) connects downtown to the city's coast. Though it may not be the fastest means of transport, it takes a scenic route once it hits the coast. Comfortable and air-conditioned, it's handy for visiting the beaches and the coastline's attractions and nightlife. The tram runs 5am to midnight Sunday through Thursday, and around the clock on Friday and Saturday. A ride from Syntagma Square to the current last stop in seafront Voula is a little over an hour.

BY TAXI

Taxis are inexpensive, and most drivers are honest. Even so, when you get into a taxi during the day and up until midnight, check the **meter.** Make sure it is turned on and set to 1 (the daytime rate) rather than 2 (the late night rate). The meter will register 1€. The meter should be set on 2 (double fare) only between midnight and 5am *or* if you take a taxi outside the city limits; if you plan to do this, negotiate a flat rate in advance. The "1" meter rate is .32€ per kilometer; the minimum fare is 2.80€. There's a surcharge of 1€ for service from a port or from a rail or bus station. Luggage costs .32€ per 10 kg (22 lb.). *Note:* These prices will almost certainly be higher by the time you visit Greece.

Don't be surprised if the driver picks up other passengers en route; he will work out everyone's share of the fare. If you plan to travel around Athens by taxi, carry a business card from your hotel, so you can show it to the taxi driver on your return trip.

BY CAR

As in other large cities, don't drive. In Athens, a car is far more trouble than convenience. The traffic is heavy, and finding a parking place is extremely difficult. Much of the central city is closed to cars, while you will be able to get to most of places you want to reach on foot or by the city's extensive public transport system. Taxis are plentiful and fairly inexpensive. If you plan on renting a car when leaving Athens, maybe to continue on to Delphi or into the Peloponnese, you'll find many rental agencies south of Syntagma Square and in Athens International Airport. Airport rentals are especially handy because you can immediately get onto the highway network that will whisk you away from the city. See p. 283 for more on renting a car in Athens. Should you find yourself with a car to stash in Athens, a centrally located garage is **Parking Menandrou,** at Menandrou 22, near Omonia Square, *②* **210/524-1027.** Also central is **Parking Syntagmas,** Filellinon 12, near Syntagma Square, *②* **210/324-4090.** At these and other central garages expect to pay 1€ an hour and 12€ to 15€ for 24 hours.

ON FOOT

Since most of what you'll want to see and do in Athens is in the city center, it's easy to do most of your sightseeing on foot. The city has created pedestrian zones around Omonia, Syntagma, and Monastiraki squares, in the **Plaka,** in **Kolonaki,** and elsewhere. **Dionissiou Areopagitou,** at the southern foot of the Acropolis, is also pedestrianized, with links to the Grand Promenade past the Ancient Agora, Thissio, and Kerameikos. Still, don't let your guard down completely: Athens's multitude of motorcyclists seldom respect the rules, and a red traffic light or stop sign is no guarantee that vehicles will stop for pedestrians.

[FastFACTS] ATHENS

ATMs Automated teller machines are common at banks throughout Athens. The **National Bank of Greece** operates a 24-hour ATM in Syntagma Square.

Banks Banks are generally open Monday through Thursday, 8am to 2pm, and Friday 8am to 2:30pm. All banks are closed on the long list of Greek holidays. (See p. 29.)

Business Hours Even Greeks get confused by

their complicated, changeable business hours. In winter, shops are generally open Monday and Wednesday from 9am to 5pm; Tuesday, Thursday, and Friday from 10am to 7pm; and Saturday from 8:30am to 3:30pm. In summer, shops are generally open Monday, Wednesday, and Saturday from 8am to 3pm, and Tuesday, Thursday, and Friday from 8am to 2pm and 5:30 to 10pm. Most stores in

central Athens, though, remain open all day. Department stores and supermarkets are open 8am to 8pm Monday to Friday and 8am to 6pm on Saturday.

Dentists & Doctors Embassies (see below) may have lists of dentists and doctors, as do some hotels. For an English-speaking doctor or dentist, also try **SOS Doctor** (*②* **1016** or 210/361-7089). There are two medical hot lines for foreigners: ℰ **210/721-2951** (day) and 210/729-4301 (night) for U.S. citizens; and ℰ **210/723-6211** (day) and 210/723-7727 (night) for British citizens.

Embassies & Consulates **Australia,** Level 6, Thon Building, corner Kiffisias & Alexandras, Ambelokipi (www.greece.embassy.gov.au; ℰ **210/870-4000**); **Canada,** 48 Ethnikis Antistaseos St. (www.greece.gc.ca; ℰ **210/727-3400**); **Ireland,** 7 Vas. Konstantinou (ℰ **210/723-2771**); **New Zealand,** 76 Kifissias Ave, Ambelokipi (ℰ **210/692-4136**); **South Africa,** 60 Kifissias, Maroussi (ℰ **210/680 6615**); **United Kingdom,** 1 Ploutarchou (www.ukingreece.fco.gov.uk; ℰ **210/727-2600**); **United States,** 91 Leoforos Vas. Sofias (athens.usembassy.gov; ℰ **210/721-2951**). Be sure to phone ahead before you go to any embassy; most keep limited hours and are usually closed on their own holidays as well as Greek ones.

Emergencies In an emergency, dial ℰ **100** for the **police** and ℰ **171** for the **tourist police.** Dial ℰ **199** to report a **fire** and ℰ **166** for an **ambulance** and the **hospital.** Athens has a **24-hour** line for foreigners, the **Visitor Emergency Assistance** at ℰ **112** in English and French.

Hospitals **KAT,** the emergency hospital in Kifissia (ℰ **210/801-4411** to -4419), and **Asklepion Voulas,** the emergency hospital

in Voula (ℰ **210/895-3416** to -3418), have emergency rooms open 24 hours a day. **Evangelismos,** a centrally located hospital below the Kolonaki district on 9 Vas. Sophias (ℰ **210/722-0101**), usually has English-speaking staff on duty. If you need medical attention fast, don't waste time trying to call these hospitals: Just go. They will see to you as soon as possible.

In addition, each major hospital takes its turn each day being on emergency duty. A recorded message in Greek at ℰ **210/106** tells which hospital is open for emergency services and gives the telephone number.

Internet Access Most hotels and many bars and cafes are Wi-Fi equipped. Also, several Wi-Fi hot spots can be found in Syntagma Square, Kotzia Square, Flisvos marina, and other public spaces; the airport also offers free Wi-Fi.

Lost & Found The police's **Lost and Found,** 173 Leoforos Alexandras (ℰ **210/642-1616**), is open Monday through Saturday from 9am to 3pm. For losses on the Metro, there is an office in Syntagma station (www.amel.gr; ℰ **210/327-9630**; Mon–Fri 7am–7pm, Sat 8am–4pm). Lost passports and other documents may be returned by the police to the appropriate embassy, so check there as well. It's an excellent idea to travel with photocopies of your important documents, including

passport, prescriptions, tickets, phone numbers, and addresses.

Luggage Storage & Lockers If you're coming back to stay, many hotels will store excess luggage while you travel. There are storage facilities at Athens International Airport, at the Metro stations in Piraeus and Monastiraki, and at the train stations.

Pharmacies Pharmakia, identified by green crosses, are scattered throughout Athens. Hours are usually Monday through Friday, 8am to 2pm. In the evenings and on weekends, most are closed, but each posts a notice listing the location of pharmacies that are open or will open in an emergency. Newspapers such as the Athens News list the pharmacies open outside regular hours.

Police In an **emergency,** dial ℰ **100.** For help dealing with a troublesome taxi driver, hotel staff, restaurant staff, or shop owner, stand your ground and call the **tourist police** at ℰ **171.**

Post Offices The main post offices in central Athens are at 100 Eolou, south of Omonia Square; and in Syntagma Square, at the corner of 60 Mitropoleos. They are open Monday to Friday, 7:30am to 8pm, Saturday 7:30am to 2pm, and Sunday 9am to 1pm.

All post offices accept parcels, but the **Parcel Post Office** is at 4 Stadiou inside the arcade (ℰ **210/322-8940**). It's open Monday through Friday from 7:30am to 8pm. It usually sells twine and cardboard shipping boxes. Parcels must remain open for inspection before you seal them at the post office.

Restrooms There are public restrooms in the underground station beneath Omonia and Syntagma squares and beneath Kolonaki Square, but you'll probably prefer a hotel or restaurant restroom. Toilet paper is often not available, so carry tissue with you. Do not flush paper down the commode; use the receptacle provided.

Safety Athens is among the safest capitals in Europe, and there are few reports of violent crimes. **Pickpocketing,** however, is not uncommon, especially in the Plaka and Omonia Square areas, on the Metro and buses, and in Piraeus. When in the Metro, always place your valuables in your front pockets. Avoid the side streets of Omonia and Piraeus at night. As always, leave your passport and valuables in a security box at the hotel. Carry a photocopy of your passport, not the original.

Taxes A VAT (value-added tax) of between 6% and 24% is added onto everything you buy. Some shops will attempt to cheat you by quoting one price and then, when you hand over your credit card, adding a hefty VAT charge. Be wary. In theory, if you are not a citizen of a EU country, you can get a refund on major purchases at the Athens airport when you leave Greece. In practice, you'd have to arrive at the airport a day before your flight to get to the head of the line, do the paperwork, get a refund, and catch your plane home.

Telephones Public phones are becoming scarce and most now accept only phone cards, available at the airport, newsstands, and **Telecommunications Organization of Greece (OTE)** offices. Cards come in several denominations, currently starting at 3€. Most OTE offices and **Germanos** stores (including the one in the airport) now sell cellphones and phone cards at reasonable prices. Some kiosks still have metered phones; you pay what the meter records. For more on phones, see p. 298.

Tipping Athenian restaurants include a service charge in the bill, but a few euro extra are appreciated. Most Greeks do not give a percentage tip to taxi drivers, but often round up the fare; for example, you would round up a fare of 2.80€ to 3€.

WHERE TO STAY IN ATHENS

Concepts of low and high seasons are a bit murky in Athens. Summer is low season for many business-oriented hotels, and some woo the family trade with good prices, but summer is high season for tourist-oriented hotels, where prices might plunge in the winter months. To find the best prices, check out hotel websites. When in doubt, ask, and bargain—if rooms are available, savvy hoteliers will be happy to negotiate. Many hotels, especially in the budget category, will ask you to pay in cash and will often give you a discount for doing so. Few hotels provide parking; in the listings below, we note those that do. Other hotelkeepers can direct you to nearby garages (see p. 62 for centrally located parking facilities). Note also that Greek hotels do not always include breakfast in their rates; in the listings below, we note places where breakfast is included.

Expensive

Electra Palace ★★ One of the largest hotels in the Plaka is also the most luxurious. Guest rooms are spacious and stylishly furnished, done in soft pastels and with beautiful marble bathrooms, and many have views of the

Parthenon. The rooms on the fifth, sixth, and seventh floors are smaller than those on lower floors, but a top-floor room is where you want to be, both for the view of the Acropolis and to escape traffic noise. (Ask for a top-floor unit when you make your reservation. Your request will be honored "subject to availability.") Service is topnotch, a lavish buffet breakfast is served in a lovely garden in good weather, and you can see the Acropolis while doing laps in the beautiful rooftop pool.

18–20 Nikodimou. www.electrahotels.gr. ℂ **210/337-0000.** 106 units. 180€ double. Rates include breakfast buffet. Parking 12€ a day. Metro: Syntagma. **Amenities:** Restaurant; bar; gym; rooftop pool; indoor pool; spa; Wi-Fi (free).

Grand Resort Lagonissi ★★

Combining a seaside getaway with city sightseeing is easy to do from this stunning luxury complex on the coast about 40 minutes outside the center (buses stop just outside the gates). Sandy beaches, a lovely pool, and accommodations that range from hotel rooms to beachfront bungalows and suites with private pools can put a nice spin on a summertime visit to Athens.

Athens–Sounion Rd. www.lagonissiresort.gr. ℂ **22910/76-010.** 370 units. 350€–500€ double. Rates include buffet breakfast. Free parking. Bus: KTEL from Aigyptou Sq. **Amenities:** 7 restaurants; 2 bars; 2 beaches; spa; pool; gym; tennis courts; volleyball courts; watersports; Wi-Fi (free).

Grande Bretagne ★★★

An Athens landmark for 160 years, the Grande Bretagne has housed royalty, celebrities, and world leaders and is still the best address in town. Enough opulence remains to let you know the place has a lineage, yet 21st-century innovations ensure maximum comfort. The choicest rooms, done up in traditional luxury, are those with balconies overlooking Syntagma Square, the Parliament building, and the Acropolis. An attentive staff looks after every detail, and the rooftop pool and adjoining bar restaurant enjoy knockout views of the Acropolis.

Syntagma Sq. www.grandebretagne.gr. ℂ **210/333-0000.** 328 units. 277€–285€ double. Some rates include buffet breakfast. Parking 15€ a day. Metro: Syntagma. **Amenities:** 2 restaurants; 2 bars; free airport pickup; concierge; health club and spa with Jacuzzi; 2 pools (indoors and outdoors); room service; Wi-Fi (free).

Hotel Eridanus ★

It only figures that trendy Gazi should have a hip hotel, and here it is, with beautiful guest rooms and lounges full of contemporary flair, modern design touches, and the occasional antique or old textile tastefully thrown in. Practical needs are looked after with such touches as in-room fridges, and the in-house restaurant is excellent.

80 Piraeus. www.eridanus.gr. ℂ **210/520-5360.** 38 units. 195€–285€ double. Rates include buffet breakfast. Free parking. Metro: Thissio/Kerameikos. **Amenities:** Restaurant; breakfast room; bar; Wi-Fi (free).

Ochre & Brown ★★

The Psyrri clubs are just outside the door, making the relaxed, intimate atmosphere here a hit with the fashion-conscious looking for a chic urban experience. Any traveler appreciates the style, highly personalized service, high-tech amenities, and beautifully designed rooms. Some

Athens Hotels & Restaurants

N

0   1/4 mile   ↗ To Larissis Station

0   0.25 km

Leoforos Konstantinoupoleos

Lenorman

Achilleos

Chiou

METAXOURGIO
M

Akominatou

Maizonos

Karolou

Anexartisias
Square

Marni

VATHI

Veranzerou

Satovriandou

Aviou Konstantinou

Deligorgi

Zinonos

Tritis Septemvriou

Patision

Kapodistriou

Akadimias

Omonia
Square

OMONIA
M

El. Venizelou
(Panipistimiou)

KERAMEIKOS

Kolokynthous

Myllerou

Leonidou

Thermopylon

Keramikou

Kolonou

P. Tsaldari

Aisilaou

Pireos

Menandrou

(Pireos)

Athinas

City Hall

22

21

Sofokleous

**Central
Market**

20

Kotzia
Square

Stadiou

GAZI

Salaminos

Plataion

Aysilaou

18

Pireos

Asomaton

Dipilou

Sarri

Evripidou

Aristofanous

Athinas

Evripidou

Aiolou

Miltiadou

Praxitelous

Mykalis

Leonidou

17
M KERAMEIKOS

THISION

KERAMIKOS
CEMETERY

16

PSIRRI

19

Kolokotroni

Perikleos

GRAND PROMENADE

To Piraeus

Thessalonikis

THISSIO
M

15

Ermou

MONASTIRAKI
M

Monastiraki
Square

Ermou

Miaouli

13

Mitropoleos

Aiolou

Poulopoulou

14

Adrianou

12

**Roman
Agora**

11

**Metropolitan
Cathedral**

Apollonos

Irakleidou

Aktaiou

Amfiktyonos

GRAND PROMENADE

Vrysakiou

Mnisikleous

Nikodimou

Adrianou

10

9

Nileos

Ersichthonos

Akamantos

Ancient Agora

AREOPAGUS

Lysiou

8

Observatory

HILL OF
THE PNYX

6

Tripodon

Ragkava

PLAKA

Thespidos

7

**THE
ACROPOLIS**

5

Pnyx

NYMPHON
HILL

1

Parthenon

**Theatre of
Dionysus**

GRAND PROMENADE

(Dionissiou Areopagitou)

FILOPAPPOU
HILL

2

Rovertou Galli St.

Propylaion

MAKRIGIANNI

Parthenonos

Hatzichristou

**Acropolis
Museum**

Makrigianni

M AKROPOLI

**Dora Stratou
Theater**

3

4

**National
Archaeological
Museum**

ATHENS | Where to Stay in Athens

4

66

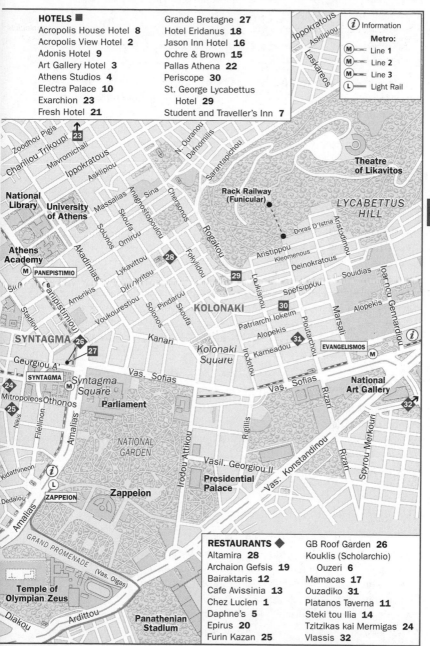

HOTELS ■
Acropolis House Hotel **8**
Acropolis View Hotel **2**
Adonis Hotel **9**
Art Gallery Hotel **3**
Athens Studios **4**
Electra Palace **10**
Exarchion **23**
Fresh Hotel **21**

Grande Bretagne **27**
Hotel Eridanus **18**
Jason Inn Hotel **16**
Ochre & Brown **15**
Pallas Athena **22**
Periscope **30**
St. George Lycabettus
    Hotel **29**
Student and Traveller's Inn **7**

ⓘ Information

Metro:
Ⓜ═══ Line 1
Ⓜ═══ Line 2
Ⓜ═══ Line 3
Ⓛ═══ Light Rail

4

ATHENS Where to Stay in Athens

RESTAURANTS ◆
Altamira **28**
Archaion Gefsis **19**
Bairaktaris **12**
Cafe Avissinia **13**
Chez Lucien **1**
Daphne's **5**
Epirus **20**
Furin Kazan **25**

GB Roof Garden **26**
Kouklis (Scholarchio)
    Ouzeri **6**
Mamacas **17**
Ouzadiko **31**
Platanos Taverna **11**
Steki tou Ilia **14**
Tzitzikas kai Mermigas **24**
Vlassis **32**

quarters overlook the surrounding streets, but the finest accommodation is the junior suite with Acropolis views from its terrace. The hotel's lounge/bar and restaurant are popular haunts.

7 Leokoriou St. www.oandbhotel.com. ✆ **210/331-2950**. 17 units. 145€–280€ double. Rates include buffet breakfast. Metro: Thissio or Monastiraki. **Amenities:** Restaurant; lounge bar; Wi-Fi (free).

St. George Lycabettus Hotel ★★ Large, nicely decorated guest rooms (each floor has a different theme, from art nouveau to minimalism) and a beautiful rooftop pool do justice to a wonderful location—the pine-scented slopes of Lycabettus hill just above the designer-boutique-lined streets of Kolonaki. Most rooms look toward the pine-clad summit; some have views of the Acropolis; and others overlook a small park or have interior views.

2 Kleomenous. www.sglycabettus.gr. ✆ **210/729-0711**. 154 units. 200€–2,259€ double. Parking 14€ per day. Metro: Syntagma. **Amenities:** 2 restaurants; 2 bars; concierge; pool; room service; Wi-Fi (free).

Moderate

Acropolis View Hotel ★★ The neighborhood around this pleasant little inn on the south side of the Filapappou Hill is leafy and quiet yet an easy walk away from Plaka and the ancient sights. Rooms are fresh and spotless, and some face the Acropolis, as does the delightful roof terrace; others overlook the Filapappou Hill, a less dramatic but pleasing prospect.

Rovertou Galli and 10 Webster. www.acropolisviewhotel.gr. ✆ **210/921-7303**. 32 units. 125€ double. Rates include buffet breakfast. Metro: Acropolis. **Amenities:** Breakfast room; bar; roof garden; Wi-Fi (free).

Fresh Hotel ★ Soothing minimalist design, along with a rooftop pool, sun deck, and Zen-like spa, put a fresh face on the gritty Omonia neighborhood. The youthful staff is helpful, the appealing in-house bar/restaurants serve light Mediterranean fare, and the laid-back ambiance is soothing. Among many modern amenities in the stylish and colorful rooms are window blinds that can be controlled from the beds. When you are adequately recharged and ready to hit the streets, the lively Central Market and hip Psyrri are nearby.

26 Sofokleous and 2 Klisthenous. www.freshhotel.gr. ✆ **210/524-8511**. 133 units. 110€–150€ double. Rates include buffet breakfast. Parking 12€ per day. Metro: Omonia/Monastiraki. **Amenities:** Restaurant/bar; pool; minispa; Wi-Fi (free).

Pallas Athena Hotel ★ Ten international artists were hand-picked to decorate the 57 "graffiti" rooms with themes ranging from Japanese and Byzantine art to comic book art—each a work of art, decorated with depictions of flowers, birds, trees, clouds, or superheroes. For those requiring more Zen-like surroundings, some of those, bathed in neutral tones, are available too, and are spacious, comfortable, and contemporary.

65 Athinas and Lycourgou. www.luxurydreamhotels.com. ✆ **210/325-0900**. 76 units. 180 €–220€ double. Metro: Omonia/Monastiraki. **Amenities:** Restaurant/bar; gym; Wi-Fi (free).

Periscope ★   The majorly minimalist decor—all grays and whites, industrial-style bathrooms, and ceilings covered with aerial views of the city—doesn't sacrifice comfort and does justice to the stylish neighborhood. Some of the city's best shopping and cafe life is just outside the door, though the lobby and rooftop bars are scenes in themselves—with the former broadcasting live images of the city shot from by a camera controlled by patrons.

22 Haritos. www.yeshotels.gr. ⓒ **210/623-6320.** 22 units. 130€–140€ double. Most rates include buffet breakfast. Metro: Syntagma. **Amenities:** Cafe/bar; restaurant; gym; Wi-Fi (free).

Inexpensive

Acropolis House Hotel ★   One of a cluster of basic but clean lodgings in a quiet corner of the Plaka, the Acropolis House occupies a 150-year-old villa and has a bit more character than its neighbors. Be sure to ask for one of the older rooms when booking—those in a newer wing are bland and their bathrooms, though private, are across the hall. Rooms 401 and 402 have good Acropolis views.

6–8 Kodrou. ⓒ **210/322-2344.** 19 units, 15 with bathroom. 70€ double without bathroom, 80€ with bathroom. 10€ surcharge for A/C. Rates include continental breakfast. Metro: Syntagma. **Amenities:** Wi-Fi (free).

Adonis Hotel ★   Room decor at this basic, value-for-money fixture in the Plaka is spruce but doesn't go much beyond a bed and chair, and bathrooms are minimal and tiny. But all have balconies, and a slight neck crane from all affords an Acropolis view. For those on a tight budget, the location (on a pleasant back street just a 10-minute walk from Syntagma Square) and an airy roof terrace may well compensate for the lack of luxury.

3 Kodrou and Voulis. www.hotel-adonis.gr. ⓒ **210/324-9737.** 26 units. 90€ double. Metro: Syntagma. **Amenities:** Cafe/bar; rooftop garden; Wi-Fi (free).

Art Gallery Hotel ★★   A 1950s house beneath Filopappou Hill was once the residence of visiting artists, who left many of their works behind. Even the vintage cage elevator evokes more gracious times. Many guests still settle in for months at a time, and the hardwood floors and polished old furniture have a homey lived-in sheen to them. A buffet breakfast (extra) and evening cocktails are served in a top-floor Victorian-era lounge and roof garden with views of the Acropolis.

5 Erechthiou. www.artgalleryhotel.gr. ⓒ **210/923-8376.** 22 units. 50€–80€ double. Metro: Syngrou-Fix. **Amenities:** Roof terrace; Wi-Fi (free).

Athens Studios ★★   These spacious apartments, with decent kitchens, plenty of space, and basic yet spiffy contemporary furnishings, are a big hit with families. So is the self-service laundry downstairs, and twin beds and separate sitting areas make the units well suited to unattached traveling companions and small groups. The Acropolis and Acropolis Museum are just a few steps away, and private balconies overlook the pleasant neighborhood.

3a Veikou. www.athensstudios.gr. ℂ **210/923-5811.** 15 units. 60€–65€ double. Rates include breakfast. Metro: Akropoli. **Amenities**: Cafe; bar; laundry; baggage storage; Wi-Fi (free).

Exarchion ★   Students (and those who still travel like students) swarm to this worn, no-frills, but homey outpost in the city's bohemian university quarter. Some nice touches are a bar that spills out onto an arcade out front and a roof terrace. Best of all for many guests, the National Archaeological Museum is just down the street.

78 Kleomenous. www.exarchion.com. ℂ **210/380-0731.** 49 units. 55€–60€ double. Metro: Omonia. **Amenities:** Restaurant; bar; roof terrace; Wi-Fi (free).

Jason Inn Hotel ★★   Don't be put off by the dull streets of the immediate vicinity—at this basic but cheerful and well-run place you are at the edge of the city's trendy enclaves of Psyrri, Gazi, and Thissio, and just steps from the busy Monastiraki cafes. The ancient Kerameikos cemetery, some of the city's most intriguing ruins, are just across the street. If the inn is full, the staff may be able to find you a room in one of their other hotels in the vicinity.

12 Ayion Assomaton. www.douros-hotels.com. ℂ **210/325-1106.** 57 units. 95€ double. Rates include American-style buffet breakfast. Metro: Thissio. **Amenities:** Breakfast room; bar; roof garden; Wi-Fi (free).

Student and Traveller's Inn ★   When location matters and budget is an issue, look no farther than this well-run and attractive hostel on a pretty pedestrian street at the edge of the Plaka. Accommodations are in multi-bunk dorms or, for those with a bit more cash to burn, in one of the private rooms, some of which have private bathrooms and are set up for families.

16 Kydathinaion. www.studenttravellersinn.com. ℂ **210/324-4808.** 65€ double with private bathroom, 55€ double with shared bathroom. Metro: Syntagma. **Amenities:** Courtyard; Wi-Fi (free).

WHERE TO EAT IN ATHENS

Dining in Athens in a real pleasure, with excellent cooking taking center stage no matter what the venue, traditional taverna or latest hotspot. Settings are wonderful, too, and restaurants often occupy old houses and shady courtyards. Probably the only restaurants to avoid are those that station waiters outside who pursue you with an unrelenting sales pitch. The hard sell is almost always a giveaway that the place caters to tourists—the meal may not be terrible, but it's likely to be mediocre at best, and you won't get the full Athenian dining experience. A meal in Athens, particularly dinner, is to be relished, never rushed and preferably enjoyed alfresco. *Note:* Many, many restaurants do not accept credit cards, especially now that money is so tight in Greece.

Expensive

Altamira ★★ EXOTIC   Fusion cuisine hits a new extreme in these elegant, old-fashioned, even operatic surroundings where dishes are infused with Middle Eastern, Indian, and Southeast Asian flavors. For an even more unusual experience, order one of the daily special preparations of reindeer, ostrich, or other wild game.

36A Tsakalof St. altamira.com.gr. ✆ **210/361-4695** or 210/363-9906. Main courses 25€–35€. Mon–Sat 1pm–1:30am; closed mid-July to Aug. Metro: Syntagma or bus: 200.

Archaion Gefsis ★★ GREEK Lying on a couch being served by toga-clad waiters may seem a bit gimmicky (or just plain decadent), but even Athenians enjoy stepping back in time here to dip into fare based on ancient recipes (accordingly, reservations are essential). Transporting as the experience can be, the food might be reassuringly familiar, if a wee bit exotic, with fig-and-pomegranate-laden salads and—a true epicurean blowout—piglet stuffed with eggs, fried liver, eggs, and fruits (only for two, and must be ordered 2 days in advance).

6 Agion Anargiron. archeongefsis.gr. ✆ **210/523-9661.** Main courses 20€–25€. Tues–Sat 6pm–1am; Sun 6pm–midnight; closed 2 weeks in Aug. Metro: Monastiraki or Thissio.

Daphne's ★★ GREEK A 1830s Plaka mansion with frescoed rooms and a leafy courtyard provides one of the city's most romantic dining experiences. Delicious hot-pepper-and-feta-cheese dip, the *stifado* (stew) of rabbit in *mavrodaphne* (sweet-wine) sauce, and other traditional fare show off some innovative flair and are served with care and charm.

4 Lysikratous St. www.daphnesrestaurant.gr. ✆ **210/322-7971.** Main courses 25€–40€. Daily 7pm–1am. Metro: Syntagma.

GB Roof Garden ★★ MEDITERRANEAN Politicians, royalty, and Hollywood stars have all raved about their meals—accompanied by knockout Acropolis views— atop the city's swankiest hotel. You can join them for dinner or (a far more economical option) just come for a cocktail at sunset. Whatever you consume, dress in "casual smart" attire to do so.

Grande Bretagne Hotel, Syntagma Sq. www.gbroofgarden.gr. ✆ **210/333-0000.** Main courses 30€–50€. Daily 7pm–2am. Metro: Syntagma.

Moderate

Café Avissinia ★★ GREEK Take refuge from the surrounding flea market in this mahogany-paneled lair, a long-standing city institution that's reason enough for many Athenians to venture into the mob scene around Abyssinia Square. Homey seafood dishes (including plump mussels roasted in wine and washed down with ouzo) star on the menu, alongside stews and other traditional fare kept warm on the stove. The house wine is delicious and encourages lingering, as does the live music that often wafts through the old rooms.

7 Kinetou St. at Abyssinia Sq. www.avissinia.gr. ✆ **210/321-7047.** Main courses 10€–15€. Tues–Sat 11:30am–1am; Sun 11am–7pm; closed mid-July to Aug. Metro: Monastiraki.

Chez Lucien ★ FRENCH You will probably have to wait for one of the shared tables in this small knick-knack-filled room that's a throwback to 1960s bohemian Paris. Reservations aren't accepted, nor are credit cards. But the French-bistro fare is delicious and much less expensive than what's on offer at some of the capital's other outposts of French cooking.

32 Troon St. ⓒ **210/346-4236.** Main courses 18€–25€. Daily 8:30pm–2am. Metro: Thissio or bus 227.

Furin Kazan ★ JAPANESE   It only stands to reason that fish, such a player in Greek cuisine, could also make an appearance in sushi and sashimi. In slick, contemporary surroundings in the busy Plaka it's a good marriage of cultures, as the crowds of Japanese businessmen and Athenians attest.

2 Apollonos St. www.furin-kazan.com. ⓒ **210/322-9170.** Main courses 10€–20€. Mon–Sat noon–midnight; Sun 2:30–11:30pm. Metro: Syntagma.

Mamacas ★ MODERN GREEK   One of the first of the city's "neo tavernas," Mamacas helped plant formerly industrial Gazi on the nightlife map. The decor is white-washed and minimalist, but the kitchen sends out the sorts of meals that Greek moms serve (the name means "mommy")—among the offerings, served by a staff who look like film stars, are trays of cooked dishes (*magirefta*) and a range of dependable and delicious grills and appetizers (the spicy meatballs or *keftedakia* are a must).

41 Persephonis St. www.mamacas.gr. ⓒ **210/346-4984.** Main courses 15€–30€. Daily 1:30pm–1:30am. Metro: Kerameikos.

Inexpensive

Bairaktaris ★ GREEK   This 150-year-old fixture in Monastiraki Square never seems to change, and that's how the loyal following likes it. A *magirefta* (one-pot meal cooked on the stove) is always on offer, along with meze and other straightforward taverna standards. Souvlaki is grilled over an open flame, gyros are succulent, and it's all served with friendly polish in a plain room lined with photos of all the famous folks who have found their way to this legendary place.

2 Monastiraki Sq. ⓒ **210/321-3036.** Main courses 5€–10€. Metro: Monastiraki.

Epirus ★★ GREEK   Butchers, fishermen, surly loners, and chic shoppers and bar-hoppers rub elbows at one of the city's favorite stops for old-fashioned home cooking. The big draw is the tripe soup, a surefire cure for a hangover and a fortifying start to the day for the market workers who pour in at dawn. Many other soups, stews, and such traditional favorites as moussaka are usually on the huge old stove—including the ever-popular *magiritsa*, with lamb offal, or for those wishing to stay away from innards, rich fish and chicken soups. Diners enjoy views of the kitchen in one direction and the market stalls in the other.

4 Filopimenos St. (inside the Central Market). ⓒ **210/324-0773.** Main courses 6€–10€. Mon–Fri 7am–7pm; Sat 5am–7pm. Metro: Omonia, Panepistimiou, or Monastiraki.

Platanos Taverna ★★ GREEK   A beloved institution, established in 1932, is a standout amid its tourist-trap neighbors. The succulent roast lamb with artichokes brings regulars back time after time, to enjoy it in a pretty courtyard beneath a plane tree (*platanos*). The wine list includes a wide choice of bottled wines from many regions of Greece, although the house wine is tasty.

A NIGHT AT THE ouzeri

For a uniquely Greek dining experience, try one of Athen's popular *ouzeris*, or ouzo taverns. The bill of fare features the traditional finger foods known as *meze*, to be washed down with plentiful amounts of the anise-flavored liqueur *ouzo*.

Kouklis (Scholarchio) Ouzeri

★★ Bring a group because this popular old standby, where the white walls are lined with paintings by customer artists, is geared to feeding a crowd. Choose from a tray of delicious appetizers—tzatziki, moussaka, taramosalata, fried eggplant, and dozens of others. The more people at the table, the more dishes you get to try.

14 Tripodon St. www.scholarhio.gr. ℂ **210/324-7605.** Meze 3€–7€. Daily 11am–2am. Metro: Syntagma or Monastiraki.

Ouzadiko

★ Tucked away in the atrium of the Lemos shopping center in Kolonaki, a big dining terrace and busy room are wildly popular with business folks, who put together meals from a

choice of dozens of meze. Fried anchovies and mountain greens are standouts and the fluffy *keftedes* (meatballs) make those at all other restaurants taste leaden. At least 40 kinds of ouzo are on offer, and the seriously overworked staff tries hard to steer you to the right ones.

Lemos International Centre, 25–29 Karneadou St. ℂ **210/729-5484.** Main courses 16€–25€; meze from 3€. Mon–Sat 12:30pm–midnight. Metro: Evangelismos.

Paradosiako

★★ The busy Plaka is the backdrop to a meal here, though the comings and goings on the busy corner are upstaged by the delicious food and friendly service. Grilled sardines, fried gavros (anchovies), and country sausages appear alongside dips and other mezes, as well as oven-cooked staples, all made fresh daily.

Voulis 44. ℂ **210/321-4121.** Meze, 4€–7€; main courses 8€–10€. Daily noon–midnight. Metro: Syntagma.

4 Dioyenous St. ℂ **210/322-0666.** Main courses 10€–11€. Mon–Sat noon–4:30pm and 7:30pm–midnight. Metro: Monastiraki or Syntagma.

Steki tou Ilia ★ GREEK/GRILL HOUSE A grill house that operates on two sides of a pedestrian street encourages a leisurely meal—part of the name, "ilias," means "hangout," and that's what many regulars come to do. The house specialty is its irresistible *paidakia*, chargrilled lamb chops served the old-fashioned way, with grilled bread sprinkled with olive oil and oregano. A second location at 5 Eptachalkou St., Thissio (ℂ **210/345-8052**) keeps the same hours.

7 Thessalonikis St. ℂ **210/342-2407.** Main courses 8€–18€. Mon–Sat 1pm–1am; Sun 1–5:30pm. Metro: Thissio.

Tzitzikas kai Mermigas ★ MODERN GREEK Kebabs, meat and vegetable pies, onions stuffed with bacon, and other traditional fare is served on tables topped with butcher paper in a whimsically retro room that evokes an old-fashioned grocery store. The food and decor is a big hit with Athenians: You'll find several other branches around town.

12–14 Mitropoleos St. www.tzitzikasmermigas.gr. ℂ **210/324-7607.** Meze 4€–8€. Mon–Sat 1pm–1am. Metro: Syntagma.

Vlassis ★★ GREEK   For a home-cooked meal, do what the Athenians do and head to this neoclassical mansion in a quiet neighborhood near the American embassy. Greeks call this kind of food *paradisiako* (traditional); dozens of salads, spreads, and small meat and seafood dishes are brought to the table and you pick what you want—be forewarned that you will be tempted to take more than you can eat.

15 Meandrou St. vlassisrestaurant.gr. 🕐 **210/646-3060.** Main courses 5€–15€. Daily 11am–1am. Metro: Megaro Mousikis.

EXPLORING ATHENS

One important thing to know about Athens: Much of what you want to see is fairly tightly clustered on and around the Acropolis Hill, so you can cover a lot of ground fairly easily on foot, and in a short amount of time. Many visitors give the capital 2 days, tops, before shipping out for the islands. That's enough time to see the **Acropolis** (see below) and the two treasure troves of ancient art, the **Acropolis Museum** (p. 78) and the **National Archeological Museum** (p. 93). That will also give you time to wander through the old Plaka and Monastiraki neighborhoods, with their rich street life, markets, and scattering of antiquities. You'll no doubt end up wanting to see more, though, and this lively, cosmopolitan, and just plain fun city has plenty else to show.

The Acropolis & Nearby Sights

The beloved 2,400-year-old landmark of Greece's Golden Age stands high above the city (Acropolis means "High City"), an enduring symbol of perfection that instills pride in even the most hard-nosed Athenians, and awe in their visitors. Wars, plunder, pollution, and neglect have taken their toll on the Parthenon, the harmonious temple to Athena, and the smaller monuments that surround it on the hilltop. Even so, in its sun-bleached beauty, the Acropolis continues to show the heights to which a civilized society can aspire.

The so-called **Grand Promenade,** a cobblestone-and-marble, pedestrian-only boulevard, skirts the Acropolis Hill, providing a stroll through the millennia accompanied by the scent of pine.

Acropolis ★★★ ANCIENT SITE/RUIN   In ancient times, worshippers and celebrants made the ascent to the Acropolis on the Sacred Way, a processional walkway that crossed the city from Kerameikos (p. 90) and ascended the Acropolis via a series of ramps and steps. The current approach, along a well-worn path through the **Beule Gate,** is no less inspiring, given the fabled ruins that lie ahead.

Beule Gate   From the ticket pavilion just off the Grand Promenade, a path ascends to this grandiose entryway built by the Romans in A.D. 280, and more recently named for the French archaeologist who unearthed the monumental entryway in 1852. (Don't be misled by the inscription on the lintel from 320 B.C.—fragments from an earlier monument were incorporated into the Roman gate.) Just beyond the gate is a pedestal that during the Roman years was topped with a succession of statuary honoring charioteers, Anthony and

Cleopatra, and finally, Marcus Agrippa, the general who defeated the couple's forces at the Battle of Actium.

Propylaia   Ancient visitors to the Acropolis passed through this symbolic entryway, an antechamber to the sacred precincts beyond. A central hall housed five gates; one was reserved for priests, worshippers, charioteers, and beasts who made their way up the Acropolis in a long procession during the Panathenaic Festival (depicted in the Parthenon Frieze, see p. 21). A forest of elegant columns remains in place, including a double row that surrounds the inner porch and dramatically frames the Parthenon, just beyond. A portion of the paneled ceiling and fragments of frescoes hint at the Propylaia's former grandeur and the awe it must have inspired in those passing through.

Temple of Athena Nike   Tucked next to the Propylaia, on a vertigo-inducing platform at the edge of the Acropolis Hill, this miniscule shrine was built between 427 and 424 B.C. as a prayer for success against Sparta in the Peloponnesian War. Square and perfectly proportioned, with four columns at either end, the temple honors Athena in her guise as the goddess of victory.

Erechtheion   Perhaps the most distinctive of all Greece's ancient temples stands on the spot where Poseidon and Athena allegedly squared off in a contest to see who would be honored as patron of the city. Poseidon struck his trident into a rock and unleashed a spring, while Athena topped him by miraculously producing an olive tree, symbol of lasting peace and prosperity (much valued but short-lived in 5th-century-B.C. Athens). Marks of Poseidon's trident can be seen in a rock on the north porch, and an olive tree still grows nearby. The god and goddess are honored in the temple, built on three levels to accommodate the slope of the Acropolis Hill and supported in part by caryatids, maidens delicately draped in pleated gowns that take the place of columns. The ones in place are copies; five of the originals are in the Acropolis Museum (p. 78).

The Parthenon   The sacred sanctuary to Athena and storehouse of the treasury of the Delian League stands at the highest point of the Acropolis. Two of the temple's most remarkable features are no longer here—an 11m-tall (36-ft.) gold-plated statue of the goddess by the great sculptor Phidias, and the 160m (530-ft.) Parthenon Frieze. Segments of the frieze are in the Acropolis Museum (p. 78) while others were carted off to London by Lord Elgin between 1801 and 1805 (see p. 79 for more on the ongoing battle to bring these treasures back to Greece). Much the worse for wear—battered by looting, the elements, pollution, and an explosion and fire ignited by Venetian artillery in 1687—the majestic temple is still the symbol of artistic perfection.

Athens Attractions

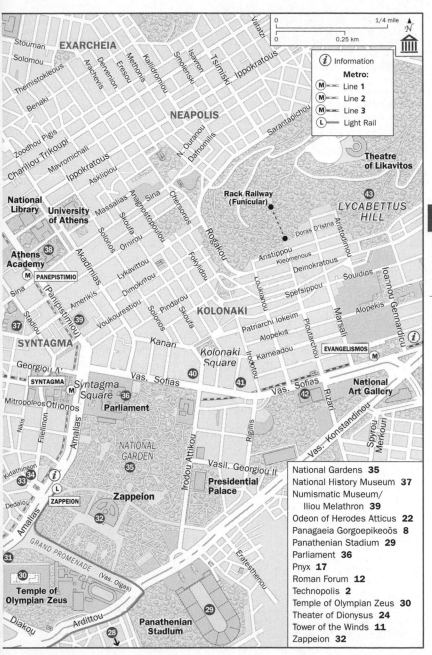

National Gardens **35**
National History Museum **37**
Numismatic Museum/
   Iliou Melathron **39**
Odeon of Herodes Atticus **22**
Panagaeia Gorgoepikeoös **8**
Panathenian Stadium **29**
Parliament **36**
Pnyx **17**
Roman Forum **12**
Technopolis **2**
Temple of Olympian Zeus **30**
Theater of Dionysus **24**
Tower of the Winds **11**
Zappeion **32**

With a sharp eye you might detect a trick of optical illusion; since straight lines appear curved, Parthenon architects slightly curved and bowed the temple's 50 columns so they seem to be perfectly straight.

Dionysiou Areopagitou St. odysseus.culture.gr. ℗ **210/321-0219.** Admission 20€, or part of the Acropolis ticket package (see p. 75). Apr–Oct daily 8am–7:30pm; Nov–Mar daily 8am–3pm. Elevator for visitors with disabilities.

Acropolis Museum ★★★ MUSEUM   The sculptures and statuary that once adorned the temples of the Acropolis—a breathtaking presence through the tall windows—are shown to beautiful advantage here, among acres of glass and marble. Caryatids (female sculptures used as architectural supports), statues of Korai (maidens) dedicated to Athena, figures of Kouri (young men), and elaborate friezes—4,000 works altogether—are displayed in the light-filled galleries. What's not here are many segments of the Parthenon Frieze, carted off to England from 1801 to 1804. Greece wants these treasures back, and stunning quarters on the museum's top floor await their return.

A walk through the galleries, with their airy views of the Parthenon, mimics an ascent up the Acropolis Hill. On the ground floor, the **Acropolis Slopes** gallery houses votives, offerings, and other finds from sanctuaries at the base of the Acropolis, where cults to Athena and other gods and goddesses worshipped; an overlook provides a look at ruins *in situ* beneath the museum. The marble floor gently slopes toward the next level, where works are arranged in the order in which ancients walking through the Acropolis would have encountered them. A head of Hermes, by Alkamenes, in the **Propylaia** collections once greeted visitors passing through the ceremonial entrance way; in the **Temple of Athena Nike** exhibit, a relief captures the goddess in the refreshingly humanlike act of

THE VISION OF pericles

Ever since the Acropolis was first inhabited, at least 5,000 years ago, the flat-topped, 156m-high (520-ft.) outcropping provided Athenians protection and views of enemies approaching, either by sea or across the surrounding plains. Such measures proved powerless, however, against the Persians, who razed Athens, and the Acropolis with it, in 479 B.C.

Athenians and Spartans banded together to rout the Persians in 449 B.C., and a year later the great general and statesman Pericles set about rebuilding the Acropolis. Plundering the state coffers, he hired the sculptor Phidias and the architects Iktinos and Kallikrates, and with the aid of the finest artisans of the day, the purest marble, and a work-force of thousands, he completed the Parthenon within 10 years and most of the other temples and monuments within a decade or two later.

The perfectly proportioned Parthenon and its neighbors on the Acropolis were showpieces for the superiority of Athens and the achievements of the Golden Age—achievements including democratic ideals, the philosophy of Socrates, the plays of Aeschylus and Sophocles, and the artistry of Praxiteles and other sculptors. Pericles bankrupted Athens by building the Acropolis, and by 404 B.C. the city had fallen to the Spartans. But the harmony and proportion Pericles achieved on the Acropolis Hill has survived the ages.

Fifty panels of the Parthenon Frieze—the remarkably animated marble frieze of maidens, priests, soldiers, worshippers, and oxen making their way to the Acropolis to honor the goddess Athena—are in the British Museum in London. Lord Elgin, onetime British ambassador to the Ottoman Empire, began removing segments of the frieze in 1801, supposedly with the permission of Turkish officials, and shipped them home. Greece is demanding the return of the treasures, carrying on a campaign that actress and minister of culture Melina Mercouri launched in the 1980s. Britain's long-standing argument that Greece can't properly care for the treasures is belied by the stunning new galleries that now stand completed, awaiting their return.

unfastening her sandal; and in the **Erechtheion** section, five famous caryatids, female figures used in place of columns on the temple's south porch, are grouped on a balcony. In the top floor **Parthenon Galleries,** friezes and metopes are arranged as they originally appeared on the temple, which can be viewed through floor-to-ceiling windows. Wrapping around the walls is a 160m-long (530-ft.) section of one of the world's greatest ancient treasures: the Frieze of the Great Panathenaia (also known as the Parthenon Frieze), a tableau of a procession in honor of Athena (see "The Frieze Fracas," p. 79).

15 Dionysiou Areopagitou St. www.theacropolismuseum.gr. ⓒ **210/900-0900.** Admission 5€, 3€ students and children under 18. Apr–Oct Mon 8am–4pm, Tues–Thurs and Sat–Sun 8am–8pm, Fri 8am–10pm. Nov–Mar Mon–Thurs 9am–5pm, Fri 9am–10pm, Sat–Sun 9am–8pm.

Agios Dimitrios Loumbardiaris ★ CHURCH   Legend surrounds this little 14th-century church nestled in a copse on Pnyx Hill. In 1645, so the story goes, the Ottoman commander of the Acropolis garrison planned to fire upon Christians gathering for services in honor of Saint Dimitrios. The night before the attack, lightning hit the cannon and gunpowder magazine and ignited an explosion that killed the commander but spared his Christian daughter. The humble stone and wood church is decorated with some delightfully primitive frescoes.

Apostolou Pavlou St., on the path opposite (south) the entrance to the Acropolis. Free admission. Hours vary. Metro: Akropoli or bus: 230.

Areopagus ★★ NATURAL LANDMARK   A bald granite outcropping next to the Acropolis, reached by treacherous steps carved out of the rock, is one of the most ancient and storied places in Athens. According to legend, the gods tried Ares here for killing Halirrhothius, son of Poseidon. (Ares was acquitted on the grounds that he was protecting his daughter from Halirrhothius' unwanted advances.) The summit was also the meeting place of the Council of the Areopagus, an assembly of citizens who heard murder trials, and for Socrates and his students, who came here to discourse away from the distractions of the city. St. Paul delivered his famous Sermon to an Unknown God from atop the Areopagus, trying to convert Athenians to Christianity. You may well encounter pilgrims from around the world who climb the hill to pay homage to Paul.

Continuation of Theorias St. opposite Acropolis entrance. Metro: Akropoli or bus: 230.

Filopappou ★★ NATURAL LANDMARK This hilly precinct just west of the Acropolis affords stunning, eye-level views of the Parthenon. In fact, the view has been mesmerizing gazers since the days of Pericles, when the general assembly (Ecckesia) met on the Hill of the Pnyx; any citizen of Athens could vote on civil matters, making this a hallowed ground of early democracy. An even better outlook is from the summit of the adjacent Lofos Mousson (Hill of the Muses).

Follow Dimitriou Aiginitou off the Grand Promenade.

First Cemetery ★ CEMETERY Since the 19th century, prominent Athenians have been laid to rest in this parklike expanse of greenery that climbs the cypress- and pine-clad slopes of Ardittos Hill behind the Temple of Olympian Zeus. Among those buried here are Heinrich Schiliemann, the archaeologist who uncovered Troy and Mycenae, and Melina Mercouri, the actress, activist, and politician who launched the battle for the return of the Parthenon Frieze (p. 79). Even some lesser-known people are laid to rest beneath spectacular monuments, many carved by stone masons from the island of Tinos. The cemetery's most beloved monument is Sleeping Lady (1877), crafted by Tiniot Yannoulis Halepas for the tomb of Sophia Afentaki, the 18-year-old daughter of a wealthy Athenian. Walking along the shaded lanes is a popular outing; many Athenians gather here to picnic near the graves of their loved ones.

Anapafseos and Trivonianou sts. ℂ **210/923-6720.** Apr–Oct 8am–8pm; Nov–Mar 8am–5:30pm. Bus: A3, A4, 057, 103, 108, 111, 155, 206, 208, 237, 856, or 227.

Grand Promenade ★★★ LANDMARK A walkway of marble and cobblestone skirts the base of the Acropolis Hill, linking some of the world's most famous ancient sites. You can follow the walkway all the way from Hadrian's Arch (see below) to Plateia Thissio and on to Kerameikos Cemetery (p. 90). Walking along this pedestrians-only boulevard is one of the capital's greatest pleasures—the great monuments of ancient Greece surround you, and the air is scented with pine.

Hadrian's Arch ★★ ANCIENT SITE This beautifully preserved, albeit soot-darkened, triumphal arch was erected in honor of the emperor in A.D. 131. The monument divided the old Greek city from the new Roman city that Hadrian—an ardent Hellenophile—endowed with many temples and monuments, naming the district Hadrianoupolis after himself. Hadrian considered Athens to be the cultural capital of the Roman Empire and struck his claims to the city by having the marble on the east side of the arch inscribed with "this is the city of Hadrian and not of Theseus" and the west side with "This is Athens, once the city of Theseus." The gate is remarkably well preserved, though ignobly besieged by a swirl of passing traffic.

Amalias Ave. and Dionysiou Areopagitou St.

Hill of the Nymphs ★ NATURAL LANDMARK   The northernmost of the hills surrounding the Acropolis is topped by the **National Observatory,** built in 1842 to designs by Theophilos Hansen, the Danish architect of the Academy at the University of Athens (p. 92) and many other public buildings around the capital. Just below is the multi-domed **Agia Marina** church, a 20th-century replacement of an earlier church honoring Saint Marina, the patron saint of childbirth. Her presence here continues the hill's long association with nymphs who were believed to protect pregnant women and sick children. Ancient Athenians would leave the garments of sick children beneath the trees in the hopes that nymphs would work a cure. In places the rugged hillsides are etched with caves, including one known as the Prison of Socrates, said to be where the philosopher was held and forced to drink hemlock after being found guilty of corrupting Athenian youth; the story is unproven and highly unlikely but adds a bit of romance to the bucolic surroundings. Also enhancing the rural prospect of the hillside are a herd of white ponies used to pull buggies on the tourist route; they're brought here to graze during off hours.

Dionysiou Areopagitou/Apostolou Pavlou sts.

Lalaounis Jewelry Museum ★ MUSEUM   Greece's millennia-long knack for crafting fine jewelry comes to the fore in the workmanship and style of internationally renowned designer Ilias Lalaounis (b. 1920). His magnificent gold and silver interpretations of Greek designs, inspired by cultures from the Minoans to the Ottomans, are displayed in the former Lalaounis workshops, alongside jewels and bling from around the world. The designer's dazzling pieces are on offer in the museum shop, but don't look for prices any lower than they are at the other tony Lalaounis shops around the world.

4 Karyatidon and 12 Kallisperi sts. www.lalaounis-jewelrymuseum.gr.© **210/922-1044.** Admission 5€. Tues–Sat 9am–3pm; Sun 11am–4pm. Metro: Akropoli. Bus: 230.

Odeon of Herodes Atticus ★ ANCIENT SITE   Wealthy statesman, scholar, and philanthropist Herodes Atticus funded works throughout Greece, including the baths at Thermopylae and a theater in Corinth. In A.D. 160 he presented this lovely theater to the Athenians in memory of his wife, Regilla. Since a 1955 restoration, audiences fill the 34 rows of seats for drama, music, and dance performances of the summertime Hellenic Festival. You may enter the theater only during performances, but you will see portions of the arched exterior and get a sense of the theater's elegant proportions on a walk around the pine-scented grounds.

Grand Promenade, Thrassilou and Dionysiou Areopagitou sts.

Panathenian Stadium ★ ANCIENT SITE   Built around 330 B.C. to host the Panathenian games, this stadium has been well used over the millennia. Greco-Roman aristocrat Herodes Atticus had the stadium reconstructed in A.D. 143–144, and the so-called Kalimarmaro (Beautiful Marble) underwent another redo by architect Ernst Ziller and Anastasios Metaxa to host the first modern Olympic Games in 1896. The stadium is still used for events; during the 2004 Olympics it hosted the archery competitions and was the finish line for the marathon.

Vas. Konstantinou and Irodou Attikou sts. Metro: Akropoli.

Pnyx ★★ NATURAL LANDMARK   The ancient Assembly met on the Pnyx during the 5th and 4th centuries B.C., which more or less makes the hilltop the birthplace of democracy. Any citizen of Athens was welcome to come here to debate and vote on matters of importance to the city. (Granted, women were not allowed to be citizens, and most residents of the city were slaves.) Pericles stood on this spot to argue for funds to build the Parthenon—which would prove to be such a distraction that in 404 B.C. the semicircle of benches was turned around so the display of glowing marble was behind the Assembly members' backs. Take a seat and gaze across to the Acropolis to see just how engaging the spectacle of the monument still is.

Dionysiou Areopagitou and Apostolou Pavlou sts. Metro: Akropoli.

Temple of Olympian Zeus ★★ ANCIENT SITE   The greatest monument that Roman emperor Hadrian bestowed upon his beloved Athens is this massive temple, the largest in Greece, completed in A.D. 131. Hadrian finished the work that the ruler Peisistratos had begun in the mid-500s B.C. (work was stopped for lack of funds). By Hadrian's time the unfinished temple, with its vast foundations and huge columns, had lain abandoned for centuries; Aristotle held the temple up as an example of the excesses with which tyrants enslaved the populace. Hadrian may have been inspired to complete the temple after seeing two of its columns in Rome, which the general Sulla had installed in the Temple of Jupiter on the Capitoline Hill in 81 B.C. Hadrian's temple lacks the grace of the Parthenon but is undeniably impressive: 104 Corinthian columns, more than 1.5m (5 ft.) in diameter, stood 16m (52 ft.) tall. The 15 that remain in place are dramatically floodlit at night. At one time, a gigantic replica of the statue of Zeus by Phidias (one of the Seven Wonders of the Ancient World) stood in an inner chamber, with a similarly grandiose statue of Hadrian himself next to it.

Vas. Olgas St. and Amalias Ave. odysseus.culture.gr. ℂ **210/922-6330.** Admission 6€ or part of Acropolis ticket (see p. 75). Apr–Oct daily 8am–7:30pm; Nov–Mar 8am–5pm. Metro: Syntagma or Akropoli.

Theater of Dionysus ★★ ANCIENT SITE   A theater has been tucked into the slope of the Acropolis Hill since the 6th century B.C., when Athenians began celebrating a Dionysus Festival to honor the god of wine and ecstasy with several days of dancing, feasting, and drinking. Celebrations became more refined during the 5th-century B.C. Golden Age, and theatergoers came from throughout the land to see the dramas of Aeschylus, Sophocles, and Euripides. The ruins you see today are of a vast marble theater begun in 342 B.C. that sat 17,000 spectators on 64 tiers of marble benches; 20 rows remain, as does a claw-footed throne, carved with satyrs, that was reserved for the priest of Dionysus.

For almost 1,500 years—from around 900 B.C. to A.D. 500—Athens was one of the most important cities in the ancient world, a center of trade and for many centuries renowned for promoting art and philosophy. Much of the ancient city you see today was built or transformed by the Romans, who gave Athens free status and financed many public works. Athens enjoyed the favor of Hadrian and other Roman emperors until the 6th century, when Justinian, a Christian, declared the famous schools of philosophy to be pagan institutions and closed them.

Grand Promenade, Thrassilou, and Dionysiou Areopagitou sts. (C) **210/322-4625.** Admission 2€ or part of Acropolis ticket (see p. 75). Apr–Oct daily 8am–7:30pm; Nov–Mar 8am–3pm.

Around Syntagma Square

This lively expanse of paving stones, overlooked by the formidable Parliament building, is figuratively and literally the center of Athens. Parliament was once the palace of Otto of Bavaria, the first monarch of a newly independent Greece, and under his less-than-stellar leadership the first constitution was adapted in 1843. Ever since, the square has been a hallowed ground of Greek nationalism, a stage for protests, celebrations, and as you'll no doubt observe, the comings and goings of everyday life in the capital. Syntagma is also geographically at the center of Athens. Tree-lined Vasillis Sofias, the city's Museum Row—home to the Museum of Cycladic Art (p. 95), the Benaki Museum (p. 90), and several other collections—leads off the Square to the east. Plaka and Anafliotika, two of the city's oldest neighborhoods, are just to the south; Omonia, the commercial center, is to the north; and the old working class neighborhoods of Monastiraki and Gazi are to the west. Before you hurry off to explore, though, stop to take a peek at the ruins of Roman baths unearthed during construction of the Metro; more artifacts are on display inside the modernistic station—a wonderful introduction to the juxtaposition of the ancient and the modern that you'll often encounter in Athens.

Folk Art Museum ★ MUSEUM The baskets, homespun textiles, pottery, and hand-hewn tools displayed here elevate even the simplest everyday items into works of art—and suggest just how labor-intensive rural life once was. Festive costumes, jewelry, pillows that brides-to-be embroidered for the marital bed, and puppets used in traveling shows show some wonderfully fanciful flourishes, too. Frescoes by Theophilos Hatzimihail, a naïve artist who lived and worked on the island of Lesbos, cover the walls of one room, and the collection spills over into the Tsisdarakis Mosque and the Loutro ton Aeridon (Bathhouse of the Winds), one of the last of the Turkish hamams that the Ottomans installed throughout Athens.

17 Kydathineon St. (C) **210/322-9031.** Admission 2€. Tues–Sun 9am–2pm. Metro: Syntagma.

In front of Parliament at Syntagma Square, two *Evzones*—soldiers of the Presidential Guard—keep watch at the Tomb of the Unknown Soldier (Amalias Avenue and Vas. Georgiou streets). It's easy to spot them, dressed as they are in the frilly white skirts and pom-pommed red shoes of their ancestors who fought to gain Greece's freedom during the War of Independence (1821–28). Every hour on the hour, the guards do some pretty fancy footwork in front of the tomb. A much more elaborate duty-rotation ceremony **(Changing the Guard)** occurs on Sunday at 11am, usually to the accompaniment of a band.

Frissiras Museum of Contemporary European Painting ★

MUSEUM   Should you begin to think that Greek art ended sometime around 400 B.C., step into these stark galleries spread across two adjoining neoclassical mansions for a look at the work of contemporary Greek artists, as well as those from other European countries. Some of the works by David Hockney and other internationally known artists will be familiar, but you will also enjoy an introduction to Costas Tsoclis and other highly acclaimed Greek artists.

3 and 7 Monis Asteriou St. www.frissirasmuseum.com. © **210/323-4678**. Admission 6€. Wed–Fri 10am–5pm; Sat–Sun 11am–5pm. Metro: Syntagma.

National Gardens ★

PARK   Queen Amalia, wife of King Otto, almost started another revolution back in the mid–19th century when she banned the Greek public from using the 16 hectares (40 acres) of paths, ponds, gardens full of exotic plants, and shady lawns behind her palace, now the Parliament. The gardens have been open to all since 1923 and are a welcome refuge from the swirl of traffic just outside the gates.

Daily 7am–10pm. Free admission.

Parliament ★

HISTORIC BUILDING   The palace that Munich architect Friedrich von Gaertner built for King Otto in 1848 probably did not do much to endear the unpopular monarch to his Greek subjects. Almost fortress-like, the massive landmark is a formidable presence on Syntagma Square, perhaps befitting its present role as home to the Greek Parliament. Among the few signs of life are two highly photogenic soldiers in traditional foustanellas (ceremonial skirtlike garments) guarding the Tomb of the Unknown Soldier outside. The most impressive thing about this austere building is the way its stone changes color throughout the day, from off-white to gold to a light blush mauve before it is lit dramatically at night.

Closed to general public.

National History Museum ★

MUSEUM   Palaia Vouli, or Old Parliament (housing the Greek Parliament from 1875–1935), is the suitable home for collections that focus largely on "modern" Greek history, from the arrival of the Ottomans in the 15th century to World War II. The Greek War of

Independence is idealistically captured with such mementoes as the sword and helmet Lord Byron (p. 91) donned when he came to Greece to take up the cause. Less than idealistic realities of the nation's past are also depicted in galleries surrounding the former assembly chamber, from the harsh yoke of Ottoman rule to the Battle of Crete.

Stadiou St. at Kolokotroni St. www.nhmuseum.gr. © **210/323-7617.** Admission 3€. Tues–Sun 8:30am–2:30pm. Metro: Syntagma.

Numismatic Museum/Iliou Melathron ★★ HISTORIC HOME/
MUSEUM   Heinrich Schliemann, the German archaeologist who unearthed the ancient kingdoms of Troy and Mycenae, commissioned German architect Ernst Ziller to design his Athens residence, which he named Iliou Melathron (Palace of Troy). Ziller emblazoned the gates with swastikas (a popular design in ancient Greece) and decorated the cavernous interior with marble, columns, and ancient-looking frescoes—just the right setting in which the learned Schliemann could entertain his dinner guests by reciting the *Iliad* from memory. The splendid rooms are enhanced by the presence of the holdings of the Numismatic Museum, one of the world's finest collections of ancient and historic coins—600,000 in all, dating from 700 B.C., including many from Troy and Mycenae. Many of the coins are arranged by the themes depicted on them, so you can loiter over the cases to compare the charming representations of gods and goddess, Roman generals and Byzantine emperors, and mythical beasts and sea creatures.

12 Panepistimiou St. www.nma.gr.© **210/364-3774.** Admission 6€. Mon 1–8pm, Tues–Sun 8:30am–3pm. Metro: Syntagma.

Zappeion ★ HISTORIC BUILDING   Amid the nationalistic fervor of the newly formed Greek nation, millionaire Evangelias Zappas sought to build a hall to host world-fair-style exhibitions as well as ceremonies for the revived Olympic Games. Theophilos Hansen, who had demonstrated his neoclassical bent in his designs for the Greek Academy (p. 92) and National Library (p. 93), designed the huge semicircular hall, inaugurated in 1888 and named for the man who financed the project. Hansen adorned the long facade with a portico and an elegant row of columns, but his pièce de résistance lies within—a vast circular atrium surrounded by a two-story arcade supported by columns and caryatids. The Zappeion was the venue for fencing competitions during the first modern Olympic Games in 1896, and in more recent years was the scene of ceremonies signing Greece into the European Union.

Entrances from the National Gardens, Amalias Ave., and Vas. Olgas and Vas. Konstantinou sts. Free admission. Daily 9am–5pm (hours vary depending on events). Metro: Syntagma.

Zappeion Gardens ★ PARK   This shady oasis adjoining the National Gardens is crisscrossed by broad promenades and surrounds the Zappeion, a vast, neoclassical exhibition hall.

Daily 7am–10pm. Free admission.

The Plaka & Monastiraki

These sprawling old quarters beneath the Acropolis are remnants of 19th-century Athens, with Byzantine churches and fragments of the ancient city sprinkled among the narrow lanes. With alleys, simple bougainvillea-clad houses, and a round-the-clock holiday atmosphere, the neighborhoods also exude the cheerful ambiance of a Greek island. Vendors hawk souvenirs (especially along Adrianou and Pandrossou streets in the Plaka and around Monastiraki Square); chicly clad young Athenians sit in cafes alongside their worry-bead wielding elders; and waiters try to lure passersby into restaurants serving some of the city's most undistinguished cuisine. It's easy to feel you've stumbled into a tourist trap as you amble through the Plaka and into Monastiraki, but this colorful heart of old Athens is also quintessentially and alluringly Greek.

Agii Apostoli Solanki ★ CHURCH   One of Athens's oldest churches was built in the Agora around A.D.1020 to honor St. Paul, who preached Christianity in the surrounding stoas and atop nearby Areopagus Hill. The Ottomans and overly zealous 19th-century renovators all but obliterated the charm of the church, but it was tenderly restored to its original form in the 1950s. A few fine early Byzantine frescoes remain in place, though some wall paintings are from the 17th century, moved here from a now-demolished church.

Dionysiou Areopagitou St., in the Ancient Agora. Free admission. Hours vary.

Ancient Agora ★★★ ANCIENT SITE   The center of commercial, administrative, and social life in ancient Athens for almost 1,000 years, starting in the 6th century B.C., the Agora is today a jumble of broken columns and crumbling foundations strewn among olive, pink oleander, cypress, and palm trees. Long ago, the city elite gathered to watch ceremonial processions pass through the Agora on the Sacred Way; so important was the Agora in the life of ancient Greece that it was ground zero, the point from which all distances throughout the Greek world were measured. With a little imagination, life at the center of ancient Athens can come alive as you encounter its monuments.

The sole remaining ancient structure is the beautifully preserved **Temple of Hephaestus,** from the 5th century B.C. Devoted to Athena and Hephaestus, god of blacksmiths, it was once surrounded by metalworking shops; a beautiful frieze atop the 34 columns depicts Hercules and Theseus, ancient Greece's popular superheroes who slew beasts and monsters and performed other amazing feats. The government's ruling body met and lived in the circular **Tholos,** while the council met in the nearby **Bouleuterion** and state archives were kept in the **Metroon.** The **Stoa of Attalos** was once the city's major shopping venue, with marble-paved colonnades that were popular gathering places; St. Paul preached Christianity here and Socrates sat on a bench expounding his philosophical principles. (The stoas—porticos—of the Agora lent their name to stoicism.) Reconstructed in the 1950s, the two-story stoa houses pottery, oil flasks, bronze disks used to cast votes, and many other

In the quiet enclave of **Anafiotika**, white-washed stepped streets and bougainvillea-clad houses climb the rocky slopes of the Acropolis. A world removed from modern Athens, Anafiotiika was settled by masons and other craftsmen who migrated from Anafi and other Cycladic islands in the middle of the 19th century to find work building the new capital. They put up these simple houses by hand in the style of their homeland and also renovated the enchanting little 17th-century church of **Agios Girogios tou Vrachou** (St. George of the Cliff), perched on the flanks of the Acropolis Hill. In the garden is a memorial to Konstantinos Koukidos, an Acropolis guard who wrapped himself in a Greek flag and threw himself off the top of the bluff when the Germans invaded in 1941.

finds evoking commercial and political life in the ancient city. Just behind is a beautiful medieval landmark, the 11th-century **Agii Apostoli Solanki** (church of the Apostles; see p. 86), and **Adrianou,** the neighborhood's most pleasant street, follows the north side of the Ancient Agora toward Kerameikos cemetery. Many of the 19th-century houses have been converted to cafes; take a seat on one of the terraces and soak in the views over the ruins to the Acropolis.

Entrances on Adrianou St. and Agiou Filippou, Monastiraki; west end of Polygnotou St., Plaka, and Thissio Sq., Thissio. odysseus.culture.gr. ℂ **210/321-0185.** Admission 4€ or part of Acropolis ticket (see p. 75). May–Oct daily 8am–7pm; Nov–Apr 8am–4pm. Metro: Monastiraki or Thissio.

Kapnikarea ★ CHURCH One of the greatest pleasures of strolling through the crowded Plaka and Monastiraki is coming upon this 11th-century gem, planted right in the middle of busy, shop-lined Ermou Street. The stone, tile-domed church was built on the site of an ancient temple to Athena, incorporates Roman columns from the Forum, and escaped demolition twice as Athens began to burgeon in the middle of the 19th century. Standing proud, slightly sunken beneath the level of the modern street, the landmark is an endearing testament to the city's long past.

Ermou and Kapnikarea sts. Free admission. Hours vary. Metro: Monastiraki.

Library of Hadrian ★★ ANCIENT SITE Roman emperor Hadrian built this lavish hall, of which a portion of a columned porch remains, for learning, discourse, and relaxation. At the center of the complex was a large inner court, surrounded by 100 columns supporting a portico overlooking the courtyard's garden and pool. Opening off the court were lecture halls, rooms for reading and conversation, and a library where papyri were stored in stone cabinets (a few of which survive). Hadrian intended the library to be his contribution to the intellectual life of Athens; he and other Romans considered the city to be the Empire's center of learning and enlightenment, and many noble families sent their sons to Athens to be educated.

4

ATHENS | Exploring Athens

Areos St. odysseus.culture.gr. ⓒ **210/923-9023.** Admission 4€ or part of Acropolis ticket (see p. 75). Daily 8am–3pm. At other times can be viewed from Aiolou St. Metro: Monastiraki.

Lysicrates Monument ★★ ANCIENT SITE   Many so-called choragic monuments like this once lined ancient Tripodon Street (Street of the Tripods), which still runs through Plaka. Choragics were producers who trained and costumed choruses and dancers for festivals; winners displayed their trophies (three-footed vessels known as tripods) atop lavish monuments. This is the only surviving example, erected by Lysicrates to show off the trophy he was awarded in the Dionysian festival of 334 B.C.

Lysikratous and Herefondos sts. Metro: Syntagma.

Mitropolis ★ CHURCH   The city's cathedral is home church to the archbishop of Athens and the chosen place of worship for the Athenian elite. Completed in 1862 amid the new capital's building boom, the massive walls incorporate marble from dozens of earlier churches around the city that were demolished to make room for roads and buildings. Among the medieval landmarks that survived is Panagia Gorgoepikoös, or Little Mitropolis (see below).

Mitropoleos St. Free admission. Hours vary. Metro: Monastiraki.

Museum of Greek Folk Musical Instruments ★ MUSEUM   The lyres and other gorgeously crafted instruments on display here, along with recorded music and occasional live performances in the attractive courtyard, deliver a delightful introduction to Greek musicology. With roots in the ancient world and the Byzantine and Ottoman Empires, Greek music goes far beyond the *Never on Sunday* theme that wandering minstrels pluck out in tourist tavernas.

1–3 Diogenis St. ⓒ **210/325-0198.** Free admission. Tues, Thurs–Sun 10am–2pm; Wed noon–6pm. Metro: Monastiraki.

Panagia Gorgoepikoös (Little Mitropolis) ★★ CHURCH   Though overshadowed by the unremarkable 19th-century Mitropolis (Metropolitan Cathedral) next door, this little church dedicated to the Virgin Mary Gorgoepikoös ("she who hears quickly") is much closer to the hearts of Athenians. The late 12th-century builders chose the site of an ancient temple to Eileithyia (goddess of childbirth and midwifery) and made use of the old stones and cornices. As you peruse the more than 90 stone reliefs, you'll be treated to layers of the past—some are ancient, depicting the Panathenaic games, others are Roman, and many are early Byzantine designs of plants and animals, brought here from other shrines around the city.

Mitropoleos and Agias Filotheis sts. at Mitropoleos Sq. Free admission. Hours vary. Metro: Monastiraki.

Plateia Monastiraki ★★ LANDMARK   This lively square, paved in gold mosaics, takes its name from a medieval monastery and poorhouse, of which only the church of Panayia Pantanassa remains. The square's most prominent feature, however, is the tiled-domed 18th-century Tzistarakis

ATHENS | Exploring Athens

Mosque, a remnant from the days of Ottoman rule. It became infamous when a Turkish administrator destroyed a column from the Temple of Olympian Zeus to extract lime for its construction; a plague soon swept through the city, which was blamed upon that desecration. You can step beyond the porch into several halls that display beautiful Turkish ceramics. A Turkish bazaar grew up around the Tzistarakis Mosque, and narrow alleyways leading off the square, especially Ifestou and Pandrosou streets, still have a souklike feel to them, lined with stalls and tiny shops. The exotic aura is especially in evidence on Sunday mornings, when a flea market snakes along Ifestou and nearby Kyntou and Adrianou streets. A 21st-century innovation in the square is a glass enclosure revealing the Iridanos River, which once flowed freely around the base of the Acropolis and was considered sacred by ancient Athenians.

Ermou and Athinas sts. Metro: Monastiraki.

Roman Forum ★ ANCIENT SITE   The well-preserved Gate of Athena Archetegis is inscribed with a notice that these now-ruined monuments—a rectangular marketplace that was the commercial center of the city under the many years of Roman rule—were erected with funds from Caesar and Augustus. Hadrian, who rebuilt so much of Athens in the 2nd century, is represented in the forum by a simple inscription regulating the sale of oil at the bazaar that operated near the entrance. In the 16th century, when Athens fell to the Ottomans, Mehmed II the Conqueror was allegedly so taken with the city's classical beauty that he prohibited destruction of the ancient monuments on pain of death. Besides converting the Pantheon to a mosque, he also built the Fethyie (Victory) mosque on the north side of this forum to celebrate his conquest. The most sought-out remnant, however, is a Roman latrine, maybe only second to the Acropolis as the most popular spot in Athens for photos.

Aiolou and Pelopida sts. ⓒ **210/324-5220** or 210/321-0185. Admission 2€ or part of the Acropolis ticket (see p. 75). May–Oct daily 8am–7pm; Nov–Apr 8:30am–3pm. Metro: Monastiraki.

Tower of the Winds ★★★ ANCIENT SITE   One of the most intriguing buildings of the ancient world stands on high ground next to the Roman Forum. Built by Syrian astronomer Andronikos Kyristes around 50 B.C., with a weather vane and eight sundials visible from afar, the structure was one of the first known versions of a clock tower. Each of the eight sides is inscribed with friezes of Boreas and other personifications of the winds; inside was a water clock that employed gears and sophisticated mechanisms to regulate the flow of water from a stream on the Acropolis Hill into a basin, allowing timekeepers to make measurements. A walk along **Aiolou Street** (named for Aeolus, god of wind) presents you with a nice view of the tower. Turn off Aiolou into Pandrossou, a pedestrian alley that was the Turkish bazaar. It's one of the city's few vestiges of the 400 years of Ottoman rule that ended in the 1820s. A bazaarlike aura still prevails; the narrow lane is chockablock with little souvenir and jewelry shops.

Near corner of Pelopida and Aiolou sts. Metro: Monastiraki.

Psyrri & Gazi

Monastiraki runs into Psyrri, by day a busy working-class neighborhood where leather crafters, tinsmiths, and basket weavers work out of small shops. When the sun sets, Psyrri transforms itself into Athens's prime showcase for night life, and nocturnal-by-nature Athenians crowd the tavernas, bars, and clubs until dawn. To the west is Gazi, where old brick smokestacks that once infamously spewed fumes and smoke now glow with colored lights, providing a beacon above the increasingly gentrified streets.

Benaki Museum of Islamic Art ★★ MUSEUM   A 19th-century neo-classical house and outbuildings display Islamic ceramics, carpets, woodcarvings, and other objects. Especially evocative are two reconstructed living rooms from the Ottoman times and a 17th-century reception room from a Cairo mansion.

22 Agion Asomaton and Dipylou. www.benaki.gr. ℂ **210/367-1000.** Admission 9€. Thurs–Sun 9am–7pm. Metro: Thissio.

Cultural Centre Melina Mercouri ★ MUSEUM   Take a romp through 19th-century Athens along a typical street of the then-newly transformed capital, painstakingly re-created in a former hat factory. Shop windows display clothing and dry goods, a door opens into a neoclassical house, and a *kafeneion* (coffeehouse) is so authentic you can almost hear the clatter of worry beads. The center evokes the memory of Melina Mercouri (1920–94), the actress and former minister of culture who launched the battle for the return of the Parthenon Marbles (see "The Frieze Fracas," p. 79). The center is in Thissio, an old neighborhood just west of the Acropolis and south of Kerameikos.

Iraklidon 66a. ℂ **210/345-2150.** Free admission. Tues–Sat 9am–1pm and 5–9pm; Sun 9am–1pm. Metro: Thissio.

Kerameikos Cemetery ★★★ ANCIENT SITE   Potters settled Kerameikos (from which the word ceramics is derived) as early as 1200 B.C., and by the 7th century B.C. the district had become the main burying ground of Athens. Generations of noble Athenians were laid to rest along the Street of Tombs, beneath monuments that seem little affected by the millennia—including a splendid marble bull atop the tomb of Dionysos of Kollytos and a marble relief of Dexileos, showing the young soldier on horseback preparing to spear an opponent (ironically mimicking his own death at the hands of the Corinthians in 394 B.C.). Not as well preserved are two gates in the ruins of the city walls. The Dipylion Gate was the main entrance to the city, while the Sacred Gate was reserved for participants in sacred processions. Celebrants of the Eleusinian mysteries followed the Iera Odos (Sacred Way) through the Sacred Gate in Kerameikos to Demeter's temple in ancient Eleusis (now modern Elefsina, 22km/14 miles west); sections of the gate and road remain, as do segments of the Long Walls that Themistocles erected in 478 B.C. Pottery, funerary sculptures, and other finds from Kerameikos are displayed in the Oberlaender Museum, next to the entrance. Kerameikos is one of the lesser-known ancient

LORD byron's ATHENS

Back in 1809, when Psyrri was known as a haven for underworld thugs and a hotbed for revolutionaries, British poet Lord Byron, an ardent Philhellene, boarded at 11 Agias Theklas St. (now a warehouse). His landlord's 12-year-old daughter, Teresa Makris, inspired his poem "Maid of Athens." Returning to Greece in the 1820s, Byron wrote part of "Childe Harold" while staying in the 17th-century Capuchin monastery, now destroyed, that once surrounded the **Lysicrates Monument** (p. 88). At the **Temple of Poseidon** (p. 99), he carved his name on one of the columns; visiting **Marathon** (p. 96), he wrote: "*The mountains look on Marathon, And Marathon looks on the sea, And musing there an hour alone, I dreamed that Greece might still be free.*"

Mementoes of Byron's involvement in the Greek independence movement can be found at the **National Museum** (p. 93) and the **Benaki Museum** (p. 95). Alas, before he could fight to free Greece, Byron succumbed to fever in the boggy, cholera-infested town of Mesolongi, where he died on April 19, 1824.

sites in Athens, so you can wander through these peaceful and storied surroundings at leisure.

148 Ermou St ⓒ **210/346-3552.** Museum and site 0€, or part of the Acropolis ticket (see p. 75). Mon–Sun 8am–7:30pm. Metro: Thissio.

Technopolis ★★ MUSEUM   Gazi translates as "gas lands," a reference to the unwelcome effect this former foundry spewing smoke and fumes from its smokestacks once had on the surroundings. The city of Athens converted the complex to an arts and culture center in the late 1990s (Technopolis means "Arts City"), and brick and stone-walled exhibition spaces surround a courtyard that is often used for concerts. Furnaces and other industrial equipment remain in place, interspersed with art exhibits and performance spaces. One hall houses the **Maria Callas Museum,** allowing a voyeuristic peek at some of the diva's personal effects and clothing. The main exhibition spaces at Technopolis are usually open until 9pm, after which you can catch a late dinner at one of the many restaurants and cafes that have sprung up in Gazi and adjoining Psyrri.

100 Pireos St. www.technopolis-athens.com. ⓒ **210/346-1589** or 210/346-7322. Metro: Kerameikos.

Omonia & Exarchia

Much of life in Athens transpires on and around busy and gritty Omonia Square, north of the Plaka. There's plenty to see—the central market, university, and National Archaeological Museum are all within easy reach—and you'll find no shortage of bustle and color. You can follow a pedestrian walkway, Aiolou, north from Monastiraki to Omonia, but walk at least part of the way along Athinas Street, a busy workaday avenue. Little shops cater to everyday needs, selling everything from tools and twine to votive candles and live chickens.

Agii Theodori ★ CHURCH   Marble tablets over the door date this squat church to the middle of the 11th century. With its sturdy stone walls and eight-sided, tile-roofed dome, the church has withstood bombardment during the War of Independence and other ravages, to stand as a sentinel from another age above the bustle of the busy streets below. Inside are many 19th-century frescoes and some charming terra-cotta reliefs of plants and animals.

Evripidou and Aristidou sts. at Klafthmonos Sq. Free admission. Hours vary. Metro: Panepistimiou.

City of Athens Museum ★ MUSEUM   Newlyweds King Otto and Queen Amalia set up temporary housekeeping in this modest 1830s house while their royal palace (now Parliament) was being built. The reception rooms, study, and library are set up to look as if the royal couple—still teenagers when they came to Athens to assume leadership of the new nation—might pop in at any moment. Most intriguingly, a plaster model to the scale of 1:1,000 shows what the city looked like in 1872, when it was home to just 25,000 souls.

7 Paparigopoulou St. www.athenscitymuseum.gr. © **210/323-1397.** Admission 5€. Mon and Wed–Fri 9am–4pm; Sat–Sun 10am–3pm. Metro: Panepistimiou.

Exarchia Square ★ SQUARE   The heart of the university district of Athens is covered in graffiti and surrounded by boho shops and laidback, shabby chic cafes. You can join the black-clad ranks of artists, intellectuals, and hordes of youth for a vicarious look at Athenian student and intellectual life. A student uprising in Exarchia on November 17, 1973, left 34 dead but eventually brought down Greece's oppressive military dictatorship.

Stournari and Themistokleous sts. Metro: Omonia.

The Hansen Buildings ★★ HISTORIC BUILDINGS   In the 1840s, Danish architects Theophilus and Christian Hansen came to Athens to take up Bavarian King Otto's mandate to rebuild the new capital in neoclassical style. They focused their energies on three adjoining buildings that are now surrounded by more functional buildings of the University of Athens. Theophilus undertook the **Greek Academy,** where two 23m-tall (75-ft.) columns topped with statues of Athena and Apollo flank an entrance portico richly embellished with statuary—most elaborate is the pediment frieze depicting the birth of Athena. In the main hall, beneath frescoes of the myth of Prometheus, is a statue of Simon Sinas, Greek consul to Vienna, who bankrolled the project. Hansen took his inspiration from the Parliament in Vienna, which he also designed, adding a few flourishes from the Erechtheion on the Acropolis (p. 74). The Academy promotes the advancement of sciences, humanities, and fine arts, and the public may step in for a look at the main hall and library. Theophilus' brother Christian Hansen, who was King Otto's court architect, in 1839 began work on the **Senate,** intended as the main building of the National and Kapodistrian University (now referred to simply as the University of Athens). Hansen was well versed in a classical sensibility, and also spent his time in Athens reconstructing the Temple of Nike on the Acropolis

Not Your Ordinary Grocery Store

The sheep heads, live chickens, calf carcasses, and other wares probably won't tempt you, and even much of the snack food on offer, such as steaming bowls of tripe soup, can seem a bit, uh, exotic. But few places in Athens are livelier and more colorful than the **Central Market** ★★ on Athinias Street. The scent of wild herbs wafting through the vast halls is transporting. The heaping piles of comestibles provide a culinary tour of Greece: You probably never knew there were so many kinds of olives or varieties of creatures in the sea. Cheese, bread, sliced meats, and other picnic fare are sold at the north end of the market. The market opens at 6am Monday through Saturday and should be in full swing by the time you arrive at a more reasonable time of the morning.

(p. 75). He showed more restraint with the Senate than his brother did, adorning the refined facade with a graceful, tall portico. The **National Library,** the third in the Hansen brothers' trilogy, was also designed by Theophilus, who indulged his bent for extravagance with a sweeping pair of curving marble staircases. It's well worth ascending them to see the exhibits—the library displays some of Greece's most rare manuscripts, including fragments of 6th-century gospels and the earliest known written versions of Homeric epics.

Panepistimiou St. www.nlg.gr. © **210/360-0207,** 210/360-0209, or 210/364-2918. Free admission. Mon–Thurs 9am–8pm; Fri–Sat 9am–2pm. Metro: Panepistimiou.

National Archaeological Museum ★★★ MUSEUM The splendor of ancient Greece comes to the fore in the world's finest collection of Greek antiquities. Galleries behind the neoclassical facade are filled with sensuous marble statues that once adorned temples throughout Greece and other treasures that span Greek history from the age of Homer to the days of the Roman Empire.

Three collections steal the spotlight. The **Mycenaean Collection** evokes the short-lived civilization that dominated much of the southern Mediterranean from around 1500 to 1100 B.C. and whose king, Agamemnon, launched the Trojan War and inspired the legends of Homer. In their royal tombs, the Myceneans left behind gold death masks and many other magnificent treasures, unearthed by Heinrich Schliemann in the 1870s. In the **Cycladic Collection** are enigmatic marble figures typical of this early civilization, some 5,000 years ago, as well as some three-dimensional pieces, including an utterly charming harp player and a life-size female figure that is the largest Cycladic piece yet to be unearthed. The **Thira Collection** showcases colorful frescoes from the Minoan settlement of Akrotiri on Santorini (also known as Thira), buried in a volcanic eruption around 1600 B.C. Hauntingly beautiful images of monkeys (indicating trade with North Africa), ships sailing past leaping dolphins, and young women gathering saffron reveal much about everyday life in such a distant past.

A CITY transformed

After Greece's War of Independence, Otto of Bavaria, then just 17, was named sovereign. One of his first orders of business was to transform what was then just a small town into a grand European capital. He imported some of the most prominent northern European architects of the day to design palaces and public buildings in a neoclassical style, inspired by the ancient culture whose enduring landmarks loom above the city on the Acropolis. While Otto's Athens never attained the grandeur of Baron Haussmann's Paris, the city is all the better for his efforts.

You can glimpse 19th-century Athens at its best a few blocks south of Omonia Square, down Athinas Street at beautifully restored **Kotzia Square.** Its grand neoclassical buildings include the Athens City Hall designed in 1874 and the National Bank of Greece. In the middle of the square, a fenced-off excavation area shows a large portion of an ancient road, along with several ancient tombs and small buildings. The square is beautiful at night when it is dramatically lit.

Some of the ancient world's most moving images are captured in the **funerary monuments,** including one from the Grave of Aristonautes in Kerameikos (p. 90), in which a boy tries to refrain a frisky horse. While most of ancient Greece's bronze statues were melted down for weaponry over the centuries, three extraordinary **bronzes** were retrieved from shipwrecks: a galloping steed with a horseman astride its back; Marathon Boy, depicting a youth, perhaps a young Hermes; and a majestic figure from around 400 B.C. that may be Poseidon or Zeus—his hands are clasped to hold a missing piece that may have been a thunderbolt or a trident.

44 Patission and 28 Oktovriou sts. www.namuseum.gr. © **210/821-7717.** Admission 10€ adults. Metro: Victoria or trolley: 2, 3, 4, 5, 6, 7, 8, 9, 11, 13, or 15.

Omonia Square ★ SQUARE   Another one of the city's hubs lacks the grace of Syntagma Square, surrounded as it is by a swirl of traffic and banal office blocks and frequented by some decidedly shady denizens. The everyday aspect of the space is not out of keeping with the square's history—when created as part of the renewal of the new capital in 1833, the space was intended to honor King Otto; after the unpopular monarch's ouster it became a hotbed of popular unrest and was renamed Omonia, which means Unity.

Athinas and Konstantinou sts. Metro: Omonia.

Kolonaki & Lycabettus

Athenians who are especially well coiffed, shod, and clothed tend to gravitate to the shady Kolonaki neighborhood, just to the north and east of Syntagma Square. You may want to follow in their footsteps—not just to sip coffee in their favorite lairs, but to spend an afternoon stepping in and out of some of the city's finest museums and window-shopping in chic boutiques. Top off the experience with an ascent to the top of Lycabettus hill for a spectacular view of the sun setting over the city.

Benaki Museum ★★★ MUSEUM   Antonis Benakis (1873–1954) spent his vast fortune satisfying his taste for anything having to do with Greek heritage, spanning the millennia from prehistory to the 20th century. More than 20,000 objects are showcased in the Benaki family's 19th-century mansion and a modern wing. Mycenaean and Roman jewelry, 5,000-year-old gold and silver bowls that mark the transition from the Stone Age to the Bronze Age, pistols Lord Byron brandished when he came to Greece in 1824 to join the fight for independence, and paintings by El Greco (who left his native Crete for Spain) are among the treasures you'll come across in the 36 rooms. Reception rooms, plush with paneling and Persian carpets, from an Ottoman mansion in Macedonia have been painstakingly re-assembled. A rooftop cafe overlooking the National Gardens (p. 84) is a great place to recharge, and the gift shop is stocked with beautiful reproductions of silver, terra-cotta, and jewelry.

Koumbari 1. www.benaki.gr. © **210/367-1000.** Admission 7€ adults. Mon and Wed–Fri 9am–8pm; Sat 9am–10pm; Sun 9am–3pm. Metro: Evangelismos.

Byzantine and Christian Museum ★★ MUSEUM   From their palaces in Constantinople, Byzantine emperors and the hierarchy of the Orthodox church ruled much of the Balkans and Asia Minor from the 6th century well into the 15th century. Few collections anywhere match this trove of icons, manuscripts, frescoes, mosaics, and sculptures from that period. One of the most enchanting pieces is an ivory depicting a lyre-playing Orpheus surrounded by animals—an allegorical reference to Christ and his followers, typical of the transition from paganism to Christianity. Mosaic floors from a 5th-century basilica and a Roman villa show similar refinement and sophistication, a testament to how Byzantine masters kept classical artistry alive through the Dark Ages.

22 Vasilissis Sofias Ave. www.byzantinemuseum.gr. © **210/721-1027.** Admission 8€. Daily 8am–8pm. Metro: Evangelismos.

Cycladic Art Museum ★★★ MUSEUM   From 3200 to 2000 b.c., one of Greece's early civilizations produced enigmatic, almost abstract marble figures that seem strikingly modern. Greece's wealthiest shipping dynasty, the Goulandris family, amassed more than 300 of these figures, housed in light-filled modern galleries. The elegant simplicity and symmetry of the pieces were not lost on such modern masters as Picasso and Modigliani, who were hugely inspired by them. Most are female, suggesting they were sculpted in honor of a goddess, though a few warriors and other males slip into the mix. Additional exhibits bring together vases, lamps, tools, and other artifacts for an enlightening and entertaining look at everyday life in ancient Greece. Temporary exhibitions are mounted in an adjoining 19th-century neoclassical mansion by Ernst Ziller, who designed many municipal buildings in Athens and elsewhere in Greece.

4 Neophytou Douka St. www.cycladic.gr. © **210/722-8321** or 210/722-8323. Admission 7€. Mon, Wed, Fri–Sat 10am–5pm; Thurs 10am–8pm; Sun 11am–5pm. Metro: Syntagma or Evangelismos.

Lycabettus Hill ★ NATURAL LANDMARK   One of the most popular rides in town is aboard the Teleferik that climbs to the pine-clad summit of the highest hill in Athens, topped with the gleaming white **church of Ayios Giorgios.** An early evening ascent via the funicular from Kolonaki usually ensures a breeze, a spectacular sunset to the west, and a moonrise to the east. The views of the Acropolis and across endless blocks of white buildings to the sea are mesmerizing. Views extend as far as the island of Aegina. Legend has it that Lycabettus is actually a piece of rock that Athena intended to use to make her temple on the Acropolis even loftier; she became distracted while winging her way over the city and dropped it, doing us all a favor. You can walk down (or up, for that matter) on one of the many well-marked paths.

Funicular leaves every 20 min. in summer from Ploutarchou St. 6€ round-trip. Metro: Syntagma or Evangelismos.

Plateia Kolonaki ★ SQUARE   In the shady Kolonaki neighborhood it's easy to get the impression that some well-heeled residents do nothing but shop, then sit at the cafes around Kolonaki Square. In the center of the square is a small, ancient column, giving the surroundings their name—"kolonaki" means "little column." Take a seat at a cafe of your choice, and enjoy a frappe (a tasty concoction of Nescafe and frothy milk) while watching the endless parade of elegant, beautifully coiffed elderly women, well-fed businessmen, wafer-thin models, and nattily attired young men on the prowl.

Off Kanari and Koumbari sts. Metro: Syntagma or Evangelismos.

Outside the Center

Monasteries, temples, and other age-old landmarks surround Athens in the hilly landscapes of Attica. Never too far from the sea, these sights are rich in myth and the labyrinthine history of Greece.

Daphni Monastery ★★★ RELIGIOUS SITE   One of Greece's finest Byzantine monuments was founded in the 6th century on the site of a temple to Apollo; you can still see one of the temple columns in a wall. Daphni takes its name from the laurels associated with Apollo, whose amorous pursuit of the goddess Daphne ended in her being transformed into a laurel tree. A prime position on the busy route to Corinth left the monastery vulnerable to sackings by medieval crusaders and some rough handling during the War of Independence. Yet its spectacular 11th-century mosaics remain intact, colorfully depicting saints, prophets, angels, and, from the center of the tall dome, Christos Pantokrator (Christ in Majesty). Daphni is located west of Athens and can be an ordeal to get to. Allow plenty of time and check that it is open before setting out.

Lera Odos, Attica, 9km (5½ miles) W of Athens. odysseus.culture.gr. © **210/581-1558.** Free admission. Tues–Sun 8:30am–3:30pm (call or check website for hours). Bus: A16, B16, E16.

Marathon ★ ANCIENT SITE   The race name we use so widely today harks back to 490 B.C. A young man, Pheidippides, ran the 42km (26 miles) from this little town at the edge of the marshy coast to Athens, burst into the

Agora, cried "We've won," then dropped dead from exhaustion. He was announcing the seemingly miraculous victory of the Athenians, outnumbered three to one, over the Persian army. It was said that the mythical hero Theseus appeared to fight alongside the Athenians, and that the god Pan put in an appearance, too. All told, the Persians lost 6,400 warriors and the Athenians just 192. Perhaps humiliated by the defeat, the powerful Persian navy returned to Asia Minor rather than attacking Athens. The Athenian heroes were buried in a mound, the Marathon Tomb, that still rises from the battlefield. There's not much else to see at Marathon, though the site of the Athenians' greatest victory is hallowed ground in Greece. A fragment of the column that the Athenians erected to celebrate independence is in the Archaeological Museum, about 1.6km (1 mile) from the tomb.

Marathonas, 42km (26 miles) NE of Athens. www.visitmarathon.gr. ⓒ **0294/55-155.** Admission 3€ for battlefield and museum. Tues–Sun 8:30am–5pm (shorter hours in winter). Buses depart from Pedion tou Areos Park station every 30–60 min; fare 5€; trip time 2 hr.

Monastery of Kaisariani ★ RELIGIOUS SITE   One of the most tranquil spots close to Athens is this simple monastery at the foot of Mount Hymettus, once carpeted with pine groves that have been decimated in recent fires. The 11th-century complex has ancient roots—it was built on the foundations of a Christian church that in turn replaced a temple to Aphrodite. The surroundings are still surprisingly bucolic, given the proximity of the sprawling city. A spring that rises on the grounds fed the River Illisos, which once flowed near the Acropolis and in antiquity supplied the capital with water. The mountainside was famous for the honey gathered from great swarms of bees. Philosophers brought their students to Kaisariani to escape the heat of the city, as many Athenians still do. Among them are brides who drink from the spring water gurgling forth near the entrance to the monastery, which is said to help induce pregnancy.

Off Academias St., Kaisariani, about 10km (6 miles) E of Athens. odysseus.culture.gr. ⓒ **210/723-6619.** Admission 2€. Tues–Sun 8:30am–5pm (shorter hours in summer). Bus 224 from Plateia Kaningos, near Syntagma; fare 1.40€; trip time 30 min. (plus 2km/1-mile walk from Kaisariani center to monastery).

Sanctuary of Artemis at Vravrona ★★ ANCIENT SITE   You'll encounter many sanctuaries in Greece where ancient cults worshipped specific deities. This one is especially quirky and charming. As legend has it, a young man killed a bear that had attacked his sister, and an epidemic soon broke out. A ceremony in which young girls wore bear masks and danced was mounted, and the epidemic subsided. So the bear-dance became a regular event, and a temple to Artemis, goddess of wild animals and the hunt, was built. In yet another twist, Iphigenia—King Agamemnon's daughter, who offered herself for sacrifice during the Trojan War to save the women of Greece—became a priestess at the temple. All that remains of the temple to Artemis are some foundations, and a cave said to be the Tomb of Iphigenia. A restored stoa is lined with bedrooms, complete with small beds and tables,

HIT THE beach

It doesn't take much to get an Athenian to the beach—and when summertime temperatures hit 46°C (115°F) in the shade, you'll see the appeal. Fortunately, it's easy to get to a beach near Athens. A nice string of sand follows the coastline south of the city, known as the Apollo Coast. You'll pay anywhere from 4€ to 7€ to get onto these beaches (reduced prices for children); once you're there you can rent sunbeds, umbrellas, and all sorts of other amenities.

In Glyfada, 17km (10 miles) south of Athens, **Asteria Glyfada** ★, 58 Poseidonos Ave. (www.balux-septem.com; ℂ **210/894-4548;** tram Metaxa St.) offers a Miami Beach vibe: white recliners, white umbrellas, even white sand (imported). A string of bars will deliver drinks to your lounge chair. The water can be a bit shallow and murky, but most patrons are too caught up in the scene to care.

Another 3km (2 miles) down the coast in Voula, the most popular beach is **Voula A** ★, 4 Alkyonidon St. (ℂ **210/895-9632;** tram Asklipiou Voulas St.). The regular crowds of 20-somethings and teenagers don't seem to mind that the beach is pebbly in spots and, unless you snag a sun bed, there's no shade. You'll find a lot more than sand and surf here: a swimming pool, a snack bar, water slides and watersports gear (skis, tubes, and boards), parachuting, pedal boats, racquetball, beach volleyball, minisoccer, some bars, and a minimarket;

its beachfront cafe and other facilities stay open at night after the beach itself closes. Nearby **Thalassea** ★, also known as Voula B (www.thalassea.gr; ℂ **210/895-9632;** buses A2, E1, E2, E22, 114, 116, 149, 340) is a bit less of a scene than its neighbor, and the waters are calm and clean, protected by breakwaters.

One of Athens' favorite beach getaways, **Vouliagmeni** ★★, Poseidonos Ave. (ℂ **210/967-3184;** bus E22) lies further on, some 25km (16 miles) south of Athens. It has a bit of everything: trees, shade, and sand and sea so sparkling that the beach has earned the European blue flag for cleanliness. There's even a ruined temple down the road, and if you desire a curative soak, Lake Vouliagmeni, just south of town, maintains a constant 24°C (75°F) temperature year-round.

Around the point from Vouliagmeni, the very popular **Yabanaki Varkiza** ★★, on Sounion Avenue in Yabanaki (www.yabanaki.gr; ℂ **210/897-2414;** buses E22, 170, 171, or 340), some 30km (19 miles) southeast of Athens, is hardly a quiet getaway, with rows of sun beds and blaring beach bars. But the drive here is a treat, winding along the spectacular cliffs of the Attica peninsula. And from here on down to Cape Sounion, the rocky coastline is etched with coves that are great for snorkeling and swimming.

where the young celebrants were housed. Masks, marble heads of the girls, and other artifacts are in the small museum.

Vravrona, 38km (22 miles) E of Athens. odysseus.culture.gr. ℂ **22920/27-020.** Admission 6€. Tues–Sun 8:30am–5pm (shorter hours in winter). Bus 304 from Athens, Zappion stop; fare 4€; trip time 1 hr.

Sanctuary of Eleusis ★★ ANCIENT SITE   It is hard to imagine that present-day Eleusis, a forest of belching refineries and warehouses, was once carpeted with fields and was the realm of Demeter, goddess of the Harvest. As the story goes, Hades, god of the underworld, kidnapped Demeter's daughter,

Persephone. Demeter came to Eleusis in search of her daughter, and, with the intervention of Zeus (Persephone's father) struck a deal with Hades that Persephone could return to earth for half the year. In gratitude, Demeter equipped Triptolemos, son of the king of Eleusis, with seeds and a chariot in which he could fly around the earth to disperse them. This story inspired the Eleusian Mysteries, rites that celebrated the cycle of life and death. Celebrants from Athens made their way here annually along the Sacred Way, which began in Kerameikos Cemetery (p. 90). At Eleusis they engaged in rituals that only the initiated could witness, under pain of death. You can follow the Sacred Way into the Temple of Demeter, where a row of seats surrounds the hall where the rites took place. Much of what remains at the site is Roman, including an arch honoring Hadrian that inspired the Arc de Triomphe in Paris.

Off I. Agathou, Elefsina, 23km (14 miles) W of Athens. ℂ **210/554-6019.** Admission 4€. Sun–Tues 8:30am–5pm (shorter hours in winter). Bus A16, 853, or 862 from Leoforos Pieros in Omonia; fare 3€; trip time 1 hr.

Temple of Poseidon ★★★ ANCIENT SITE   Fifteen of the original 34 columns still surround this temple to the god of the sea, commissioned in 444 B.C. by the statesman Pericles (who also built the Parthenon) and commanding a 29m (95-ft.) bluff at the southernmost tip of Attica. The rugged coast below the temple has changed little since ancient times, making it easy to imagine the joy the landmark elicited in sailors, a sign they were nearing home. Gazing out over the sea from the temple, you can understand its role as a lookout post where sentinels kept watch for approaching warships during the Peloponnesian Wars. Many visitors come to watch the sunset from the temple. For an especially memorable view up to the ruins, enjoy a swim in the view just below the temple. *Note:* The easiest way to visit Sounion is on an organized tour.

Cape Sounion, 70km (43 miles) E of Athens. ℂ **22920/39-363.** Admission 4€. Daily 10am–sunset. Bus departs every half-hour. from Pedion tou Areos Park station; fare 6€; trip time 2 hr. (plus 1km cab ride or walk to temple).

ORGANIZED TOURS

Athens is an easy city to navigate and explore on foot, and most of what you will want to see is concentrated beneath the Acropolis around Syntagma, Monastiraki, and Omonia Squares. That said, guided tours quickly show off the highlights and can help make sense of the layers of facts and myths of Greek history. Three agencies with especially good itineraries and well-informed guides are **CHAT Tours,** 4 Stadiou (www.chatours.gr; ℂ **210/323-0827**), **Fantasy Travel,** 19 Filelinon (www.fantasytravel.gr; ℂ **210/331-0530**) and **Key Tours,** 4 Kalliroïs (www.keytours.gr; ℂ **210/923-3166**). All offer half-day and full-day bus tours of the city, as well as excursions to Corinth, Delphi, and other sights outside Athens (see chapter 5). **Athens Walking Tours** (www.athenswalkingtours.gr; ℂ **210/884-7269**) leads excellent forays into the city's ancient sites as well as food and shopping tours. *Pame Volta*

(**Let's Go for a Ride**), 20 Hadjichristou, Acropolis (www.pamevolta.gr; ℂ **210/922-1578**) offers bicycles for rent and **bicycle tours** around the city.

The old standby, **CitySightseeing** (www.city-sightseeing.com) is a good way to get the lay of the land and a look at the major sites in one go. Open-top double-decker buses begin and end a 90-minute circuit at Syntagma Square, with stops at the Acropolis, Temple of Zeus, Plaka, the university, Omonia Square, Kerameikos, Monastiraki, Psyrri, Thission, the Benaki Museum, the National Gallery, the Central Market, and the Panathenaiko Stadium. Prerecorded commentaries are available in English, Greek, Spanish, French, German, Italian, Russian, and Japanese. Tickets are valid for 24 hours and buses depart every half-hour from 9am to 9pm. Tickets cost 22.50€ for adults, 9€ for children.

SHOPPING

Many of the best shops catering to Athenians and their visitors are within a fairly small area in the triangle bounded by Omonia, Syntagma, and Monastiraki squares. The Plaka can seem like one giant souvenir shop, though some excellent shops are tucked along the narrow lanes, as are department stores. Pedestrians-only Ermou Street, running west from Syntagma Square to skirt the Plaka and Monastiraki, is the city's main shopping strip. The Kolonaki neighborhood, on the slopes of Mount Likavitos, provides the best window shopping—much of what you see in the boutiques is imported and expensive. Voukourestiou, Tsakalof, Skoufa, and Anagnostopoulou streets are other main shopping avenues.

Collectibles

Antiqua ★   One of Athens's oldest and finest antiques dealers sells 19th-century watercolors, icons, coins, and other easy-to-carry high-end souvenirs. 2 Amalias Ave. www.antiqua.gr. ℂ **210/323-2220.** Metro: Syntagma.

Astrolavos-Dexameni ★★   This highly touted gallery plays a big part in bringing attention to the Greek art scene, showing well-known and up-and-coming artists. Kolonaki branch: 11 Irodotou St. www.astrolavos.gr. ℂ **210/722-1200.** Metro: Evangelismos.

Attention, Bargain Hunters

Monastiraki lives up to its reputation for bargain hunting along **Ifestou Street,** a narrow lane lined with shops selling tacky souvenirs and second-hand knick-knacks. The environs are especially lively on Sunday mornings, when a flea market sets up in **Abyssinia Square** and the surrounding streets. Some worthy antiques can be unearthed, but the mounds of vintage clothing and old housewares make it clear why the square is also known as Paliatzidika (the "secondhand-shop district").

Ekklisiastika Eidi ★ A large showroom and workshop on the premises can supply an icon of any saint you'd like. 9 Agias Eirinis St. ✆ **210/325-2047.** Metro: Monastiraki.

Ikastikos Kiklos ★ One of Athens's largest and sleekest galleries showcases contemporary Greek artists; besides this one, there are a few other Kiklos locations around the city. 20 Karneadou St. www.ikastikos-kiklos.gr. ✆ **210/724-5432.** Metro: Syntagma.

Old Prints ★ The extensive stock of old maps, books, and drawings here includes some beautiful prints of flowers and birds. 15 Kolokotroni St. antique booksandprints.com. ✆ **210/323-0923.** Metro: Syntagma or bus: 200.

Zoumboulakis ★ Athens's oldest gallery has introduced the work of many Greek artists over the decades; the Syntagma store specializes in silkscreens, poster art, and ceramics, while a branch on Kolonaki Square shows contemporary work. 26 Kriezoutou St. www.zoumboulakis.gr. ✆ **210/363-4454.** Metro: Syntagma.

Books & Magazines

Eleftheroudakis ★ Browse Athens's largest selection of English titles, with a huge selection of travel books, then pull up a seat in the pleasant cafe to linger over your selections. 17 Panepistimiou St. www.books.gr. ✆ **210/331-4480.** Metro: Panepistimiou.

Kiosk ★ Athens's best-stocked foreign-press **periptero** (kiosk) never closes, which is fortunate for news and magazine junkies. 18 Omonia Sq. at Athinas St. ✆ **210/322-2402.** Metro: Omonia.

Stoa tou Vivliou ★ An entire shopping arcade devoted to books—including rare volumes, current editions (some in English), and rare bindings—is a bibliophile's delight. 5 Pesmzoglou St. ✆ **210/325-3989.** Metro: Omonia.

Department Stores

Attica ★ Up-and-coming Greek designers are among those showcased throughout eight floors of fashionable clothing. The store also sells high-end furniture and housewares. 9 Panepistimiou St. www.atticadps.gr. ✆ **211/180-2500.** Metro: Syntagma.

F-Fokas ★ Brand-name sportswear and casual wear sold here, including many lines for children, are from Greek and international designers. 41 Stadiou St. www.fokas.gr. ✆ **210/325-7770.** Metro: Syntagma.

Hondos Center ★ The flagship store of this toiletries chain has all the grooming items you'll ever need, along with clothing for men and women, kitchenware, linen luggage, and many other accessories for you and your home. Don't leave without checking out the lavish perfume counters or stopping on the top floor to enjoy the view of the city over coffee. 4 Omonia Sq. www.hondos.gr. ✆ **210/528-2800.** Metro: Omonia.

Notos Home ★ Everything for the home, including fine crystal, fills eight floors of the Omonia outpost. 5 Kratinou St. at Kotzia Sq. www.notoshome.gr. ⊘ **210/374-3000.** Metro: Omonia.

Food & Wine

Aristokratikon ★ Athens's premier purveyor of chocolate has been turning out decadently rich creations since 1928. 9 Karayioryi Servias. www.aristo kratikon.com. ⊘ **210/322-0546.** Metro: Syntagma.

Bahar ★ Spices and dried herbs from Greek mountainsides are accompanied by herbal oils and other elixirs; the bags of herbs and mountain teas are ideal for easy-to-carry gifts. 31 Evripidou St. www.bahar-spices.gr. ⊘ **210/321-7225.** Metro: Omonia or Monastiraki.

Karavan ★ The dessert deprived can sate their cravings here; bite-sized, honey-soaked baklava and kadaifi (Greek pastry with nuts and syrup) are the specialties. 11 Voukourestiou St. www.karavan.gr. ⊘ **210/364-1540.** Metro: Syntagma.

Loumidis ★ This old-fashioned coffee roaster has been around since 1920. You can choose from a huge variety of Greek and Turkish coffees and the *briki* (traditional little coffee pots) in which to brew them. 106 Aiolou St. at Panepistimiou St. ⊘ **210/321-6965.** Metro: Omonia.

Mastihashop ★ *Loukoumi* (Turkish delight), intoxicating liqueurs, soaps, salves, gum, and all sorts of other products sold here are made from mastic harvested on the island of Chios. Panepistimiou and Kriezotou sts. ⊘ **210/363-2750.** Metro: Syntagma.

Gifts

Amorgos ★★ Wooden utensils, finely embroidered linens, shadow puppets—anything Greek-made seems to find a place on the crowded shelves here. 3 Kodrou St. ⊘ **210/324-3836.** Metro: Syntagma.

Center of Hellenic Tradition ★ Genuine folk arts and crafts from around Greece, including pottery, decorative roof tiles, and old-fashioned painted-wood shop signs, are on offer, as is delicious light fare in the shop's cafe. 36 Pandrossou and 59 Mitropoleos sts. ⊘ **210/321-3023.** Metro: Monastiraki.

Ekavi ★ Tavli (backgammon) sets—the game of choice for Greece's *kafeneion* (cafe) crowd—and chess sets with pieces resembling Olympic athletes and Greek gods are handmade by the Manopoulos workshops in wood, metal, or stone. 36 Mitropoleos St. www.manopoulos.com. ⊘ **210/323-7740.** Metro: Monastiraki or Syntagma.

Ethnikos Organismos Pronias (National Welfare Organization) ★ Traditional Greek designs include rugs, tapestries, and beautifully embroidered linens made by disadvantaged women around the country. Prices start at 20€ for a small embroidery. 6 Ypatias St. ⊘ **210/325-0524.** Metro: Syntagma.

Kombologadiko ★ Komboloi ("worry" beads) sold here are fashioned from bone, stone, wood, and antique amber—and can be worn as jewelry as well as used as a stress reliever. 6 Koumbari St. www.kombologadiko.gr. © **212/700-0090.** Metro: Syntagma.

Konstantopoulou ★ Lekka Street is one long row of silver shops; Konstantopoulou carries the largest selection of table settings, candlesticks, cutlery, and the like. 23 Lekka St. www.silverware.gr. © **210/322-7997.** Metro: Syntagma.

Mala (Komboloi Club) ★ Beautiful amber worry beads are the house specialty, though *komboloi* fashioned from many other materials are also available; prices run from 15€ to 9,000€. 1 Praxitelous St. www.komboloiclub.com. © **210/331-0145.** Metro: Panepistimiou.

Roussos Art and Jewelry ★ This store's porcelain dolls, dressed in traditional costumes, are made at a workshop in western Athens. Other handcrafted Greek-made trinkets are also available. 121 Adrianou St. at Kydathineon St. www.roussosantiques.gr. © **210/322-6395.** Metro: Akropoli.

Shoes

Stavros Melissinos ★★★ Sophia Loren, Jackie O., and Anthony Quinn are among the international roster of celebs who have sported the house's trademark, handmade leather sandals, first created in 1954. The son of the famous Stavros, known as the "poet shoemaker," now runs the enterprise. 2 Agias Theklas St. www.melissinos-poet.com. © **210/321-9247.** Metro: Monastiraki.

NIGHTLIFE & ENTERTAINMENT
The Performing Arts

Athens's biggest performing arts event, the **Athens and Epidaurus Festival,** brings drama, opera, symphonies, ballet, and modern dance to venues throughout the city from June through August. Audiences come from all over the world to see dazzling performances by an international roster of stars. The **Odeon of Herodes Atticus** (© **210/324-2121** or 210/323-2771) hosts many of the performances; the sight of the Acropolis looming overhead is no small part of the spectacle. The remarkably well-preserved **Epidaurus Theater,** about 2 hours south of Athens, stages many of the festival's productions of classical drama; packages include transport by bus. The festival box office is at 39 Panepistimiou St. (www.greekfestival.gr; © **210/327-2000**). The same box office offers tickets for the summertime **Lycabettus Festival,** where the outdoor theater atop Lycabettus Hill is a magical setting for summertime concerts of popular music featuring such headliners as Bob Dylan, Diana Ross, and scores of other international stars.

Athenaeum International Cultural Centre ★ Dedicated to Greek-American opera legend Maria Callas, this center pursues a mission of promoting music in Greece; it sponsors many classical concerts, including a winter and spring series at the center's neoclassical headquarters. The Maria Callas

Grand Prix competition for operatic vocalists and pianists brings international talent to the city in March, and an annual September 16 concert commemorating the singer's death is one of the city's big events, staged at the Odeon of Herodus Atticus. 3 Adrianou St. www.athenaeum.com.gr. ℭ **210/321-1987.** Metro Thissio or Monastiraki.

Dora Stratou ★★   This beloved Athenian institution has been performing traditional Greek folk dances at a beautiful garden theater on Filopappou Hill since 1953. 8 Scholiou St. www.grdance.org. ℭ **210/324-4395.** Metro: Petralona. Bus/ trolley: 15, 227.

Gagarin 205 ★   This cavernous modern hall hosts rock concerts, with a lineup of Greek and international stars playing to crowds of 1,300 or more. Check the website to see who's performing. In summer, the action moves to various Gagarin venues on the coast. 205 Liosion Ave. www.gagarin205.gr. ℭ **210/854-7601.** Metro: Attikis.

Megaron Mousikis ★   Exceptionally fine acoustics make this sleek modern venue a standout on the classical musical circuit. Recitals, symphonic performances, and other programs by an international roster of musical talent run from September to June. Vas. Sofias and Kokkali sts. www.megaron.gr. ℭ **210/729-0391** or 210/728-2333. Metro: Megaron Mousikis.

Olympia Theater ★   The Greek National Opera performs its regular September to June season in new quarters on the coast in Palaio, designed by Italian architect Renzo Piano, and a grand old hall in Omonia. Akadimias 59–61. www.nationalopera.gr. ℭ **210/362–2100.** Metro: Panepistimio.

Technopolis ★★   Occupying what was once a fume-spewing factory, this is now Athens's trendiest art center and the dramatic backdrop for cutting-edge concerts and dance performances. In the first 2 weeks of July, Technopolis hosts the **Athens International Dance Festival,** with performances by modern-dance companies from throughout the world. 100 Piraeos St. www.technopolis-athens.com. ℭ **210/346-1589** or 210/346-7322. Metro: Kerameikos.

Nightlife

It's pretty easy to find a club or bar in Athens. When in doubt, head to **Psyrri,** once a nighttime nest of hooligans and these days the place to be for anyone who wants to partake of nightlife. **Gazi** is the city's up-and-coming gay district, with bars and clubs that tend to cater to men and women, straight and gay. Clubs and bars in **Exarchia** are popular with students, not surprisingly, given the presence of Athens University. The pedestrian streets and squares of **Plaka** and **Thissio** are chockablock with outdoor cafes and bars, many with gardens or rooftops.

Venues come and go all the time, and many of the bigger dance clubs close up shop in Athens in the summer and move out to the sea coast. Most nightspots don't heat up until midnight, and many don't even open until 11pm or later and stay open until 5 or 6am—all the more amazing considering that many of the habitués have to report for work in the morning.

BARS & LOUNGES

45 Degrees ★★   Bypass the crowded bar downstairs and head straight to the rooftop terrace overlooking the Acropolis—a mellow place to begin or end your nighttime explorations of the surrounding Gazi bars and clubs. 18 Iakhou, at Voutadhon. © **210/347-2729.** Metro: Thission.

Akrotiri Lounge ★   One of Athens's most popular seaside playgrounds, Akrotiri is stylish and just plain fun, with tropical decor, a beach, a big swimming pool, many dance floors and bars, very decent Mediterranean cuisine, and excellent music that runs the gamut from Greek to hip-hop and R&B. It's about 6.8km (4¼ miles) from central Athens, along the coast. Leof Vas Georgiou B5, Agios Kosmas. www.akrotirilounge.gr. © **210/985-9147.** Tram: Elliniko.

Baraonda ★★   A location at the edge of Kolonaki near the big international hotels helps make this the most glamorous outdoor spot in Athens, catering to international business people as well as Athenians out for a polished night on the town. In winter, the move inside brings red velvet curtains, candles, stone and tiled walls, and chandeliers. Tsocha 23. www.baraonda.gr. © **210/644-4308.** Metro: Ambelokipi.

Balthazar ★★★   A beautiful courtyard garden and the elegant interiors of a neoclassical mansion attract a well-heeled crowd who enjoy lounge music and a light menu. Tsoha 27. www.balthazar.gr. © **210/644-1215.** Metro: Ambelokipi.

Mamacas ★★   Just as stylish and popular as the restaurant of the same name across the street, this bar is almost a mandatory stop for those who make the nighttime scene in the trendy Gazi neighborhood. 41 Persefonis St. www.mamacas.gr. © **210/346-4984.** Metro: Kerameikos.

Mike's Irish Bar ★   An outpost for ex-pats (with a strong contingent of Americans), Mike's serves a decent pint of Guinness and offers all sorts of diversions, from darts to televised soccer matches to karaoke and, on some nights, live rock and funk. 6 Sinopis St. www.mikesirishbar.com. © **210/777-6797.** Metro: Ambelokipi.

Podilato ★★   Laid-back, stylishly retro, and perpetually crowded, the "Bicycle" in Exarchia caters largely to chatty students who seem determined to drink and talk until dawn. 48 Themistokleous St. © **210/330-3430.** Metro: Omonia.

Thirio ★★   You'd have to be pretty thick-skinned not to get in the mood for romance at this Psyrri nightspot. Jazz and Latin music wafts through two levels are divided into little cubbyholes, lit by candles, and decorated with African tribal artifacts. 1 Lepeniotou St. thirio.gr. © **210/321-7836.** Metro: Monastiraki.

HOTEL LOUNGES

Air Lounge ★★★   This is the place to get away from it all, in an outdoor garden that surrounds the pool and overlooks the Acropolis—hands-down one of the most relaxing spots in the busy, gritty center of town. Fresh Hotel, 26 Sofokleous St. www.freshhotel.gr. © **210/524-8511.** Metro: Omonia.

Alexander's ★★ Alexander the Great, centerpiece of an 18th-century tapestry, hangs over the bar, keeping an eye on what many seasoned travelers claim is the best hotel lounge in the world. A clubby atmosphere, along with a huge selection of single malt Scotches and cigars (dispensed from a walk-in humidor), give the place an old-boy aura, but in these upscale environs the "old boy" next to you may well be a prince or oil baron. Try the house's signature drink, a delicious concoction laced with the oils of Sicilian tangerines. Hotel Grande Bretagne, Syntagma Sq. www.grandebretagne.gr. ☎ **210/333-0000.** Metro: Syntagma.

Frame Garden ★ A slightly retro ambiance prevails at this stylish lounge that spills off an airy portico into a beautifully lit garden. International music, sometimes live, accompanies a menu of light fare and grown-up cocktails. St. George Lycabettus Hotel, 78 Kleomenous St. www.sglycabettus.gr. ☎ **210/729-0711.** Metro: Evangelismos.

Galaxy Bar ★ This landmark bar on the top floor of the Hilton comes with a gorgeous view of the Acropolis. Hilton Hotel, 46 Vas. Sofias Ave. www.hiltonathens.gr. ☎ **210/728-1000.** Metro: Evangelismos.

Periscope ★★ A drink or light meal in the lounge of one of the city's hippest hotels is a sightseeing experience—sofas and chairs are the seats of Morris Minis and Ferrari-red tables are equipped with joysticks that allow you to maneuver panoramic views of the city that spin overhead. For an exotic flourish, get on the dance floor and sway to the tracks of world music. Periscope, 22 Haritos St. www.periscope.gr. ☎ **210/729-7200.** Metro: Syntagma. Bus: 022, 060, 200.

MUSIC BARS & DANCE CLUBS

Bios ★ This Psyrri hotspot does multi-duty as a club, screening room, art gallery, and cafe, and often adds to the mix with excellent music in a basement nightclub and a hip roof garden. 84 Pireos St. www.bios.gr. ☎ **210/342-5335.** Metro: Kerameikos.

Booze Cooperativa ★★★ Occupying three floors of an old factory, Booze Cooperativa offers a little bit of everything—coffeehouse, bar, dance club, art gallery, screening room, meeting place. Music is often live, and at other times provided by some of the city's most popular DJs. Should you still wish to smoke while clubbing, this is the place to do so; Booze is registered as a political headquarters, exempting it from the city's smoking ban. Kolokotroni 27. www.boozecooperativa.com. ☎ **210/324-0944.** Metro: Syntagma.

Envy ★ This big mainstream club caters to well-heeled youth, who dance to hip-hop, R&B, and, on Sundays, Greek music. Agias Eleousis St. www.dubliner.gr. ☎ **210/331-7801** or 210/331-7802. Metro: Monastiraki.

Gallery Club ★ A slightly older crowd drops in to this Kolonaki club to dance to music that runs the gamut from Greek to disco to Western nostalgia. 17 Amerikis St. ☎ **210/362-3901.** Metro: Syntagma.

Half Note ★★ The city's most popular venue for jazz, tucked away in a quiet corner behind the Temple of Olympian Zeus, has hosted the greats for the past 30 years. 17 Trivonianou St. www.halfnote.gr. ☎ **210/921-3310.** Bus: A3, B3, 057.

Rebetika Clubs

Rebetika, the Greek equivalent of blues, originated with immigrants from Asia Minor in the 1920s and 1930s and is a popular fixture of the club scene. One of the most popular of the many rebetika clubs around the city is **Rebetiki Istoria** ★, 181 Ippokratous St. (www.rebetikiistoria.com; ℂ **210/642-4937;** Metro Omonia), a smoky lair in Exarchia that attracts a crowd of older regulars and enthusiastic students. At **Stamatopoulos** ★★, 26 Lissiou St. (www.stamatopoulostavern.gr; ℂ **210/322-8722;** Metro Syntagma), wall murals re-creating life in early-20th-century Athens set the mood for a night of fine traditional rebetika and bouzoukia music, accompanied by good taverna fare and decent house wine. Many rebetika legends show up regularly to perform at storied 1930s-era **Stoa Athanaton** ★★★, tucked away in the Central Market, Sofokleous 19, ℂ **210/321-4362;** Metro Omonia). A late lunch crowd can get their rebetika fix at matinee sessions from 3:30 to 7:30pm. Note, however, that this place closes down in the summer.

Kalua ★   One of the city's oldest discos, Kalua is still going strong, appealing to everyone from visiting businessmen to die-hard dance fans. 6 Amerikis St. ℂ **210/360-8304.** Metro: Syntagma.

Mad Club ★   The favorite place to dance in popular Gazi plays 1980s rock for an enthusiastic crowd that wasn't even born when this music came on the scene. 53 Persefonis St. ℂ **210/346-2007.** Metro: Kerameikos.

Rodon ★★   Some of the biggest names in rock have appeared at Rodon since it opened in the 1980s—in fact, Rodon basically brought rock and pop to Athens when the city was just emerging from the era of military rule. Local and foreign acts from the pop charts still make regular appearances. 24 Marni St. ℂ **210/524-7427.** Metro: Omonia.

Six D.O.G.S. ★★   Four adjoining bars in Monastiraki join forces to create one of the city's most exciting and hippest venues. It combines a laid-back library, sleek cocktail lounge, and huge dance hall/performance space. The design is sleek and minimalist and the music, provided by popular DJs and bands, is enhanced with remarkable acoustics that bring dancers out in force. Avramiotou 6–8. www.sixdogs.gr. ℂ **210/321-0510.** Metro: Monastiraki.

Vanilla Project ★   A rather glamorous and prosperous crowd comes here to enjoy two DJ-manned dance floors and a huge bar. 37 Sarri St. ℂ **210/322-0647.** Metro: Monastiraki.

Venti ★   An open-air dance floor and Greek pop music make this Psyrri club a hit with young Athenians, especially in summer when most other clubs move to the seaside or shut down entirely. 29 Lepiniotou St. ℂ **210/325-4504.** Metro: Thissio.

GAY & LESBIAN BARS & CLUBS

My Bar ★   More intimate and less rowdy than its Gazi counterparts, this Monastiraki bar is just as energetic and all the better for its grown-up vibe. 6 Kakourgiodikiou. www.mybar.gr. ℂ **210/86-2161.** Metro: Monastiraki.

Noiz Club ★ Big and noisy, this Gazi club offers two dance floors and two DJs. It's especially popular with gay women but welcoming to all. Leof. Konstantinoupoleos 78. ℰ **210/346-7850.** Metro: Kerameikos.

Sodade ★ A mainstay in the gay-friendly district of Gazi, Sodade is popular with men and women, whatever their tastes might be. It gets packed on weekend nights. 10 Triptolemou St. www.sodade.gr. ℰ **210/346-8657.** Metro: Kerameikos.

CASINOS

Club Hotel Casino Loutraki ★ In the seaside resort town of the same name, 80km (50 miles) south of Athens, this complex has 80 gaming tables, 1,000 slot machines, a luxury hotel, a restaurant, and a spa. Many older gamblers come to soak in curative hot springs between bouts at the slots. The casino's Casino Express bus (ℰ **210/523-4188** or 210/523-4144) makes frequent runs to and from Athens. 48 Poseidonos Ave. www.clubhotelloutraki.gr. ℰ **27440/65-501.**

Regency Casino Mont Parnes ★ A cable car takes you up Mount Parnitha, 18km (11 miles) north of central Athens, to this casual, laid-back casino complex with 53 table games and 508 slot machines. You can't get away with wearing shorts, though no one's going to insist on a jacket and tie, either. Entrance fee is 6€. You can also make the ascent by car, a 30km (19 miles) drive from the center of the city. Aharnon. www.regency.gr. ℰ **210/242-1234.**

AROUND ATHENS

Fire up the imagination and get ready for some time travel. To the south of Athens in the Peloponnese, and to the west at Delphi, you'll be visiting some of the most legendary sites of Greek history and myth. These places are more than just piles of old stones: They're the haunts of superheroes, villains, willful gods and naughty goddesses, all brought to life by Homer and ancient playwrights. King Agamemnon launched the Trojan War from his palace at stony Mycenae; centuries later, Saint Paul preached at Corinth, where vast ruins are all that remains of one of the largest, most cosmopolitan cities in the ancient world. Emperors and the elite came from all over the Mediterranean world to consult the oracle at Delphi, maybe the most beautiful and mysterious of all ancient sites. Athletes traveled from as far away as the Black Sea to complete in the games at Olympia, far more raucous than the modern-day events to which the pine-scented ancient site has lent its name. Visiting these sites brings the thrill of stepping back through the millennia and reliving the great epics of western civilization.

On a more hedonistic note, west of Athens in the Saronic Gulf are a clutch of island getaways, all an easy sail away from the capital. Which one you set your sights on depends on what you're in the mood for—a taste of cosmopolitan leisure, Spetses; sophisticated getaway, Hydra; old-fashioned island life, Aegnia; or sandy beaches, Poros.

All of these nearby attractions are within day-trip distance from Athens, though an overnight or two makes the experience all the better.

STRATEGIES FOR SEEING THE ANCIENT SITES

Athens-based companies such as **CHAT Tours,** 4 Stadiou (www. chatours.gr; © **210/323-0827), Fantasy Travel,** 19 Filelinon (www. fantasytravel.gr; © **210/331-0530) and Key Tours,** 4 Kalliroïs (www.keytours.gr; © **210/923-3166**) offer tours to Delphi and ancient sites in the Peloponnese. Typical day excursions might cover just Delphi or a pair of Peloponnesian sights—Mycenae and Epidaurus, for example, or Mycenae and Corinth. Two- to three-day tours tend to make a full loop, going to Corinth, Epidaurus, and Mycenae, then swinging through Olympia before heading up to Delphi and back to Athens. Whatever option you choose, try to avoid seeing too much in too short a time—beware of those ambitious day tours that pack Corinth, Mycenae, Epidaurus, and Nafplion into one day. That's an exhausting jumble of ruins, and this is a vacation, after all. Costs range from about 80€ for a 1-day tour to about 300€ for multi-day tours, including lodging and transportation and often admission fees (or at least discounts on admission).

Independent travelers may want to consider spending a night or two in Nafplion as a base for visiting the surrounding sites, and/or an overnight in Olympia, with a stop in Delphi on the way back to Athens.

THE PELOPONNESE

Greece's southern peninsula, divided from the mainland by the Corinth Canal, is virtually a grab bag of famous ancient sites: the awesome palace of king Agamemnon at Mycenae; the mysterious thick-walled Mycenaean fortress at Tiryns; the magnificent classical temples at Corinth, Nemea, and Olympia; and the monumental theaters at Argos and Epidaurus, still used for performances today. These are all within easy reach of Athens, and presented below in order of their proximity to the capital. Also in the Peloponnese is Nafplion, one of the most beautiful towns in Greece and, with its neoclassical mansions facing the Gulf of Argos and beaches, a favorite place for Athenians to spend a day or weekend. It's your top choice for an overnight when you're visiting the ancient sites, although Olympia also has a lively, friendly vibe and some nice places to stay and eat.

Where to Stay & Eat Near the Peloponnese Sites

NAFPLION

Antica Gelateria di Roma ★★★ SWEETS/COFFEE A little bit of Italy comes to Nafplion in this delightful shop. It serves delicious espresso, but even that takes second place to what many regulars consider to be the best ice cream in Greece. Sometimes it seems that the Athenians who flock to Nafplion on weekends come only to stop here to try yet another flavor.

3 Pharmakopoulou and Kominou. © **27520/23-520.** Sweets and sandwiches 4€–12€. Daily 10am–midnight.

Family Hotel Latini ★★ This stylish little guest house in a former sea captain's mansion has a prime location, one of the best in town, near the port and steps from Syntagma Square. Rooms are large, bright, and surprisingly quiet, and many have balconies and sea views. A top-floor suite tucked under the eaves is especially attractive and commodious. Downstairs, a welcoming bar-breakfast room opens to a sidewalk terrace.

47 Othonos. www.latinihotel.gr. ℂ **27520/96470.** 10 units. 70€–85€ double. Rates include breakfast. **Amenities:** Bar/cafe; Wi-Fi (free).

Hotel Perivoli ★★★ A hillside planted with citrus and olive groves is a magical setting for this smart, comfortable little resort. The handsome rooms all open to terraces and balconies facing a pool and, sparkling in the distance, the Gulf of Argos. Nafplion is just a few minutes' drive away, but home-cooked meals served poolside are reason enough to stay put for a quiet evening. In-room fireplaces help make this a cozy year-round retreat.

Pirgiotika. 8km (5 miles) E of Nafplion. www.hotelperivoli.com. ℂ **27520/47905.** 18 units. 130€ double. Rates include breakfast. **Amenities:** Bar; restaurant; pool; Wi-Fi (free).

Marianna Hotel ★★★ On a perch high above the old town, just below the Acronafplia, this delightful hotel has extremely attractive and comfortable rooms. Most are view-filled, and many have stone walls and other character-rich architectural touches. The setting is enhanced by the hospitality of the Zoltos brothers, who provide platters of oranges and fresh-squeezed juice from their farm and help lug bags up the steps from the lanes below. A breezy terrace is just one of many outdoor spaces available to guests, from balconies and patios to a shady communal courtyard garden.

Ilia Potamianou 9. www.pensionmarianna.gr. ℂ **27520/24256.** 20 units. From 85€ double. Rates include breakfast. **Amenities:** Bar; Wi-Fi (free).

Ta Phanaria ★ GREEK A shaded table under Ta Phanaria's enormous scarlet bougainvillea is the prettiest place in the center of town for lunch or dinner, and the old-fashioned taverna fare has been a hit with locals and visitors for years. Aside from such standbys as moussaka, many vegetable dishes, stews, and grilled chops fill out the big menu.

13 Staikopoulo. ℂ **27520/27-141.** Main courses 7€–15€. Daily around noon–midnight.

Taverna Old Mansion (Paleo Archontiko) ★★ GREEK You'll long remember a meal here as a quintessential Greek experience, enjoying good traditional Greek *spitiko* (home) cooking—stews, chops, and usually several vegetarian choices—on a narrow lane in the Old Town. Every once in a while musicians stroll in to complete the picture-perfect scene.

7 Siokou. ℂ **27520/22-449.** Main courses 8€–15€. Daily 7pm–midnight; summer weekends noon–4pm.

OLYMPIA

Europa Best Western ★★ The most luxurious accommodations in Olympia are the large and well-appointed rooms at this airy hilltop retreat. Many have sunken sitting areas that open to balconies, providing lots of space for relaxation. The many amenities include a pleasant garden surrounding a large pool, and the hotel's outdoor taverna can't be beat for a meal on a summer evening.

Around Athens

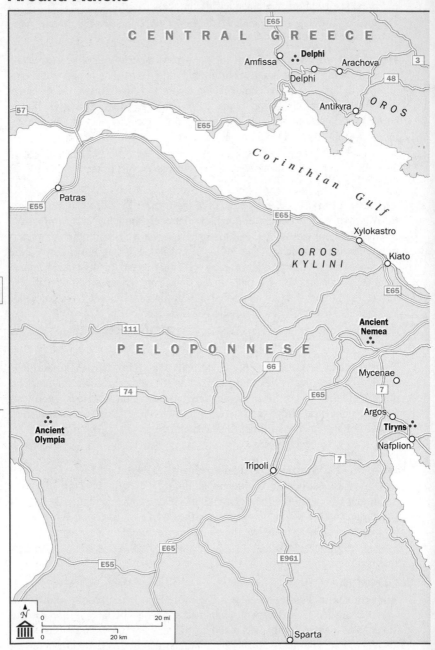

Psachna

EUBOEA

Larymna

E75

Nea Artaki

Livadia

Chalkida

44

Vathy

Vasiliko

44

Lepoura

E75

11

Euboic Gulf

ELIKON

Thespies

Thebes

Thivsi

OROS

Erythres

PARNITHA

E75

E962

Vilia

ATTICA

Mandra

Kamatero

Pefki

GERANEIA

Dafni

Vrilissa

Megara

E94

Athens

Stavros

Perama

Artemis

Corinth

Kineta

Salamina

Vyronas

Zografou

(Loutsa)

Ag.

Karakiani

Piraeus

Athens Int'l.

Theodori

Selinia

Airport

Ancient

Isthmus

Markopoulo

Corinth

Salamina

Saronic Gulf

Saronic Gulf Islands

Voula

Vari

Keratea

ONIA

Vouliagmeni

ORI

Souvala

91

Lagonisi

Aegina

Agia Marina

Saronida

Anavyssos

Skala

Aegina

Thimari

Angistri

Methana

Legrena

Ligourio

Epidaurus

Peninsula

Patroklou

Sanctuary of

Dryopi

Methana

Asklepios

Poros

Tracheia

Trizina

Poros

Kantia

Galatas

Ag. Georgios

Ermioni

Aegean Sea

Argolic

Kranidi

Gulf

Hydra

Hydra

Dokos

Spetses

GREECE

Athens

Aegean

Sea

Area of detail

Mediterranean

Sea

CRETE

Oikismou Drouba, above modern town. www.hoteleuropa.gr. ✆ **26240/22650.** 80 units. 90€–105€ double. Rates include buffet breakfast. **Amenities:** 2 restaurants; bar; pool; Wi-Fi (free).

Hotel Pelops ★★★ Offering spruce and appealing rooms on a quiet back street, the Hotel Pelops is an easy walk away from the ruins and museums. Small terraces overlook the surrounding hills, and the Spiliopoulou family is on hand with gracious hospitality. Guests can use the beautiful swimming pool of the Hotel Europa (p. 111), just up the hill.

2 Varela. www.hotelpelops.gr. ✆ **26240/22543.** 26 units. 50€ double. Rates include buffet breakfast. **Amenities:** Bar; lounge; Wi-Fi (free).

Taverna Bacchus ★★ This appealing countryside taverna with a large terrace has good-sized guest rooms upstairs, with lots of character and nice touches like wood ceilings, tile floors, and beautiful views over the rolling hills; some studios with kitchenettes are in an adjoining cottage. A swimming pool sparkling in the garden is most welcome after a day exploring the ruins, a pleasant hike away through the woods. Delicious home-cooked meals are served in the dining room clustered around a huge hearth and a wide terrace overlooking the surrounding olive groves.

Ancient Pissa, 3km (2 miles) E of Olympia. www.bacchustavern.gr. ✆ **26240/22298.** 11 units. 70€–90€ double. Rates include breakfast. **Amenities:** Restaurant; bar; pool; Wi-Fi (free).

Isthmus of Corinth ★

80km (50 miles) W of Athens

The name Peloponnese means "Pelops Island," but for centuries this region west of Athens was not really an island, but connected to the mainland by this narrow neck of land, only 6.3km (4 miles) wide. As a result, ships approaching Athens were forced to sail an extra 400km (240 miles) around the Peloponnese. Over the millennia, numerous schemes for shortcuts were attempted. The ancient Greeks built a stone road, the Diolkos, to cart goods and small ships between the Gulf of Corinth to the west of the isthmus and the Saronic Gulf to the east. (Portions of the stone ramp still run alongside the modern canal.) The Romans attempted to dig a canal several times but eventually settled for rolling ships across the isthmus on logs, similar to the way the Egyptians had transported blocks of granite across the desert to build the Great Pyramids. The Emperor Nero revived attempts in A.D. 67 and set 6,000 slaves to work with spades, but that endeavor was soon determined to be too costly and impractical. It was not until the Suez Canal was completed in the 1870s that interest turned again to digging a similar water route across the isthmus, and a Greek team completed the job in 1893, making the Peloponnese a bona fide island at last.

Most highway traffic zooms across the Isthmus, but you can pull off into the Canal Tourist Area and a well-marked overlook for a look at the ribbon-like waterway, the ship traffic, and, most impressively, the 86m-high (282-ft.) walls of rock through which the canal was cut. An added attraction is the daredevil antics of bungee jumpers, for whom the chasm is a big draw. The lookout is also popular with thieves who prey on gawking tourists, so be sure to lock your car doors and watch for pickpockets.

Corinth ★★★

89km (55 miles) W of Athens

Now lying in vast ruins and surrounded by fertile plains, Corinth—one of the most important cities in the world for well over a thousand years—still evokes wealth and power. A prime location on the narrow Isthmus of Corinth gave the huge city, with a population of 100,000 by 400 B.C., not one but two ports, gateways to sea routes to the Middle East as well as Italy. Goods from all over the known world once flowed into Corinth. A player in the Trojan and Persian Wars, the city was a major sea power with a huge fleet and established a colony at Siracusa on the island of Sicily that became another of the world's great Greek cities. Corinth's citizens were known for their love of luxury, reflected in the so-called Corinthian Order of architecture, in which columns are topped with elaborate capitals decorated with acanthus leaves and scrolls. They were also known for their free-wheeling lifestyle, exemplified by the Temple of Aphrodite's 1,000 sacred prostitutes—morals that later vexed St. Paul when he came here to preach Christianity in the 1st century A.D. What you see today is actually the remains of two cities, for the Romans destroyed much of Corinth when they overran Greece in the 2nd century B.C. Julius Caesar ordered the city's reconstruction in A.D. 52, and much of today's site dates to that era.

ESSENTIALS

Many longtime travelers to Greece never thought they'd see the day, but it's now possible to travel to Corinth from Athens easily by train. Service is not terribly fast but it's efficient and fairly frequent, via the **Proastiako** suburban railway system from Larissa Station in Athens (p. 285). The trip takes about 2 hours. For up-to-date schedules and fares (about 12€ for Athens to Corinth) visit www.trainose.gr; given the bewildering nature of the website, you may also want to ask at the tourist office in Athens or at Larissa Station. If you're driving, you can shoot over to Corinth in an hour or so on the **E94 toll road.** KTEL **buses** leave from Athens' Stathmos Leoforia Peloponnisou (Peloponese) station, 100 Kifissou (✆ **210/512-4910**), about every hour and the trip takes 1 to 2 hours, depending on traffic and the number of stops. For schedules, check www.ktelargolida.gr. The fare is about 11€. If you arrive by train or bus, you'll have to a catch a taxi or local bus from the station to the ancient site.

EXPLORING ANCIENT CORINTH

Acrocorinth ★★★ RUINS   Standing sentinel some 540m (1,700-ft.) above the coastal plain, the acropolis of ancient Corinth has been a lookout post, place of refuge, and shrine since the 5th century B.C. Byzantines, Franks, Venetians, and Turks all added to the ancient walls, creating three rings of massive fortifications, pierced by gates, that ramble across the craggy mountaintop. The ruins of the Temple of Aphrodite stand atop the highest reaches of the peak. In ancient times the reward for the climb was the company of one of the temple's 1,000 prostitutes; trekkers who make the 3-hour climb now settle for views that sweep across the sea to the east and west and a broad swath of southern Greece. The less adventurous can make the ascent by car or in one of the taxis that wait at the bottom of the peak.

Ancient City ★★ ANCIENT SITE   The most imposing remnant of the Greek city are those of the **Temple of Apollo,** on a low hillock from which 7 of the temple's original 38 Doric columns still rise. Most of the rest of the city that remains was built by the Romans, whose shops line the **forum** ruins. On the Bema, a raised platform for public speaking in the forum, St. Paul appeared before the Roman prosecutor Gallio in A.D. 52 to plead his innocence against accusations that he was persuading the populace to worship God in unlawful ways. The Romans refurbished the **Greek Theater,** adding rows of seats and engineering the arena so it could be flooded for naval battles. Two fountains of the ancient city also remain. Glauke, daughter of the king of Corinth, allegedly threw herself into the **Glauke Fountain** when Medea, the scorned wife of Jason (who had sailed the Mediterranean with his Argonauts in search of the Golden Fleece), presented her with a wedding dress that burst into flames. The **Fountain of Peirene,** rebuilt by the Romans with arches and arcades, surrounds a spring that allegedly began to bubble forth when Peirene, a Greek woman, wept at the death of her son until she dissolved into a stream of water.

The Archaeological Museum ★ MUSEUM   Display cases groan under the weight of the famous Corinthian pottery, decorated with red-and-black figures of birds, animals, and gods and humans, often in procession. Among the city's chief exports was black figure pottery, the most common style of ancient Greek vases, in which figures turn black after firing. Given the city's prominence as a port, the wares of Corinthian potters could be found throughout the ancient world. From the Roman city come several mosaics, including a delightful one in which Pan pipes away to a clutch of cows. The museum keeps an extensive collection of graphic representations of afflicted body parts from the Shrine of Asclepius (god of medicine) behind closed doors; if you express a scholarly interest, a guard may unlock the room for you.

Old Corinth, on the site of ancient Corinth. odysseus.culture.gr. ℂ **27410/31207.** Admission 8€, includes ancient Corinth and Archaeological Museum; Acrocorinth 2€. Summer daily 8am–8pm; Oct 1–15 daily 8am–7pm, Oct 15–31 8am–6pm; winter daily 8am–3pm.

Ancient Nemea ★★

25km (15 miles) SW of Corinth; 115km (72 miles) SW of Athens

Gently folded into the foothills of the Arcadian Mountains and surrounded by the famous Nemean vineyards, this once-great city was famous throughout the ancient world for the Nemean Games held every two years. Like those at Delphi, Olympia, and Corinth, the games attracted athletes from throughout the Greek world.

The Nemean Games: Born in Legend

The most popular legend has it that the Nemean games were founded to honor Hercules, who slew a ferocious lion lurking in a den outside Nemea—the first of 12 labors he was assigned by King Eurystheus in penance for killing his own children. According to another myth, however, the games were founded to honor Opheltes, son of the Nemean king. The oracle at Delphi predicted the baby prince would remain healthy if he remained off the ground until he could walk. One day his nursemaid set him down in a bed of parsley while she showed soldiers the way to a spring; in her absence, a serpent strangled the boy. This story explains why judges at the games wore black in mourning, and the victor was crowned with a wreath of parsley.

ESSENTIALS

From Athens, take the highway to Corinth and then continue southwest toward Tripolis to the Nemea turnoff. About five buses a day travel here, usually via Corinth, from the Stathmos Leoforia Peloponnisou station in Athens, 100 Kifissou (© **210/512-4910**). Allow about 3 hours for the trip. Ask to be let off at the ancient site of Nemea (Ta Archaia), on the outskirts of the hamlet of Archaia Nemea, not in the village of Nea Nemea. For schedules, check www.ktelargolida.gr; one-way fare is about 12€.

EXPLORING ANCIENT NEMEA

Coins from every Greek city have been unearthed among the ruins here, proof of how the Games attracted competitors from far and wide. Those coins, along with athletic gear and other artifacts, are on display in a small **museum** at the site. The 4th-century-B.C. **stadium** is still largely intact—in fact, races are still sometimes held on its running track. Be sure to note the vaulted **tunnel** that leads from a dressing room to the track—this tunnel is one of the great marvels of ancient engineering, and sheds new light on the development of the arch, once thought of as a Roman innovation. This arch's presence in a pre-Roman structure suggests that troops traveling with Alexander the Great during his India campaign in 326 B.C. may have introduced the architectural concept to the Mediterranean world.

Nemea was also famous for its **Temple to Zeus,** several columns of which remain, although they were mined extensively for a Christian basilica nearby.

Outside modern Nemea. odysseus.culture.gr. © **27460/22739**. Admission 3€. Daily 8am–3pm.

Mycenae ★★★

50km (31 miles) S of Corinth; 120km (75 miles) SW of Athens

Just looking at this ruined city with its still-massive fortifications, it's easy to imagine what Homer meant when he said that "Mycenae was once rich in gold." The sprawling ruins, tucked beneath massive cliffs, suggest all the one-time might of what was once the greatest city in the western world.

The short-lived Mycenaean civilization dominated much of the southern Mediterranean from around 1500 B.C. to 1100 B.C. and built their power base on a bluff above the fertile Agrolid Plain, surrounded by deep ravines between two barren craggy peaks. It's a somber setting, befitting the tragic story told by Homer and later embellished by playwrights Aeschylus, Sophocles, and Euripides. In effect, they laid out the world's first great soap opera, and it all comes to life in Mycenae: The King, Agamemnon, launched the Trojan War when the beautiful Helen—wife of his brother, Menelaus—was abducted by the Trojan prince Paris. Upon Agamemnon's return from Troy, his wife, Clytemnestra, and her lover Aegisthus killed him; Agamemnon's son and daughter, Orestes and Electra, slew Aegisthus in turn.

The wealthy Mycenaeans also left behind many magnificent treasures, which German archaeologist Heinrich Schliemann unearthed in the 1870s; most are now on display at the National Archeological Museum in Athens (p. 93), but a few remain here in the site's small museum.

ESSENTIALS

If you're driving, you'll probably stop at Corinth first then continue to Mycenae on the toll road, **E64,** to the Nemea exit, and follow signs to Mycenae from there. KTEL **buses** from the Stathmos Leoforia Peloponnisou station in Athens, 100 Kifissou (© **210/512-4910**), stop about a mile from the site, at Fithia; the bus trip from Athens requires a change in Corinth.

EXPLORING ANCIENT MYCENAE

So steeped in legend is Mycenae that it is difficult to separate fact from fiction; even Heinrich Schliemann was convinced that a golden death mask he found in a tomb was that of Agamemnon, though the mask predates the king by many centuries. Some of these artifacts are in a small museum near the entrance, though most of the treasures, including the famous mask, are in the National Archaeological Museum in Athens (p. 93).

You enter the city through a fortified entrance, the **Lion Gate ★★**, which is topped by a relief of two lions, now headless, who face each other with their paws resting on a pedestal. You can still see the holes for the pivots that once supported a massive wooden door sheathed in bronze. An adjacent **round tower** provided a vantage point from which guards could unleash arrows on invaders who breached the gate.

Uphill, the **Main Palace ★** may have been the palace of King Agamemnon, the Mycenaean king who fought in the Trojan War. Traces of a central hearth and supporting columns are still visible in the throne room. Archaeologist Heinrich Schliemann, who rather romantically intertwined myth and historical fact, conjectured that a bathtub in an apartment adjoining the ceremonial hall was the very one in which the king was slain by his adulterous wife, Clytemnestra. Other ruins include a **granary** where massive quantities of wheat were kept on hand in the event of a long siege. The ruins of **houses** cover a nearby slope, and a wooden staircase descends into a vast subterranean **cistern ★★**—do climb down to appreciate the enormous amount of water, delivered by a secret channel, that could be stored. **Grave circles** are another haunting feature of the site. Here archaeologist Heinrich Schliemann found a trove of face masks, cups, and jewelry, all fashioned from gold—14 kilos (31 lb.) worth—now displayed at Athens' National Archaeological Museum (p. 93).

On another hill, the largest and grandest Mycenaean tomb, called **The Treasury of Atreus ★★**, consists of a narrow passageway, fashioned out of massive blocks, that leads to a high domed subterranean chamber. Evidence shows the tomb was too early to be the final resting place of King Atreus, but it was so richly decorated, it must have been built for royalty.

Off Nafplion–Argos and Corinth–Argos rds. odysseus.culture.gr. ℂ **27510/76585.** Admission 8€. Apr daily 8am–7pm; May–Oct daily 8am–8pm; Nov–Mar daily 8am–3pm.

Nafplion ★★★

145km (90 miles) SW of Athens

If not the most beautiful city in Greece, Nafplion is certainly a top contender—and this storied port on the Gulf of Argos is more than just pretty. For centuries, Byzantines, Franks, Venetians, and Turks fought over the city; their once-mighty forts and castles are now spectacular viewpoints. For a few years after Greece achieved independence in 1828, Nafplion was even the nation's first capital. Elegant Venetian houses, neoclassical mansions, churches, and mosques line the streets that surround the marble expanses of Plateia Syntagma (Constitution Square), where Nafpliots sit at cafe tables to sip coffee, chat, and watch the parades of passers-by. You may well want to combine a visit to Nafplion with a visit to Epidaurus, with its well-preserved ancient theater, only half an hour away.

ESSENTIALS

If you're driving, you can get here from Athens in less than 2 hours on the **E94/E65** toll roads. KTEL **buses** leave hourly from Athens Stathmos Leoforia Peloponnisou station in Athens, 100 Kifissou St. (ℂ **210/512-4910**); the trip takes 2 to 3 hours, depending on traffic and the number of stops. For schedules, check www.ktelargolida.gr; one-way fare is 18€.

EXPLORING NAFPLION

Wedged onto a narrow promontory between the sea and the heights dominated by the Acronafplia and Palamidi fortresses, old Nafplion is a delightful place. Tall townhouses line narrow lanes that lead off lovely **Plateia Syntagma** (Constitution Square), and two broad, airy seaside promenades, the **Bouboulinas** and **Akti Miaouli,** are lined with cafes and patisseries. Palaces, churches, and mosques are remnants of the Venetians and Turks who occupied the city for centuries; other monuments are from Nafplion's brief tenure as the first capital of Greece, from 1829 until 1834, when King Otto moved the capital to Athens.

Acronafplia ★★ RUINS   Fortifications have stood at the southeastern heights of Nafplion for some 5,000 years. Until the Venetians arrived in the 13th century, the entire town lived within the walls, out of harm's way from pirates. Scattered among the pine-scented hilltops are the ruins of several castles and forts, a testament to the Byzantine, Frankish, and Venetian powers who have fought for control of Nafplion and the rest of the Peloponnese. A well-fortified Venetian castle, the **Castello del Torrione,** is the best-preserved of the fortifications.

Daily dawn–dusk. Free admission.

Archaeological Museum ★★ MUSEUM   A thick-walled Venetian storehouse houses assorted artifacts from the many ancient sites that surround Nafplion. The Mycenaeans steal the show with their splendid craftsmanship, unearthed at Mycenae, Tiryns, Dendra, and other nearby settlements. These include a bronze suit of armor so heavy that scholars have concluded the wearer could only have fought while riding in a chariot. There are also death masks and offerings from the extensive network of tombs at Mycenae (p. 117).

Plateia Syntagma. ✆ **27520/27-502.** Admission 2€. Daily 8:30am–3pm.

Bourtzi ★ FORT   This picturesque 15th-century island fortress in the harbor has witnessed pirate attacks, served as headquarters for the town executioners, and was once equipped with a massive chain that the Turks could draw across the harbor to block entry. From anywhere in town the crenellations and sturdy sexagonal watchtower look like a mirage shimmering across the water. Boats chug out to the Bourtzi from Akti Maouli, the town quay.

Harbor. Free admission. Daily dawn–dusk. Boat is usually about 5€.

Palamidi ★★ FORT   The mightiest of the three fortresses that defend Nafplion is Venetian, completed in 1714 and surrounded by massive walls and eight bastions. So secure were the Venetians with these defenses that upon completing the Palamidi they left only 80 soldiers in Nafplion; the Turks easily seized the fortress just one year later. Greek rebels then took the fortress from the Turks during the War of Independence in 1821. Prisoners unfortunate enough to be confined in the Palamidi dungeons over the centuries were forced to cut the 999 steps that climb the cliffface from the town below.

Above Old Town. ✆ **27520/28-036.** Admission 3€. Apr–Oct Mon–Fri 8am–7pm, Sat–Sun 8am–3pm; Nov–Mar daily 8am–3pm.

Peloponnesian Folklore Foundation Museum ★★★ MUSEUM   In this handsome neoclassical house, the emphasis is on beautiful textiles, along with looms and other equipment used to make clothing—harking back to the days when just about all everyday items were made at home. Peloponnesian families donated many dowry items and embroidery, though the holdings come from all over Greece, including such rarities as *sperveri,* tents that surround bridal beds in the Dodecanese. Overstuffed drawing rooms from the homes of well-to-do 19th-century Nafpliots provide a glimpse into the comfortable lives of the bourgeoisie.

Vasileos Alexandrou 1. www.pli.gr. ✆ **27520/28-947.** Admission 4€ day. Mon–Sat 9am–2:30pm; Sun 9am–3pm.

Promenade ★★★ WALKWAY   All that remains of the lower walls that were constructed in 1502 to encircle the city is one bastion, the so-called Five Brothers, intended to defend the harbor and named for five Venetian cannons, all bearing the lion of St. Marks. A beautiful seaside promenade extends beyond the Five Brothers, skirting the southeastern tip of the peninsula, following a ledge between the Acronafplia above and the rocky shore below. Arvanitia beach, at the end of the promenade, is popular with residents who gather here to chat and swim from the rocks and a pebbly shoreline.

Tou Sotiros (Church of the Transfiguration) CHURCH   The oldest church in Nafplion was a convent for Franciscan nuns during the 13th-century Frankish occupation; later it was refurbished as a mosque by the Turks. A distinctly Christian presence has prevailed since 1839, when Otto, the Bavarian king who served as monarch of a united Greece, presented the church to Greek Catholics and the so-called Philhellenes, the foreigners who fought alongside Greeks for independence from the Turks. The names of the Philhellenes, among them the British poet and adventurer Lord Byron, are inscribed on the columns.

Old Town. Free admission. Daily 8am–7pm.

OUTSIDE NAFPLION

Argos ★ TOWN/RUINS   What's now an agreeable farm town was once one of the most powerful cities of the ancient Peloponnese. Ancient Argos saw its heyday in the 7th century B.C., under the tyrant Phaedon, until it was eventually eclipsed by Sparta. The scant remains scattered around the modern town include a theater that, with room for 20,000 spectators in 89 rows of seats, was one of the largest in the ancient world (summertime performances are still held here). The Romans re-engineered the arena so it could be used for mock naval battles and channeled the water into the adjacent baths. A small archaeological museum on Plateia Ayiou Petrou (odysseus.culture.gr; ⓒ **27510/68-819**) shows off local finds; among them is a clay figure of a squat, heavy-thighed woman, unearthed at nearby Lerna, thought to be the earliest representation of the human body yet to be found in Europe. Figures in Roman mosaics in the museum's shady courtyard are far less primitive: They're bundled up in cloaks and leggings in the cold months, and casually dressed in light tunics and filmy cloaks in the summer months. A 7th-century-B.C. clay krater (vessel) shows a determined Ulysses blinding the one-eyed Cyclops Polyphemus. Admission is 2€; 6€ with theater and other ruins.

High atop the town are two citadels, famous in antiquity. The **Aspis** was the city's first acropolis, abandoned when the higher (274m/905 ft.) **Larissa** was fortified in the 5th century B.C., with an inner and outer system of walls and several towers, the ruins of which are still visible. You can drive to both on rough roads, or make the ascent on a rugged, steep path from the ancient theater; allow at least 3 hours for the ascent and descent and bring water. The piles of sun-baked old stones at the top really aren't the draw: your reward for the climb is spectacular views of fertile plains and the sparking blue waters of the Gulf of Argos. The site is always open and admission is free.

Tiryns ★★ RUIN   A jumble of massive stones—appropriately known as Cyclopean and some weighing as much as 15 tons—were once part of the walls surrounding this fortress-town that may have been the seaport for ancient Mycenae. Homer praised the city as "mighty-walled Tiryns," and the sheer power the place exudes gave rise to the ancient belief that it was the birthplace of Hercules. A modern observer, the writer Henry Miller, observed that the ruined city "smells of cruelty, barbarism, suspicion, isolation." Not all about Tiryns was barbaric, however: A palace within the walls was once decorated with splendid frescoes of women riding chariots and other scenes, now in the National Archaeological Museum in Athens (p. 93). In a series of storage galleries and chambers on the east side of the citadel, the walls of one long passageway with a corbeled arch have been rubbed smooth by generations of sheep sheltered here after Tiryns was abandoned—a graphic example of how the mighty can fall.

5km (3 miles) N of Nafplion, off Nafplion–Argos Rd. (Take Nafplion–Argos bus and ask to be let off at Tiryns.) odysseus.culture.gr. ✆ **27520/22657.** Admission 2€. Apr–Oct daily 8:30am–7pm; Nov–Mar daily 8am–5pm.

Epidaurus ★★★

32km (20 miles) E of Nafplion; 63km (39 miles) S of Corinth

Just as the stadium at Olympia (p. 123) brings out the sprinter in many visitors, the theater at Epidaurus tempts many to step stage center to recite poetry or burst into song. One of the best-preserved classical Greek theaters in the world, Epidaurus is a magnificent arrangement of 14,000 limestone seats set into a hillside. Pausanias, the 2nd-century-A.D. Greek traveler and chronicler, commented, "Who can begin to rival . . . the beauty and composition?" Or, he might have added, the acoustics? They are so perfect that a whisper onstage can be heard at the last row of seats, as demonstrated at productions of the summertime Hellenic Festival. To the ancients, Epidaurus was best known for the Sanctuary of Asklepios, a healing center that featured such remedies as dream interpretation and the flickering caress of serpent tongues.

ESSENTIALS

If you're coming from Athens or Corinth, turn left for Epidaurus immediately after the Corinth Canal and then follow the coast road to Ancient Epidaurus (or Epidaurus Theater), not to Nea Epidaurus or Palea Epidaurus. From Nafplion, follow the signs for Epidaurus and keep an eye out for signs for the Theater (the theater and sanctuary are poorly signposted, but there are some road signs saying ANCIENT THEATER). Two buses a day run from the Stathmos Leoforia Peloponnisou station in Athens, 100 Kifissou (✆ **210/512-4910**), to Epidaurus. The trip takes about 3 hours and the fare is 15€; for schedules, go to www.ktelargolida.gr. There are three buses a day from the Nafplion bus station, off Plateia Kapodistrias (✆ **27520/27-323**); extra buses are scheduled when there are performances at the Theater of Epidaurus. This bus takes about an hour and the fare is 5€.

The Sanctuary and Museum ★★ RUINS   The Sanctuary of Asklepius at Epidaurus was one of the most famous healing centers in the Greek world. Asklepius, son of Apollo and god of medicine, was worshipped in the beautiful **temple** at Epidaurus (like much of the sanctuary, undergoing restoration) by cure seekers who were housed in an enormous guesthouse, the **Katego-geion.** They were treated in the **Abaton,** where Asklepius came to them in drug-induced dreams and dispensed advice on cures. The round **Tholos** appears to have housed healing serpents, which could allegedly cure ailments with a flicker of the tongue over an afflicted body part; it's believed the snakes lived in the labyrinth-like inner foundations. The **Excavation Museum** helps put some flesh on the bones of the confusing remains with an extensive collection of architectural fragments from the sanctuary, including lovely acanthus flowers from the mysterious tholos. Assorted terra-cotta body parts were votive offerings that show precisely which part of the anatomy needed to cured; a display of surgical implements will make you grateful that you didn't have to go under the knife in ancient times—although hundreds of inscriptions record the gratitude of satisfied patients.

The Theater ★★★ ANCIENT SITE   The magnificent open-air theater at Epidaurus is one of the best preserved from the ancient world. Buried for close to 1,500 years, the stage and 55 tiers of seats—divided into a lower section of 34 rows and an upper section with 21 rows—remain much as they were. Acoustics are so sharp that a stage whisper can be heard at the top of the house. Researchers have demonstrated that the theater's superb acoustics are due to its limestone seats, which deaden the low-frequency murmurs of the audience while magnifying the higher-frequency voices of the actors.

Epidaurus. odysseus.culture.gr. ✆ **27530/22-009.** Admission 12€, includes theater, sanctuary, and museum. May–Oct daily 8am–7pm; Nov–Apr daily 8am–3pm.

A PERFORMANCE AT EPIDAURUS

Classical performances at the ancient theater are usually given Friday and Saturday and sometimes Sunday at around 9pm June through September. Many productions are staged by the **National Theater of Greece,** some by foreign companies. Ticket prices range from 20€ to 60€. For the latest ticket prices and other information, contact the **Athens and Epidaurus Festival,** at the Epidaurus theater or in Athens at 39 Panepestimiou (greekfestival.gr; ✆ **210/928-2900**). Most of Nafplion's travel agencies sell tickets on the day of a performance. The ancient tragedies are usually performed, either in classical or modern Greek; programs usually have a full translation or synopsis of the play.

Olympia ★★★

311km (193 miles) W of Athens

One of the most popular archaeological sites in the world, the stadium, gymnasium, training hall, and dormitories at the foot of the Kronion Hill evoke Olympia's famous ancient games, inaugurated in 776 B.C. It's easy to see why the ancients, with their knack for finding the most beautiful settings for their creations, favored this spot, where the forested hillsides, pine-scented mountain air, and the Alpheios and Kladeos rivers rushing past the remains of temples and public buildings are still transporting. Little wonder that before Olympia became a sports venue, the site was a sacred place, a sanctuary founded around the 10th century B.C. to honor Zeus and his older sister and wife, Hera. Like ancient worshippers and spectators, you'll probably find that visiting the mountainside site is a bit of a spine-tingling thrill.

ESSENTIALS

Olympia is about a 3½-hour drive from Athens, and a little over 2 hours from Nafplion, via the new **Corinth-Tripolis toll road.** There are several **buses** a day to Olympia from the Stathmos Leoforia Peloponnisou in Athens, 100 Kifissou (*(C)* **210/512-4910**), requiring a change in Pirgos and sometimes in Corinth. The total trip time is long, about 7 hours. Trains run twice daily from the Stathmos Peloponnisou (train station for the Peloponnese) in Athens (www.trainose.gr; *(C)* **210/513-1601**), though the trip requires a change of trains in Patras and a change to a bus in Pirgos, for a total trip time of almost 7 hours.

Modern Olympia is a one-street town; the few things you do not find on Praxitelous Kondili will be just off it. The tourist office, on the way to the ancient site near the south end of the main street, is officially open daily, in summer from 9am to 10pm, and in winter from 11am to 6pm.

EXPLORING ANCIENT OLYMPIA

The superheroes who bring most visitors to Olympia are not gods and artists but ancient athletes. Remnants of the city's games, inaugurated in 776 B.C., are copious; the stadium, gymnasium, training hall, and dormitories are scattered around the foot of the Kronion Hill. Athletes from throughout Greece were granted safe passage to the games under the Ekecheiria, a truce that promoted the notion of a united Greece. In their footsteps came spectators, touts, vendors, poetry reciters, entertainers, and prostitutes. The aim of the five-day festivities was for city-states to commingle peaceably; in part, however, they were also a wine-fueled bacchanal.

Ancient Olympia ★★ ANCIENT SITE   Fifth-century Roman Emperor Theodosius II, ruling that the Olympic games were pagan rituals, cleared much of ancient Olympia, and earthquakes and mudslides over the centuries finished the job. Enough rubble remains, however, to lend a sense of the layout and magnificence of the ancient city. The entrance is just west of the modern village, across the Kladeos River. The first ruins are those of the **gymnasium,** with a field surrounded by porticoes where athletes could train in bad weather, and the **Palaestra,** a training ground for wrestlers and runners. Just beyond is the **Workshop of Phidias,** where the great sculptor crafted his gold-sheathed statue of a seated Zeus that became one of the Seven Wonders of the Ancient World; archaeologists found the sculptor's tools here, along with a cup inscribed with "I belong to Phidias." The **Leonidaion** was a luxurious hostel for visiting dignitaries, next to the **Theokoleon,** chambers of the

Legend tells us that Hercules, assigned 12 heroic labors for slaying his children, rerouted the Alpheios River to clean out the foul stables of King Augeas. Then he relaxed by mapping out the Olympia stadium with his toe and running its length—192m (630 ft.)—without taking a breath, just to work off steam. In so doing, he established the city and the games.

priests who oversaw the Altis, the sacred precinct of Zeus. Within the Altis complex stood the **Temple of Hera** and the **Temple of Zeus,** once surrounded by 36 columns, one of which was re-erected in honor of the 2004 Athens Olympic Games. The Temple of Zeus was the site of Phidias's famous statue of Zeus that once rose 13m (43 ft.) above the temple floor (it was carted off to Constantinople in the 5th century, where it was destroyed in a fire). The Temple of Hera had its own great art work, *Hermes Carrying the Infant Dionysus,* the only work by the great sculptor Praxiteles to survive the centuries (it's now in Olympia's Archaeological Museum, see below).The **Metroon** is shrine to Rhea, mother of the gods, and the **Pelopeion** honors Pelops, legendary king of the Peloponnese; his altar was drenched nightly with the blood of a black ram. Philip of Macedonia erected his own shrine when he overran Greece in 338 B.C., the **Philippeion.** A perpetual flame burned in the **Prytaneion,** a banqueting hall where victorious athletes were feted. The most powerful city-states stored their equipment and valuables in the **treasury,** and next to it is the **Nymphaeum,** a grandiose, column-flanked fountain house from which water was channeled throughout the city. To the east of the Altis are the **stadium** and **hippodrome.**

The Archaeological Museum ★★★ MUSEUM This collection makes clear Olympia's astonishing wealth and importance in antiquity: Every victorious city and almost every victorious athlete dedicated a bronze or marble statue to Olympia, making the city something of an outdoor museum of the finest bronze and marble sculpture. Among the collection's highlights is a monumental sculpture from the **west pediment of the Temple of Zeus** showing the battle of the Lapiths (Greeks who lived in Thessaly) and centaurs—the triumph of civilization (the Lapiths) over barbarism (those brutish centaurs)—as the magisterial figure of Apollo, the god of reason, looks on. On the **east pediment,** Zeus oversees the chariot race between Oinomaos, the king of Pisa, and Pelops, the legendary figure who sought the hand of Oinomaos's daughter. Crafty Pelops loosened his opponent's chariot pins, thereby winning the race, the girl, and the honor of having the entire Peloponnese named after him. At either end of the room, sculptured **metopes** show scenes from the Labors of Hercules, including the one he performed at Olympia: cleansing the stables of King Augeus by diverting the Alpheios River.

The museum's standout, *Hermes Carrying the Infant Dionysus,* has a room to itself. The glistening white marble (the torso said to be worn smooth

5

AROUND ATHENS | The Peloponnese

THE THRILL OF VICTORY, THE agony OF DEFEAT

For the ancients, the Olympic Games were the greatest show on earth, staged every 4 years in honor of Zeus, king of the gods. For nearly 12 centuries, they drew athletes from as far as the shores of the Black Sea. Behind them followed prostitutes, pushy vendors, orators, and tens of thousands of spectators, including diehard fans such as Plato and the tyrant Dionysus of Syracuse. Roman Emperor Nero demanded that the Games take place a year early, in A.D. 67, when his schedule would allow him to travel from Rome to compete. After bribing officials to disqualify competitors, he won six events—including a race he didn't finish after falling from his chariot.

Conditions were primitive, but most attendees were happy to sleep under the stars to watch the world's greatest athletes perform—and to curry favor with Zeus and the other gods who were worshipped during the proceedings. In the earliest years, the only event was a simple foot race on a straight strip of grass the length of the stadium—a unit of measure known as a stade (185m/610 ft.). By 500 B.C., wrestling, boxing, discus throwing, and more than 50 events took place over the course of 5 days in the hippodrome, gymnasium, stadium, and other arenas. The most popular event was the *pankration*, a combined wrestling-boxing-kicking match with only two rules: no biting or eye gouging. Strangulation was perfectly acceptable. The game ended when one athlete quit, passed out, or died. Polydamas, a pankration champ, was as famous for his exploits off the field as on. He slew a lion with his bare hands, stopped a speeding chariot in its tracks, and singlehandedly defeated a trio of Persia's mightiest warriors.

Regardless of social status, any free, Greek-speaking male without a criminal record could enter the games. Victors won money, tax emption, free meals for life, laurel wreaths, the favor of the gods, and the services of Hetaeras, high-class escort girls, at the victors' table. Only virgins and certain priestesses could attend the men's games. Trespassers, if caught, were tossed from a cliff.

One brave female, Kallipateira, dressed as a trainer to watch her son compete but accidentally revealed her sex while climbing over a wall. Her life was spared, but from then on trainers, like athletes, were not allowed to wear clothes—though boxers were allowed to wear metal knuckle bands to add sting to their punches. Competitors rubbed themselves with olive oil and sand, an ancient sunscreen, and ate ground lizard skin, their version of steroids.

by the admiring hands of temple assistants) depicts the divine messenger Hermes about to deliver the newborn Dionysos to the mountains, where he was raised by nymphs. As legend has it, Zeus conceived Dionysus with his mortal lover Semele but was forced to hide the infant from his ever-jealous wife, Hera. The plump baby thrived and grew up to become the god of wine, revelry, and theater. The work is typical of Praxiteles, the 4th-century-B.C. sculptor whose graceful, intimate creations in marble often depicted the gods as humanlike. Transporting as the work is, scholars have long been debating the possibility that it's a copy by a contemporary or even a Roman master.

Other Museums Historical exhibits scattered around Ancient Olympia explore the games and the site. The **Museum of the History of the Olympic**

Games in Antiquity ★★ engagingly covers the ancient contests, finger-breaking and eye-gouging and all, with text panels, illustrations, and some gee-whizz artifacts, such as ancient chariot wheels. The **Museum of the History of the Excavations in Olympia ★**, in the former home of German archaeologists, documents the excavations of Olympia with photos, journals, and letters, beginning with 1766, when British antiquarian Richard Chandler discovered the ruins.

Olympia. odysseus.culture.gr. © **26240/22517.** Admission 12€, includes site and museums. May–Oct daily 8am–8pm; Nov–Apr daily 8am–5pm.

DELPHI ★★★

178km (110 miles) NW of Athens

No other ancient site is quite as mysterious and alluring as this sanctuary to Apollo, nestled high above the Gulf of Corinth on the flanks of Mount Parnassus. It's easy to see why the spot was so transporting for the ancients. Look up and you see the cliffs and crags of Parnassus; look down, and Greece's most beautiful plain of olive trees stretches as far as your eyes can see toward the Gulf of Corinth. Since Delphi is just about 180km (112 miles) from central Athens, you can easily visit the site in a day. The ruins look their best in the spring, when they are surrounded by wildflowers and the mountain above them is still covered in snow, but they are spectacular any time you visit.

Essentials

There are usually five KTEL buses daily to Delphi from Athens' Liosson Terminal B bus station at 260 Liossion (www.ktel-fokidas.gr; © **210/831-7153** or 210/831-7096). One-way fare is 16€.

To drive to Delphi **from Athens,** allowing at least 2 hours, take the National Road toward Corinth and then the Thebes turnoff. If you are approaching Delphi **from the Peloponnese,** cross over the Rio-Antirio Bridge into Central Greece and follow the coastal road as it climbs upwards from Itea to Delphi (65km/40 miles). The road is spectacular, but with many curves and almost as many tour buses.

The **tourist office** (© **22650/82-311;** www.visitdelphi.gr), in the town hall, is usually open Monday through Friday from 8am to 2:30pm, and sometimes reopens from 6 to 8pm in summer. The museum and ancient site (signposted) are about 1km (½ mile) out of town, on the Arachova Road. Parking spots are at a premium both in the village and at the site. If you can, park your car near your hotel and walk everywhere.

Where to Stay & Eat in Delphi

Epikouros Restaurant ★★★ GREEK Views and wonderful home cooking are a winning combination in this rather sophisticated dining room and glassed-in terrace. An extensive menu feature local mountain cheeses and homegrown vegetables, along with lamb with fresh tomato sauce, *keftedes* (grilled round meatballs), and *sousoutakia* (rice-and-meat balls, stewed in tomato sauce), and other old-fashioned classics. You'll feel you're enjoying an authentic Greek experience even when the tour groups pack in.

Vasileos Pavlou and Frederikis. *©* **22650/83-250.** Main courses 9€–18€. Daily lunch, dinner.

Hotel Varonos ★★   At one of the nicest and best-value lodgings in town, comfortable guest rooms, painted in soothing pastels, overlook the plains below town. With lots of plants and a fire when it's chilly outside, the lobby is a cozy place to relax. The Varonos family could not be more helpful, and their shop next door is filled with local honey, herbs, preserves, and other goodies.

25 Vasileos Pavlou. www.hotel-varonos.gr. *©* **22650/82-345.** 12 units. 65€–90€ double. Rates include buffet breakfast. **Amenities:** Lounge; Wi-Fi (free).

Taverna Vakchos ★★ GREEK   The family who cook and prepare the excellent meals here pride themselves on serving only the freshest vegetables and just-picked mountain herbs. You can put together a delicious meatless feast from daily offerings of greens or *briam,* a juicy vegetable stew; simple, grilled and oven-roasted meat dishes are also on offer. Vakchos, of course, is Greek for Bacchus, and the wine god makes an appearance in excellent local wines and in a mural decorating rooms that open to a large terrace overlooking Delphi and the plains below town.

31 Apollonos. www.vakhos.com. *©* **22650/83-186.** Main courses 7€–10€. Daily 11:30am–4pm and 6–11pm.

Exploring Ancient Delphi

Archaeological Museum ★★★ MUSEUM   These spacious, well-lit galleries show off treasures from the Delphi temples and shrines. Seeing these magnificent works helps bring the importance of the sanctuary to light; time permitting, walk around the site, then tour the museum, then do another round of the site, using your imagination to put these treasures in place. A bronze statue of a charioteer, one of the great works to come down from ancient Greece, honors a victory during Delphi's Pythian games. (He is believed to have stood next to the Temple of Apollo.) Some of the most fascinating finds are friezes depicting the feats of the gods, the superheroes of the ancient world. A 4th-century-B.C. marble egg (omphalos), a reproduction of an even older version, honors Delphi's position as the mythical center of the ancient world. Legend has it that Zeus released two eagles from Mount Olympus to fly around the world in opposite directions; where they met would be the center of the world and that, of course, was Delphi.

Ancient Delphi ★★ ANCIENT SITE   Slightly below the ancient site, the terraced **Sanctuary of Athena** was the first stop for many pilgrims climbing up the slope from the sea. They would pause to pay homage at such shrines as the exquisitely beautiful and photogenic **Tholos** (Round) temple, dedicated to an unknown goddess. A shrine has stood on this spot since 1500 B.C., when the Mycenaeans established a sanctuary here to the earth goddess Gaia. The formal entrance to the site was the monumental walkway known as the

Sacred Way ★, once lined with magnificent temples that city-states erected as votive dedications to Apollo—and as a bit of one upmanship to see who could outdo one another. These were some of the greatest works of antiquity, filled with treasures. Only foundations remain of all but the **Athenian Treasury,** restored in the 1930s. The 4th-century-B.C. **theater** ★★ and nearby **stadium** ★★ hosted the musicians, performers, and athletes who came to Delphi for the Pythian Games, held every 4 years in honor of Apollo. Both afford magnificent views over the sanctuary and surrounding mountains.

The main attraction, however, was (and still is) the **Temple of Apollo** ★★★. Six limestone columns and rocky foundations, set against craggy cliffs, are all that remain of the temple begun in the 7th century B.C. that, according to legend, was designed by Trophonios and Agamedes, gods who labored as earthly architects. Over the centuries, the temple was financed by Greece's most important families and foreign powers. Funding the temple was not only a mark of status but also a sound investment in the future, because here one might receive life-altering words of wisdom. Allegedly, questions inscribed on stone tablets would be presented to a Pythian priestess who had undergone a cleansing and purification ritual. Speaking for Apollo, she would utter garbled verse to priests, who interpreted them and passed along enigmatic statements (setting a precedent adapted by today's politicians). Among the supplicants were rulers and generals who came from throughout the Mediterranean world seeking advice. Perhaps the most famous piece of advice was given to King Croesus of Lydia, who asked if he should attack the Persians. If he did so, he was told, he would destroy a great empire. He did attack, and he did destroy a kingdom—his own.

Delphi. odysseus.culture.gr. ⓒ **22650/82-312.** Admission 12€ to museum and site. Open daily; summer 8am–7:30pm, winter 9am–3pm. (Check times when you arrive in Delphi; they can change without warning.)

ISLAND ESCAPES NEAR ATHENS

When the heat in Athens gets to be too much, do as the Athenians do—get on a boat and head to a nearby island in the Saronic Gulf. Aegina, Poros, Hydra, and Spetses dot the waters between Athens and the Peloponnesian Peninsula. To reach any of them, all you need to do is take the Metro to Piraeus and board a hydrofoil; the farthest of the four main islands, Spetses, is less than 2 hours away.

The question is, which island to choose for your getaway? Each serves up a taste of island life, but with a distinct character all its own. **Aegina** retains the old-world atmosphere of a fishing port and also has one of Greece's best-preserved temples, dedicated to the mysterious Aphaia. **Poros** promises miraculous cures at its Monastery of Zoodochos Pigi, as well as a long stretch of lemon-grove-backed sand that's not on the island at all, but along its mainland holdings in the Peloponnese. **Hydra,** with its rugged landscapes and handsome stone mansions, wins the prize for beauty and a sense of getting away from it all (the island is car-free)—even the dearth of beaches doesn't detract from the island's overdose of charm. **Spetses** combines both—lots of worldly elegance, with palm-shaded neoclassical mansions, and plenty of sand.

Essentials

Car ferries and excursion boats for the Saronic Gulf Islands usually leave from **Piraeus's main harbor;** hydrofoils leave both from the main harbor and from **Marina Zea** harbor. Hydrofoil service is at least twice as fast but more expensive. Often, in order to continue to another Saronic Gulf island by hydrofoil, you must return to Piraeus to transfer. Schedules can change, so double-check information you get—**www.gtp.gr** is a useful site for ferry schedules.

Hydrofoil and ferry service is offered by **Hellenic Seaways** (www.hellenic seaways.gr; ☏ **210/419-9200**). **Saronikos Ferries** (www.saronicferries.gr; ☏ **210/417-1190**) takes passengers and cars to Aegina, Poros, and Spetses (cars are not allowed to disembark on Hydra). **Euroseas Ferries** (www.fer ries.gr/euroseas; ☏ **210/411-3108**) offers speedy catamaran service from Piraeus to Poros, Hydra, and Spetses.

Where to Stay & Eat in the Saronic Gulf Islands

Proximity and boat service makes it easy to visit the Saronic islands on a day trip from Athens, but if you're not rushing back, hands-down the nicest island on which to stay is Hydra.

Economou Mansion ★★ While Spetses seems more geared to day trippers and wealthy Athenians with island homes than it does to overnight guests, this 19th-century sea captain's mansion is the exception. The shady garden is enlivened with sea-motif mosaics and a pool, while in the cozy and elegant sea-view guest rooms, handsome tile floors are covered with old carpets and big iron bedsteads are dressed with fine linens.

Kounoupitsa, Spetses Town. www.economouspetses.gr. ☏ **22980/73-400.** 8 units. 200€ double. Rates include buffet breakfast. **Amenities:** Breakfast room; pool; Wi-Fi (free).

Hotel Miranda ★★ Oriental rugs, antique cabinets, wooden chests, marble tables, nautical prints, and contemporary paintings do justice to a beautifully restored 1820 captain's mansion on Hydra. There's even a small art gallery downstairs; upstairs are bedrooms and suites of varying shapes and sizes, many with such enhancements as frescoed ceilings and large balconies overlooking the town and port.

Miaouli, Hydra. www.mirandahotel.gr. ☏ **22980/52-230.** 14 units. 150€–225€ double. Rates include breakfast. **Amenities:** Breakfast room; Wi-Fi (free). Closed Nov–Feb.

Lazaros Taverna ★ GREEK Spetses gets downright homey at this friendly place that caters to locals. Potted ivy, family photos, and big kegs of homemade retsina line the walls, and a small menu sticks to such basics as grilled meats and goat in lemon sauce.

Dapia, Spetses Town. No phone. Main courses 7€–14€. Daily 6:30pm–midnight. Closed mid-Nov to mid-Mar. Inland and uphill about 400m (1,312 ft.) from the waterfront.

The Saronic Gulf Islands

Aegina **1**

Hydra **3**

Poros **2**

Spetses **4**

Maridaki ★ GREEK   One of string of old-fashioned tavernas and ouzeri along the waterfront in Aegina's port comes with a ringside seat of the sparkling water and all the comings and goings on land. You'll fit right in with the locals with a plate of grilled octopus (dried on a line in front of the seafront terrace) and a glass of ouzo, though all the mezedes are good, as are souvlaki, moussaka, and other taverna fare.

Port, Aegina Town. ℭ **22970/25-869.** Main courses 8€–20€; some fresh seafood priced by the kilo. Daily 8am–midnight.

To Steki ★★ GREEK   A few blocks up from the quay end of the harbor, this Hydra mainstay has simple food and reasonable prices. Murals portray a picturesque version of island life that has long since vanished (and was probably never so idyllic), though the island life passing by the terrace is certainly colorful. The kitchen does a fine job of maintaining old ways: The moussaka, oven-roasted lamb, and stuffed tomatoes are delicious, and the fish soup is memorable.

Miaouli, Hydra Town. ℭ **22980/53-517.** Main courses 7€–18€. Daily noon–3pm and 7–11pm.

Aegina ★★

30 km (19 miles) SW of Piraeus

The largest island in the Saronic Gulf is so close to Athens that many islanders commute to the capital for work. A walk along the waterfront of Aegina Town shows off Aegina at its best, giving a glimpse into island life that, despite the presence of Athenian teenagers staring into their iPhones, seems to have never changed over the decades. Fishing boats bob at the docks; a covered fish market, the Psaragora, does a brisk business in the morning; and fishermen hang out on the terraces of *ouzeris*. A walk inland along winding stone streets to the corner of Thomaidou and Pileos shows off **Markelos Tower,** a Venetian-era fortified house that in 1827 hosted meetings of the first government in Greece; the pink-and-white landmark now occasionally hosts art exhibits.

Aegina was at one time a rival to Athens, and the island's most splendid ancient monument—in fact, one of the best-preserved, though unsung, antiquities in Greece—attests to its onetime wealth and power. The majestic **Temple of Aphaia** ★★, set above the sea in a pine grove 12km (7 miles) east of Aegina Town (odysseus.culture.gr; ℭ **22970/32-398**) commands a promontory facing Athens and the coast of Attica. It's so close to the mainland, in fact, that both the Parthenon and Temple of Poseidon can be seen on a clear day (with the aid of binoculars); to the ancients, these three sanctuaries constituted a Sacred Triangle. Built in the late 6th or early 5th century B.C., on the site of earlier shrines, Aegina's temple was dedicated to Aphaia, a goddess with the enviable ability to vanish into thin air to avoid unwanted amorous advances (see box, p. 133). Although 25 columns of the temple remain standing, the finest feature is missing: a magnificent pediment frieze depicting scenes from the Trojan War, now in the Glyptothek in Munich. Still, the setting is so beautiful, you'll hardly miss it. Admission is 4€; the temple is open daily April to November 8:30am to 7pm, December to March 8:15am to 3pm.

While the **Temple of Aphaia** (p. 132) is Aegina's most evocative ruin, no one really knows who Aphaia was. It seems that she was a very ancient, even prehistoric, goddess who eventually became associated both with Artemis and Athena. According to some legends, Aphaia lived on Crete, where King Minos—usually preoccupied with his labyrinth and Minotaur—fell in love with her. When she fled Crete, Minos pursued her, until she finally threw herself into the sea off Aegina to escape him. She became entwined in fishing nets and was hauled aboard a boat. A sailor then fell hopelessly in love with the beautiful creature. So she jumped overboard again, swam ashore on Aegina, and, as her smitten admirer watched from his boat, vanished right before his eyes (*afandos* means "disappear").

The crumbling remains of the island's longtime capital, **Palechora ★**, sprawls across a hillside 5km (3 miles) east of Aegina Town. Abandoned in the early 19th-century when an end to piracy made it safe to settle along the coast again, the ghost town is, quite literally, inhabited by spirits of a sort. More than 30 Byzantine churches remain, and a dozen or so are still in use. Many of these are decorated with faded frescoes, with the best covering the walls of the church of **Ayioi Anargyroi.**

One of the island's nicest seaside perches is **Perdika,** a leisure and fishing port 9km (5½ miles) south of Aegina Town and easily reached via the island bus (see below). Aside from a lively waterfront, with a long line of fish tavernas, the town's sandy beach, Klima, is maybe the island's nicest. For an extraspecial getaway, and a refreshing swim, take a boat from the pier in Perdika to **Moni,** a pine-clad island nature preserve; boats come and go about every hour and charge 5€ round-trip.

Good bus service around Aegina leaves from Plateia Ethneyersias, near the ferry dock in Aegina Town. Buses leave hourly in summer for the Temple of Aphaia (3€; purchase tickets before boarding). Every Saturday and Wednesday in summer, **Panoramic Bus Tours** (© **22970/22-254**) offers a 3½-hour bus tour of the island (6€; leaving Aegina Town 10:35am), taking in the Temple of Aphaia, several beaches and villages, and the **Hellenic Wildlife Hospital** (© **22970/28-267**) at Pachia Rachi, where monkeys, wild boar, crocodiles, owls, and other exotic creatures are rehabilitated and housed before being returned to the wild.

Hydra ★★★

79km (46 miles) SW of Piraeus

Still an alluring beauty, this rugged little island has been admired and appreciated for centuries. Seafaring merchant families built proud mansions of honey-colored stone on Hydra in the late 18th and early 19th centuries, artists and writers began arriving in the 1960s, and in their wake came the rich and famous and the simply rich. They keep a low profile, however, and with the absence of cars (transport is by foot or mule), Hydra seems wonderfully removed from the modern world.

The captains' lasting legacy, their handsome stone *archontika* (mansions) overlooking the harbor, still give Hydra town its distinctive character. The curved, picturesque harbor and these worldly houses overlooking the blue waters (many housing bars and expensive shops), are especially striking because they're enclosed by barren gray and brown mountainsides. The only places on Hydra that are habitable, in fact, are Hydra Town and some small collections of pretty seaside houses at neighboring Kamini and Vuchos, making the island seem even more like a privileged getaway.

In earlier days, Hydra was a prosperous port that sent ships as far away as America; that history comes to the fore at the harborside **Historical Archives and Museum ★** (© **22980/52-355**), which displays old paintings, carved and painted ship figureheads, and costumes. Admission is 4€; the museum is open daily, 9am to 3pm and 7 to 8pm. The hilltop **Koundouriotis mansion ★**, built by an early-19th-century Albanian family who contributed generously to the cause of independence, is now a house museum displaying period furnishings and costumes. It's usually open from April until October, daily except Monday, 10am to 4pm; admission is 4€. If you wander the side streets on this side of the harbor, you will see more handsome houses, many of which are being restored by wealthy Athenians and other Europeans, for whom Hydra is a favorite retreat.

Six monasteries are tucked away in the island's remote, barren hinterlands, and hiking to them across the herb-scented countryside is a popular outing for some sturdy souls. (This is certainly not an excursion for a hot summer's day.) Most popular is the pilgrimage up to the **Monastery of the Prophet Elijah ★**, on the flanks of Mount Eros, at 500m (1,650 ft.) the island's highest peak—which might suggest the level of difficulty of the 2-hour trek along a well-marked route from Hydra Town. Many visitors make the trip by donkey, with rates starting at a highly negotiable 60€. Once there, the monks will offer you a glass of cold water in their shady courtyard and probably try to sell you some needlework made by the nuns at **Ayia Efpraxia ★**, on the hillside just beneath the monastery. The nuns there occasionally allow visitors in to see their charming chapel as well.

Far more relaxing is a swim from the rocks of the rugged shoreline, an exhilarating way to enjoy the warm Aegean waters. A pleasant waterside walk west from Hydra Town brings you to especially nice spots at **Spilla** and **Kaminia.** Still farther west are the pine-lined coves of **Molos, Palamida,** and **Bisti** (all three as sandy as it gets on Hydra), best reached by water taxi from the main harbor (about 10€). Excursion boats from the harbor also set sail for **Ayios Nikolaos,** a pebble beach with sun beds and refreshment concessions on the south coast (the cost is about 8€ a person round-trip).

Poros ★

51km (32 miles) SW of Piraeus

Barely an island at all, Poros is separated from the mainland by a channel only 370m (1,214 ft.) wide—Poros means "straits." Ferries bring cars and visitors to Poros on summer weekends, but you may wish to do the reverse and head over to the mainland beaches (see below) after taking a quick look around.

The scant remains of the **Temple of Poseidon** ★ (5km/3 miles south of Poros Town) are associated with Demosthenes, the great 4th-century-B.C. Athenian orator who took refuge here when Macedonians attacked Athens. When discovered, he asked to write one last letter—and bit the nib off his pen to release concealed poison. The orator's remains allegedly lie beneath a monument at the **Monastery of Zoodochos Pigi** (3km/2 miles from Poros Town; ℂ **22980/22-926**), with its heavily frescoed church. The monastery also has a famous orphanage that once housed as many as 180 boys and girls whose parents had lost their lives in the Greek War of Independence. A spring is believed to have curative powers—discovered when a 17th-century archbishop, hovering near death, took a sip and sprang back to life. Similar miracles have been reported ever since, and you can fill a bottle or two at the spring to test the life-giving for yourself. The monastery is open daily 8am to 1:30pm and 4:30 to 8:30pm (closes at 5:30pm Oct–Apr). Buses from Poros Town will take you to either the temple or the monastery; the conductor will charge you according to your destination.

Paradoxically, the best beach experience on Poros is actually back on the mainland. A 5-minute ferry ride will take you across the strait to Galatas, which is part of the island's holdings; a 10-minute taxi ride from the ferry brings you to **Aliki,** a lovely stretch of sand on a spit wedged between the bay and a lake. In spring and early summer, the shoreline is scented with lemons grown in surrounding groves.

Spetses ★★

98km (58 miles) SW of Piraeus

The greenest of the Saronic Gulf islands was known even in antiquity as Pityoussa (Pine-Tree Island). Many of Spetses's pine trees became the masts and hulls of vessels, and in time, Spetses was almost as deforested as its rocky neighbor Hydra. In the early 20th century, local philanthropist Sotiris Anargyros bought up more than half the island, then replanted barren slopes with pine trees. He also built an ostentatious mansion, the first of many to come on this island now noted for its handsome *archontika,* or fine houses, flanked by palm trees.

Today, pine groves and architecture are the island's greatest treasures. Many of the handsome mansions have lush gardens and pebble mosaic courtyards that can be viewed only in a glance when gates are left ajar. Yes, Spetses is a world of privilege of which most of us can only catch a glimpse. We can also read about island life: English author John Fowles taught at the island's exclusive prep school in the early 1950s and set his novel *The Magus* on Spetses.

Spetses Town (aka **Kastelli**) meanders along the harbor and inland in a lazy fashion, with most of its neoclassical mansions partly hidden from envious eyes by high walls and greenery. Much of the town's street life takes place on the main square, the **Dapia,** the name also given to the harbor where the ferries and hydrofoils arrive. The handsome black-and-white pebble mosaic on

SHE swore LIKE A SAILOR!

A monumental bronze statue on the Spetses Town waterfront honors one of the greatest heroes of the War of Independence, **Laskarina Bouboulina.** The daughter of a naval captain from Hydra, she was the widow of two more sea captains, who left her with nine children and a large fortune. Bouboulina financed the warship *Agamemnon*, oversaw its construction, served as its captain, and took part in the successful naval attacks on the Turks at Nafplion, Monemvassia, and Pylos. She was said to be able to drink any man under the table, and strait-laced citizens sniped that she was so ugly and ill-tempered the only way she could keep a lover was with a gun. Bouboulina remained on shore long enough to settle into the **Laskarina Bouboulina House** (www.bouboulinamuseum-spetses.gr; *©* **22980/72-077**) just off the port in Spetses Town; she was shot in a family feud years after retiring from sea. The house keeps flexible hours (posted outside), but is usually open mornings and afternoons from Easter until October. An English-speaking guide often gives a half-hour tour. Admission is 5€. In the **Spetses Mexis Museum** (*©* **22980/72-994**), in the stone Mexis mansion (signposted on the waterfront), you can see Bouboulina's bones, along with archaeological finds and mementos of the War of Independence. In the nearby boatyards you can often see caiques being made with tools little different from those used when Bouboulina's mighty *Agamemnon* was built here.

Dapia commemorates the moment during the War of Independence when the first flag, with the motto "Freedom or Death," was raised. Spetses played an important part in the fight for freedom, routing the Turks in the Straits of Spetses on September 8, 1822.

Spetses has a decent bus network, though bikes are widely available and an excellent way to get around, given the flat terrain; rentals from one of the many travel agencies near the harbor run about 12€ per day. The traditional mode of transport on the island is horse-drawn carriages, a good way to tour the mansion-lined back lanes. Fares for these are highly negotiable.

The best way to get to the various **beaches** around the island is by water taxi. **Ayia Marina,** about a 30-minute walk southeast of Spetses Town, is the best beach close to town and terribly popular; it's the place to see and be seen for a chic Athenian crowd, some of whom arrive in high style via horse and buggy. On the forested west coast, 6km (4 miles) west of Spetses Town, **Ayii Anaryiri** has one of the best sandy beaches anywhere in the Saronic Gulf, a perfect C-shaped cove lined with trees, but almost more bars and tavernas than greenery. Also on the west coast, about 10km (6 miles) west of Spetses Town, is the beach at **Ayia Paraskevi,** bordered by pine trees. The idyllic stretch of sand figures in *The Magus,* though it's no longer the isolated strand it once was. West over some rocks is the island's official nudist beach.

THE CYCLADES

Whether it's the experience of sailing into Santorini's volcanic caldera, getting a glimpse of the windmills lining stark hilltops on Mykonos, or seeing the ancient temple doorway that looms over the port on Naxos, your first sightings of the Cyclades will likely make quite an impression. Even the commonplace seems spectacular in this archipelago of 24 inhabited islands and hundreds of islets floating southeast of the mainland. From afar, dazzling white villages of the islands' distinctive cubical houses look like stacks of sugar cubes or a dusting of snow. Rising out of all that glaring white are the brilliant blue domes of chapels and churches. Memorable moments will keep coming as you travel through the rugged, often barren Cyclades, so named—from the ancient Greek word for circle—because the islands encircle Delos, the birthplace of the god Apollo and one of ancient Greece's most sacred religious sanctuaries.

MYKONOS ★★

Small, dry, and barren, Mykonos is one of the least naturally attractive of the Cyclades. But it's a testament to the island's charms that Mykonos is now among the most famous of all the Greek isles. Attractions include beautiful Mykonos Town, better known as Hora, and a south coast full of sandy beaches, but this small hunk of rock in the middle of the Aegean is maybe most famous for people-watching. Ever since Jackie O. and other celebs started stepping ashore from their yachts in the 1960s, Mykonos has been a place to see and be seen. You may love the scene or want to flee from it on the next boat, but do stick around for a bit, because in one way or another Mykonos tends to work its sybaritic spells eventually on even the most resistant visitors.

Essentials

ARRIVING   Mykonos is very well connected to Athens by several flights daily. **Olympic Airways** (www.olympic-airways.gr; ✆ **210/966-6666**) operates several flights a day in season (and at least once daily in off season), and one flight daily from Mykonos to Iraklion (Crete) and Santorini. **Aegean Airlines** (www.aegeanair.com; ℂ **210/998-8300**) also operates daily service between Athens and Mykonos in summer.

Frequent **ferry** service runs to and from Piraeus, and high-speed **catamarans** go to and from Rafina and Lavrio, both outside Athens. In season there are daily ferry connections between Mykonos and Andros, Paros, Naxos, Santorini, Siros, and Tinos; five to seven trips a week to Ios; four a week to Iraklio, Crete; several a week to Kos and Rhodes; and two a week to Ikaria, Samos, Skiathos, Skyros, and Thessaloniki. The island has two ports: the old port, just at the edge of Hora, generally handles the high-speed catamarans, while the new port, 2km (1 mile) north of Hora in Tourlos, accommodates ferries. However, be sure to check which port you'll be arriving in and from which you'll be departing. Keep in mind that due to winds, boats often run late. The website www.gtp.gr is a useful resource for checking out the many ferries that serve Mykonos, but your best bet for getting up-to-date schedules is to check at individual agencies. Reputable agencies on the main square in Mykonos (Hora) town include **Delia Travel** (ℂ **22890/22322**) and **Sea & Sky Travel** (www.seasky.gr; ℂ **22890/22853**).

VISITOR INFORMATION **Mykonos Accommodations Center,** at the corner of Enoplon Dhinameon and Malamatenias (www.mykonos-accommodation.com; ℂ **22890/23-160**), helps visitors find accommodations and functions as a tourist information center. **Windmills Travel ★** (www.windmills travel.com; ℂ **211/800-4668**) has an office at Fabrica Square, where you can get general information, book accommodations, arrange excursions, and rent a car or moped.

GETTING AROUND You can reach many places on the island by boat or bus. **Caiques** to Super Paradise, Agrari, and Elia beaches depart from Platis Yialos beach, on the island's south side, every morning, weather permitting; there is also service from Ornos beach in high season (July–Aug) only. Caique service is highly seasonal, with almost continuous service in high season and no caiques October through May. Mykonos has an excellent **bus** system, with frequent service to towns and beaches around the island. Depending on your destination, a ticket costs about 1€ to 4€. There are two bus stations in Hora: one near the Archaeological Museum and one on the other side of town (both are well marked). You may want to rent a **car, moped,** or **all-terrain vehicle** for a day to explore some of the farther-flung beaches on the island, especially those on the north coast. Expect to pay at least 35€ per day for a small car with manual transmission, 20€ for a bike (prices rise to even more in July and Aug). Among the many rental agencies on the island is **Amenos,** with offices in Hora near the School of Fine Arts and in Plata Gialos (www.mykonosrent car.com; ℂ **22890/24607**). Rentals include free parking in a lot at the edge of Hora—a huge plus, since parking is tight around Mykonos Town. If you stash your car in a no-parking area, the police will remove your license plates and you—not the rental office—will have to find the police station and pay a steep fine to get them back.

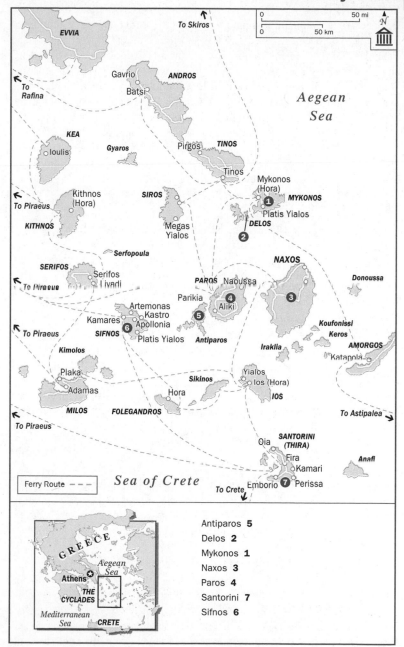

Where to Stay on Mykonos

EXPENSIVE

Belvedere ★   Should you have any doubt that Mykonos is the epitome of Euro-chic, you need only step into this super-cool retreat in the palm-shaded Fine Arts District of Hora. Rooms look out toward the distant sea, lush gardens, and a shimmering pool. A study in white-on-white simplicity, these quarters are so stylish with handcrafted island furnishings fashioned from rich woods that you won't notice their small size. One of the in-house restaurants is the very hip open-air sushi emporium **Matsuhisa Mykonos** (an offshoot of the Matsuhisa-Nobu family in London, Los Angeles, Miami, New York, and elsewhere around the world). A spa and pool bar are among the other amenities.

Off Odos Ormou Agi-Agou Ioanni (aka Ring Rd.), School of Fine Arts District, Hora. www.belvederehotel.com. © **22890/25122.** 48 units. 320€–500€ double. Rates include buffet breakfast. **Amenities:** 2 restaurants; 3 bars/lounges; fitness center; Jacuzzi; pool; sauna; spa; Wi-Fi (free). Closed Nov–Mar.

Cavo Tagoo ★★★   One of the island's most sophisticated getaways is just north of Hora above the new marina. A sumptuous outdoor lounge surrounds the infinity pool, while an indoor pool is the centerpiece of a hedonistic spa. Huge rooms and suites, set amid beautiful gardens, are filled with high-tech gadgetry, gorgeous handcrafted furnishings, and sunken tubs and other soothing comforts. Décor features golden stone accents amid acres of soothing white, with splashes of blues and greens. Most rooms and suites have sea-facing terraces, many with private pools; built-in divans and dining tables surrounded by exotic plantings provide a thoroughly decadent alfresco island experience. It's a ten-minute walk into Hora, but along a very busy road without a sidewalk or shoulder—it's best to let the hotel car whisk you back and forth.

Tagoo, coast rd. to Tourlos. www.cavotagoo.gr. © **22890/23692.** 70 units. 400€–600€ double. Rates include buffet breakfast. **Amenities:** Restaurant; bar; 2 pools; spa; Wi-Fi (free).

Mykonos Grand ★★   On the island's west end, this sprawling resort above the sea (where the film *Shirley Valentine* was set) breaks the generic Greek resort mold with exceptional service that seems more typical of much more intimate surroundings, along with endless amenities that ensure guests feel pampered. Many of the sea-facing rooms are equipped with deep whirlpool tubs and steam rooms, while stylish decor makes the most of some fairly small spaces. A beautiful pool sparkles above the private sandy beach, and a spa, tennis courts, and in-house bars and restaurants make staying put a pleasant alternative to coping with high-season crowds.

Agios Yiannis. www.mykonos grand.gr. © **22890/25555.** 100 units. 250€–4500€ double. Rates include buffet breakfast. **Amenities:** 2 restaurants; 3 bars; pool; beach; spa; Wi-Fi (free). Closed Nov–Mar.

Petasos Beach ★★★   For sheer drama it's hard to top this rather extravagant resort at the north end of Platis Yialos beach, on the island's southwest coast. Many of the accommodations, while brightly and sharply appointed, are fairly standard size, but little matter—just beyond their glass doors and balconies lies a huge swimming pool, lavish sun terraces, and, of course, the sparkling Aegean. The beach at Platis Yialos is more crowded than a rush-hour bus, but the Petasos has its own seaside aerie, a rocky peninsula from which a ladder descends into the heavenly waters. Dining is on a perch above the sea. For those without a car, Hora and the south coast beaches are within easy reach by bus, caique, or taxi.

Platis Yialos. www.petasos.gr. *ⓒ* **22890/23437.** 133 units. 350€–650€ double. Rates include buffet breakfast. **Amenities:** 2 restaurants; bar; pool; beach; spa; fitness center; sauna and steam room; Wi-Fi (free).

MODERATE

Apanema ★★ Comfortable and casually elegant, this small retreat surrounds a sea-facing terrace and pool above the marina just north of Hora. The large, airy rooms are simply but tastefully done, awash in creamy white with a slightly contemporary twist. Handcrafted pottery and woven rugs on the cool tile floors create a homey feeling amid all the refinement. All rooms have terraces or balconies. An alluring poolside restaurant and bar may persuade you to forgo the short trip into town and stay put for an evening or two of your stay.

Tagoo, coast rd. to Tourlos. www.apanemaresort.com. *ⓒ* **22890/28590.** 17 units. 200€–300€ double. Rates include buffet breakfast. **Amenities:** Restaurant; bar; pool; Wi-Fi (free).

Elysium ★★ Mykonos is not quite the gay mecca it once was, but you would hardly know it from this hilltop retreat above the Fine Arts District. It's a great place to stay even if you aren't a beautiful young male, though the poolside parties are definitely geared to those who are, as are the sunset cabaret shows. Rooms are pleasant though not fancy, of the white-wall, plain contemporary furniture variety, enlivened with some bright fabrics and portraits of male nudes. The real draws are the pool, sauna, hillside views of Hora and the sea, and the friendly ambience.

Hillside above Fine Arts District, Hora. elysiumhotel.com. *ⓒ* **22890/23952.** 42 units. 180€–300€ double. Rates include breakfast. **Amenities:** Restaurant; bar; pool; sauna; spa; Wi-Fi (free). Closed Oct–Apr.

Leto Hotel ★ The location on the harbor at the edge of Hora is the big plus, along with a seaside garden complete with pool, bar, and restaurant. Plain rooms maintain basic standards of comfort with not a hint of chic, but any style shortcomings are offset by the hospitality, shady pool terrace, and convenient location. The lovely Leto garden is a justifiably popular spot for weddings, so when booking, make sure an all-night party won't be interrupting your sleep.

Waterfront, off Polikandrioti near Old Harbor, Hora. www.letohotel.com. *ⓒ* **22890/22207.** 25 units. 300€–350€ double. **Amenities:** Restaurant; bar; pool; Wi-Fi (free).

INEXPENSIVE

Carbonaki Hotel ★★ One of the island's oldest hotels, tucked away on the back lanes of Hora, is family-run with a well-deserved reputation for hospitality and exceptional service. Just about all of the simply furnished but stylish rooms surround a beautiful, multilevel courtyard garden with a plunge pool, ensuring quiet (especially welcome at night, when late-night diners make their way home along the little lane out front). Downstairs is an attractive bar and lounge; breakfast (extra) is served here and in the garden. The hotel can only be reached on foot, but it's a short walk from the bus station, a parking lot, and a taxi stop along the ring road that skirts Hora.

23 Panachrantou St., Hora. carbonaki.gr. ⓒ **22890/24124.** 21 units. 120€–210€ double. **Amenities:** Garden; plunge pool; Wi-Fi (free).

Philippi Hotel ★★   It's hard to believe that Mykonos could still have a simple, family-run Greek-style hotel, but here it is, right in the heart of Hora, with a pretty garden to boot. Rooms are simply furnished but spacious, stylish, and nicely topped off with a smattering of antiques and family pieces. All are different, and many have balconies; those off the street are pleasantly quiet. Amenities are few, but the shops and restaurants of Hora are just outside the door.

25 Kalogera St., Hora. www.philippihotel.com. ⓒ **22890/22294.** 13 units. 100€–210€ double. **Amenities:** Garden; Wi-Fi (free).

Where to Eat

In Mykonos, you can eat like a king—well, at least like a shipping magnet or film star—or a mere commoner, in some highly acclaimed and unabashedly glitzy hotspots or in some delightfully simple tavernas focusing on fresh fish and traditional recipes. Wherever you choose to dine, remember that the lanes of Hora were laid out to baffle invading pirates and can still have the same effect on those looking for a specific address. Even locals often navigate by benchmarks—"the little lane after the big tree," whatever, so when in doubt simply ask for the nearest landmark. Not all Mykonos dining prices are daunting: there are many grill houses in Hora, serving up gyros for about 5€, including **Sakis,** near the Alpha Bank at Kalegora 7 (sakisgrillhouse.yolasite.com; ⓒ **22890/24848**).

Fish Taverna Kounelas ★★   SEAFOOD   This plain upstairs room with a cramped garden below is a Hora institution, living up to its reputation with simple preparations of the freshest catch available. Prices are fair but vary with weight. That said, you may have to negotiate with the rushed and sometimes surly staff to make sure they don't foist a lavish seafood feast on you. Instead, just go to the kitchen and pick out the fish, shrimps, or other seafood you want.

Savoronou 1, near Old Harbor and town hall, Hora. kounelas-myconos.com. ⓒ **22890/22890.** Main courses 8€–20€. Daily 7pm–midnight.

Kiki's ★★   GREEK   One of the island's great pleasures is a simple one: a swim at beautiful Agios Sostis on the north shore followed by a lazy lunch beneath the flowering vine that shades Kiki's seaside terrace. Fish and meat are grilled outdoors, and you'll step into the kitchen to choose one of the delightfully fresh salads. The place has no electricity and shuts up at sundown.

Agios Sostis. No phone. Main courses 6€–8€. Daily noon–7pm. Closed Nov–Mar.

La Maison de Catherine ★ GREEK/FRENCH   One of the island's most iconic restaurants was serving fusion cuisine long before that became a trend—wonderful seafood soufflés, French leg of lamb infused with island spices, and an apple tart with light Greek pastry. The candlelit room in the heart of old Hora is lovely and so blessedly quiet you won't mind not being outdoors, but if you need to be, ask to sit at one of the tables out front.

Ayios Gerasimos and Nikou, near Old Harbor, Hora. ✆ **22890/22890.** Main courses 20€–35€. Daily 7–11pm.

Niko's Taverna ★ GREEK   These tables sprawling across a square in the heart of Hora are never empty, and the moussaka, cabbage stuffed with feta, and other basic tavern fare is reliably good. Avoid lunch and early evening, when the cruise-ship crowd packs in; those who wait to dine late are rewarded, because lingering into the wee hours beneath the trees and stars is quite a nice experience.

Agios Moni Sq. near Parapotianis, Hora. tavernanikos.gr. ✆ **2289/024320.** Main courses 6€–10€. Daily noon–midnight.

To Maereo ★★★ GREEK   Mykonos could use about a dozen more places like this one—simple and atmospheric, serving good traditional fare at reasonable prices. Most Mykonites feel the same way, so come early or late to avoid the crush. Ask for a table on the little street, and tuck into country sausage, meatballs, zucchini fritters, and other delicious fare, offered on a small menu and in daily specials.

16 Kalogera, Hora. ✆ **22890/28825.** Main courses 9€–14€. Dinner 7pm–midnight.

Exploring Mykonos Town (Hora) ★★★

No matter how crowded the narrow streets may be, like legions of other international travelers, you will soon succumb to the Cycladic charms of Mykonos Town (better known as Hora). Wooden balconies hang from white cubical houses, outdoor staircases are lined with pots of geraniums, and oleander and hibiscus scent the air. The experience is made all the more pleasant by the absence of motorized traffic, mostly prohibited beyond **Plateia Mando Mavrogenous.** This busy square is named for the island heroine who pushed back a fleet of invading Turks in the War of Independence in 1822. Despite her fame, the beautiful and aristocratic Mando Mavrogenous died forgotten and in poverty on Paros, but she is now honored with a marble bust here, gazing out over the harbor.

Matoyanni Street, lined with expensive boutiques, leads south from the square into the Old Quarter. The glittering wealth on this street, with its distinctive white-outlined paving stones, belies the fact that until tourism transformed the island in the 1960s, bleak sun-parched Mykonos was the poorest island in the Cyclades.

On Dinameon Street, you'll find one of the island's favorite landmarks, the **Tria Pagadia (Three Wells).** Legend has it that a virgin who drinks from all three wells will soon find a husband. The water is no longer potable—but then, virgins are few and far between on worldly Mykonos these days.

For centuries before the jet set arrived, the island residents of Mykonos made a humble living from the sea. In fact, the Mykonites were also once corrupt corsairs, and by the 17th century the harbor at Mykonos had become an infamous pirates' nest. Only in the 19th century, when the piracy business went out of fashion in the Aegean, did islander traders and merchants become respectable.

In the heart of the Old Quarter, you can pore over the navigational bric-a-brac displayed at the **Aegean Maritime Museum** at 10 Dinameon street (odysseus. culture.gr; © **21081/25547;** admission 3€). The little museum is open 8:30am to 3pm in winter (Nov–Mar); in summer (Apr–Oct), it's open 10:30am to 1pm and 6 to 9pm. It's closed on Sundays and Mondays. Next door you'll find **Lena's House,** the overstuffed home of a 19th-century sea captain (© **22890/ 22591;** free admission). The house is open daily from April to October, 6pm to 9pm.

Perhaps the most famous icons of Mykonos are the **windmills** that line Alefkandra Ridge on a point of land just south along the waterfront from the Old Quarter. Alefkandra means "whitening"—women used to wash their laundry in the surf and string it out on the ridge to take advantage of the same breezes that once propelled the giant blades—and still do, on special occasions. Other windmills line a barren ridge above Hora to the east. Until a few decades ago 16 of these conical, thatch-roofed mills were in operation around Mykonos to grind grain.

Archaeological Museum ★ MUSEUM   Filling a couple of stark rooms off the harbor, this museum displays funerary sculptures and vases excavated from the purification pit on the island of Rhenea. The artifacts were originally buried with the dead on the sacred island of Delos; in the 5th century B.C., the oracle at Delphi advised the Athenians to cleanse Delos to reverse their defeats in the Peloponnesian War, so human remains and funereal offerings were removed to the necropolis on Rhenea. From Mykonos comes a large pythos (vase) from the 7th century B.C. painted with vivid depictions of the fall of Troy at the hands of soldiers emerging from the wooden horse.

Agios Stefanos. odysseus.culture.gr. © **22890/22325.** Admission 4€. Tues–Sun 8:30am–3pm.

Folklore Museum ★ MUSEUM   A evocative throwback to times past is filled with household implements, costumes, and a re-created 19th-century kitchen. Stringed instruments reflect the island's long-standing musical traditions—even islanders who partake of modern Mykonos' cosmopolitan nightlife probably also know the ages-old laments sung during feasts at the island's more than 400 churches. The museum is also the final resting place of Petros, a pelican who took shelter on Mykonos during a storm in the 1950s and soon became the island's mascot. Since the island began to prosper from the arrival of well-heeled visitors not long afterward, Petros may well have brought good luck with him. Petros met his own bad fortune under the wheels of a car in 1985 and was stuffed for posterity.

Near Church of the Paraportiani. © **22890/22591.** Free admission. Apr–Oct Mon–Fri 6:30–9:30pm.

Little Venice ★★★ NEIGHBORHOOD   The esplanade that follows the harbor is especially pleasant in evening, when Mykonites and their visitors stroll and sit at cafe tables to catch a sea breeze. Eventually it leads west to the area now known as Little Venice. Many of the island's sea captains built homes at water's edge here, on the west side of Hora; the houses are so close to the sea that waves wash against the lower floors—an arrangement that is reminiscent of houses along the canals of Venice. Of course, those Italian waterways are more placid than the Aegean, and a drink on the seaside balconies of the bars in the captains' former dwellings often comes with a shower of sea spray. At the north end, the waterside **Church of the Paraportiani** (Our Lady of the Postern Gate) is actually four little churches pieced together into a squat, rambling, lopsided assemblage that is both homely and utterly charming. In the absence of straight lines, the whitewashed walls look lumpy and rumpled, like a poorly iced cake, and they fascinatingly reflect the shadowy shades of the sea that crashes against the foundations.

Exploring Ano Mera ★

The only sizable settlement on Mykonos besides Hora, Ano Mera is set amid stark, rolling hills in the center of the island, 8km (5 miles) east of Hora. To one side of the shady plateia is the **Monastery of Moni Panagias Tourlianis ★,** where intricate folk carvings cover the marble bell tower. Inside are elaborate baroque altar screens and incense holders fashioned in the shape of dragons. Even a water spout in the courtyard is decorated with the carved figure of a woman wearing a crown, is accordingly known as the Queen. The monastery is the repository of an icon of the Virgin that has been working miracles since it was found in the countryside several centuries ago. Every August 15, the feast of the Virgin, the icon is carried in a procession across the island to the Church of **Agia Kyriaki** in Hora (© **0289/71249**). Admission to the monastery is free, but it's open randomly; you can always see the exterior carvings, however.

Mykonos Beaches

Beaches on Mykonos are not the best in Greece, but they are among the most popular. The beaches on the island's **south shore** have the best sand, views, and wind protection, but they are so well-patronized that from June into September you'll have to navigate through a forest of beach umbrellas to find your square meter of sand. A few (**Paradise, Super Paradise**) are known as party beaches, and guarantee throbbing music and loud revelry until late at night—actually, until dawn. Others (**Platis Yialos** and **Ornos**) are quieter and more popular with families. With all the south coast beaches, keep in mind that most people begin to arrive in the early afternoon; you can avoid the worst

Prevailing winds on Mykonos (and throughout the Cyclades) blow from the north, which is why the island's southern beaches are usually calmer. Periodically, however, a hot southern wind occurs during the summer, kicking up Sahara-like sandstorms on the south-coast beaches. On such days, in-the-know sun worshippers head instead to the northern beaches—and you should do likewise. In Mykonos town, particularly hot temperatures and calm in the harbor are a pretty good sign that the southern wind is coming.

As for the north coast, on many days during July and August into September, the strong *meltemi* winds blowing from the north tend to whip up awesome and unrelenting waves—which is when the water there is filled with surfers.

of the crowds by going in the morning. The **north coast beaches,** such as Ayios Sostis and Panormos, are much less developed but just as beautiful. Buses make infrequent trips to some of them, but it's more convenient to reach them by car or scooter.

Beaches Near Hora   For those who can't wait to hit the beach, the closest to Mykonos Town is **Megali Ammos (Big Sand)** ★, about a 10-minute walk south—it's very crowded and not particularly scenic. To the north, the beach nearest town is 2km (1 mile) away at **Tourlos;** however, because this is now where many ships dock at the new harbor, it's neither scenic nor relaxing. **Ornos** ★, popular with families, is about 2.5km (1½ miles) south of town and has a fine-sand beach in a sheltered bay, with hotels backing the shore. Buses to Ornos run hourly from the South Station between 8am and 11pm.

Platis Yialos ★, with back-to-back hotels and tavernas along its long sandy beach, is extremely easy to get to from Mykonos Town by car or bus. It has pristine aqua-blue waters and a variety of watersports, but it is usually so packed with beach chairs that you can't even see the sand, and its almost-tawdry boardwalk is lined with mostly mediocre eateries. From here, however, you can catch a caique to the more distant beaches of Paradise, Super Paradise, Agrari, and Elia (see below), as well as a small boat to Delos. The bus to and from North Station in Hora runs every 15 minutes from 8am to 8pm, then every 30 minutes until midnight. *Tip:* The first stop on the bus from town to Platis Yialos, **Psarou** ★★, is a higher-brow version of its neighbor, with white sand and greenery overlooked by the terraces of tavernas and hotels.

The South Coast Beaches   Buses from Hora's North Station serve the south coast beaches, with service every half hour throughout the day. Caiques to Super Paradise, Agrari, and Elia depart from Platis Yialos (see above) every morning, weather permitting; there is also service from Ornos in high season (July–Aug). Note that there are no caiques October through May. **Paradise** ★ is the island's most famous beach, with golden sands washed by breathtakingly beautiful water, but no one comes here for the sea. Lined with bars, tavernas, and clubs, Paradise is the premier party beach of the island. (One beach party on Paradise that revelers won't want to miss is the **Full Moon Party,** a once-a-month bacchanal that would make Dionysus blush. The only other party that compares to it is the **Closing Party** every September that has become an island institution.) The more adventurous arrive at Paradise by moped on roads that are incredibly narrow and steep. Seeing how very few leave this beach sober, it is in your best interest (even if you have rented a moped) to get back to town by bus. As in most of the island, the water here is breathtakingly beautiful.

Super Paradise (Plindri) ★, in a rocky cove just around the headland from Paradise, is somewhat less developed than its neighbor, but no less crowded. The left side of the beach is a nonstop party in summer, with loud music and dancing, while the right side is mostly nude and gay. The waters here are beautiful but very deep, so it isn't the best swimming option for families with small children. You can get to the beach by bus or by caique; if you go by car or moped, be very careful on the extremely steep and narrow access road. Farther east across the little peninsula is **Agrari** ★★, a lovely cove sheltered by lush foliage, with a good little taverna and a beach that welcomes bathers in all modes of dress and undress.

One of the longest beaches on the island, **Elia** ★★ is a sand-and-pebble beach surrounded by a circle of steep hills. Despite its popularity, there is no loud bar/club here, so the atmosphere is more sedate than the Paradise beaches. It's a 45-minute caique ride from Platis Yialos and on the bus route from Mykonos Town. The next major beach is **Kalo Livadi (Good Pasture)** ★. Located in a farming valley, this long, beautiful beach is about as quiet as a beach on Mykonos's southern coast gets. Adjacent to the beach are a taverna and a few villas and hotels on the hills.

The last resort area on the southern coast accessible by bus from the north station is **Kalafatis** ★. This fishing village was once the port of the ancient citadel of Mykonos, which dominated the little peninsula to the west. A line of trees separates the beach from the rows of buildings that have grown up along the road. The waters are pristine, there's a good beach restaurant and bar, and hotels along the sands offer water-skiing, surfing, and windsurfing lessons. Boats are available to take you to **Dragonisi,** an islet with caves ideal for swimming and exploring. You might also catch a glimpse of rare monk seals at the islet; its caves are reportedly a breeding ground for them. Adjacent to Kalafatis in a tiny cove is **Ayia Anna** ★, a short stretch of sand with a score of umbrellas. Several kilometers farther east, accessible by a good road from Kalafatis, is **Lia** ★, which has fine sand, clear water, bamboo windbreaks, and a small, low-priced taverna.

North Coast Beaches   The island's north coast beaches are unspoiled, often windswept, and much less crowded than those in the south. The huge Panormos Bay has three main beaches. The one closest to Hora, **Ftelia** ★★, is a long fine-sand beach, easily one of the best on the island. Two well-sheltered northern beaches are **Panormos** ★★★, where a long stretch of fine sand is backed by low dunes, and another 1km (¾ mile) down the road, **Ayios**

Offshore breezes, underwater scenery, and crystal-clear waters make Mykonos one of the Aegean's favorite playgrounds for watersports enthusiasts. For diving and snorkeling excursions and instruction, try the **Mykonos Diving Center** on Paradise Beach (www.dive.gr; ℂ **22890/** 24808) or the **Kalafati Dive Center** on Kalafati Beach (www.mykonos-diving. com; ℂ **22890/71677**). For windsurfing board rental and instruction, try the **Wind Surf Center** on Kalafati Beach (www.pezi-huber.com; ℂ **22890/72345**).

Sostis ★★, a lovely small crescent just below a tiny village. There isn't any parking at Ayios Sostis; leave your vehicle along the main road and walk down past the church and excellent small taverna, a perfect spot for lunch. Buses run from Mykonos Town to Panormos four times a day in high season. Farther east, **Fokos** ★★, north of Ano Mera, is a superb swath of sand set amid raw, wild scenery.

Mykonos Shopping

Fashion designers such as Christian Dior and Givenchy were chief among the international travelers who began to visit Mykonos in the 1950s. They discovered the island's distinctive textiles, often woven by hand in a striped pattern, and they incorporated the designs into their creations. Young Mykonites began designing their own fashions, and these were soon taken up by Jacqueline Onassis and other well-heeled visitors. The tradition continues. **Yiannis Galatis,** who applies island designs to thin, multicolored textiles, shows his famous gowns and other creations, including men's clothing, in his beautiful shop in Hora on Plateia Mando Mavrogenous (ℂ **22890/22255**). **Dimitris Parthenis,** another innovative island designer, showcases his work and that of his daughter, Orsalia, in a shop near Little Venice on Plateia Alefkandra (ℂ **22890/23080**). **Ioanna Zouganeli** carries on the family weaving craft and sells silk and mohair shawls, scarves, and other pieces from a delightful little shop facing Paraportiani (ℂ **22890/22309**).

Efthimiou, on Zouganeli St., sells almond sweets, a traditional Mykonos favorite, and wine made on the island (ℂ **22890/22281**). You can find sweets at **Pantopoleion,** 24 Kaloyerou (ℂ **22890/22078**), along with Greek organic foods and natural cosmetics; the shop is in a beautifully restored 300-year-old Mykonian house. **Gioras Wood Medieval Mykonian Bakery** (ℂ **22890/ 27784**) is a magical spot, down some steps off Efthimiou Street, where cheese pies, breads, and baklava and other delectable pastries emerge out of a centuries-old wood oven.

Mykonos After Dark

Many visitors to the island don't creep out of their lairs until sunset, and they have no lack of venues for nighttime escapades when they do. Little Venice is the island's most popular spot at sunset, with four especially pleasant waterside bars—**Kastro** (www.kastrosmykonos.com; ℂ **22890/23072**), **Montparnasse** (www.thepianobar.com; ℂ **22890/23719**), **Katerina's** (katerinaslittlevenice mykonos.com; ℂ **22890/23084**), and **Galeraki** (ℂ **22890/27188**) serving up views from their balconies, along with refined music, sophisticated clientele, and decent cocktails (to be sipped slowly, at about 10€ a drink). Bars in the center of Hora are popular for after-dinner drinks and people-watching, pleasures that go on well into the wee hours. **Aroma** (ℂ **22890/27148**) and **Uno** (ℂ **22890/26144**), on Matoyanni Street, are the perennial favorites. **Pierro's** (ℂ **22890/22177**), also on Matoyanni, is the island's most popular gay club, with nearby **Icarus,** on Agias Kiriakas Square (ℂ **22890/22718**), holding its own with all-night music and drag shows.

The late-night scene is liveliest at Paradise Beach, where **Cavo Paradise** (cavoparadiso.gr; ℂ **694/850-4989**) and the **Paradise Club** (www.paradise clubmykonos.com; ℂ **694/946-8227**) get going at about 2am and charge hefty covers (at least 25€) for the privilege of dancing till dawn. The sobering morning swim is included. The Mykonos scene changes each season, however, so check out what's new and hot once you get to the island.

A Side Trip to Delos ★★★

No one stays on Delos, but day-trippers arrive by the boatload from Mykonos and the other Cyclades, flocking to this uninhabited isle to see one of the most important—and haunting—archaeological sites in the Aegean.

Even in antiquity, Delos was set apart from the rhythms of everyday life: no one was allowed to be born, to die, or to be buried there (the remains of locals were placed in a purification pit on Rhenea; you'll see some of these at the Archeological Museum in Hora, see p. 144). As the legendary birthplace of Apollo, Delos was one of ancient Greece's most sacred religious sanctuaries. It even had a second robust act, developing under the Romans into a flourishing center of trade, with a huge slave market, on the shipping routes between the Aegean world and the Middle East. Delos was gradually abandoned, however, after most of the population was massacred in a wave of attacks beginning in A.D. 88. Except for occasional visits by Venetians and crusaders, the temples, mosaics, and shrines were left to the elements—as you'll see them today.

GETTING THERE From Mykonos, organized guided and unguided excursions leave starting about 8:30am about four times a day Tuesday through Sunday at the harbor's west end. Every travel agency in town advertises its Delos excursions (some with guides). Individual caique owners also have signs stating their prices and schedules. The trip takes about 30 minutes and costs about 12€ round-trip; as long as you return with the boat that brought you, you can (space available) decide which return trip you want to take when you've had enough. The last boat for Mykonos usually leaves by 4pm. The site is closed on Mondays, and boats usually do not make the crossing in rough weather.

Warning: If you're heading to Delos just to see the Avenue of the Lions, double-check to see if the lions are in place. Recent restoration activity and staff cutbacks have forced some of the noble beasts to endure the indignity of being put into storage. Some replicas have been substituted on the site.

EXPLORING THE ISLAND

In myth, Delos is the birthplace of Apollo, god of music and light, begotten of Zeus and his lover Leto. When Zeus fell in love with Leto and she became pregnant, Zeus's furious wife, Hera, ordered the Python, the earth dragon, to pursue Leto. Poseidon took pity on Leto and provided her a safe haven by anchoring Delos to the sea floor with four diamond columns. She first stopped on nearby Rhenea to deliver Artemis; then she gave birth to Apollo on Delos, grasping a sacred palm tree on the slopes of Mount Kynthos, the highest hill on the island, as Zeus watched from the summit.

The island grew to be the center of an Apollo cult, hosting the annual Delian festival in his honor. Its power as a trade center grew, and for a few decades in the 5th century B.C., Delos was important enough to be the headquarters of the Delian League, the confederation of Greek city-states, and the repository for its treasury. By 100 B.C., under Roman occupation, Delos had a cosmopolitan population of 25,000, drawn from throughout the Mediterranean world; its market sold 10,000 slaves a day.

Next to the harbor, you can see what's left of the **Agora of the Competialists,** a Roman-era domain of members of trade guilds known as Competialists. Just to the east of it is the **Delian Agora,** site of the slave market.

Pilgrims once made their way from the harbor to the **Sanctuary of Apollo** along the Sacred Way, past two long, columned porticoes. After the 2nd century B.C., they would enter the sanctuary through the **Propytheria,** a triple-arched marble gateway that opened to a precinct of temples and shrines. Some of the oldest remains on Delos are here, including a shrine thought to be Mycenaean, from as early as 1300 B.C. Three great temples to Apollo were erected in the 6th and 5th centuries B.C. One of them, the **Porinos Naos,** housed the treasury of the Delian League from 477 to 454 B.C.

Just beyond the eastern perimeters of Apollo's precinct are the ruins of the long **Sanctuary of the Bulls,** so called for a pair of carved bull heads over the entryway. Two former headquarters of state are next to the sanctuary, the **Bouleterion (Council House)** and the **Prytaneion (Senate).**

A slight depression in the earth is all that remains of the Sacred Lake, now dry. On its shores stood the enormous **Agora of the Italians,** once bordered by 112 columns, and the 50m-long (164-ft.) promenade, the **Terrace of the Lions,** where five of nine original marble lions still stand ready to pounce.

North of the lake is the **House on the Lake,** a once-elegant residence; the **Granite Palaestra,** a gymnasium and bath complex; and beyond that, the **stadium,** where the Delian Games were first staged in the 5th century B.C. A nearby **synagogue** was built around 80 B.C. to serve Syrian and Lebanese Jews who came to Delos during the island's heyday as a trading center.

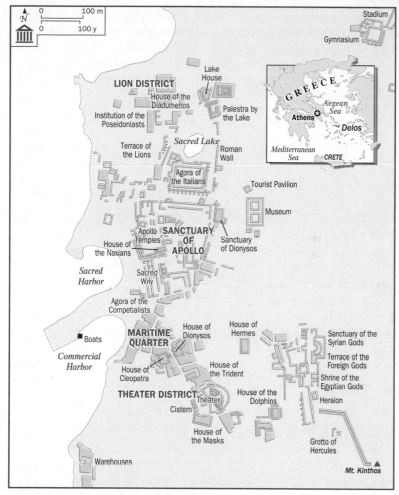

East of the harbor, in what was once the residential district of the island, you can see a **theater** carved into a hillside that could seat 5,000 spectators. Elaborate villas built by wealthy merchants and bankers in this area include the **House of the Dolphins, House of the Masks** (perhaps a boardinghouse for actors), and the lavish **House of Dionysus.** Behind this rises Mount Kynthos, which you can ascend on a stepped path for a stunning view of the sea and ancient city.

A small archaeological museum on the island displays many artifacts, including statues of Apollo and Artemis, and pottery and other household objects that residents left behind. A snack bar sells beverages and light meals.

Site and museum: odysseus.culture.gr. ℂ **22890/22259.** Admission 12€ (included on most organized tours). Tues–Sun 8:30am–3pm.

SANTORINI ★★★

Do yourself a favor: Arrive by boat rather than by plane, because sailing into Santorini is one of the great Greek experiences. From the deck of the ferry, you will be looking up the 300m-high (1,000-ft.) cliffs that form the western flanks of the main island. The bay, some 10km (6 miles) long and as deep as 400m (1,312-ft.) in places, is actually the flooded caldera of a volcano, whose eruptions caused the center of a once-large island to collapse. Gaze back west to the islets on the west side of the bay, Therasia and Aspronissi, and you'll see that they were originally fragments of the rim.

From the sea the towns and villages that line the caldera look almost like apparitions. At first the clusters appear to be natural formations of white stone, until blue domes come into focus and you notice white cubical houses practically teetering on the sides of the cliffs.

Little wonder that Santorini is the most visited of the Greek isles. You won't encounter too many vestiges of authentic Greece here or explore wild terrain, but you will never tire of soaking in the natural beauty of one of the world's most spectacular natural settings. When you tear yourself away from the views of the volcanic caldera, you can bask on black sand beaches and encounter the remains of prehistoric civilizations at Akrotiri and Ancient Thera.

Essentials

ARRIVING **Olympic Air** (www.olympicair.com; ✆ 810/114-4444) and **Aegean Airlines** (www.aegeanair.com; ✆ 810/112-0000) fly several times a day between Athens and the Santorini airport, **Monolithos** (✆ 22860/31-525), which also receives European charters. There are frequent connections with Mykonos and Rhodes, and service two or three times per week to and from Iraklion, Crete. A bus to the largest town, Fira (4€) meets most flights; the bus stop is beside the airport entrance. A taxi to Fira costs about 13€.

BY BOAT Ferry service runs to and from Piraeus at least twice daily; the trip takes 9 to 10 hours by car ferry on the Piraeus-Paros-Naxos-Ios-Santorini route, or 4 hours by catamaran, if you go via Piraeus-Paros-Santorini. Boats are notoriously late and/or early; a travel agent or the **Santorini Port Authority** (✆ 22860/22-239) will be able to give you updates. In July and August, ferries connect several times a day with Ios, Naxos, Paros, and Mykonos; almost daily with Anafi and Siros; five times a week with Sikinos and Folegandros; and twice weekly with Sifnos. Service to Thessaloniki (a trip that takes 17–24 hr.) is offered four to five times per week. There is an almost daily connection by excursion boat with **Iraklion** in Crete, but because this is an open sea route, the trip can be an ordeal in bad weather and is subject to cancellation.

Almost all ferries dock at **Athinios,** where buses meet each boat for the trip to Fira (one-way to Fira costs 3€); taxis are also available from Athinios, at nearly five times the bus fare. Athinios is charmless; when you come here to catch a ferry, it's a good idea to bring munchies, water, and a good book.

The exposed port at **Skala,** directly below Fira, is unsafe for the larger ferries but is often used by small cruise ships, yachts, and excursion vessels. If your boat docks here, head to town either by cable car (5€), mule, or donkey (5€); or you can do the 45-minute uphill walk.

VISITOR INFORMATION Nomikos Travel (www.nomikosvillas.gr; (© **22860/23-660**), **Bellonias Tours** (© **22860/22-469**), **Pelican Travel** (www.pelican.gr; © **22860/22-220**) and **Kamari Tours** (© **22860/31-390**) are well established on the island, offering bus tours, boat excursions around the caldera, and submarine tours beneath the caldera.

GETTING AROUND The **central bus station** is just south of the main square in Fira. Most routes are served every hour or half-hour from 7am to 11pm in high season. A conductor on board will collect fares, which range from 2€ to 5€. Destinations include Akrotiri, Athinios (the ferry pier), Ia, Kamari, Monolithos (the airport), Perissa, Perivolas Beach, Vlihada, and Vourvoulos.

A **car** is not really necessary, except for maybe a 1-day excursion to visit Pyrgos, wineries, Akrotiri, Ancient Thera, or the island's famous volcanic

A caldera forms when molten rock, known as magma, is ejected from a volcanic crater during an eruption. Without the support of underlying magma, the land surrounding the crater collapses. A volcanic eruption several hundred thousand years ago created the caldera in Santorini, when the center of a circular island collapsed and the sea rushed in to fill the caldera. Volcanic debris from other eruptions has refilled the caldera many times over the millennia, only to collapse again. By the time of the last eruption around 1500 B.C., the Santorini caldera was almost entirely ringed with land, except for one narrow channel.

One of the largest eruptions on record, the 1500 B.C. explosion blew open additional channels, creating the present-day appearance of the caldera.

Which leads to the million-dollar question: Is Santorini Atlantis? Plato tells us that Atlantis "disappeared into the sea depths" some 9,000 years before his time—but that's only one zero off from 900 years (a mistake passed down through the ages, perhaps?). Plato wrote in the 5th century B.C., so the missing-zero theory places the destruction of Atlantis tantalizingly close to the time of Santorini's last eruption.

beaches. Many travel agents on the island rent cars, however, charging about 60€ a day in high season for a small car with unlimited mileage. If you park in town or in a no-parking area, the police will remove your license plates, and you, not the car-rental office, will have to pay a steep fine to get them back.

If you decide to rent a **moped** or **ATV,** keep in mind that many roads on the island are narrow and winding. Between local drivers who take the roads at high speed, and visiting drivers who aren't sure where they're going, the island's high accident rate should be no surprise. If you're determined to use these modes of transportation, expect to pay about 25€ per day, less during off season. Greek law now requires wearing a helmet.

The **taxi** station is just south of the main square. In high season, book ahead by phone (✆ **22860/22-555** or 22860/23-951) if you want a taxi for an excursion; be sure that you agree on the price before you set out. For most point-to-point trips (Fira to Ia, for example), the prices are fixed. If you call for a taxi outside Fira, you'll be charged a pickup fee of at least 2€; you're also required to pay the driver's fare from Fira to your pickup point. Bus service shuts down at midnight, so book a taxi in advance if you'll need it late at night.

Where to Stay on Santorini

Many hotels along the caldera are accessible only via very long flights of steep steps. Staff members are usually on hand to carry your bags, but if you're not up to some fairly rigorous climbs, many of these places are not for you—and many are not suitable for young children. Ask about accessibility when booking and, if that's an issue, seek out lodgings on level ground.

EXPENSIVE

Aressana Spa Hotel ★★ Travelers put off by the steps of caldera-view hotels will find a welcome refuge in this stunning retreat set around a dramatic swimming pool and lush gardens in the middle of Fira. The surroundings can be aggressively hip, but the stylish rooms are large and offer every comfort; most rooms have balconies or terraces, often facing the pool and quiet gardens, and many have the high barrel-vaulted ceilings typical of this island.

Fira. www.aressana.gr. © **22860/23-900.** 50 units. 300€–350€ double. Rates include buffet breakfast. **Amenities:** Cafe; bar; pool; room service; Wi-Fi (free). Closed mid-Nov to Feb.

Astra Apartments ★★★

Dramatic eagle's-eye views over the caldera and the Skaros promontory set the scene for some of the most pleasant lodging in Santorini. Stylishly appointed suites and apartments surround a lovely pool and cling to the side of the caldera, looking like a tiny, whitewashed village. This amazing setting is the backdrop for extremely tasteful, comfortable accommodations, with vaulted ceilings, beautiful tile work, and handsome wood and fabrics. Everything is just right, and the management and staff, a large part of what makes Astra so special, go out of their way to ensure it remains that way, providing service that focuses on every detail.

Imerovigli. www.astrasuites.com. © **22860/23-641.** 27 suites. 300€–800€ double. **Amenities:** Bar; restaurant; pool; spa services; Wi-Fi (free).

Ikies ★★

On an island famous for dramatic settings, this aerie tucked away on the side of the caldera ranks high on the gee-whiz scale. All units are different, though each is a greatly enhanced cliff house with a kitchenette, living area, and bedroom or two. Many are on two levels, and each open to its own terrace with a private hot tub and eye-filling views. Stonework, domed ceilings, bright-blue shutters, and other architectural details provide plenty of exotic island ambiance, while furnishings are a design-magazine-worthy mashup of contemporary and traditional styling. Attentive, low-key service accentuates the feeling that you are in a world of your own with the sparkling Aegean at your feet.

Ia. www.ikies.com. © **22860/71311.** 11 units. 350€–500€ double. Rates include breakfast. **Amenities:** Room service; pool; Wi-Fi (free). Closed Nov–Mar.

MODERATE

Aura Marina ★★

A hillside above the village of Akrotiri at the south end of Santorini is the quiet setting for airy, handsomely furnished apartments that look over the sea and the caldera. All of the beautifully designed, handsomely furnished units have sitting rooms, kitchenettes, and bedrooms/sleeping lofts, and all open to large terraces with private plunge pools. You'll need a car to reach this pleasantly remote place, but you'll be near the island's best beaches as well as the archeological sites.

Near Akrotiri. www.aura-marina.com. © **2286/083101.** 9 units. 150€–250€ double. **Amenities:** Private pools; Wi-Fi (free). Closed Nov–Mar.

Esperas ★★★

You'll feel like a cliff dweller at this welcoming enclave of traditional houses teetering on the edge of the caldera at the edge of Ia. Shops and restaurants are just steps (in the literal sense) away, and a path leads to stairs descending to Ammoudi's beach Even so, this enchanted perch seems like a world unto itself, set apart from the busy Ia scene. Views are stupendous from the private terraces (many with hot tubs) or the beautiful pool and terrace, and the comfortable and tasteful accommodations, filled with traditional island furnishings, invite seclusion (a rare commodity on the crowded caldera these days). The in-house restaurant shows off local produce in delicious salads, wonderful seafood dishes, and a slow-cooked lamb shank.

Ia. www.esperas.com. ⓒ **22860/71088.** 17 units. 280€–450€ double. Rates include buffet breakfast. **Amenities:** Restaurant; bar; pool; Wi-Fi (free). Closed Nov–Mar.

Zannos Melathron ★★ Pyrgos, an atmospheric medieval citadel in the island's center that was once the capital, is the setting for this distinctive and luxurious hideaway, part of the Relais & Chateaux group. Two exotic 18th- and 19th-century neoclassical mansions are set in lush gardens behind high walls. Restrained old-world ambience fills the frescoed lounges, guest rooms, and suites, all facing patios and a pool. Wine and food are first-rate, views from this vantage point (some of the highest ground on the island) are extensive, and the welcoming lanes of Pyrgos are just outside the door.

Pyrgos. www.zannos.gr. ⓒ **22860/28220.** 12 units. 265€–330€ double. Rates include buffet breakfast. **Amenities:** Restaurant; bar; airport pickup; concierge; Jacuzzi; pool; room service; Wi-Fi (free).

INEXPENSIVE

Hotel Keti ★ You don't have to take out a second mortgage to afford a caldera view. This delightful and reasonably priced inn clinging to the cliff face below the center of Fira is full of eye-catching scenery, enjoyed from a sunny communal terrace. Rooms are pleasantly vaulted, whitewashed, and traditionally furnished. All open onto a shared terrace overlooking the caldera, while bathrooms, at the back of the rooms, are carved into the cliff face. The fanciest accommodation in the house is a suite with an outdoor Jacuzzi. You'll do some climbing to get in and out of this hideaway, but your efforts are well rewarded.

Fira. www.hotelketi.gr. ⓒ **22860/22324.** 7 units. 150€–200€ double. Rates include breakfast. **Amenities:** Bar; Wi-Fi (free). Closed Nov to mid-Mar.

Paradise Hotel ★ If you're willing to forgo the caldera views, you'll be lucky to find yourself in this delightful spot near the island's ancient sites and lava beaches. Pleasantly plain, tile-floored rooms surround a flowery garden and enormous pool, living up to the standards of a Best Western affiliation. Though the nearby sea is just out of sight, the scene of village life unfolding all around you is a spectacle in itself.

Akrotiri. www.hotelparadise.gr. ⓒ **22860/81277.** 40 units. 130€–175€ double. Rates include breakfast. **Amenities:** Pool; Wi-Fi (free). Closed Nov–Mar.

Where to Eat on Santorini
EXPENSIVE
Restaurant-Bar 1800 ★ GREEK/CONTINENTAL A 200-plus-year-old sea captain's house in the center of Ia is one of Santorini's favorite dining spots, and little wonder. Fresh fish beautifully sauced with capers, tender lamb

chops with green applesauce, and other inspired cuisine does justice to the exquisite decor—and, for that matter, to the views from the roof terrace. After you eat, you can decide whether the owner (an architect and chef) deserves more praise for his skill with the decor or with the cuisine.

Main St., Ia. www.oia-1800.com. © **22860/71485.** Main courses 18€–35€. Daily 8pm–midnight.

Selene ★★★ GREEK   This elegant retreat, occupying an old manor house in Pyrgos, consistently tops best-in-Greece lists and works its magic from the moment you step into the handsome dining room or onto the candlelit terrace overlooking vineyards and the distant sea. Dishes such as octopus with smoked eggplant, fava balls with capers, and herb-encrusted rabbit make creative use of local ingredients; the baked mackerel with caper leaves and tomato wrapped in a crepe of fava beans and *brodero* (seafood stew) are legendary, stars of haute-cuisine magazines. The beautiful surroundings, perfect ambience and service, and memorable meals come together to form the perfect Santorini evening that many travelers talk about for years after. For something a little more casual, and less expensive, you can enjoy a meal or light bite at the adjacent bistro-cafe-patisserie-wine bar (main courses from 12€; open daily noon–11pm).

Pyrgos. www.selene.gr. © **22860/22-249.** Main courses 17€–30€. Daily 7–11:30pm. Closed Nov to early Apr.

MODERATE

Kandouni ★★ GREEK   It's hard to pass by this 19th-century sea captain's house, where pork fillets stuffed with apricots, pasta with salmon and caviar, and other innovative dishes are served in an enticing candlelit garden and in charming old rooms amid antiques and mementos of old Santorini. The Korki-antis family takes care of guests with warmth and style, and will encourage you to linger over wine late into the evening.

Ia. © **22860/71616.** Main courses 10€–25€. Daily noon–midnight.

Katina's ★★ SEAFOOD   Fish tavernas line the quay at Ammoudi, the fishing port below Ia. All are good, and given the discerning taste of the islanders when it comes to seafood, none would stay in business for long if offerings were to fail the freshness test. Family-run Katina's stands out because it is one of the oldest and most revered places on the waterfront, yet it never lets down its high standards. At all these tavernas, the fresh fish, calamari, or octopus you choose from the iced display cases will be grilled and served with fresh salads and vegetables. Lapping waves and bobbing fishing boats provide a suitably nautical backdrop. What more could one ask for? Maybe a taxi back up the hill when it's time to leave. Just ask your waiter and a taxi will appear.

Amoundi, at bottom of steps from Ia. © **22860/71280.** Main courses 10€–25€ or more; fish sold by weight. Daily noon–midnight.

Metaxy Mas ★★★ GREEK/CRETAN   An out-of-the-way location in the countryside outside Pyrgos doesn't seem to deter eager diners, who pack into the stone-walled dining room and terrace from noon until the wee hours. The name means "between us," but no one's chosen to keep this buzzing place a secret. The draws are simple time-honored dishes made with the freshest ingredients: Delicious salads, perfectly grilled fish, heavenly shrimp *saganaki*, simply roasted eggplant, tomato fritters—everything that comes from the kitchen is memorable. If service seems a bit rushed, you'll certainly understand.

Pyrgos, Exo Gonia. www.santorini-metaximas.gr. *©* **22860/31323.** Main courses 7€–12€. Daily noon–midnight.

INEXPENSIVE

Taverna Nikolas ★ GREEK   An authentic Greek taverna seems almost out of place in Fira these days—but that, of course, is the appeal of this simple, whitewashed room that has been serving old favorites, from a good moussaka to lamb in lemon sauce, for more than 50 years. Nikolas is usually on hand to make sure his guests are happy—and they are, especially in light of the down-to-earth prices. Arrive early or late, and bring cash, as the place is always busy, and reservations and credit cards are not accepted.

Just up from the main square in Fira. *©* **22860/24550.** Main courses 7€–10€. Daily noon–midnight.

Roka ★★ GREEK   A neoclassical house with a colorful garden on the back streets of Ia is a welcome retreat from the busy scene on the caldera rim. The traditional taverna fare sticks close to the basics, making the most of island ingredients. Peppers stuffed with rice and pine nuts, vegetable pies, and grilled meat and fish are unfailingly delicious.

Ia. *©* **22860/71896.** Main courses 8€–15€. Daily noon–midnight.

Zafora ★ GREEK   From a seat on the terrace, you can take in the action of this pleasant village (near the ancient site of the same name) while sampling tomato fritters, pasta with seafood, stuffed peppers, and other local favorites. This is a good lunch stop if you're exploring the southern end of the island.

Akrotiri. *©* **22860/83025.** Main courses 7€–12€. Daily noon–midnight.

Exploring the Ancient Sites

Archaeologists have unearthed two ancient sites on Santorini: Ancient Thera, from around the 9th century B.C., and Akrotiri, settled by Minoans from Crete around 3000 B.C. Many of the treasures from these ancient settlements are now in the National Archeological Museum in Athens and elsewhere. Even so, the island makes a good showing of delicately painted cups, jugs, *pithoi,* and other artifacts from both in Fira's **Museum of Prehistoric Thera**, near the bus station, with some wonderful fresco fragments, and the nearby **Archaeological Museum,** to the north on Erithrou Stavrou, founded in 1902 (*©* **22860/22217** for both). They're open daily except Monday, 8:30am to 3pm. Admission to each is 2€ or part of combined ticket (see p. 159).

Ancient Akrotiri ★★★ ANCIENT SITE   One of the best-preserved ancient settlements in the Aegean, the so-called Minoan Pompeii was settled by Minoans who sailed over from Crete as early as 3000 B.C. By 2000 B.C., Akrotiri

Ancient Sites Ticket Package

For 14€, you can purchase a ticket package that includes all of Santorini's archeological sites and museums: Ancient Akrotiri, Ancient Thera, the Archaeological Museum, the Museum of Prehistoric Thera, and the Collection of Icons and Ecclesiastical Artifacts at Pyrgos. The ticket is good for 4 days.

was a flourishing urban center that grew olives and grain, created fanciful art, wove beautiful textiles, sent trade ships to ports as far away as Egypt, and took peace so much for granted that residents saw no need to build defensive walls.

Buried deep in ash during the eruption of 1600 B.C. Akrotiri was not uncovered for another 3,300 years, by workers mining ash and pumice in 1860. No human remains and valuables were ever found, suggesting that the inhabitants had enough warning to flee the city. What they could not take with them were the magnificent paintings that once covered the walls of their public buildings and homes. Those are now in the National Archaeological Museum in Athens (and stunningly re-created in Fira; see p. 160), but on site you can still see some 40 stores, warehouses, and houses lining Akrotiri's main street, which are remarkably well preserved, as well as many giant *pithoi* (earthenware jars) and their contents of oil, fish, and onions. More than two-thirds of the town still remains covered and may one day reveal more treasures and secrets of the past. One of the island's famously colored beaches, Paralia Kokkini (Red Beach), is next to Akrotiri and is at most times pleasantly uncrowded.

6km (4 miles) W of Pyrgos. odysseus.culture.gr. © **22860/81366.** Admission 12€ or part of combined ticket (see above). Tues–Sun 8:30am–3pm.

Ancient Thera ★★ ANCIENT SITE   This ancient city high atop a rocky headland reaffirms the notion that the ancients never underestimated the value of a good location. The town was settled in the 9th century B.C., and since then Egyptian sanctuaries, Greek temples, Roman baths, and Byzantine walls have risen atop the seaside cliffs. The ruins are a jumble left behind by these different cultures, but the views are so dizzying you probably won't mind a little confusion. Most striking is the **Stoa Basilike** (Royal Porch), a colonnade 40m (131 ft.) long and 10m (33 ft.) wide, built in part by Egyptian troops of Ptolemy, garrisoned on Santorini in the 3rd century B.C. The large **Terrace of the Festivals** in front of the **Temple to Apollo Karneios** was the stage for the Karneia, a Greek festival in which Ephebes, adolescent males undergoing strict military training, danced naked; the display was more than a little erotic, and it's been suggested that the spectacle inspired a large phallus carved onto a nearby wall with the inscription "to my friends." The youth trained in the **Gymnasium of the Ephebes** and bathed afterward in facilities that the Romans fashioned into elaborate baths. Below the promontory is the most famous beach on Santorini: Kamari—a dramatic swath of silky black sand.

6km (4 miles) E of Akrotiri, 10km (6 miles) SE of Fira. odysseus.culture.gr. © **22860/31366.** Admission 4€ or part of combined ticket (see above). Tues–Sun 8am–3pm.

Thera Foundation: The Wall Painting of Thera ★★MUSEUM The island's greatest archaeological treasures are the stunning frescoes found virtually intact in Akrotiri, among the largest and most intact artworks to come down from such a distant past. While the originals were carted off to the National Archaeological Museum in Athens (p. 93), where they are star attractions, these reproductions, re-created in sophisticated three-dimensional photographs, are stunning. The images of monkeys (indicating trade with North Africa), ships sailing past leaping dolphins, cows, and young women gathering saffron reveal much about this early society that disliked war and admired beauty. The view over the caldera from the museum terrace is as memorable as the scenes depicted.

Petros M. Nomikos Conference Center, Fira, on caldera path past cable car. www. idryma-theras.org.gr. ℂ**22860/23016.** Admission 4€. May–Sept daily 10am–8pm.

Around the Island

FIRA ★

The island capital surrendered its soul to tourism several decades ago, but the cliffside setting remains as intoxicating as ever. From **Ypapantis,** the walkway that follows the rim of the caldera, the view is never less than staggering. The blue sea sparkles some 300m (984 ft.) below, cliffs take on multicolored hues in the sun, and white houses appear to tumble from the cliff tops. This extraordinary vista is especially dramatic from the stepped path that winds down the cliff face to the little harbor of **Fira Skala,** or you can board a cable car for the descent and ascent. Tour guides will try to cajole you into mounting a donkey for the ride down and up the cliff-face, but leave the poor sway-backed beasts in peace; the cable car makes the trip in 2 minutes, runs every 15 minutes from 7:30am to 9pm, and costs 3€.

A good refuge from the crowds along shop-lined Erythron Stavron street is the nearby **Megaro Gyzi Cultural Centre ★★**, next to the Cathedral of St. John (www.megarogyzi.gr/en; ℂ 22860/22244). Fascinating photographs show Santorini as it looked before and just after the last catastrophic seismic event, the earthquake of 1956, which leveled much of the island. The handsome 17th-century mansion that houses the museum is one of the few historic homes in Fira that withstood the quake. Admission is 3€; the museum is open Monday through Saturday 10am to 9pm, Sunday 10am to 4pm. The center is closed from November through April.

CALDERA PATH ★★★

Walking even a portion of the 10km (6-mile) cliff-top path from Fira to Ia is one of the best experiences you will have on Santorini. Looking over the bay and the crescent of cliffs is like staring into the Grand Canyon—an ever-changing scene in which the rock seems to switch color before your eyes. What looks like a patch of snow takes shape as a cluster of houses; an islet suddenly catches your notice.

Santorini is actually the eastern rim of a volcano and the largest fragment of an island that was blown apart by a series of massive eruptions (the 1600 B.C.

blast was one of the largest volcanic eruptions ever recorded). Looking across the bay, you can see other remnants of the rim, the isles of Therasia and Aspronisi (White Island); in the center are two isles of blackened earth, Nea and Palea Kaimeni (New and Old Burnt Isles), the cones of volcanoes. This geology reveals itself slowly, and its unique beauty seems to intensify with every step you take along the caldera path. Allow at least 2 hours for the walk from Fira to Ia; it's a good idea to start in the morning, before the heat of the day.

FIROSTEFANI ★

This quiet outpost north of Fira is a good place to appreciate the island's beautiful architecture (see box, p. 164). Fira, Firostefani, and many other villages on Santorini were built atop cliffs to protect them from pirates who once marauded around the Aegean. As you walk down any of the lanes descending from the cliff top, note how the white cubical houses huddle together on narrow lanes, one on top of another, many dug into the side of the cliff—impossibly picturesque.

IA ★★★

Santorini's most picturesque village clings to the northwestern tip of the caldera. Once populous and prosperous, home of many of the island's wealthy maritime families, Ia was all but leveled in the earthquake of 1956. Most residents fled, leaving behind a spooky yet beguiling ghost town of half-ruined houses overlooking the caldera. Recent years have been kinder to Ia, however. Nikolaou Nomikou, the main pedestrian way, is lively once again, and the blue Aegean sparkles enticingly below cave houses reclaimed as comfortable hotels.

One of the town's neoclassical mansions, once home to sea captains, now houses the **Naval Maritime Museum** ★ (© 22860/71156). Its figureheads, ship models, and old photographs recall a time when, in the middle of the 19th century, Santorini launched one of the largest merchant fleets in the Aegean. By 1850, more than 200 Santorini vessels were shipping the island's wine to Russia, transporting Russian wheat to ports of call around Europe, and sailing to Athens laden with volcanic pumice from the island, prized for the building craze then transforming Athens, the new nation's capital. Admission is 3€; the museum is open Wednesday to Monday 10am to 2pm and 5 to 8pm.

A small fishing fleet bobs in the sea far below the town in the little port of **Ammoudi,** reached by a flight of 300 stone stairs that wind down the cliff. The quay is lined with a row of tavernas that serve fresh fish right off the boats, and a small pebble beach serves well for a quick swim.

Many visitors flock to Ia to watch the sunset from the walls of the open-air remains of the **Kastro,** at the western edge of town—a spectacular sight, but no more so here than anywhere else on the caldera.

IMEROVIGLI ★★

At the edge of this enchanting little village, tucked into the highest point on the caldera rim further north from Fira, are more of the visual treats so common on Santorini—views of the caldera and Skaros, a rocky promontory below. Skaros was once crowned with an ancient city and later the fortified town of

Rocca, the seat of Venetian nobility and Turkish administrators. After descending the stepped, quiet streets of Imerovigli, then a precipitous drop down a cliff path, you'll reach the rocky heights that connect Skaros to the rest of Santorini. Then it's uphill for 2km (1 mile) or so, along a cliff face of volcanic rock, to the ruins of the fortifications, toppled by earthquakes over the years, and a small chapel. Your rewards for the excursion are phenomenal views over the bay and up the walls of the caldera to the villages glistening on the cliff tops.

PYRGOS ★★

The longtime capital of the island under the Venetians and Turks, Pyrgos is inland, far out of the way of harm that could arrive by sea. Pyrgos makes a striking appearance as you approach from the flat, arid landscapes of the coastal plain: A cone of tiered houses rises on the flanks of a hill beneath a Venetian citadel. Built back-to-back and one on top of the other, the compact white houses provided a phalanx against invaders, and the lanes that tunnel beneath them could be blockaded to keep out invaders. The once mighty castle at the top of this medieval maze was indeed impenetrable—but not immune to earthquakes, one of which toppled the walls and towers half a century ago. The overgrown ruins afford views across the island. Pyrgos is 6km (4 miles) south of Fira and easy to reach by bus.

The **monastery of Profitis Elias** ★★ crowns a nearby peak, the tallest on Santorini at almost 1,000m (3,281 ft.). Islanders make their way to these breezy heights not just for the views but to pay tribute to the community that provided a place of refuge and kept Greek traditions alive at a secret school during Turkish rule in the 18th and 19th centuries. A shady series of rooms off the courtyard houses some of the rare books the monks safeguarded, as well as icons. Admission to the monastery is free, though hours are irregular and vary with the comings and goings of the caretakers.

The enterprising monks also produced excellent wine on their steep hillsides, shipping the output all over Europe on their own merchant ship, which flew the monastery banner. Vineyards still grow around Pyrgos and nearby Megalochori. Their vintages, and those of Santorini's other canavas (wineries), rank among the top Greek wines (see box, p. 163). You may want to stop at one or two in your travels around the island.

Beaches on Santorini

Santorini's beaches may not be the best in the Cyclades, but they have the distinction of being carpeted with black and red volcanic sand. They are clustered at the south end of the island, away from the high rim of the caldera. **Kamari** ★★ and **Perissa** ★★, both with black sand, are crowded and backed by hotels and tavernas. Perivolos, an extension of Perissa, in season teems with beautiful people (many topless). **Red Beach (Paralia Kokkini)** ★★, at the end of the road to Ancient Akrotiri, is usually a bit less crowded than other beaches on the island.

Volcano Diving Center (www.scubagreece.com; © **22860/33-177**) at Kamari, offers guided snorkel swims for around 25€ and scuba lessons for

The eruption of 1500 B.C. covered Santorini with ashy volcanic soil that is extremely hospitable to the Assyrtiko grape, a hardy variety that yields the island's distinctly dry whites and *vin santo*, a sweet dessert wine. Some 36 other varieties grow on Santorini as well, including the white Athyri and Aidani and the red Mantilaria and Mavrotagano. Growers twist the vines into low-lying basket shapes that hug the ground for protection against the wind, and nighttime mists off the sea provide just enough moisture. Several wineries offer tastings and tours; most of the larger operations cater to busloads of passengers from cruise ships, so don't expect a winery visit to be low-key. Some of the top wineries that offer tastings are **Boutari,** in Megalochori (℡ **22860/81011**); **Antoniou,** in Megalochori (℡ **22860/23557**); and **Santo,** in Pyrgos (℡ **22860/22596**). The enormous tasting rooms and terraces at Antoniou and Santo overlook the caldera, adding a bit of drama to enhance your tippling. For an introduction to Santorini wines, visit **www.santorini. org/wineries**. On minibus excursions with **Santorini Wine Tours** ★★★, professional sommelier and informative and gracious guide Vaios Panagiotoulas takes his guests to several distinctive wineries, with tastings and descriptions of the ins and outs of Santorini grape-growing and winemaking; for information, go to www.santoriniwinetour.com (℡ **22860/28358**).

around 60€. The **Santorini Dive Center,** at Perissa, also has scuba and snorkel facilities and instruction (www.divecenter.gr; ℡ **22860/83-190**).

Excursion from Santorini

A fleet of excursion boats take visitors to **Nea Kaimeni (New Burnt Isle),** one of the cones of the volcano that still smolders in the caldera, and they often also stop for a swim in the hot springs that bubble up off **Palea Kaimeni (Old Burnt Isle).** Boats then continue to the quiet island of **Therasia,** a fragment of the rim across the caldera from Santorini, for lunch. All in all, this is a pleasant outing but not essential, especially if your time on Santorini is short. Excursions usually cost about 20€ and can be arranged with any of the legion of tour operators on the island; most boats leave from Armeni, below Ia.

Santorini Shopping

Santorini is an island of jewelers. The most renowned shop, with lovely reproductions of ancient baubles, is **Kostas Antoniou** (℡ **22860/22-633**), on Ayiou Ioannou, north of the cable car station in Fira. **Porphyra** (℡ **22860/22-981**), near the Orthodox cathedral, also has impressive work. The **Bead Shop** (℡ **22860/25-176**), by the Museum of Prehistoric Thira, sells beads, of course, most carved from island lava.

In Firostephani, **Cava Sigalas Argiris** (℡ **22860/22-802**) stocks all the local wines, including their own. Also for sale are locally grown and prepared foods, often served as *mezedes: fava,* a spread made with chickpeas; *tomatahia,* small pickled tomatoes; and *kapari* (capers).

Cycladic Architecture

On Santorini and other Cycladic Islands, houses were crowded together, one on top of another with common walls, to make optimal use of the land, provide protection, and save money and labor when materials often had to be transported on the backs of donkeys. Many houses on Santorini were built into the cliff face for extra economy (some of the most luxurious hotels on the island now occupy such cave dwellings). Walls were thick for warmth in the winter and for coolness in the summer, and windows were small. Often the only windows were in the front of the house, on either side of a windowed door, above which a clerestory window was placed to emit light and let hot air trapped near the ceiling escape—still a feature in many Santorini hotel rooms. Local materials on Santorini were red and black volcanic stone and "Theran earth," a volcanic ash that served as mortar. Roofs were vaulted, an efficient way to bridge interior spaces without using support beams and to allow rain to run off into cisterns, where it was stored for drinking and irrigation. Even many flat-roofed houses are vaulted, with parapets built atop the vaults to serve as terraces or passageways to more houses.

Replica (✆ **22860/71-916**), on the main street in Ia, is a source of contemporary statuary and pottery as well as museum replicas. **Atlantis,** an English-language bookshop down the street (www.atlantisbooks.org; ✆ **22860/72346**), is a haven for visitors hungry for good literature, and is a friendly meeting spot as well.

Santorini Nightlife

Witnesses have been celebrating the quality of light in Santorini for centuries, probably even millennia: It's ethereal. It's transcendent. It's, to sum it up, romantic, especially at sunset. Many visitors traipse to Ia to watch the end-of-day spectacle from there, while other discerning viewers enjoy the fiery scene as a backdrop for a cocktail on the terrace of **Franco's** (www.francos.gr; ✆ **22860/24428**) or **Palaia Kameni** (www.paliakameni.com; ✆ **22860/ 22430**), caldera-side bars in Fira. As the evening wears on, the young usually find their way to the string of ever-changing discos on the seaside in Kamari, on the island's east coast. Quieter venues in Fira include the stunning Pool Bar at the **Aressana Hotel** (www.aressana.gr; ✆ **22860/23900**) and the very mellow **Cori Rigas Art Café** (coririgasartcafe.com; ✆ **22860/25251**), just off the caldera path below the Museum of Prehistoric Thira. The **Kira Thira,** just south of the Archaeological Museum on Ipapantis (✆ **690/909-7271**) is a serious, adult jazz bar with live music some nights and muted, conversation-inducing selections on others. In Ia, **Restaurant-Bar 1800** (www.oia-1800.com; ✆ **22860/71485**) keeps the evening going with a lively bar scene well into the wee hours.

SIFNOS ★★★

Sifnos is the favorite getaway of too many people to be a well-kept secret, but it's still one of the most beautiful—even, at times, serene—islands in the

Cyclades. The mountains that frame Sifnos's deep harbor, Kamares, are barren, but as the road climbs from the port, you will see elegantly ornamented dovecotes above cool green hollows, old (no one really knows just how old) fortified monasteries, and watchtowers that stand astride the summits of arid hills. The beautiful slate and marble paths across the island, *monopati,* are miracles of care—you'll come across islanders washing them—and Sifnos is a walker's delight. It's astonishingly green, not only in spring but well into the summer. Beaches along the southern coast offer long stretches of fine amber sand; several smaller rocky coves are also excellent for swimming. Sifnos does not have much in the way of nightlife and has no must-see sights, but the allure is just wandering those green hillsides and dazzlingly white villages, and finding a place to enjoy the water along the cove-etched coastline. In the interest of full disclosure, if you decide to visit Sifnos in August, when much of well-to-do Athens seems to be transplanted to the island, you might have a decidedly less favorable impression.

Essentials

ARRIVING   By Boat   Weather permitting, there are at least four boats daily from Piraeus, including car ferries and fast boats, some of which take cars. They arrive at Kamares, the island's port. From Kamares the road climbs through a narrow gorge, past olive groves, and emerges at **Apollonia,** the island's main settlement, about 5km (3 miles) southeast. Ferries travel on ever-changing schedules to other islands, including **Serifos, Kimolos Milos, Tinos, Paros,** and **Kithnos.** Boats are notoriously late and/or early; your travel or ticket agent will give you an estimate of times involved in above journeys. If you have time to kill waiting for your boat, have a seat by the dock at the Poseidon Café, where an ouzo and *mezedes* cost only a few euro.

VISITOR INFORMATION   The best place on the island for information and help getting a hotel room, boat tickets, car, motorbike, or hiking excursion is **Aegean Thesaurus Travel and Tourism ★★**, with offices on the port (www.thesaurus.gr; ⓒ **22840/32-152**) and on the main square in Apollonia (ⓒ **22840/33-152**). Just off the main square in Apollonia, **Xidis Travel** (www. xidis.com.gr; ⓒ **22840/32-373**) is another good travel agent.

GETTING AROUND   Apollonia's central square, Plateia Iroon (which locals simply call the Plateia or Stavri), is the main **bus** stop for the island. Buses run regularly to and from the port at Kamares, north to Artemonas and Cheronisso, east to Kastro, and south to Faros, Platis Yialos, and Vathi. Apollonia's main square is also the island's primary **taxi** stand. There are about 10 taxis on the island, each privately owned; you can get their mobile phone numbers from travel agents and some cafes. Most hotels, restaurants, and shops will call a taxi for you; offer to pay for the call.

Many visitors come to Sifnos for the wonderful hiking and mountain trails, but still want the convenience of a **car, motorcycle,** or **ATV** (all-terrain vehicle). Reliable agencies include **Aegean Thesaurus** (ⓒ **22840/33-151**), in Apollonia and **Proto Moto Car** (www.protomotocar.gr; ⓒ **22840/33-792**),

Sifnians were among the wealthiest of the ancient Greeks, thanks to the silver and gold they mined. They flaunted their riches and made especially lavish offerings to Apollo on the sacred island of Delos (p. 149). One year the greedy Sifnians decided to substitute gilded lead for their offering of gold. Apollo, of course, detected the ruse and wreaked his revenge by conjuring an earthquake that caused the mines to flood. The mines on Sifnos did indeed stop yielding riches, but on account of natural causes. Many of the mines were dug beneath sea level and eventually filled with water; others were simply depleted of their precious minerals over time.

with a quayside office in Kamares and offices in Apollonia and Plati Yialos. In high season, you should reserve ahead. The daily rate for an economy car with full insurance is from 30€; a moped or ATV rents from 20€.

Where to Stay on Sifnos

Akti Hotel Plati Yialos ★★   The island's nicest beach hotel overlooks the cove in Plati Yialos, set apart from the rest of the town's densely populated beach strip. The sand beach slopes gently into the sea, ideal for children, and ground-floor guest rooms, with patios facing the garden and water, are also well suited to young travelers. Rooms on upper floors command sweeping sea views from their balconies. All the accommodations are bright and attractive, studies in white on white (white furnishings against white floors and walls) with the blue sea beyond. A flagstone sun deck extends from the beach to a dive platform at the end of the cove.

Platis Yialos. www.platys-gialos.gr. © **22840/71-324.** 21 units. 100€-200€ double. Rates include breakfast. **Amenities:** Restaurant; bar; Wi-Fi (free). Closed Oct–Mar.

Elies Resort ★   Sifnos has always been sophisticated, but quietly so, and this swank retreat on a hillside above Vathy brings a big dose of glossy glamour to the island. Whether this is a welcome change depends on your taste and budget (many islanders resent the intrusion). Lavish rooms and suites are full of contemporary style and comforts, many with private pools; indoor/outdoor restaurants are excellent; and a large swimming pool sparkles above a sandy beach. Best of all, the beautiful seaside village of Vathy is just beyond the gates.

Vathy. www.eliesresorts.com. © **22840/34000.** 32 units. 240€–340€ double. **Amenities:** Restaurant; bar; pool; beach; spa; tennis courts; Wi-Fi (free). Closed Oct–Apr.

Hotel Anthoussa ★   These rooms above the very popular Gerontopoulos Cafe are right in the center of town. They face a flowery garden or look out to the surrounding hills, but even so, all of Sifnos seems to congregate outside the windows, so don't expect a quiet getaway. Rooms are simple yet appealing, with crisp blue fabrics and homey furnishings, and the location makes a handy base for exploring the rest of the island by bus. The open-air cafe downstairs is a great place to linger.

Apollonia. hotelanthousa-sifnos.gr. © **22840/31431.** 15 units. From 90€ double. **Amenities:** Cafe; garden; Wi-Fi (free). Closed Oct–Apr.

Petali Village Hotel ★★★ This comfortable perch is high above Apollonia, requiring a walk uphill from the square but ensuring views across the villages and the rolling interior hills to the sea. The extremely comfortable rooms and suites are large and attractive and face well-kept gardens from large terraces. All the village sights and services are within walking distance, and the pool and the summertime-only restaurant are most welcome after a day of sightseeing.

Apollonia. sifnoshotelpetali.com. © **22840/32152.** 25 units. 120€–200€. Rates include breakfast. **Amenities:** Restaurant; bar; pool; Wi-Fi (free).

Where to Eat on Sifnos

Sifnos is famous for its olive oil and sophisticated cooking; in fact, "Tselementes," a Greek slang term for cookbook, is a tribute to the famous 20th-century Sifnian chef and cookbook writer, Nikos Tselementes. As you travel around Sifnos, you'll notice a lot of bakeries (a bakery is called a *furno* in Greece) and sweet shops. Among the island's most popular bakeries are **Katerina Theodorou,** on the main street in Aretmonas, and **Gerontopoulos Pastry Shop** in the Hotel Anthousa in Apollonia.

Boulis Taverna ★★ GREEK   It's worth the trip down to the port just to enjoy a meal at this friendly taverna lined with wine casks. Many of the tavernas in town are good and do a brisk business with diners coming and going from the port, but Boulis is the best, serving delicious salads and grilled chicken and lamb that the family produces on its farm. You can follow up a meal with a walk on the town's sandy beach.

Kamares. © **22840/31648.** Main courses 6€–12€. Daily noon–midnight.

Chrysopigi ★★ GREEK/SEAFOOD   You can see the seaside monastery of the same name from the shady terrace of this very relaxed taverna on Apokofto Beach. Caper salad and other Sifnos specialties are made daily, and fresh fish from the fleet at Faros, just around the headland, is grilled to perfection.

Apokofto. © **22840/71295.** Main courses 5€–15€. Daily noon–11pm. Closed Oct–Apr.

A Baker's Dozen

A Sifnian baker named Benios (pronounced *Ve-ni-os*) once had 13 children—a baker's dozen—and almost all the children and their children's children and successive generations of the Venios family became bakers. Several bakeries in Sifnos to this day are owned by one or another member of the Venios family. Many families, and even some restaurants, send their *revithia* (chickpeas) in a Sifnian clay pot to a Venios bakery to be slow-cooked overnight for a traditional Sunday dinner.

To Liotivi ★★ GREEK   One of the oldest and best-known restaurants on Sifnos has introduced legions of travelers to caper salad, chickpea croquettes, and other island specialties. Service is not always first-rate, but a meal on the square out front or in a cozy dining room is still a memorable experience. Artemonas ©**22840/31246.** Main courses 8€–15€. Daily noon–11pm.

Exploring the Apollonia Villages ★★

The island's capital, Apollonia, is really a cluster of six villages (or five or seven, depending on whom you ask) that tumble across the inland hills in haphazard fashion, a jumble of whitewashed houses and blue-domed churches interspersed with vineyards, orchards, and gardens. Flagstone footpaths delicately outlined in whitewash wind through the villages and converge on **Plateia Iroon** (Hero's Square). A bus from the port in Kamares makes the trip up here to the square hourly from about 6am to midnight every day in summer. To one side of the square, the **Popular and Folk Art Museum** (admission 2€) is a showplace for island embroidery and weaving, along with the earthenware pots and jars that Sifnians once loaded onto ships in exchange for staples. The museum is generally open July to mid-September, daily 10am to 1pm and 6 to 10pm. A short walk west up a path brings you to the **Panagia Ouranophora** (Church of Our Lady of the Heavenly Light), where a relief of St. George crowns the doorway. A marble column and a few other fragments of a temple to Apollo are scattered about the shady courtyard.

Artemonas ★ VILLAGE   The path from Plateia Iroon rises through the quiet village of Ano Petali, drops down to a stone bridge across the Marinou River, then climbs into the most beautiful of the Apollonia villages. The remains of a temple to Artemis, sister of Apollo and goddess of virginity and the hunt, are said to be buried beneath the **Kochi,** one of several churches that rise above the village rooftops. **Panagia tou Barou** (Church of Our Lady of the Baron) is named for one of the Italian nobles who ruled Sifnos from the 15th through early 17th centuries. The baron allegedly fell in love with a nun in a nearby monastery and turned his unrequited ardor toward local women; his offspring soon populated the quarter, known ever since as the Barou in his honor.

A bust of a more respectable resident, Nicholas Chrysogetos, stands near the village square. The surroundings have changed little since this hero of the 1821 War of Independence taught in Artemonas before becoming Greece's first minister of education. This is a nice spot in which to linger and sip a coffee before resuming your wanderings along any of the lanes that lead off the square.

Exambala ★ VILLAGE   The name of the southernmost of the Apollonia villages translates as "trouble in the night"—a reference to the days under Turkish rule when the village was famous for spirited, independence-oriented rhetoric and song that often got out of hand as the nights wore on. On a hillside just outside the village the large, whitewashed monastery of **Kyria Vryssiani** (Sacred Spring) stands among olive groves. The cool spring that still bubbles forth in the courtyard is said to supply the freshest water on the island.

Around Sifnos

The island is not known for its beaches, though **Chrysopigi** (p. 167) and **Vathy** (p. 170) are beautiful places to get into the water. **Kamares,** the port, has a nice sandy beach. **Plati Yialos,** on the island's south coast, is the only bonafide beach resort on Sifnos. This one-street town is pleasant enough but pretty much devoid of character and exists only for tourism during high season.

Ayios Andreas ★★ CHURCH/ANCIENT SITE   One reason to make a vigorous 20-minute hike up to this hilltop church is to enjoy the almost 360-degree view of Sifnos and neighboring islands. (Less sportingly, a road also climbs to the summit.) Another reason is to explore the excavations of an **ancient acropolis,** and its excellent small site museum. People have lived on this spot from perhaps the 13th century B.C. until at least the 4th century B.C. Massive walls that once stood some 6m (20 ft.) high (shorter versions still stand here) encircled the settlement, with its sanctuary of Artemis and small houses. From the site, you can see the remains of some of Sifnos's more than 80 stone towers that were used for defense and for communication: bonfires could flash messages quickly across the island from tower to tower. All this and more is explained in the excellent museum, where everything is labeled both in Greek and English.

2km (1 mile) S of Apollonia. Free admission (but fee may soon be imposed). Tues–Sun 8:30am–3pm.

Chrysopigi ★★★ LANDMARK/RELIGIOUS SITE   The Monastery of Panagia Chrysopigi (the Golden Wellspring) has been close to the heart of Sifnians since it was founded atop a rocky islet in 1650 to house an icon of the Virgin Mary that fishermen found washed up on the rocks. The image soon miraculously intervened to save the island from the plague—and came to the rescue again in 1928, when locusts descended upon the island. Yet another miracle occurred when two women fled to the monastery to escape pursuing pirates. They prayed to the Virgin, who interceded by creating a deep chasm in the rocks to separate Chrysopigi from the mainland (a bridge now crosses the rift above the churning sea). Fishermen bring their sons to the monastery to be baptized in a font on a rocky point at the very edge of the surf, and in so doing ensure that the boys will forever be safe from the perils of the seafaring life. You can contemplate the beautiful, still-active monastery with its simple church from a sandy beach, Apokofto, nestled alongside an adjacent cove. A stone path leads around a headland to **Faros,** a small fishing village that takes its name from the lighthouse that guides the fleet past the rocky shoreline.

8km (5 miles) SE of Apollonia. Church open occasionally, hours vary; courtyard always open.

Kastro ★★ TOWN   While the villages of Apollonia are light and airy, Kastro, is somberly medieval, a fortress hugging a rocky promontory above the surf. The capital of Sifnos under Venetian rule, it was virtually unassailable, made so by a row of connected houses that form a solid defensive wall around the inner town. Tunnel-like passages lead into a maze of little lanes and tiny squares lined with tall Venetian-era houses—and littered here and there with sarcophagi left behind by the Romans who occupied Sifnos. The two-room **Archaeological Museum** (free admission) displays bits of pottery and friezes from the ancient city that occupied these heights 3,000 years ago. The museum is open Tuesday through Sunday, 8:30am to 3pm. The **Church of the Eftamartyres (Seven Martyrs)** sits atop a sea-girt promontory far beneath a clifftop promenade that skirts the town's outer flanks. The scene of the white chapel practically floating on the waves is remarkably picturesque, especially when wind-whipped waves buffet the sturdy white walls.

4km (2½ miles) E of Apollonia. Frequent bus service from Apollonia.

Profitis Elias o Pilos ★★ LANDMARK/RELIGIOUS SITE   The highest mountain on the island rises 850m (2,789 ft.) and is topped by an isolated monastery. O Pilos means "high one," a term that takes on special meaning as you make the 1-hour-long climb on a well-worn path, the only means of access, and regard the panoramic views across what seems like most of the Aegean Sea. A monk is often on hand to show you around the thick-walled courtyard and chapel and offer a glass of cool water. The monastery celebrates the feast of Elias around July 20, when hundreds of celebrants make a night-time pilgrimage up to the monastery carrying torches.

Well-marked trail begins 2km (1 mile) W of Apollonia in Katavati, a tiny hamlet just south of Exambala, and involves a steep ascent.

Vathy ★★ TOWN   Until a new road was laid about 15 years ago, the only way to reach Vathy was on foot, donkey, or boat. Even with this road linking it to the rest of the island, Vathy remains a serene getaway, a small collection of houses alongside a beach of fine sand and backed by a verdant valley. This setting is made all the more beautiful by the presence of the **Monastery of the Taxiarchis Evangelistrias (Archangel of the Annunciation),** so close to the seaside that the whitewashed walls and a bell tower seem to rise out of the water. *Note:* If you follow the *monopati* footpath across the island to Vathy from Chrysopigi, at the top of the peninsula above the Bay of Platos Yialos you'll notice the **Aspro Pirgos,** or White Tower, a lookout post built round 500 B.C., when the mines of Sifnos still yielded gold and the island was an important Aegean outpost.

12km (7 miles) W of Chrysopigi by road, 5km (3 miles) by path.

Sifnos Shopping

Famed in antiquity first for its precious metals, then for its ceramics, Sifnos still produces some wonderful brown glaze pottery with minimalist white decorative swirls. As you crisscross the island, you'll see signs advertising pottery workshops. **Simos and John Apostolidis** (✆ **22840/71-258**) are among the few potters who still have a workshop in the resort town of Plati Yialos, once a pottery center. In Kamares, **Antonis Kalogerou** (✆ **22840/31-651**) sells folk paintings of island life as well as pottery manufactured in his showroom, from the deep gray or red clay mined in the inland hill region. In Apollonia, Kastro, and Artemonas a number of shops sell pottery, but it's mostly from neighboring Paros (p. 178)—Parian pottery is distinguished by its bright colors, shiny glazes, and scenes of fruit, flowers, and island life. For those in search of distinctive jewelry, Spyros Koralis's **Ble** (*C* **22840/33-055**), in Apollonia, does innovative work in silver and gold.

NAXOS ★★

One of the first tourists to visit Naxos must have been the god Dionysus, who descended to the island to sweep the jilted Ariadne off her feet. It's easy to see why he chose Naxos for his amorous pursuit. It's the largest and greenest island in the Cyclades, with fertile valleys overlooked by proud villages, abundant fields (potatoes are a famous staple), long stretches of sand, and even the highest mountain in the Cyclades—Mount Zas, associated in antiquity with Zeus, who felt at home on lofty eminences.

Rising from these scenic landscapes are temples, Venetian towers, and Byzantine churches. Despite such a wealth of natural beauty and monuments, Naxos is, blessedly, also one of the lesser traveled of the major Cyclades. While the justifiably popular beaches are a magnet for throngs of sun-loving northern Europeans, the villages and countryside can often seem appealingly isolated.

Essentials

ARRIVING The Naxos airport handles two to four **Olympic Air** flights a day to and from Athens, depending on the season (www.olympicair.com; *C* **810/114-4444**). **Aegean Airlines** offers a few flights a week (www. aegean air.com; *C* **801/11 20000**). Planes are small, and seats sell out quickly, so in high season especially, book early if you plan to fly. The island is also well connected by at least twice-daily boat service to and from Piraeus, with both high-speed and regular ferries. There's fairly frequent service as well to and from **Paros, Santorini, Mykonos, Siros,** and the other Cyclades. For ferry tickets, try **Zas Travel** (www.zastravel.com; *C* **22850/23-330**), on the Paralia opposite the ferry pier, or any of the other agents along the waterfront. The website **www.gtp.gr** is a useful resource for ferry schedules, but keep in mind that due to winds, boats in the Cyclades often run late.

VISITOR INFORMATION Naxos does not have a municipal tourist office, though several agencies along the Naxos Town waterfront can provide maps and information. The website **naxostoday.com** is also a good resource.

GETTING AROUND The **bus** station is on the harbor, and schedules are posted there (though they are not always up to date). In summer, there's service every 30 minutes to the nearby south coast beaches at Ayios Prokopios, Ayia Anna, and Plaka. Buses also run several times a day to and from other places on the island. In summer, the competition for seats on the beach routes can be fierce, so get to the station well ahead of time.

Where to Stay on Naxos

Chateau Zevgoli ★★   A medieval mansion tucked next to the walls of the Kastro, high above the harbor, has so much charm and character that you will not mind the trek through the narrow lanes to the front patio—taxis can't get anywhere close. Once inside the three-story landmark, a welcoming, beamed lounge surrounds a fireplace and is filled with family heirlooms of owner Despini Kitini. Marble-floored, tastefully done guest rooms surround a plant-filled courtyard. Several have sea-view balconies, and all exude a vaguely exotic, old-world flair, with dark furnishings and a few antiques here and there. Two apartments have been fashioned out of a 13th-century Venetian house nearby. Ms. Kitini is an energetic host who will ensure that your stay is close to perfection and that you experience the best of the island.

Bourgo, just below Kastro. www.naxostownhotels.com.© **22850/25201.** 14 units. 90€–120€ double. Rates include breakfast. **Amenities:** Bar; Wi-Fi (free).

Studios Kalergis ★★   Agios Yeoryios (St. George) beach is at the southern edge of Naxos Town, about a 10-minute walk away from the center and surrounded by a pleasant neighborhood of white houses and small hotels. Facing a luxuriant garden and the sands are these bright, attractive studios with well-equipped kitchenettes, all stylishly decorated with painted wood ceilings and handsome traditional pieces. Upper floor units open off a big terrace and have breezy sea-view balconies, while those on the lower floor share many shady nooks tucked amid the garden greenery, with the beach just on the other side of a low wall. An adjacent beachside cafe serves an excellent breakfast (not included in room rates), as well as snacks and drinks into the early evening.

Agios Yeoryios, Naxos Town. studios-kalergis.com.© **22850/22425.** 18 units. 80€–120€ double. **Amenities:** Cafe; beach; Wi-Fi (free).

Villa Marandi ★★★   A stone and stucco villa set in seaside gardens surrounding a large pool fulfills just about anyone's fantasy of a Greek island retreat. Beautifully designed and maintained rooms are large, stylish, and supremely comfortable, with crisp fabrics and casually elegant custom pieces. All have large, well-furnished terraces, most with sea views. A private strip of beach is at the end of the garden path, while the island's spectacular west coast beaches, Naxos Town, and other island sights are all an easy drive away. Even so, it's hard to pull yourself away from the beautiful garden, where an expert staff serves cocktails and inspired Mediterranean-style meals and plenty of shady spots encourage hours of lazy idling.

Stelida, 5km (3 miles) W of Naxos Town© **2285/024652.** 16 units. 150€–220€ double. Rates include buffet breakfast. **Amenities:** Restaurant; bar; beach; Wi-Fi (free).

Where to Eat on Naxos

Fortify your wanderings around Naxos with local cheeses and olives from **Tirokomika Proionda Naxou** (© **022850/22230**), a fragrant, old-fashioned food emporium on Papavasiliou, Naxos Town's main inland shopping street, just off the waterfront. Accompany your choices with a selection of island wines from **Pamponas** on the waterfront Paralia (✆ **22850/22258**); the shop also stocks *kitro,* a lemon liqueur for which many Naxian households have a secret recipe. You will be offered a free tasting here—and you're likely to stagger away with a bottle or two.

Lithos ★★★ MODERN GREEK   A stylishly contemporary dining room tucked far away from the clamor of the waterfront beneath the walls of the Kastro is a quiet refuge of glistening white walls and floors accented with bright colors. In good weather, the kitchen's simple yet satisfying creations are also served by a friendly sister and brother team at tables strung out along the steep lane out front. A small but tempting menu offers a refreshing change from standard taverna fare: *kritharoto* is a creamy risotto with sausage and feta, carmelized pork belly is succulent and delicious, and seafood linguine is laden with clams and fresh fish. If you're on the island long enough, you'll probably want to return a few times to try everything on the menu.

Just beneath Trani Porta. Naxos Town. ✆ **2285/026602.** Main courses 5€–10€. Daily noon–midnight.

Taverna Lefteris ★★ GREEK   Aprianthos, the prettiest of the Tragaea Valley villages (p. 175), is the setting for one of the island's nicest dining spots, where a traditional tavern meal might be the focus of a trip into the mountains—a drive through the valley and a meal here are the components of a near-perfect day on Naxos. The freshest of vegetables and meats are prepared with admirable subtlety in such staples as fava beans with carmelized onions, peppers and feta, and simply grilled pork fillets. Meals are enhanced with hearty homemade bread, capped with delicious sweets, and served in a marble-floored dining room and on terrace shaded by two massive walnut trees.

Aprianthos. ✆ **22850/61333.** Main courses 5€–10€. Daily 11am–11pm.

Taverna to Kastro ★★ GREEK   An animated table-filled square just outside the south gate of the Kastro makes an ideal spot for a meal on a summer evening. Views extend over the rooftops to the sea and St. George's beach, and there's a wonderful sense of calm in this hillside aerie. Simply grilled meats and fish dishes are accompanied by roasted, locally grown potatoes and other fresh island produce; the house specialty is rabbit stewed in red wine with onions, spiced with pepper and cinnamon.

Braduna Sq., Naxos Town. ✆ **22850/22-005.** Main courses 7€–15€. Daily 7pm–2am.

Exploring Naxos Town

From the harbor, it's an easy climb along little lanes through Bourgo, the lower town, up to the hilltop Kastro, the mighty fortress of the Venetians who ruled Naxos from 1207 until it fell to the Turks in 1566. The name Kastro also applies to the neighborhood of handsome Venetian-style mansions that huddle beneath the fortress walls.

Bourgo ★ NEIGHBORHOOD   Along the waterfront today, cafes line pedestrian-only Parali, entry to the busy streets of the Bourgo, the lower section of the Old Town. During Venetian rule, the grandees lived above in the Kastro, while the Bourgo was home to the Greek citizens of Naxos. But even long before that, Mycenaeans, classical Greeks, Romans, and early Christians inhabited this stretch of shoreline. This long past comes to light in the extensive excavations in front of the **Mitripolis** (cathedral), on Cathedral Square just inland from the waterfront, where bits and pieces of ancient chapels, temples, and an agora are well marked. Inside the cathedral, coats of arms of Venetian families litter the marble floor, and Byzantine icons showing Western subjects reflect the mix of Eastern and Western traditions on the island. The excavations are an open site, where you can wander for free. The church is open Tuesday to Sunday, 8am to 2:30pm; admission is free.

Kastro ★★★ NEIGHBORHOOD   Any of the narrow streets winding uphill from the Bourgo lead into the Kastro, the Venetian fortress, and the neighborhood of tall houses, chapels, and convents within its walls. Of the 12 towers once rising above the fortification, only the Tower of Crispi remains. The most impressive way to make the transition from the bustle of the Bourgo into the medieval world of the Kastro is though **Trani Porta** (Strong Gate), via Apollon Street at the northern end of the port. An incision on the right column of the arch marks the length of a Venetian yard, used to measure the cloth merchants brought to Naxos for aristocratic households. The coats of arms of noble medieval Venetian families appear above many doorways, and flowering vines trail over the walls surrounding well-kept gardens. Many residences are still occupied by members of the families who built them; the home of the Dellarocca-Barozzi clan is open to the public as the **Domus Venetian Museum** (© **22850/22387**), next to the Trani Porta. Salons are filled with the furnishings the family has collected during their 800 years of residency, and the garden is the setting for summertime concerts. Admission is 4€; the house is open June to August, daily 10am to 3pm and 7 to 10pm.

Portara ★★★ ANCIENT SITE   A great unfinished doorway stands on the islet of Palatia at the western end of Naxos Town harbor, providing a dramatic backdrop for an approach to the island by sea. According to myth, the god Dionysus built this for Ariadne, daughter of King Minos of Crete. Ariadne helped the youth Theseus escape the maze of the Minotaur at Knossos (p. 196), but Theseus abandoned her on Naxos. Dionysus took pity on the lovesick princess and swept down in a chariot borne by leopards to marry her; the Portara was the gateway to their bridal palace. (This story inspired both Titian's beautiful painting *Bacchus and Ariadne* and the opera *Ariadne auf Naxos* by Richard Strauss.) The more prosaic story is that this was part of a temple begun by the ruler Lygdamis in 530 B.C. in homage to Apollo and abandoned when he was overthrown in 506 B.C. A thousand years later the Venetians carted off much of the temple's marble to build their hilltop Kastro, but this doorframe and lintel, constructed from slabs weighing 20 tons each, were too heavy to move. Along the shore just north of the Portara are some of Greece's oldest antiquities—the submerged remains of houses and steps constructed by Cycladic peoples who lived on the island as long as 5,000 years

Naxos was both Venetian and Turkish for many centuries. In 1210, Venetian duke Marco Sanudo began ruling the Cyclades on behalf of Constantinople; Venetian rule under lax Turkish oversight lasted into the 18th century. The fact that a French School was founded here by Roman Catholic Jesuits in 1627 is testimony to how permissive the Turkish administrators were. Nikos Kazantzakis, the famous Cretan author of *Zorba the Greek* and other modern classics, attended that school in 1896. The island made a lasting impression on the young Kazantzakis, who always remembered it as a land of "great sweetness and tranquility." However, he left abruptly when his father appeared at the door with a torch, demanding, "My boy, you papist dogs, or else it's fire and the ax!" The school's former building is now the **Archaeological Museum** (odysseus. culture.gr; © **22850/22725;** admission 3€), a showplace for sensuous, elongated, white marble Cycladic statuettes that date to 3000 B.C. yet strikingly resemble the work of 20th-century Italian sculptor Amedeo Modigliani. The galleries are open Tuesday through Sunday, 8:30am to 3pm.

ago. You can take a look at the underwater antiquities while swimming off the rocks below the temple door.

Exploring the Tragaea Villages ★★★

Spreading across the center of Naxos, the beautiful Tragaea Valley epitomizes the gorgeous scenery that makes Naxos different from the other Cyclades. Olive groves and lemon orchards climb the slopes of mountainsides, and chapels, monasteries, and small villages overlook countryside that has changed very little from the days of the Byzantines.

Begin in **Moni ★★**, some 18km (12 miles) east of Naxos Town. This lovely mountain village is known throughout Greece for the **Church of Panagia Drosiani (Our Lady of Refreshment),** with its dome and walls of rough-hewn rock. Legend has it that during a drought in the 8th century, Naxians brought icons of the Virgin from churches across the island to the sea to pray for rain: Only the icon from this church yielded results. Some of the oldest frescoes on the walls of the three simple chapels date to the 7th century and are rich with imagery not always seen in Orthodox art. Hours vary, but the church is generally open daily, 8am to 1pm and 4 to 6pm; admission is free but donations are welcome.

Chalki ★, 5km (3 miles) southwest of Moni, surrounds a beautiful plaza, shaded by plane trees. In the 1,500-year-old tile-roofed **Church of Panagia Protothrone (Our Lady Before the Throne),** layers of frescoes date to the 6th century, with the oldest depicting the Apostles. The 17th-century Pirgis Frankopolous, a Venetian tower house, is sometimes open to the public, and from the upper floors you can see a broad swath of the Tragaea Valley.

The white houses of **Filoti ★**, 3km (2 miles) southeast of Chalki, sparkle on the flanks of Mount Zas—which, at a little more than 1,000m (3,281 ft.), is the tallest peak in the Cyclades. The tower of the **Church of Kimisis tis**

Theotokou (Assumption of the Mother of God) stands above the rooftops, a beacon to the revelers who come from all over Naxos in mid-August for the island's biggest *paneyeri* (feast), in honor of the Virgin. Hours vary, but the church is generally open daily, 8am to 1pm and 4 to 6pm; admission is free but donations are welcome. From the village, a trail climbs the face of the mountain to the **Arghia Cave,** one of several caverns in Greece said to be the birthplace of Zeus. The cave is spectacular, entered through a wide natural arch that leads into a main chamber spanning more than 4,000 square meters (43,056 sq. ft.) without support. Tools found in the cave suggest human habitation more than 5,000 years ago.

Wind up your tour in **Apiranthos ★**, 7.5km (4½ miles) northeast of Filoti, where the streets are paved in marble, and the houses are made of rough, gray stone hewn from the mountain. The village is barely distinguishable from the hillside out of which it is carved—as you approach, it seems to appear magically, like some sort of mountain mirage.

Around Naxos

Away from the spectacular yet crowded beach strip on Naxos' southwestern coast are lush valleys, craggy hillsides, and lovely old villages that surround shady squares. Among these rural landscapes you'll find an enticing scattering of antiquities and Byzantine chapels and monasteries.

Agios Mammas ★ CHURCH   One of the oldest churches of Naxos was built under the Byzantines in the 9th century as the island's cathedral, seat of the Greek Orthodox archbishops of the Cyclades. Though abandoned through much of the Middle Ages, the stone church is still a commanding presence on the herb-scented hillside. If you're lucky, the church may be open, but even if it isn't, you can admire its rough-hewn exterior. Views extend far across the countryside where sheep and goats graze—an apt tribute to Mammas, the patron saint of shepherds.

3km (2 miles) S of Pirgos Bellonia on a lane off the road to Sangri, 8km (5 miles) S of Naxos Town.

Apollonas ★ VILLAGE   This once-quiet fishing village on the northern tip of the island is a popular, though undistinguished, summer resort. Besides the good sandy beach, many travelers are attracted here to see a huge *kouros* statue, 10m (33 ft.) tall, which still stands abandoned in the quarry where it was being carved in the 7th century B.C.—most likely because it cracked when it was shifted.

37km (22 miles) NE of Naxos Town.

Melanes ★ ANCIENT SITE   Melanes (also known as Flerio) lies in one of the many verdant vales that carpet the interior of Naxos. In the shady garden of a Venetian estate nestled in a gorge at the end of the valley lies a *kouros,* a huge marble statue of a beautiful youth reclining on a pillow. Some 6m (20 ft.) long, the statue was carved in the 6th century B.C., probably intended for the Sanctuary of Apollo on Delos (p. 149). You can admire the boy's peaceful repose as you sip a beverage at a cafe run by the garden's owner.

About 7km (4 miles) E of Naxos Town on road to Kinidharos. Free admission. Open site.

Pirgos Bellonia (Pirgos Tower) ★ HISTORIC SITE   Venetian overlords built tall fortified towers across Naxos, not only to provide refuge from pirate attacks, but also to keep an eye on their estate workers from the upper stories. When danger was imminent, tower dwellers lit fires on the flat roofs to warn their neighbors. These stone castles may seem like a romantic, fairytale presence in the countryside today, but back in the day they could be most unwelcoming when residents drew up drawbridges and poured boiling oil through the loopholes. An especially elaborate example, the Bellonia tower was once the home of the Venetian archbishop of Naxos—look for an emblem of the Lion of St. Mark, symbol of the Venetian Republic, embedded above the doorway. The tower is a private residence today, though it is sometimes possible to slip into the adjoining twin chapels, one for Roman Catholics and one for Orthodox Catholics.

5km (3 miles) S of Naxos Town, near village of Galando.

Sangri ★★ TOWN   Old tower houses and cypress trees rise from the end of a valley to mark the entrance to Sangri, a cluster of three small villages that tumble into one another on a hillside. **Mount Profitis Elias,** topped with a chapel and a ruined Byzantine fortress, overlooks the villages. At the foot of the mountain is a beautiful fortified monastery, **Timios Stavros (the True Cross),** now abandoned. In the 18th and early 19th century, before Naxos became part of a united Greece, monks here secretly taught Greek language and culture, which had been neglected under the centuries of Venetian and Turkish rule. Sangri's most notable monument is the ruined **Temple of Demeter,** about 5km (3 miles) outside the village on a well-marked dirt road (free admission). Archaeologists have only recently re-erected its columns and pediments, which had lain scattered about the site for centuries. As you gaze upon it, look around: It's only fitting that a temple dedicated to the goddess of grain should be surrounded by fertile fields.

13km (8 miles) SE of Naxos Town.

Naxos Beaches

The capes and promontories of the southwest coast shelter the island's finest beaches, some of the best in the Cyclades. The sandy strands closest to Naxos Town, especially Agios Yeoryios and Agios Prokopios, are fine but crowded; **Agios Yeoryios** ★ is right at edge of town, so can't be topped for convenience if that's where you're staying; its shallow waters are ideal for young swimmers. Busy **Agios Prokopios** ★ is about 8km (5 miles) south of Naxos Town, the first of a long stretch of golden sand along the southwest coast. If you have a car, it's well worth continuing just a little farther south to its less-crowded neighbors **Plaka** ★★, backed by sand dunes and bamboo groves, and **Kastaraki** ★★, etched with rock formations. Both stretch for miles, leaving plenty of room for everyone. **Pyrgaki** ★★★, the southernmost beach on this stretch of coast (though still only 21km/13 miles from Naxos Town), seems a world removed, with empty white sands and crystalline waters edged with fragrant cedar forests. Summertime bus service from Naxos Town serves most of these beaches, running about every half-hour.

PAROS ★★

Marble dug out of Paros quarries was the pride of the ancient world, fashioned into such masterworks as the *Venus de Milo*. The island still yields up all sorts of glittering prizes, making Paros a favorite of travelers who relish a mix of antiquities, sand, sun, and quiet coves—minus the crowds and hype of Mykonos and Santorini. The narrow lanes of Parikia, or Paros Town, are cooled by marble fountains and wind their way to a medieval castle built with chunks pillaged from ancient temples. One of the world's oldest churches, Panagia Ekatontopylani, is a Byzantine masterpiece with a lemon-scented courtyard and a purported 100 doors. Shorelines open to gentle bays, sandy beaches, and little ports like chic Naoussa, where tiny lanes dead-end at the sparkling blue water. In the mountainous hinterlands, Lefkes and other medieval villages are tucked onto terraced hillsides crisscrossed with marble Byzantine paths. And in the highly unlikely event Paros fails to deliver enough of an island getaway, little Antiparos is just a short ferry ride away.

Essentials

ARRIVING   The Paros airport runs several flights a day to and from Athens on **Olympic Air** (www.olympicair.com; ✆ **810/114-4444**). The island is also served by 2 or 3 boats a day from Piraeus in season, and daily ferry and hydrofoil service links the island with **Naxos, Ios, Mykonos, Santorini,** and **Tinos.** Several times a week, boats depart for **Folegandros, Sifnos,** and **Siros.** For general ferry and other travel information, try **Santorineos Travel** (✆ **22840/ 24-245**) or **Polos Tours** (✆ **22840/22-092**), both on the harbor in the island's capital and largest town, Parikia.

VISITOR INFORMATION   A tourist information office on the Parikia waterfront is open daily in summer, and the many nearby travel agencies will also provide information. The island has a number of helpful websites, including **www.parosweb.com** and **www.paroslife.com**.

GETTING AROUND   A good bus network will take you where you need to go on Paros, so a car is not necessary. The main **bus** station (✆ **22840/21-395**) in Parikia is on the waterfront, to the left as you face the windmill. There is often hourly service between Parikia and Naoussa, from 8am to midnight in high season. Other buses run frequently, from 8am to 9pm, in two general directions from Parikia: south to Aliki or Pounda, and southeast to the beaches at Piso Livadi, Chrissi Akti, and Drios, passing the Marathi Quarries and the town of Lefkes along the way. Schedules (not always up-to-date) are usually available at the Parikia bus office.

Where to Stay on Paros

Hotel Dina ★★★   If you're not looking for luxury, you may find these simple rooms that open to balconies and terraces to be your Parian paradise. You reach the nicely old-fashioned accommodations—almost an island institution, having housed guests for the past 35 years—through a narrow, plant-filled courtyard at the quiet end of Parikia's Market Street. There's something about stepping into such a charming, almost-secret enclave that makes you want to slow down and take time to smell the gardenias and savor the serene island **atmosphere.** The choicest of the tidy, plain but comfortable rooms is number 8, at the back, with a balcony that faces a little chapel, so close you can almost reach out and touch the blue dome. Dina Patellis is a gracious and helpful hostess and will tell you what you need to know about seeing the island. Her husband wrote the excellent *Guide Through Ekatontapiliani,* available in local bookshops.

Market St., Parikia. www.hoteldina.com. ⒸⒸ **22840/21-325.** 8 units. 50€–85€ double. **Amenities:** Wi-Fi (free).

Lefkes Village Hotel ★   You'll glimpse this handsome, estate-like enclave on an adjacent hillside as you wander through Lefkes; staying here as a guest will net you similarly stunning views over the town and sea. In fact, with these views, and a delightful swimming pool, you may not mind being away from the beaches and Parikia, 10km (6 miles) away down the mountainside. Bright tile-floored guest quarters are scattered among stone and stucco houses set up to resemble the surrounding village, where joining the residents for an early-evening wander through streets and squares is one of the pleasures of a stay.

Lefkes. www.lefkesvillage.gr. ⒸⒸ **22840/41-827.** 25 units. 200€–210€ double. Rates include buffet breakfast. **Amenities:** Restaurant; bar; Jacuzzi; pool; Wi-Fi (free). Closed Oct–Apr.

Yria Hotel Resort ★★   Like many resorts around Greece, this handsome assemblage on the coast just south of Parikia imitates a Cycladic village, with rooms and suites tucked away in well-tended gardens that are all the more appealing with the blue sea glistening in the distance. A sandy beach is about 150m (500 ft.) down the lane, and the choicest accommodations have sea views. Yet the grounds are so green and soothing that you won't feel deprived if you don't have one, and the pleasant-if-unexciting decor (lots of soft pastels with bright blue and white motifs) and well-furnished terraces are geared to hours of quiet relaxation, as are a huge swimming pool, spa, and tennis courts.

3km (2 miles) S of the port, in Parasporos. www.yriahotel.gr. ⒸⒸ **22840/24-154.** 60 units. From 2750€ double. Rates include breakfast. **Amenities:** Restaurant; bar; concierge; fitness center; pool; tennis; spa; Wi-Fi (free). Closed mid-Nov to Apr.

Where to Eat on Paros

Barbarossa Ouzeri ★ GREEK/MEZEDES   Sitting in an *ouzeri* on the waterfront is part of the Naoussa experience, and this is one of the oldest and best. You can linger for hours over milky ouzo in water in the company of wind-burned fishermen, chic Athenians, and French tourists who seem to enjoy the experience in spite of themselves. Small portions of grilled octopus, olives, and other meze accompany it well; or, if you want more, try the deftly prepared fish.

Naoussa waterfront. ✆ **22840/51-391.** Mezedes 6€–15€. Daily 1pm–1am.

Distrato ★★ GREEK/INTERNATIONAL   It's hard to resist taking a seat beneath the spreading branches of an enormous ficus tree on the street that runs from the cathedral to Market Street. In fact, it seems many habitués never leave, starting the day here with a coffee and croissant and ending it with wine and one of the tasty pasta dishes. The kitchen also serves an assortment of crepes, sandwiches, and salads. A shop stocks nicely packaged organic Greek produce. If there are no tables at Distrato, try **Symposio,** a few steps away, with tasty snacks (great mozzarella and tomato baguette sandwich), minus the shady tree.

Paralia. ✆ **22840/22-311.** Snacks and main courses 8€–15€. Daily 10am–midnight.

Happy Cows ★ GREEK/INTERNATIONAL   The name of this brightly colored room on a little lane off the waterfront suggests a break from traditional taverna fare, and a talented young chef delivers this with flair, without straying too far from the basics. Meat, fish, and produce are all fresh and served in inventive-yet-simple preparations, with several vegetarian options. Pita is topped with juicy tomatoes and creamy feta, salads brim with garden produce, prawns are served in linguine with creamy tomato sauce—all best enjoyed at an outside table.

Off Market St., behind National Bank, Parikia. ✆ **0698/105-3607.** Main courses 8€–15€. Daily 7pm–midnight.

Porphyra ★★ GREEK/SEAFOOD   There's nothing fancy about this waterfront seafood house—strictly utilitarian, the place looks like a big garage—yet the fish and seafood is reputed to be the freshest and best on the island. The owner cultivates the shellfish himself, resulting in exceptional mussels saganaki (mussels cooked with tomato, feta, and wine) and a great fish soup. The tzatziki (cucumber-yogurt dip) and other traditional cold appetizers are also very good.

Parikia waterfront, near the pier. ✆ **22840/22-693.** Main courses 8€–20€. Daily 6:30pm–midnight. Closed Jan–Feb.

Exploring Parikia ★★

In Old Parikia, a pretty cluster of whitewashed Cycladic houses, lanes of paving stones etched with fresh white paint open into shady squares. Here you'll find marble fountains, built under French-Ottoman rule in the late 18th century, inscribed with a jaunty verse that ends, "Come, good folk, every one, take drink but be sparing of me." A stepped street leads into the Kastro, the seaside fortress the Venetians cobbled together in the early 13th century from marble fragments of ancient temples. Pediments and chunks of columns are pieced randomly into the walls, presenting a jumbled glimpse of the classical-era days when Paros grew wealthy from marble quarried on the island by tens of thousands of slaves. The fortress provided the Venetians little protection against pirates, however; they were eventually chased off the island by Barbarossa, the most famous medieval brigand of them all.

Archaeological Museum ★★★ MUSEUM A rich depiction of Greece's distant and often mythic past, the Parian Chronicle—intricately carved in marble quarried on the island—commands pride of place in these galleries. The fragment here tells only the tail end of the story, from 356 to 299 B.C., highlighting in complex imagery the march of Alexander the Great and the birth of the poet Sosiphanes. (To follow the entire chronicle, you need to travel to England, where the other slab, covering 1581–356 B.C., has been on display at the Ashmolean Museum in Oxford since 1667.) Among other intriguing remnants scattered about the museum is a marble frieze of the 7th-century-B.C. poet Archilochus, who was born on Paros and died on the island in a battle against the Naxians. He is shown reclining on a couch, as if he is about to utter one of his famously ironic verses laden with such timeless insights as "for 'tis thy friends that make thee choke with rage."

Near waterfront, behind church. odysseus.culture.gr. **22840/21231.** Admission 2€. Tues–Sun 8:30am–3pm.

Panagia Ekatontopylani (Church of the Hundred Doors) ★★★ CHURCH One of the oldest churches in the world is also, from the moment you step through the gates into the lemon-scented courtyard, one of the most transporting. The surroundings are steeped in legend. Helen, mother of Constantine, the first Christian emperor of the Roman Empire, took shelter on Paros during a storm on her way to the Holy Land in 326 A.D. Here, it is said, she had a vision of finding the True Cross (the one on which Christ was crucified) during her voyage, and she vowed to build a church on Paros if she did. Her dream came to pass, and Constantine completed the basilica upon his mother's death. Emperor Justinian rebuilt the church in the mid-6th century, sending Isidoros, the architect of the Hagia Sofia in Constantinople, to Paros to build the dome. Isidoros handed the commission over to his apprentice Ignatius, then was so filled with envy when he saw the splendid structure that he pushed the apprentice off the church roof. Ignatius grabbed Isidoros as he fell; the two men plummeted to their deaths. A sculpture on the gate near the Chapel of St. Theodosia shows Isidoros rubbing his beard, a sign of apology, and Ignatius rubbing his head, perhaps plotting revenge. (More likely, the figures are satyrs who once adorned a temple of Dionysus that stood on the spot.) Only 99 of the eponymous 100 doors have been found; the last will not be located, legend has it, until Constantinople is Greek once again. A thick wall, embedded with monks' cells, surrounds a shady entrance court. Within the cross-shaped church, frescoes, icons, and a sea of columns of Parian marble are bathed in soft light. The church, one of Greece's most important shrines to the Virgin Mary, is much visited on her feast days, when pilgrims arrive from throughout Greece.

Near waterfront. **22840/21243.** Free admission. Daily 8am–8pm.

Around Paros

Byzantine Road ★ HISTORIC SITE   A section of this stone and marble roadway, paved in the Middle Ages and once the main route across the island, descends from the mountain village of Lefkes (see below) through olive groves and grazing land to Prodomos on the coastal plain below. The well-marked walk is easy—only about 4km (2½ miles), mostly downhill, from the bottom of Lefkes. Prodomos is a fascinating little place, where whitewashed houses, squat little chapels, and gardens with bougainvillea spilling over the walls are confusingly arranged in a bull's-eye pattern radiating from a central *plateia*—a maze intended to thwart invaders and still ensured to do so today. Check schedules for buses from Prodomos back to Lefkes or Parikia, or you could be stranded for hours.

Christos sto Daos ★ RELIGIOUS SITE   The convent of Christ of the Wood, on a hillside just above the Valley of Petaloudes (reached by a path), is the final resting place of St. Arsenios, a 19th-century schoolteacher and abbot noted for his ability to conjure up rain in times of drought. In a famous exchange, he told a group of farmers who sought out his divine services, "If you truly have faith, why have none of you brought umbrellas?" The nuns sometimes allow visitors, but women only, to come into their walled compound to view the tomb and share sweeping views of the sea and surrounding farmlands.

5km (3 miles) S of Parikia off the airport rd. Free admission, donations welcomed.

Lefkes ★★ VILLAGE   The medieval capital of Paros sits high atop an interior mountain, out of harm's way from the pirates who once raided the coast. Brigands who made their way this far inland were further thwarted by the town's mazelike arrangement of narrow lanes, cascading down the mountainside from the beautiful plateia. Rising high above the cluster of white houses are the impressive twin towers of the **Church of Agia Triada,** an enormous 19th-century marble edifice (open daily 8am–6pm). Windmills on an adjoining ridge are still used to grind grain, grown in a tidy patchwork of terraced fields interspersed with olive groves.

5km (3 miles) S of Marathi, 10km (6 miles) SE of Parikia.

Marathi Quarries ★★ ANCIENT SITE   Translucently white and luminescent, the highly-prized white marble of Paros was dug out from three shafts in Marathi. Some of the greatest works of antiquity were crafted from Parian marble, among them *Hermes Carrying the Infant Dionysus* by Praxiteles, now in the Archaeological Museum in Ancient Olympia; the *Venus de Milo,* the most prized ancient treasure of the Louvre in Paris; and temples on the sacred island of Delos. Thousands of slaves worked the dank quarries night and day, wearing oil lanterns strapped to their heads that gave the marble the name lynchnites, "won by lamplight." French engineers came to Marathi in 1844 to mine marble for Napoleon's tomb at Les Invalides in Paris, the last people to work the quarry. Visitors can now descend (bring a flashlight and wear shoes with a good grip) into the 91m-deep (300-ft.) tunnels to see millennia-old chisel marks and, in the middle quarry, a 3rd-century-B.C. relief of the gods.

5km (3 miles) E of Parikia, off Parikia–Lefkes Rd. (ask bus driver to get off). Free admission. Dawn to dusk (site is unattended).

Naoussa ★★ TOWN   Many players in the Mediterranean have anchored in this ancient port on a broad gulf: Persian and Greek warships, Venetian galleons, Russian frigates taking on supplies during the Turko-Russian War of 1768–1774, and the French pirate Hugue Crevelliers. Reminders of this storied past—a Venetian watchtower, the submerged ruins of the seaside *kastro* fortress, and a medieval gateway—today lend a colorful backdrop for fishing boats bobbing in the harbor and an animated resort life that transforms the quiet village during the summer. Even when the town is busiest, you can still get lost in tiny lanes winding uphill from the harbor or come to a dead-end next to the sparkling blue water. Perch on the shady terraces of the seaside *ouzeries* and explore the shady, whitewashed lanes of the old town. The **Church of Agios Nikolaos Mostratou** reflects Naoussa's maritime traditions with models and plaques of ships that mariners have left as offerings of thanks for salvation from drowning; it's open daily 8am to 6pm and admission is free. Some of the best sands on the island flank Naoussa: Santa Maria and Langeri to the east, Kolimbithres to the west.

10km (6 miles) E of Parikia.

Scropios Museum ★ MUSEUM   The Cyclades are magically re-created in a lovely garden, where you'll see carefully crafted models of the pigeon towers of Tinos, the lighthouse of Andros, the Kastro in Parikia, and other monuments of the Cyclades. All are the creation of Benetos Skiadas, who is often on hand to show off the model ships he builds and will make to order upon request.

Aliki Rd., near airport, about 8km (5 miles) S of Parikia. www.benetos-skiadas-folkartist-paros-gr.com. © **22840/91129.** Admission 3€. May–Sept daily 9:30am–2pm (hours vary).

Valley of Petaloudes (Valley of the Butterflies) ★★ NATURE SITE   On the grounds of a Venetian estate spread across a small vale, you'll discover a surprisingly verdant landscape watered by several springs, one of the greenest patches on this dry island. The valley is especially enticing in the spring and early summer, when flowers bloom in wild abandon against a backdrop of cypress trees, and the air hums with the flapping wings of swarms of butterflies—actually, a species of tiger moth with spectacular brown and coral red wings. The best time to experience the spectacle is in the early evening, when moths by the thousands awaken from their daytime slumber and flutter upward toward the cool air. When the creatures are not alight, feel free to scold visitors who clap and shout to alarm the butterflies and make them fly, often causing the fragile insects to collapse.

5km (3 miles) S of Parikia off airport rd. Admission 3€. Mid-May to mid-Sept daily 9am–8pm.

This islet off the southwestern coast of Paros was once a place to get away from it all, and still is. These days, though, villas along the cove-laced coastline have become the not-so-secret hideaway of some famous film stars, while rates at some nice yet charmless hotels have soared up to accommodate the less-privileged. Still, the open countryside is beguiling, beaches at Glyfa and Soros are sandy, the water is sparkling, and life in white-washed Antiparos Town and other settlements is relaxed. All this makes the crossing to Antiparos a pleasant and worthwhile detour. Boats run hourly throughout the day from Parikia (3€ each way, about 20 min.), and a ferry shuttles all day from Pounda (3.50€ each way for car and driver). A bus makes the rounds of villages and sights on Antiparos. The island's big attraction is Antiparos Cave ★★ (off coast road, 10km/6 miles south of Antiparos Town; admission 3€; open Apr–Aug 10am–6pm). Legions of travelers have climbed into the grotto, including 19th-century British poet Lord Byron (see box, p. 91). The most noted visitation was on Christmas Eve, 1673, when a French nobleman arranged a candlelight mass for 500 celebrants in a 40m-tall (131-ft.) cavern known as the Cathedral. An inscription on the base of a stalagmite, known as the Altar, commemorates the event. Near the entrance to the cave, the monastery of **Agios Ioannis Spiliotis (St. John of the Cave)** was built around a grotto etched out of the hillside. Here, a miracle occurred when St. John turned the doors to stone to protect residents who had taken refuge inside from marauding pirates.

Paros Beaches

Some of the island's most popular beaches are on either side of the gulf of Naoussa. **Santa Maria ★★★**, popular with windsurfers, is the most beautiful beach on the island, with especially clear water and shallow dunes of fine sand along the irregular coastline. The **Santa Maria Surf Club** (✆ 22840/52-490) provides windsurfing gear and a brief lesson for about 20€ per hour. **Kolimbithres ★★** is interspersed with huge boulders that divide the gold-sand beach into several tiny coves. Both can be reached by boat or bus from Naoussa.

The southeastern shores of the island are also lined with fine beaches, including the long strip of golden sands at **Chrissi Akti (Golden Beach) ★★**, where the annual World Cup windsurfing championships take place every August (offshore winds make it one of Europe's best windsurfing spots). The Aegean Diving College (www.aegeandiving.gr; ✆ 22840/43-347) at Chrissi Akti offers scuba lessons and certification and excursions to shipwrecks and other submerged sites.

Paros After Dark

Nightlife on Paros is no match for that on Mykonos or Santorini. Nevertheless, islanders and their visitors enjoy sitting outdoors to enjoy an evening. Just behind the windmill in Parikia, the local landmark **Port Café ★** (✆ 22840/27354), a basic *kafenion* lit by bare incandescent bulbs, is filled day and night with tourists waiting for a ferry, bus, taxi, or fellow traveler. **Pirate Bar ★**

(© **6979/194074**), on Market Street within the old quarter behind the harbor, often has classical music and good jazz. **Alexandros Cafe ★** (alexandros-cafe.gr; © **6930/671269**), in a restored windmill by the harbor, is a perfect spot to enjoy the sunset and watch the passing evening scene.

In Naoussa, **Agosta ★** (© **22840/51345**) is a popular harborside spot for an after-dinner drink, while **Palio Agora** (© **22840/51847**), tucked into the old lanes behind the waterfront, is a wonderfully old-fashioned place to snack and drink. **Vareladikos ★** (© **22840/5325**), by the bus station in Naoussa, is an all-night disco.

CRETE

The birthplace of Zeus, the cradle of Minoan civilization, the site of Zorba's feats—Crete is steeped in at least 5,000 years of myth, history, and culture. Greece's largest island is 257km (159 miles) long and 60km (37 miles) at its widest; it sometimes feels more like a separate country, with wildly diverse landscapes. You can go from the remote sandy beaches of the south coast to the snowy heights of the White Mountains to the Venetian harbors of the island's port cities in a day. The Minoan palaces, Venetian Rethymnon and Chania, the precipitous Samaria Gorge, luxury beach resorts—if ever an island could claim to be loaded with sheer variety it's Crete. Maybe the greatest offerings, however, are the many simple pleasures on hand. The spectacular mountains that form the island's spine are laced with trails for hikers and peaks for climbers. Wildflowers and flowering bushes bedeck the landscapes, and the island is home to many species of birds. Crete's terrain can be rugged and raw, its ancient sites austere, and its inland villages geared to the rigors of rural life. But for those looking for scenic beauty and glimpses of the long-ago past, with a dash of exoticism thrown in, Crete never fails to deliver.

ESSENTIALS

Arriving

BY PLANE **Olympic Airways** (www.olympicairlines.com; ✆ **210/926-9111**) and **Aegean Airlines** (www.aegeanair.com; ✆ **801/112-0000**) offer several daily flights from Athens to Crete's two main airports, in **Iraklion** and **Chania.** It's 50-minute flight to either airport. **Sky Express** (www.skyexpress.gr) operates a daily flight between Athens and Iraklion. Olympic also offers at least one direct flight a week between Iraklion and **Rhodes.** Many carriers also operate service between Iraklion and Chania and European cities outside of Greece, making it possible to fly directly to Crete from London, Paris, Frankfurt, and elsewhere.

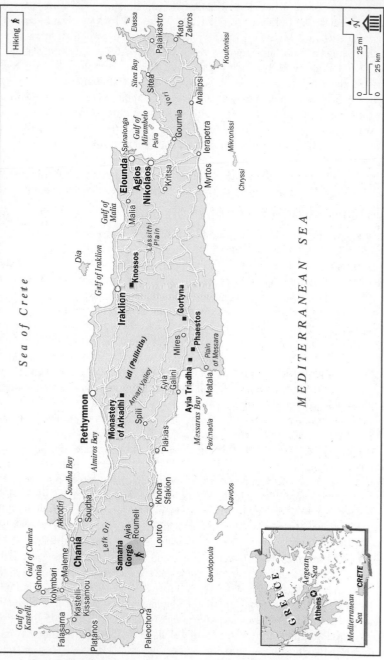

Hiking 𝑘

Sea of Crete

MEDITERRANEAN SEA

Elassa
Palaikastro
Kato Zakros
Koufonissi
Sitea Bay
Sitea
Vori
Analipsi
Spinalonga
Gulf of Mirambelo
Psira
Gournia
Ierapetra
Mikronissi
Chryssi
Myrtos
Elounda
Agios Nikolaos
Kritsa
Malia
Gulf of Malia
Lasithi Plain
Dia
Gulf of Iraklion
Knossos
Iraklion
Gortyna
Phaestos
Mires
Idi (Psiloritis)
Ayia Galini
Ayia Triadha
Plain of Messara
Matala
Messaras Bay
Paximadia
Rethymnon
Spili
Monastery of Arkadhi
Amari Valley
Plakias
Khora Sfakion
Gavdos
Almiros Bay
Soudha Bay
Akrotiri
Soudha
Loutro
Ayia Roumeli
Samara Gorge
Lefk Ori
Chania
Maleme
Kolymbari
Ghonia
Gulf of Chania
Kastelli-Kissamou
Falasarna
Platanos
Paleochora
Gavdopoula

GREECE
Aegean Sea
Athens
CRETE
Mediterranean Sea

25 mi
25 km

BY BOAT Boats from Piraeus regularly serve the island's main ports in Iraklion and Chania, with one daily sailing to Chania on **ANEK Lines** (www. anek.gr) and two to Iraklion, on ANEK and **Minoan Lines** (www.minoan.gr). These are 9- to 10-hour overnight journeys on well-equipped ships with berths, lounges, and dining rooms. In the summer, ANEK Lines ferries also run about twice a week between Irakilon and Rhodes (stopping at Karpathos, Kassos, and Khalki, the islands between the two). Catamarans operated by **Hellenic Seaways** (hellenicseaways.gr) and **Seajets** (www.seajets.gr) link Iraklion with several Cycladic islands (Santorini, Ios, Paros, Naxos, and Mykonos). In high season, occasional cruise ships from Italy, Cyprus, and Israel put into Iraklion. For information on all ships, search online at www. gtp.gr.

Iraklion's harbor is within walking distance of the city center; Chania's port is in Souda, a 20-minute bus ride from town. Buses and taxis meet the ships.

Getting Around Crete

Most visitors prefer to tour the island by **car.** The five largest cities—Chania, Rethymnon, Iraklion, Agios Nikolaos, and Sitea—are all on the north coast and within easy striking distance of each other. Sights on the south coast are rarely more than an hour or 90 minutes' drive from the north. The **National Road,** three lanes wide in a few places, skirts the north coast, providing a fast way for cars and buses to travel from one end of the island to the other. It's 270km (162 miles), a 4-hour drive, between Chania in the west and Sitea in the east. It's 72km (43 miles), about 1 hour, between Chania and Rethymnon; 78km (47 miles), 1 hour and 15 minutes, between Rethymon and Iraklion; 69km (41 miles), 1 hour, between Heraklion and Agios Nikolaos; and 70km (42 miles) between Agios Nikolaos and Sitea. Rental agencies abound at both major airports and in the larger town centers, with many along 25th Avgusto street in Iraklion. Rentals begin at about 35€ a day for a small car with manual transmission. Insurance is usually included, with a 500€ deductible.

Moped and **motorcycle rentals** are also popular, but be careful: injuries are common among even experienced riders navigating chaotic urban traffic, and mountain roads can be dangerous, with few shoulders but lots of potholes and gravel. Helmets are required by law. Expect to pay about 20€ a day for a bike.

Buses on Crete are cheap, relatively frequent, and connect to all but the most isolated locales. The downside: Remote destinations often have schedules that cater to locals, not tourists. The long-distance bus system is operated by **KTEL,** which serves all of Greece. The group does not have a singular web presence, but you can find many schedules at **www.cretetravel.com** or ask a travel agency for bus information. By phone, call ✆ **2810/221-765** to find out more about KTEL buses to Rethymnon-Chania and points west. For buses to Agios Nikolaos, Sitea, Ierapetra, and points east, call ✆ **2810/245-019.** For buses to Phaestos and other points south, call ✆ **2810/255-965.** Iraklion has bus terminals in two locations—along the harbor for arrivals from the west, east, or southeast—Chania or Rethymnon, for instance, or Ayios Nikolaos or

Sitea—and a terminal at Chania Gate, on the southwest edge of town, for buses to and from the south, from such towns as Phaestos and Matala.

Visitor Information

Crete Travel (www.cretetravel.com; ℗ 28250/32-690) is a valuable resource when planning a trip to the island, with a helpful website full of resources. Its office is in the village of Monoho near Chania.

IRAKLION ★

Many visitors linger in Crete's busy capital, the fifth largest city in Greece, just long enough to visit the remarkable Minoan relics in the Archaeological Museum and the outlying Palace of Knossos. Give the city a little time, however, and you'll discover much more: A large old quarter, enclosed within massive walls, that's filled with animated streets and squares and remnants of the city's Venetian and Turkish past. As untidy and ramshackle as much as modern Iraklion appears, throughout the old city you'll encounter the legacy of four centuries of Venetian rule.

ARRIVING   Iraklion's **Kazantakis International Airport** is about 5km (3 miles) east of the city coast. (Plans are afoot to build a long-delayed new airport at nearby Kasteli, perhaps opening by 2020.) Major car-rental companies have desks at the airport. A **taxi** to Iraklion costs about 15€; public **bus** no. 1 also connects the airport with the city center (fare 4€).

VISITOR INFORMATION   The **National Tourist Office** (www.west-crete.com; ℗ 2810/228-225) is at 1 Xanthoudidou, opposite the Archaeological Museum. Hours are Monday through Friday 9am to 5pm. The office is a good source for maps and other material, including details on the many Minoan sites across the island. Another good source for local information is the **municipal tourist office** on Lions Square (www.heraklion.gr); it's open Monday through Friday, 8:30am to 2:30pm. Among many reliable travel agencies is **Creta Travel Bureau,** 49B Dikeossinis (www.cretatrv.gr; ℗ 2810/300-610).

Where to Stay in Iraklion
EXPENSIVE

Capsis Astoria ★★   A prime location across animated Plateia Eleftherias from the Archaeological Museum is one great asset of this hotel. The rooftop swimming pool and sun terrace are another, especially for summertime guests who have spent the day visiting dusty archeological sites. Among many other perks are the soothingly contemporary-style rooms, done with handsome wood veneers and colorful fabrics and all with balconies, and a bar/coffee shop off the lobby.

Plateia Eleftherias. www.capsishotels.gr.℗ **2810/343080.** 130 units. 110€–140€ double. Rates include buffet breakfast. **Amenities:** Restaurant; bar; pool; Wi-Fi (free).

Hotel Galaxy ★★   Once you get past the bland facade and airport-modern lobby, you might find something relaxing about the sleek international style of the Galaxy's small but extremely comfortable and well-equipped guest rooms. (They're popular with business folks who use the hotel's conference facilities.) Many rooms have sea-facing balconies, while others overlook a greenery-filled courtyard and huge swimming pool, the largest in Iraklion. The two restaurants include a pastry/coffee shop that's a popular gathering spot. The hotel is just outside the center, on the road to Knossos, but sights are an easy walk away.

75 Leoforos Dimokratias. www.galaxy-hotel.com. ℂ **2810/238812.** 127 units. 120€–130€ double. Rates include buffet breakfast. **Amenities:** Restaurant; bar; pool; Wi-Fi (free).

MODERATE

Lato Hotel ★★★ Everything about this city-center refuge seems geared to soothe—from the pleasing contemporary decor to the Jacuzzi and steam room. The location above the Venetian harbor and fortress ensures wonderful sea views from many rooms (be sure to ask for one), most with balconies, as well as from the terrace of the excellent rooftop restaurant, open in summer.

15 Epimenidou. www.lato.gr. ℂ **28102/28103.** 58 units. 90€–100€ double. Rates include buffet breakfast. **Amenities:** Restaurant; bar; Wi-Fi (free).

Marin Dream Hotel ★★ The extremely helpful staff here seems determined to prove that genuine Cretan hospitality is still flourishing in busy Iraklion. A perch on a hillside between the center and the harbor puts these comfortable, nice-sized rooms within easy reach of the port, bus station, Archaeological Museum, and other city sights. Request one of the higher-floor rooms with a harbor-view balcony; the sunny rooftop cafe and breakfast room gets great harbor views as well.

12 Epimenidou 46. www.marinhotel.gr. ℂ **2810/300019.** 50 units. 80€–90€ double. Rates include buffet breakfast. **Amenities:** Cafe; bar; Wi-Fi (free).

Megaron Hotel ★★★ A long-abandoned office building/warehouse high above the harbor has been revamped as Iraklion's most stylish and luxurious getaway, with stunning results that combine splash with warmth and comfort at a very good value. Public spaces surrounding an atrium include an intimate library and are warm and inviting; high-ceilinged guest rooms are large, with lots of wood and a sleek combination of contemporary and traditional style. Many have sea-facing balconies. Among the many indulgences on offer is a dramatic rooftop terrace and swimming pool that seems to hang over the city.

9 Beaufort. www.gdmmegaron.gr. ℂ **2810/305300.** 46 units. 100€–140€ double. Rates include buffet breakfast. **Amenities:** Restaurant; bar; pool; Wi-Fi (free).

INEXPENSIVE

El Greco ★ This basic, good-value choice is not luxurious—you should look elsewhere if you want pampering beyond a plain breakfast or any amenities fancier than minimal bathrooms. But the location, just steps from Ta Liontaria, can't be beat, nor can the price. Rooms are a bit outdated but most are

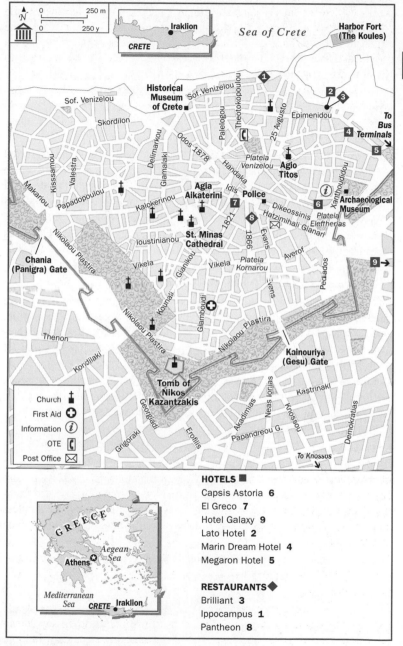

Iraklion

0   250 m
0   250 y

N

CRETE

Iraklion

Sea of Crete

Harbor Fort
(The Koules)

**Historical
Museum
of Crete**

Sof. Venizelou
Skordilon

Sof. Venizelou

Theotokopoulou

Paleologou

25 Avgusto

Epimenidou

To
Bus
Terminals

Delimarkou

Giamalaki

Odos 1878

Handaka

Plateia
Venizelou

**Agio
Titos**

Makariou

Kississou

Valestra

Papadopoulou

Kalokerinou

**Agia
Aikaterini**

Idis

Police

Dikeossinis

Xanthoudidou

Archaeological
Museum

Hatzimihali Gianari

Plateia
Eleftherias

Ioustinianou

Gianikou

1821

1866

Evans

Plateia
Kornarou

Averof

Pecados

Chania
(Panigra) Gate

Nikolaou Plastira

Vikela

**St. Minas
Cathedral**

Vikela

Evans

Kounali

Giamboudi

Nikolaou Plastira

Nikolaou Plastira

**Kainouriya
(Gesu) Gate**

Thenon

Kordilaki

Georgiadi

**Tomb of
Nikos
Kazantzakis**

Grigoraki

Erofilis

Akadimias

Neas Iorias

Papandreou G.

Knossou

Kastrinaki

Demokratias

To Knossos

Church †
First Aid ✚
Information ⓘ
OTE 🄲
Post Office ✉

GREECE

Athens

Aegean
Sea

Mediterranean
Sea

CRETE   Iraklion

HOTELS ◼

Capsis Astoria **6**
El Greco **7**
Hotel Galaxy **9**
Lato Hotel **2**
Marin Dream Hotel **4**
Megaron Hotel **5**

RESTAURANTS ◆

Brilliant **3**
Ippocampus **1**
Pantheon **8**

7

CRETE | Iraklion

good-sized, and those overlooking the interior garden are blissfully quiet—a real blessing here in the center of town, where nightlife goes on until dawn.

4 Odos 1821. www.elgrecohotel.gr. © **2810/281071.** 90 units. 55€ double. Rates include buffet breakfast. **Amenities:** Garden; Wi-Fi (free).

Where to Eat in Iraklion

Cretan fare is as likely to appear on menus in Iraklion's urbane restaurants as it is in mountain-village tavernas. Among many staples are *marathopita* (fennel pie) and *bougatsa* (sugar-sprinkled cheese turnover), along with plenty of fresh seafood, homemade cheeses and yogurt, and home-grown tomatoes, strawberries, and watermelons.

Brilliant ★★★ Greek   The excellent Lato Hotel (p. 190) provides Iraklion's most chic and arguably best dining experience, in a sleek room accented in shiny black and vibrant colors. The ingredients are basically Greek—and often local Cretan—but they appear in some in unexpected combinations like tomato-brie puff pie and goat cheese with prosciutto. The menu changes frequently, with specials offered most nights; meals are accompanied by the best wines from the island. In summer, service moves upstairs to Herb's Garden, a dramatic rooftop overhanging the harbor.

15 Epimenidou. © **28103/34959.** Main courses 20€–25€. Daily 1pm–midnight. Closed June–Oct.

Ippocampus ★★★ SEAFOOD/MEZES   You'll dine in true Greek fashion at this wildly popular *mezederia,* where you can assemble a memorable meal from a wide choice of small plates that might include zucchini fritters, delicately fried baby squid, and *tzatziki* and other spreads, then move on to servings of mussels in wine sauce and grilled fresh fish. A big crowd of regulars lines up to eat on the seafront terrace or clamorous room inside, so come early for dinner or late for lunch if you don't want to wait—and bring cash, as credit cards are not accepted.

3 Mitsotaki. © **28102/82081.** Small plates 5€–8€. Mon–Fri 1–3:30pm and 7pm–midnight.

Pantheon ★★ GREEK   Diners are assured of savory home-style cooking at this local favorite, tucked away in the covered market. The atmospheric lane (unappetizingly known as Dirty Alley) is about as authentically Cretan as you'll find in the busy city center. Menu offerings, including the spit-roasted lamb that's usually available, are as simple as the decor and invariably delicious. *Note:* Here, as at most other eateries in the market, you can pay only in cash.

2 Theodosaki. © **28102/41652.** Main courses 7€–15€. Mon–Sat 11am–11pm.

CAFE SOCIETY

Dozens of cafes line the narrow streets between Plateia Eleftheria and Plateia Venizelou. Many are on Korai, a narrow passage just north of Dedalou, the main passageway through the center; these are perfect if you enjoy shouting to be heard above pumping dance music and the cacophonous clatter of what must be the entire student body of the Iraklion-based University of Crete.

Some of the choicest perches are those surrounding the Lions' Fountain on Plateia Venizelou; none provide a better view than the **Four Lions Roof-Garden Cafe** (✆ **2810/222333**). Down toward the seafront, **Cafe Veneto,** Epimenidou (✆ **2810/223686**), affords wonderful views of the harbor and the Venetian fortress through its tall windows and from the terrace.

Where to Stay & Eat Outside Iraklion

Kalimera Archanes Village ★★★ The village of Archanes, about 15km (9 miles) east of Iraklion, is surrounded by miles of vineyards; it's a good base for exploring Knossos and the other sights, as well as some of the island's leading wineries. Fresh whitewash and lots of blooming flowerboxes give the lively lanes and squares of neoclassical houses of Archanes an unusually tidy appearance. Tucked away in a lush walled garden are four meticulously restored 19th-century stone houses, tastefully and traditionally furnished and equipped with well-outfitted bathrooms and kitchens. Several are two level; all open to terraces and are enhanced with fireplaces, beamed ceilings, and other architectural flourishes.

Theotokopoulou, Archanes. www.archanes-village.com. ✆ **2810/752999.** From 180€ double. Rates include breakfast. **Amenities:** Garden; Wi-Fi (free).

Kronio ★★★ GREEK This cozy and welcoming establishment serves the finest food on the Lasithi Plateau, 50km (30 miles) southeast of Iraklion. Everything, from thick lamb stews to homemade bread and cheese-stuffed pies, is prepared and served with great care and warmth. The proprietors, Vassilis and Christine, are gracious hosts and willing advisors on how to see the best of the plateau. They also offer rooms and an apartment to rent in their beautiful home, with a sparkling swimming pool, set in beautiful countryside just outside town and a good base for hiking and exploring.

Tzermiado, Lasithi Plateau. www.kronio.eu. ✆ **28440/22375.** 50€ double. Restaurant: Main courses 5€–10€. Daily noon–3pm and 7–10:30pm. Closed Nov–Mar.

Taverna and Studios Sigelakis ★★ GREEK In the heart of a little farm village near the south coast, excellent meals, accompanied by friendly service and often a complimentary dessert and homemade *raki,* are served on a terrace or in a stone-walled dining room. Down the road, host Giorgios Sigelakis also offers attractively furnished and extremely comfortable studios, with kitchens, living and sleeping areas, and terraces. They're a little more sophisticated that you'd expect to find in such rural surroundings. Set amid well-tended gardens and olive groves, they're near Kommos beach and other sights in this part of southern Crete.

Sivas, 6km (4miles) NE of Matala. www.sigelakis-studios.gr. ✆ **28920/42748.** 8 units. 50€ double. Restaurant: main courses 6€–10€, daily 7pm–midnight.

Exploring Iraklion

Start your explorations at **Fountain Square** (also known as Ta Liontaria and officially as Plateia Eleftheriou Venizelou, see p. 197), after trying a *bougatsa* at **Kir-Kor,** a much-cherished cafe. You can enjoy this flaky pastry filled with sweet cream custard or soft cheese—introduced by Armenian Greeks—while watching passersby hurry to and from the nearby market and Leoforos Kalokerinou, the main shopping street.

Agia Aikaterina ★★ MUSEUM   Northwest of Kornarou Square next to St. Minas Cathedral, this small 15th-century church named for St. Katherine houses a museum of icons, most by Cretan artists. Under the Venetians, Crete became an important center of religious art, and many islanders—including Domenikos Theotocopoulos, the future El Greco (p. 195)—were sent to Venice to perfect their craft.

Karterou. Admission 5€. Mon–Sat 10am–1pm; Tues and Thurs–Fri also 4–6pm.

Agios Titos ★ CHURCH   This beloved landmark just east of the Loggia honors Crete's favorite saint, Titus, who appears in scripture alongside Paul in Ephesus, Corinth, and Rome; in the 1st century A.D., Paul commissioned him to convert Crete to Christianity and ordained him Bishop of Gortyna, then the Roman capital (p. 200). Founded long after his death, in the 10th century, this church was destroyed in an earthquake in 1856 and rebuilt over the next few years as a mosque (Crete was then Turkish). The minaret was removed in the 1920s when the structure was rededicated as a church. A silver vault houses one of the island's most sacred artifacts, the skull of Titus, who died in A.D. 107 at the age of 95.

25 Avgostos. Free admission. Daily 8am–7pm.

Archaeological Museum ★★★ MUSEUM   The Minoans, whose civilization thrived on Crete some 4,000 years ago, come spectacularly to life in this museum, which houses the world's most extensive collection of the artifacts they left behind. It's a mandatory first stop on a tour of Crete's many Minoan sites. Here you'll see large **round "seal" stones,** inscribed with an early form of Greek known as Linear B script, that have revealed a wealth of information about the Minoans. (One of the most elaborately inscribed stones—called the **Phaestos Disk,** for the palace near the southern coast where it was unearthed—remains a mystery: It's elaborately inscribed in Linear A, a script predating Linear B that has yet to be deciphered.) Beautiful **frescoes** portray proceedings at a Minoan court; *The Prince of the Lilies* depicts an athletic priest-king, wearing a crown with peacock feathers and a necklace decorated with lilies, leading an unseen animal to slaughter; other works show muscular men and trim women leaping over bulls—either a religious rite or an athletic contest. A whimsical fresco of court ladies in skirts, from the palace of Knossos (p. 196), earned the nickname Les Parisiennes for its subjects' resemblance to ladies on the grand boulevards of the French capital. As early as 2000 B.C., Minoan craftsmen were producing **pottery** known as Kamares ware; other decorative pieces are made of stone, ivory, and a glass paste known as faience. Many pieces illustrate life in Minoan towns and palaces: One vase depicts a harvest ceremony, another a boxing match. A barebreasted faience goddess holds writhing snakes, perhaps part of a religious

El Greco: Crete's Star Artist

The most famous Cretan artist of all, Domenikos Theotocopoulos (1541–1614), best known as El Greco, allegedly studied at the **Agia Aikatarina** monastery school and soon became known for his skillful blending of Byzantine and Western traditions. He left the island forever in 1570 and perfected his distinctive expressionist style in Rome, Venice, and, finally, Toledo, Spain, where he died in 1614. Despite the painter's long exile from his native land, he was forever known as El Greco (the Greek), and he continued to sign his works with the Greek letters of his given name. His only two works in Crete hang in Iraklion's Historical Museum (see below).

ritual. *Rython,* vases for pouring libations, are carved in the shape of bulls' heads and other elaborate designs—yet more evidence that this ancient culture had a sophisticated flair for living.

Plateia Eleftherias. odysseus.culture.gr. *©* **2810/224630.** Admission 10€; combined ticket for museum and Palace of Knossos 16€. Apr–Oct daily 8am–7:30pm; Nov–Mar Mon 11am–5pm, Tues–Sun 8am–3pm.

Historical Museum of Crete ★★ MUSEUM Fascinating artifacts from Crete's long colorful past fill the rooms of this neoclassical mansion near the harbor. The *Baptism of Christ* and *View of Mount Sinai and the Monastery of St. Catherine* are the only works on the island by Crete-born artist Domenikos Theotocopoulo, known as El Greco (see box, above). They take their place among ceramics, sculpture, icons, and artifacts from the island's Roman, Byzantine, Venetian, and Ottoman past. Several rooms document the bloody revolutions against Turkish rule in the 18th and 19th centuries and the very brief period when Crete was an independent state in the first years of the 20th century. Especially evocative are the re-creations of the library and study of novelist Nikos Kazantzakis, and a simple farmhouse interior, typical of the island today.

Sofokli Venizelou. www.historical-museum.gr. *©* **28102/83219.** Admission 5€. Apr–Oct Mon–Sat 9am–7pm; Nov–Mar Mon–Sat 9am–3:30pm.

Koules ★★ LANDMARK The Venetians put up this mighty, wave-lapped fortress between 1523 and 1540 to protect Iraklion from attack by sea, and to assure safe harbor for the fleets constantly making the three-week journey between Crete and Venice. Within thick walls topped by rambling ramparts are workshops, warehouses, and vaulted *arsenali,* workshops where ships were repaired and outfitted, as well as officers' quarters and a prison. An inscription over the main entrance announces that the fortress stands on the remains of a fort erected by the Genoese in 1303; as you wander about, look for three plaques bearing the symbol of the Venetian republic, a lion. Crete was a prize for Venice, awarded to the republic after Constantinople was sacked in 1204 and the holdings of the Byzantine Empire disbursed. Crete

Crete's Romeo & Juliet

One of Iraklinion's busier squares, **Plateia Kornarou** (p. 197), is named in honor of Vitsentzos Kornaros (1553–1617), a Cretan who is widely acclaimed as one of Greece's greatest poets. Even though you may not be familiar with his epic work, *Erotokritos*—a 10,000-verse romance of love, honor, friendship, and courage that is not dissimilar to *Romeo and Juliet*—you may well encounter segments of the poem in your Cretan travels: The verses are often set to folk music and sung at performances of traditional music. A statue in the square depicts the poem's eponymous hero, Erotokritos, who is on horseback bidding farewell to his beloved, Aretousa.

provided Venice with agricultural bounty, timber for shipbuilding, and a strong presence in the Mediterranean. Venice lost control of Crete to the Ottoman Turks in the middle of the 17th century. The view from the ramparts takes in a good swath of coast, the brooding mountains behind, and the inner and outer harbors, jammed today with pleasure craft, fishing boats, and ferries going to and from the mainland and islands.

Old Harbor. © **2810/246211.** Admission 1.50€. July–Oct daily 8am–9:30pm; Nov–June daily 9am–3pm.

Market ★★ MARKET   One long outdoor market stretches from Ta Liontaria to Plateia Kornarou. Stalls are piled high with fresh produce grown on the island, along with thick Cretan olive oil and *raki,* the fiery digestive for which every Cretan household has a special recipe.

Palace of Knossos ★★★ ANCIENT SITE   Cretan merchant and archaeologist Minos Kalokarinos discovered the remains of the largest Minoan palace complex atop Kephala Hill in 1878; British archaeologist Sir Arthur Evans began excavating the site in earnest in 1899, soon after Crete was liberated from three and a half centuries of Turkish occupation. Employing an enormous workforce, Evans brought the complex to light in relatively short order. His work showed that the 1,300-room palace was originally built around 1900 B.C., rebuilt after an earthquake around 1700 B.C., and taken over by the Mycenaeans around 1400 B.C. The palace was the center of Minoan culture in every way—not just the court of royalty and an important religious and ceremonial center, but also an administrative headquarters and a huge warehouse where the Minoans stored everything: the honey they cultivated; the wheat, figs, and barley they grew; the elephant tusks and saffron they imported from Africa and the Middle East. As you tour the palace, you'll see ample evidence of these various functions: tall clay jars in which wine, oil, and grain were stored; a splendid grand staircase that ascends from a ceremonial court up four flights through a light well; and the elaborate apartments of the queen, complete with a bathtub and toilet that would have drained into the palace's elaborate sewage system. What's missing from Knossos (and other Minoan palaces and towns) are defensive walls. This culture seems to have been peace-loving and unconcerned about invasion—for better or for worse. While the decline of the Minoans remains a mystery, it has been attributed to attacks from outsiders as well as earthquakes and tsunamis after the eruption of the nearby Santorini volcano. Evidence suggests that Mycenaeans from mainland Greece took over the palace and other parts of Crete around 1400 B.C., but by 1200 B.C. they, too, had vanished. Evans rebuilt parts of the palace, reconstructing the courtyards and rooms as they were under the Minoans and painting them vibrant colors—a sacrilege to purists that nonetheless richly re-creates Minoan life for today's visitors.

Knossos Rd., 5km (3 miles) S of Iraklion. odysseus.culture.gr. © **2810/231940.** Admission 10€; combined ticket for Knossos and Archaeological Museum 16€. Apr–Oct daily 8am–7:30pm; Nov–Mar Mon 11am–5pm, Tues–Sun 8am–3pm. Take bus no. 2, departing every 15 min. from Odos Evans in Iraklion city center; fare 1.15€.

Plateia Kornarou ★ SQUARE   This busy square south of Ta Liontaria is named for poet Vitsentzos Kornaros (see box, p. 196), although many locals refer to the square as Falte Tzami—a corruption of the Turkish Valide Camil, or Queen Mother—the name of a church-turned-mosque that once dominated the square and was demolished in the 1960s. This history is still reflected in the square's two fountains, one Turkish and one Venetian.

Ta Liontaria ★★ SQUARE   The busy hub of Iraklion is officially listed as Plateia Eleftheriou Venizelou, for the Crete-born revolutionary and ever-popular prime minister (from 1910–20 and again from 1928–32), often considered the father of modern Greece. Any Irakliot, however, refers to the square as Ta Liontaria (the Lions), in honor of the famous Venetian-era **fountain,** adorned with four leonine symbols of the Venetian Republic. The water that once streamed from their mouths filled a basin ornately carved with mythological figures. The platcia has been the center of island life since the 9th century, when the Arab rulers of the island staged a large slave market here. Today cafe tables fill the square, while the handsome 13th-century **Agios Marcos Church**, named for the patron saint of Venice, houses art exhibitions. The adjacent 17th-century **Loggia**—a replica of architect Andrea Palladio's elegant basilica in Vincenza—was once the seat of Venice's island government and is now Iraklion's city hall.

Walls ★★ LANDMARK   The mighty walls that still surround much of old Iraklion are a sturdy remnant of the past amid the untidy sprawl of the modern city. Venetians began building the walls soon after they arrived in the 13th century, eventually erecting a circuit 5km (3 miles) long and up to 40m (131 ft.) thick atop a network of defensive ditches that the city's Saracen and Byzantine inhabitants dug. In the middle of the 17th century the Venetian fortifications almost thwarted the vast Ottoman armies—in the longest siege in European history, Iraklion held out for 21 years after the Ottomans overran the rest of the island, finally surrendering in 1669. The Turks allegedly lost 100,000 men, the Venetians 30,000. When the Venetians finally agreed to lay down their arms, they were allowed to leave the city in ships laden with their belongings and important documents. Two elegant gates still punctuate the walls, the **Chania Gate** (also known as the Pantocrator Gate or Panigra Gate) in the west and the **Kainouryia Gate** (Gate of Gesu) in the southeast. At seven points, the walls thicken into arrowhead-shaped defenses known as bastions. The southernmost of these, **Martinengo Bastion,** is the final resting place of Nikos Kazantzakis (1883–1957), the Cretan author of *Zorba the Greek* and other modern classics who was born and died in Iraklion and lies beneath a simple stone inscribed with his own words: "I expect nothing, I fear nothing, I am free." Irakliots come to pay tribute and take in the airy views across the straggling outskirts to the mountainous interior of the island, dominated by the craggy peak of Mount Iouktas, attributed in legend to be the head of Zeus.

Open sunrise–sunset.

Outside Iraklion

Acquaplus Waterpark ★ AMUSEMENT PARK   You might not see why the slides, tunnels, and pools of this 23-hectare (57-acre) water park outside the hideously overbuilt resort town of Chersonissos are any more appealing than Crete's lovely seas, but your young traveling companions certainly will. At times it seems as if every youngster in Greece has converged on this popular place. (If you're in the mood for peace and quiet, go elsewhere.)

About 25km (15 miles) E of Iraklion, outside Chersonissos. www.acquaplus.gr. ℭ **28970/24950.** 27€ adults, 16€ children 5 and older, children under 5 free. May to mid-Oct 9am–sunset. Take national hwy. E to Chersonissos and follow signs. Frequent bus service from Iraklion central station to Chersonissos; transfer to local bus to water park.

Cretaquarium ★ AQUARIUM   Jellyfish, sharks, and 2,500 species of fish and other marine life that thrive in the Mediterranean swim through beautiful re-creations of Crete's offshore seascapes. Submersible periscopes and other high-tech gizmos make a walk past the 60 enormous tanks, designed by the Hellenic Center for Marine Research, fun as well as enlightening.

Outside Gournes, 16km (10 miles) E of Iraklion on national hwy. www.cretaquarium.gr. ℭ **28103/37788.** Admission 9€ adults, 6€ children 17 and under. June–Sept 9:30am–9pm; Oct–May 9:30am–5pm. Regular bus service runs directly to aquarium from Iraklion's central station.

Lasithi Plateau ★★★ NATURAL WONDER   Few experiences on Crete top the sensation of making the final steep, vertiginous ascent over the crest of the Dikti Mountains and getting your first glimpse of the Lasithi Plateau. At your feet, a tidy patchwork of orchards and fields with more than 7,000 windmills spreads out to the encircling hills. A road skirts the rim of the plateau, passing through small villages and the largest town, **Tzermiado.** Residents of the plateau are famous on Crete for their deft weaving and embroidery, executed in front of the fire on winter evenings; they sell these wares to the busloads of daytime visitors who arrive from resort towns on the north coast. You can see some especially fine examples at the **Cretan Folk Museum** in Agios Giorgios; admission is 3€, and it's open mid-April to

AN ANCIENT tale of woe

Legend has it that the Cretan palace of Knossos was once home **to King Minos,** son of Zeus and Europa. Minos prayed to Poseidon to send him a white bull from the sea as a sign that he had the blessing of the gods to rule; he claimed he would sacrifice the bull in thanksgiving. The bull appeared, but Minos could not part with the beautiful creature; his wife, **Pasiphae,** too, was smitten, and she seduced the bull and gave birth to the **Minotaur.** Minos ordered the architect **Daedalus** to build a labyrinth to imprison this monstrous half-man, half-bull creature.

Meanwhile, after the Athenians killed Minos's son, Androgeos, Minos demanded the city send him seven boys and seven girls every nine years to be sacrificed to the Minotaur. When Minos' daughter Ariadne fell in love with one of these youths, **Theseus,** she gave Theseus a sword to slay the Minotaur and a ball of red fleece he could unravel to find his way out of the maze.

Minos blamed Daedalus for Theseus' escape and imprisoned him in a tower. The architect crafted waxen wings for himself and his son, **Icarus,** so the pair could make a daring airborne escape. Icarus, however, failed to heed his father's advice and flew too close to the sun: His wings melted, and he fell into the azure waters off northern Crete now known as the Icarian Sea, and drowned.

Nor does the unhappiness end there: Theseus and Ariadne fled Crete and the vengeful Minos, but Theseus abandoned Ariadne on the island of Naxos (p. 171) as they made their way to Athens. The spurned Ariadne put a curse on Theseus, and under her spell, he changed the sails of his ship to black. As he returned home to Athens, his father, Aegeus, saw the black-sailed ship approaching, assumed his son was dead, and fatally leapt from a cliff into the sea that to this day bears his name.

mid-October, daily 10am to 4pm. By midafternoon, the plateau is caught up in working the land that has been cultivated since the Minoans. Votive offerings suggest these ancient residents worshiped in the **Psychro Cave,** outside the village of the same name. According to some legends, the cave was the birthplace of Zeus, though the sacred associations of the cavern are lost amid the touts and shills who crowd the entrance. Admission to the cave is 4€; it's open June and September daily from 8:30am to 3pm, and July and August daily 8am to 7pm. As frenetic as a visit to the cave can be, a walk along any of the paths that crisscross the plateau's orchards and fields quickly restores a sense of the beauty of this high haven.

About 70km (43 miles) E of Iraklion. Take national hwy. E toward Chernossisos then follow signs up to Lasithi Plateau.

Excursion to the South Coast

From Iraklion a well-traveled road crosses the mountains then drops onto the Messara Plain, some of the most fertile agricultural land in Greece, a patchwork of olive groves, vineyards, vegetable fields, and greenhouses. **Vori,** 63km (39 miles) southwest of Iraklion off the road to Mires, is a pleasant and unspoiled farming village that's home to the island's finest collection of

A Beach Resort for the Ages

About 70km (43 miles) south of Iraklion, the pleasantly low-key beach resort of **Matala** may seem bland at first glance—but it has been popular with visitors for millennia. Legend has it that Zeus, taking the form of a white bull, wooed Europa on the beach at Matala. In classical Roman times, Brutus was said to be among the Romans who encamped in the caves that riddle a seaside bluff. These same caves housed hippies during the 1960s and now present a picturesque backdrop to a fine sandy beach. Matala is a nice place to relax, but the surrounding farm villages on the Messara Plain are more authentic—**Pitsidia, Kamilari,** and **Sivas** are geared to farming and laid-back tourism and offer nice tastes of rural Crete. They're especially popular with German visitors, who descend in droves from the north during the summer months to bask in the sun and easygoing lifestyle.

folkcraft, the **Museum of Cretan Ethnology** (www.cretanethnologymuseum. gr; ✆ **28920/91112**). Handsome, well-designed displays provide an intriguing look at farm equipment, basketry, pottery, weavings, and furnishings. Admission is 3€ and it's open daily, 10am to 6pm.

Besides the beach at **Matala** (see box, above), there are fine beaches at **Kommos,** 3km (2 miles) north of Matala off the road to Phaestos, and **Red Beach,** reached by a 20-minute hike over a headland on the south side of Matala.

Gortyna ★★ ANCIENT SITE   Layers of history overlap at this ancient site in the Messara Plain. It began as a small Minoan settlement, but flourished so under the Greeks that by the 5th century B.C., its citizens were governed by laws they literally set into stone—the Code of Gortyna, on display in a small building at the site. A small Greek theater and other structures remain, but most of what you see at Gortyna is Roman. After the Romans conquered Crete in 69 B.C., after years of bloody warfare, they made Gortyna the administrative center of Cyrenaica, a province that included Crete as well as parts of Northern Africa. Under their jurisdiction, roads, aqueducts, and other public works soon appeared throughout Crete. A Roman bath and theater stand amid the rubble of what was once a city of 10,000. When the Roman Empire divided into East and West regions in the 4th century, Crete came under the rule of Byzantium. The most intact remains, however, belong to the 6th century, when Christianity had gained a stronghold across the island under the Byzantine Empire. The ruins of a magnificent Byzantine basilica, destroyed during 9th-century Arab raids, stand on the site of a simple church erected in the 1st century by St. Titus, dispatched by Paul to convert the Cretans.

Outside Agii Deka, on the Iraklion–Mires Rd., 47km (29 miles) SW of Iraklion. odysseus. culture.gr. ✆ **28920/3114**. Admission 6€. Apr–Oct daily 8am–7:30pm; Nov–Mar daily 8:30am–3pm.

Phaestos ★★★ ANCIENT SITE   Italian archaeologists began unearthing the second-greatest Minoan palace about the same time Sir Arthur Evans was excavating Knossos. Unlike Evans, though, the Italian team left the ruins much as they found them, and the overall results evoke Minoan life even more effectively than reconstructed Knossos. Lavish apartments, ceremonial areas, granaries, and warehouses suggest the importance of the palace complex, probably a key center of trade with Egypt and other parts of northern Africa, just across the Libyan Sea. The **Phaestos Disk**—found encased in a vault of mud brick at the palace during excavations—is one of the great mysteries of archaeology. (It's now on display at the Archaeological Museum in Iraklion, p. 194.) Elaborately inscribed on both sides in Linear A script, it is covered with concentric circles filled with four distinct symbols. Its purpose is unknown, but theories abound, ascribing the disk and its symbolism to everything from a prayer wheel to a board game.

Off Mires–Timpaki Rd., 63km (39 miles) SW of Iraklion. odysseus.culture.gr. ℭ **28920/42315.** Admission 8€. May–Oct daily 8:30am–8pm; Nov–Apr daily 8am–5pm.

RETHYMNON ★★

72km (45 miles) E of Chania; 78km (50 miles) W of Iraklion

Old Rethymnon, crowded onto a peninsula, is an inviting maze of Venetian and Turkish houses, mosques, and a massive seaside fortress, all looking as they have for centuries. Narrow lanes, shady squares, and a long sandy beach invite lingering, and magnificent mountain and valley scenery, monasteries, and other distinctly Cretan landmarks are within easy reach.

ARRIVING   Rethymnon is about 1 hour from the Chania airport and 1½ hours from the Iraklion airport. Rethymnon is not served by ship from Piraeus (though talk of restoring service runs rife); travelers take the boat to Chania or Iraklion and continue to Rethymnon by car or bus, an easy trip along the national highway. Buses to and from Iraklion and Chania run virtually every half-hour from early in the morning until midevening. In high season, buses depart Rethymnon as late as 10pm. The **KTEL** bus station (ℭ **28310/22-212**) is at Akti Kefaloyianithon, at the city's western edge (so allow an extra 10 min. to get there).

VISITOR INFORMATION   The **National Tourism Office** (ℭ **28310/29-148**) is on Venizelou, the main avenue that runs along the town beach. In high season, it's open Monday through Friday from 8am to 2:30pm; off-season, its hours are unpredictable. The many private travel agencies in town include **Ellotia Tours** at 155 Arkadhiou (www.rethymnoatcrete.com). If you're arriving with a car, look for the well-marked public parking lot at Plateia Plastira, at the far western edge, just outside the old harbor. Free parking is also available along the seaside road that skirts the Fortezza.

Where to Stay in Rethymnon
EXPENSIVE
Avli Lounge Apartments ★★   One of Crete's most renowned restaurants (p. 203) also offers so-called Lounge Apartments that surround the

restaurant garden and occupy an old house across the street. Decor combines Greek antiques, Asian pieces, and contemporary styling, all set against stone walls and wood beams, to provide surroundings that are full of design-magazine flair; they're also enormous, and come with such amenities as soaking tubs and a rooftop terrace and whirlpool. So-called Candy Suites, in another annex, are smaller and less luxurious, though priced accordingly and decorated with color and flair.

22 Xanthoudidou. www.avli.gr. ℭ **28310/58250.** 7 Lounge Apartments, 5 Candy Suites. 135€–330€ double. Rates include buffet breakfast. **Amenities:** Restaurant; bar; Wi-Fi (free).

MODERATE

Hotel Leo ★★ A former home from 1450 is now a character-filled, intimate inn on a quiet side street. Stone walls, wood beams, fine fabrics, and a handsome blend of antiques and contemporary furnishings (including curtained beds) give off a romantic aura, making this an alluring alternative to large resorts for honeymooners and other couples. Amenities include beautifully equipped bathrooms and a pleasant bar and sidewalk cafe, perfect for sitting and watching town life go by.

Vale and Arkadiou. www.leohotel.gr. ℭ **28310/26197.** 8 units. 100€–140€ double. Rates include breakfast. **Amenities:** Cafe; Wi-Fi (free).

Kapsaliana Village Hotel ★★★ A rustic hamlet of honey-colored stone in hilly countryside about 18km (11 miles) above Rethymnon was once part of the holdings of the Arkadi monastery (p. 206); it has now been shaped into a unique country getaway. Village houses along the old lanes have been redone with designer flair, with contemporary furnishings in terraced guest rooms offset by stone walls, arches, and wood beams. Amid well-tended gardens you'll find lounges (one fitted out in a former olive mill), an outdoor dining terrace where Cretan specialties are served, and a sparkling pool. Beaches are a short drive away, as is Arkadi and the beautiful Amari Valley (p. 206).

Kapsaliana. www.kapsalianavillage.gr. ℭ **28310/83400.** 17 units. 120€–180€ double. Rates include buffet breakfast. **Amenities:** Restaurant; bar; pool; Wi-Fi (free).

Palazzino di Corina ★★ Several of Rethymnon's old Venetian palaces have been converted to hotels, but few with such panache as this one, tucked away on a quiet back street near the harbor. Rooms, named after Greek gods or goddesses, have different shapes and sizes; all are smartly decorated with a mix of traditional pieces, along with jutting beams and stone walls. Some rooms require a climb up a steep staircase, while others open off a lovely courtyard with a small pool, perfect for a refreshing plunge followed by a cocktail.

7–9 Dambergi. www.corina.gr. ℭ **28310/21205.** 21 units. 120€–150€ double. Rates include buffet breakfast. **Amenities:** Bar; pool; Wi-Fi (free).

Vetera Suites ★★★ No end of care has gone into creating these distinguished lodgings in a centuries-old Venetian/Turkish house, where much of the old wood and stonework remains. Rooms are painstakingly furnished with antique pieces and tasteful reproductions, while modern conveniences, such as bathrooms and kitchenettes, are tucked into alcoves and sleeping lofts are nestled beneath high ceilings. Breakfast is delicious, but costs extra.

9 Kastrinogiannaki. www.vetera.gr. ℂ **28310/23844.** 4 units. 100€–150€ double. **Amenities:** Wi-Fi (free).

INEXPENSIVE

Fortezza Hotel ★ Many return visitors to Rethymnon swear by this comfortable, convenient choice in a quiet part of town, only a few blocks from the inner Old Quarter (and a couple of blocks from the town beach and the Venetian Harbor). Rooms are fairly standard, but nicely furnished with good beds and handsome, Cretan-style wood pieces, and most have balconies. You'll get a better night's sleep if you ask for a room facing the courtyard and the large pool—a rarity in the Old Quarter, where small courtyards usually accommodate only tiny plunge pools. Ample parking is nearby, making it easy to explore the surrounding coast and countryside.

10 Melisinou. www.fortezza.gr. ℂ **28310/55551.** 52 units. 75€–90€ double. Rates include buffet breakfast. **Amenities:** Restaurant; bar; pool; Wi-Fi (free).

Where to Eat in Rethymnon

Rethymnon residents like to relax next to the sea in Koumbes, a little enclave just west of Old Town, past the Venetian fortress. A string of tavernas line the shore, offering drinks, coffee, and seafood meals. Among the most popular are **Tabakario,** 93 Stamathioudaki (ℂ **28310/29276**), and **Maistros,** 7 Akrotiriou (ℂ **28310/25492**). The seaside terraces at both perch just above the surf crashing onto the rocks below.

Avli ★★ GREEK/CRETAN   This veritable temple to Cretan cuisine, part of the noted hotel (p. 201), introduces you to the freshest island ingredients. Fish and lamb appear in many different guises, as do mountain greens and other fresh vegetables, all served in a delightfully romantic garden, an arched dining room, and the narrow lane in front of the hotel. Avli also operates an *enoteca* that offers a wide choice of serious Greek wines and a shop selling local foodstuffs.

22 Xanthoudidou. www.avli.gr. ℂ **28310/28310.** Main courses 15€–30€. Daily noon–3pm and 7:30–11:30pm.

Kyria Maria ★ GREEK/CRETAN   Excellent plain cooking and friendly service are the hallmarks of this old favorite, where tables are set along a narrow lane near the Rimondi fountain, beneath a trailing grape vine. Even a simple salad, brimming with garden-fresh vegetables, is a treat, as are the array of generously sized appetizers and such taverna staples as pastitsio, lamb in lemon sauce, and octopus on a bed of orzo. A chorus of caged parakeets and canaries serenades diners.

Moshovitou. ℂ**28310/29078.** Main courses 5€–10€. Daily 9am–midnight.

Othonos ★★ GREEK/CRETAN   It would be easy to walk by what looks like another Old Town tourist trap, but looks can be deceiving. Locals pour in for traditional dishes based on age-old recipes: excellent lamb dishes; pork with honey, madeira, and walnuts; or chicken roasted with garlic and lemon. An attentive staff that seems to have been around for years serves with pride and takes the onslaught of summer visitors in gracious stride.

27 Plateia Pethihaki. ⓒ **28310/55500.** Main courses 8€–15€. Daily noon–3pm and 7pm–midnight.

Prima Plora ★★ GREEK/CRETAN   It's a 20-minute walk or short cab ride out to this seaside spot, west of the town center, beyond Koumbes. The distance doesn't deter legions of diners from packing into the seafront terrace and lofty, whitewashed dining room, where it's a toss-up as to what is fresher—the vegetables or the seafood. All appear in simple yet wonderful creations, such as grilled shrimp on a bed of orzo or risotto with cuttlefish.

4 Akrotiri St., near west entrance to national hwy. ⓒ **28310/56990.** Main courses 10€–20€. Daily noon–1am.

Exploring Rethymnon

A maze of narrow lanes and squares crisscrossing a narrow peninsula jutting into the Sea of Crete, Rethymnon is enticing and exotic, a warren of Venetian palaces, wooden Ottoman houses, mosques, and fountains. While Rethymnon was inhabited through the ages by Minoans, Mycenaeans, ancient Greeks, Romans, and Byzantines, the historic city that remains today is largely the creation of the Venetians and Turks, who occupied Rethymnon for almost 800 years, until the late 19th century. For Venetians, the city was an important way station on the sea route between Iraklion and Chania, and they left many landmarks. The Turks built fewer monuments, though wooden balconies, surrounded by lattice work to ensure the privacy of Muslim women, project from many of the old houses. Rising high above the tile roofs is the minaret of the **Mosque of the Nerantzes,** converted from a former monastery and church when the Turks took Rethymnon in 1646. Nerantzes now houses a school and music school, open only when concerts are performed.

Two Venetian remnants are nearby: the **Rimondi Fountain,** where streams of water gush from the mouths of three lions, symbols of the Republic, and the **loggia,** once the meeting house of Venetian nobility. The **Venetian Harbor,** at the eastern edge of the Old Town, is surrounded by a high breakwater and overlooked by a 13th-century lighthouse. Rethymnon never became a major port for Venice, in part because this claustrophobically small harbor was not well suited to large Venetian galleys. Today, a jumble of cafe tables crowd the quayside and a fleet of colorful fishing boats are moored chockablock against one another.

Archaeological Museum ★ MUSEUM   Built by the Turks next to the Fortezza gate as part of the town defenses, and later used as a prison, this sturdy stone pentagon now houses a smattering of ancient artifacts unearthed in caves and other ancient sites around Rethymnon. You won't come across the Minoan frescoes and jewels that bedazzle visitors to the Archaeological

Museum in Iraklion (p. 194), but the prehistoric stone tools, figurines, Roman oil lamps, and other finds warrant a passing glance, if only as more reminders that Crete has been inhabited for millennia.

Next to main gate of Fortezza. ℂ **28310/29975.** Admission 2€. Daily 8:30am–3pm.

Fortezza ★★ HISTORIC SITE   Rethymnon's most prominent landmark rises next to the sea on a high promontory at the northern end of the Old Town. Ancient Greeks built a Temple of Artemis and a Sanctuary of Artemis on the hill, and the Venetians erected a small fortress that proved useless in defending the city against pirates who attacked with 40 galleys in 1571. After that, the Venetians rebuilt the fortress with a labor force of more than 100,000 conscripted Cretans, but the thick walls, bastions, and embrasures were also ineffective in stopping the Turks who overran Rethymnon in 1646. The vast rock-strewn space is now overgrown and barren. Inside the massive battlements are two simple churches, a mosque, and several former barracks (which in later years became the town brothels). Every summer, the forlorn atmosphere is enlivened by musical and theatrical performances of the Rethymnon Renaissance Festival (contact tourist office, p. 201, for details).

Above the sea at the edge of Old Town. Admission 3€. Daily 8:30am–7pm.

Historical and Folk Art Museum ★ MUSEUM   A restored Venetian mansion is the setting for beautiful basketry and hand-woven textiles, along with farm implements, traditional costumes, and old photographs that pay homage to Cretan traditions. These well-displayed collections are not merely a repository of the past. Many items—from lyres and other musical instruments to embroidery fashioned from techniques that date back to the Byzantines—are still a widespread part of island life.

30 Vernardou. ℂ **28310/23398.** Admission 3€. Mon–Fri 10am–2pm.

HIT THE BEACH

To the east of the Old Town, Rethymnon stretches along several miles of sandy beach. In recent years this asset has turned Rethymnon into a beach resort, and hotels and apartments of recent vintage now line the waterfront. This strip is not terribly attractive, but the sand and water are clean and welcoming. Much of the beach is taken up by concessionaires, from whom you can rent two beach lounges and an umbrella for about 12€ a day. *Tip:* You can also plop yourself down on the sand for free.

Shopping in Rethymnon

While Rethymnon's lanes are all-too-crowded with souvenir shops, some standouts include Nikolaos Papalasakis's **Palaiopoleiou,** 40 Souliou, crammed with some genuine antiques, old textiles, jewelry, and curiosities. **Haroula Spridaki,** 36 Souliou, has a nice selection of Cretan embroidery. **Avli Raw Materials,** at 22 Xanthoudidou 22 (part of the hotel and restaurant fiefdom; see p. 203), is an enticing stockpile of olive oils, spices, herbs, wines, cheese, and other Cretan products.

Day Trips from Rethymnon

Many travel agencies arrange tours to sights around Rethymnon. You can explore the countryside on foot with an excellent excursion from the **Happy Walker** ★★★, Tombazi 56 (www.happywalker.com; © **28310/52920**), which provides in-town pickup for day hikes in the surrounding mountains and gorges, as well as multiday hikes on Crete and elsewhere in Greece.

Amari Valley ★★★ NATURAL LANDSCAPE Some of the island's most beautiful rural scenery lies in this highland valley just south of Rethymnon. As you travel the narrow roads, you'll pass through small villages, come upon Byzantine churches, and be surrounded by vineyard- and orchard-covered mountain slopes and the omnipresence of tinkling goat bells. You'll need your own car to see the valley, along with a good map of Crete. You'll find tavernas and cafes in some of the villages; you won't find many English speakers. The village of **Thronos** surrounds a little church decorated with 14th-century frescoes and, on the exterior, a mosaic from a 4th-century Byzantine church that originally stood on the spot. A path from the village center leads to **Sivrita,** an early Greek settlement that is now being excavated; rough and unpolished, the site gives you the sense that you're stumbling upon an ancient town in its original state. The **monastery of Moni Asomaton,** about 5km (3 miles) south, was founded in the 10th century, but its present building dates from the Venetian period. Walled and fortified, it's a remnant of the fierce resistance once put up to Turkish occupation; many objects from the 15th-century church are in the Historical Museum of Crete in Iraklion (see p. 195). In **Amari,** about 2km (1 mile) west, a Venetian clock tower looms over the main square, and the Church of Agia Anna is decorated with some of the oldest church frescoes in Crete, from 1225.

From Rethymnon, take beach rd. E 5km (3 miles) to Platanias. Drive S to Apostoli, then to Thronos.

Arkadi Monastery ★★★ HISTORIC SITE The ornate Italianate-Renaissance facade of this monastery, built on a high plateau under Venetian rule in 1587, rises out of pretty pastureland in a high valley at the base of Mount Ida. As serene as the setting is, Arkadi is a place of pilgrimage for many Cretans, for it was the seat of Cretan revolutionary fervor. By 1866, rebellious zeal against the occupying Turks was at fever pitch across Crete. Arkadi and many other monasteries across the island supported the rebels, and hundreds of men, women, and children took refuge there. A Turkish force of some 15,000 men besieged the monastery, but the Cretans refused to surrender. In November 8, just as the Turks broke through the gate and swarmed the compound, the abbot ordered that the gunpowder store be ignited. The explosion killed hundreds of Cretans and Turks, and the event has become synonymous with Crete's long struggle for independence. (November 8 is celebrated as a holiday in Crete.) Arranged around the vast rectangular inner courtyard, behind fortress-like walls, are a large church, monks' quarters, and the former

Mount Ida: Cradle of Zeus

Among the rugged peaks defining the Amari Valley (p. 206), **Mount Ida,** at more than 2,600m (8,530 ft.), is the tallest mountain on Crete. (The mountain is also called Psiloritis, which means "highest" in Greek.) Zeus was allegedly raised on Mount Ida in the **Idaian Cave.** Rhea, Zeus's mother, hid him in the cave out of harm's way from Kronos, his father. Kronos had already eaten five of his offspring—Hades, Poseidon, Hera, Hestia, and Demeter—in an effort to outwit a prophecy that one of his sons would rob him of power. Zeus later gave Kronos an emetic that caused him to regurgitate the five siblings, and in turn, they appointed their brother the god of gods. From the village of **Fourfouras,** serious hikers can begin the ascent to Ida's summit, a strenuous climb that takes about 8 hours.

refectory, now filled with vestments and other belongings of the community from over the centuries.

25km (15 miles) SE of Rethymnon; take national hwy. E to Maroulas, then well-marked road to Arkadi. Frequent bus service runs from Rethymnon. Admission 2€. Daily 8am–8pm.

Moni Preveli ★★★ HISTORIC SITE   One of Crete's most beautiful and beloved monasteries is perched in isolation high above the south coast, due south of Rethymnon. More than a thousand years old, the Preveli monastic community long enjoyed the direct patronage of the Patriarch of Constantinople, and its long history is commemorated in a small on-site museum. The main attractions, though, are the peaceful terraces that look across olive-studded hillsides to the Libyan Sea. This remote location and proximity to the sea account for the monastery's widespread fame, arising from the role it played in 19th- and 20th-century resistance movements—against the Turks, as early as 1821, when the abbot organized and outfitted the first rebels to take up arms against the Ottoman occupiers, and then against the Germans who invaded the island in 1941. During those long World War II years, the monastery became a rallying point for the Allies, sheltering British, Australian, and New Zealand soldiers left behind when Germans occupied the island in the aftermath of the Battle of Crete. Many of these men were saved by the monks and the residents of neighboring villages, who hid them until they could be picked up by submarine from the beach below. A **memorial** on the hillside just outside the monastery gates commemorates the Allied soldiers, Cretan resistance fighters, and others who lost their lives in the war. **Palm Beach,** reached by a steep path from the monastery grounds, is one of the most beautiful stretches of sand on Crete, enclosed within rocky cliffs and shaded by palms that grow along the banks of the Potamas River as it flows into the sea.

40km (25 miles) S of Rethymnon; take well-marked road S into the mountains to Spilli; 5km (3 miles) past town, take turnoff on right onto narrow road through gorges to monastery. Admission 2€. Daily 9am–7pm.

CHANIA ★★★

72km (45 miles) W of Rethymnon; 150km (93 miles) W of Iraklion

One of the most beautiful cities in Greece, Chania has been settled for nearly 4,000 years. While power changed hands many times over those centuries, much of today's city is Venetian and Turkish. Minarets rise above tile roofs and bell towers, and life still centers around a remarkable harbor built to foster Venice's power here in the southern Mediterranean. Old Chania is still a cosmopolitan and vibrant place, and is also a handy jumping-off point for excursions into the White Mountains, the west and south coasts, and the Samaria Gorge—some of the most spectacular scenery in Greece.

ARRIVING The **Chania** airport is 15km (10 miles) out of town on the Akrotiri Peninsula. Public buses meet all flights except the last one at night, but almost everyone takes a taxi (about 20€). The main **bus station** is south of the Old Town, off Plateia 1866 at 25 Kidonias (✆ **28210/93-306**).

VISITOR INFORMATION The **GNTO tourist office** is at 40 Kriari, off 1866 Square (www.west-crete.com; ✆ **28210/92-943**); it keeps unreliable hours but is usually open 9am to 1pm and 4pm to 7pm. Among many private agencies that can arrange tours is the excellent **Diktynna Travel,** 6 Archontaki (www.diktynna-travel.gr; ✆ **28210/43-930**).

Free parking is available along the sea to the west of the harbor; follow the signs as you enter town. One lot is for visitors and one is reserved for residents with permits, as is much of the street parking; observe signs carefully. You can get anywhere you want to go in town on foot, though you'll probably want to rent a car to explore the surrounding mountains and coastlines.

Where to Stay in Chania
EXPENSIVE

Casa Delfino ★★★ The engaging staff here works overtime to ensure guests feel at home, and quite a home it is! Owner Manthos Markantonakis has transformed his family's 17th-century Venetian palazzo into a remarkable place to stay, combining luxury with character. Many rooms are enormous and all are distinctive, filled with art work, Cretan antiques, and specially designed contemporary pieces; many are two-level, with sleeping lofts above living areas (make it known upon booking if steps are a problem). Guest enjoy a quiet haven amid the Old Town bustle in the mosaic-floored courtyard or a roof terrace overlooking the harbor.

9 Theofanous. www.casadelfino.com. ✆ **28210/87400.** 20 units. 195€–210€ double. Rates include breakfast. **Amenities:** Cafe; bar; roof terrace; Jacuzzi; room service; Wi-Fi (free).

Villa Andromeda ★★ A seaside estate that housed the German High Command during World War II is now a luxurious enclave of eight suites surrounding a garden and swimming pool. Several units spread over two levels, and some face the sea; all are comfortably and tastefully furnished with fine

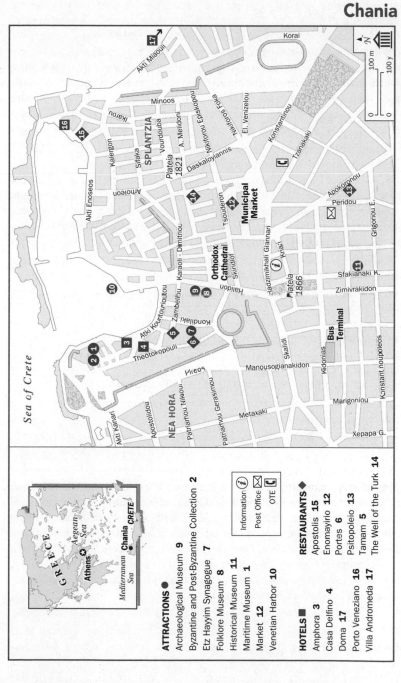

ATTRACTIONS ●

Archaeological Museum **9**
Byzantine and Post-Byzantine Collection **2**
Etz Hayim Synagogue **7**
Folklore Museum **8**
Historical Museum **11**
Maritime Museum **1**
Market **12**
Venetian Harbor **10**

Information ℹ
Post Office ✉
OTE ☎

HOTELS ■

Amphora **3**
Casa Delfino **4**
Doma **17**
Porto Veneziano **16**
Villa Andromeda **17**

RESTAURANTS ◆

Apostolis **15**
Enomayirio **12**
Portes **6**
Psitopoleio **13**
Tamam **5**
The Well of the Turk **14**

carpets, original art, and excellent beds. For a dip into history, you can dip your toes into a small pool in the garden in which it's said German general Rommel, a.k.a. the Desert Fox, once cooled off; there's also a larger pool that's more conducive to doing laps.

150 Venizelou. www.villandromeda.gr. *(C)* **28210/28300.** 8 units. 145€–240€ double. **Amenities:** Bar; pool; Wi-Fi (free). Closed mid-Nov to mid-Apr.

MODERATE

Amphora ★★   Plenty of old-world ambience is on hand at this beautiful 14th-century Venetian mansion just above the outer harbor. The sprawling rooftop terrace and many rooms look across the water· and the Old Town to the mountains beyond. Many rooms have balconies, as well as kitchenettes. Guests receive a discount at the hotel restaurant, one of the best on the waterfront—in fact, one of the few in town that maintain old-fashioned standards of service and honest home-cooking (one taste of the lemon soup, the house specialty, will convince you). Breakfast, served in a stone-walled room down the lane from the hotel entrance, is not included in room rates.

Theotokopoulou. www.amphora.gr. *(C)* **28210/93224.** 20 units. 110€–130€ double. **Amenities:** Restaurant; bar; roof terrace; Wi-Fi (free).

Doma ★★★   One of the most gracious hotels on Crete, Doma offers simple yet elegant accommodations in a seaside mansion that once served as a consulate. Antiques, historic photos, and a museum-quality collection of Asian headdresses fill the lounges and top-floor breakfast room, and a garden is accented with architectural bits and pieces. Traditional Cretan furnishings decorate the plain, handsome guest rooms; some face the sea, but the quietest overlook the garden. The airy penthouse suite, tastefully furnished with old Cretan pieces and kilims and opening to view-filled terraces, may well be the choicest accommodation in Chania.

124 Venizelou, along waterfront E of town center. www.hotel-doma.gr. *(C)* **28210/ 51772.** 25 units. 110€–120€ double. Rates include breakfast. **Amenities:** Bar; garden; Wi-Fi (free). Closed Nov–Mar.

Porto Veneziano ★★   On the harbor at edge of the Old Town, these newer and extremely spiffy premises may not have the historic pedigree of the surrounding Venetian landmarks, but the best of old-fashioned Cretan hospitality still abounds. Most of the large and pleasantly decorated, contemporary-style rooms face the sea and have airy balconies. Blue color palettes, and sea views through large expanses of glass, give the impression you're on a ship. Service is deft and personal; coffee, drinks, and snacks are served in a pleasant little garden and on a quayside terrace.

Akti Enosseos. www.portoveneziano.gr. *(C)* **28210/27100.** 57 units. 120€–140€ double. Rates include buffet breakfast. **Amenities:** Cafe; bar; room service; Wi-Fi (free).

Where to Eat in Chania

Apostolis ★★ SEAFOOD   Haniots have definite opinions about who serves the freshest fish in town, and this brightly-lit place next to the harbor is inevitably near the top of the list (**Karnagio** on nearby Plateia Katehaki is another top choice). No need to consult the menu: the waiters will show you the fresh catch, displayed on a bed of ice, then recommend the best way for it to be prepared. *Kalitsounia* (sweet cheese pie), *dakos* (rusk topped with feta and tomato), and other Cretan specialties accompany a meal.

Akti Enoseos. ℂ **28210/43470.** Main courses 7€–20€. Daily 11am–1am.

Enomayirio ★ SEAFOOD You can satisfy the cravings that a walk through Chania's market is sure to instill by taking a seat in this cramped, decidedly unstylish corner of the big hall. Since the fish and other seafood, along with vegetables and other ingredients, come from the surrounding stalls, freshness is guaranteed.

In the public market, at the "arm" with the fish vendors. Main courses 5€–18€; platter of mixed fish for 2 is 26€. Mon–Sat 9am–3:30pm.

Portes ★★ GREEK Owner-chef Susanna Koutloulaki is Irish by birth, but her takes on such traditional staples as moussaka, shrimp saganaki, and grilled chops are excellent, as are her innovations such as roasted vegetable salad and spicy chicken livers. The friendly environs spill onto a quiet backstreet along the walls in an out-of-the-way corner of Old Town. Although you're not on the harbor, a candle-lit table against the old stones provides plenty of atmosphere.

48 Portou. ℂ **28210/76261.** Main courses 7€–13€. Mon–Sat noon–1am; Sun 5pm–1am.

Psitopoleio ★ GREEK The butcher block and grill in the plain room make it clear that this is a meat-eater's paradise. Most of the clientele are Cretans who come here for the renowned chops, ribs, organ meats, and other carnivorous offerings, all from local suppliers and deftly prepared. To call the long, bare space "basic" is an understatement, and the dining experience is not for the faint hearted—meat is butchered in front of you, then grilled in great clouds of aromatic smoke. Specialties are lamb chops, pork chops, kidneys, spareribs, and sausages; excellent French fries, salads, and *tzatziki* accompany them. Bring cash and a willingness to leave any vegetarian leanings behind.

48 Apokorono, near municipal market. ℂ **28210/91354.** Main courses 6€–12€. Daily noon–3pm and 7:30pm–1am.

Tamam ★ GREEK/MEDITERRANEAN A former Turkish bath lends one of Chania's most popular restaurants its name, and the offerings are pan-Mediterranean, from as far away as Turkey. Peppers grilled with feta, salads made with mountain greens, vegetable croquettes, and kebabs are served, both along a lane out front and in a tall, tiled room that once housed the cold pools of the bath.

49 Zambeliou. ℂ **28210/96080.** Main courses 5€–14€. Daily noon–3pm and 7:30pm–1am.

Well of the Turk ★★ MIDDLE EASTERN You can find your way to this all-but-hidden restaurant at the heart of the old Turkish quarter, south of the Venetian Harbor, by keeping your eye on the minaret and asking for directions as you go. An enticing selection of Greek and Middle Eastern appetizers, juicy lamb dishes, meatballs mixed with eggplant, *laxma bi azeen* (a pita-style bread with a spicy topping), and other specialties are served on the ground floor of a Turkish house and in a lovely courtyard.

1–3 Kalinikou Sarpaki (on small st. off Daskaloyiannis). ℭ **28210/54-547.** Main courses 7€–20€. Wed–Mon 7pm–midnight.

Exploring Chania

Thick fortifications once surrounded the landward side of the Old Town. These walls did not ultimately repel the Turks who invaded in 1645, but the Venetian defenses proved so hard to topple that the invaders lost 40,000 men, an indignity for which the Turkish commander lost his head upon returning to Constantinople. The Turks subsequently fortified the walls. No amount of brick and mortar, however, could withstand the German bombs that rained down upon the city during the Battle of Crete in 1941, sparing only the western and eastern flanks that still separate the Old Town from Chania's eversprawling newer sections. In the Old Town surrounding the harbor, the palaces of the city's most prominent 15th- and 16th-century Venetian families line a warren of narrow stepped lanes.

Archaeological Museum ★ MUSEUM   Over the ages, Chania and the surrounding lands of western Crete have passed through the hands of the Minoans, Greeks, Romans, Genoese, Venetians, and Turks. Relics of this tumultuous past are on display in the former 16th-century Church of San Francesco. The artifacts here are more likely to charm than to overwhelm: a stone carved with Minoan houses standing next to the sea; a toy dog found in the tomb of a Greek boy; several colorful mosaics that once carpeted the floor of a Roman town house. A small garden, embellished with a 10-sided Turkish fountain and a Venetian doorway, is one of the most soothing spots in town. Just across the street is a remarkable-looking assemblage of 12 domes sitting atop a stone box. Under the Turks, this was Chania's largest *hamam* (baths). The city's Muslim inhabitants built their facility on the site of Roman baths, fed by a fresh supply of spring water; the *hamam* in turn became part of the Venetian Monastery of Saint Clara and is now a bronze foundry.

30 Halidon. ℭ **28210/90334.** Admission 2€, combined ticket with Byzantine and Post-Byzantine Collection 3€. Tues–Sun 8:30am–3pm.

Byzantine and Post-Byzantine Collection ★ MUSEUM   Christianity took root as early as the 1st century in Crete, and the Franciscan Monastery of San Salvatore, established by the Venetians next to the Firkas, houses many religious works from all the centuries that followed. Many pieces—mosaics from early basilicas, fragments of wall paintings of saints, bronze lamps used during services, and icons—were fashioned when Crete was under Byzantine and even Venetian rule, when Byzantine art continued to thrive on the island.

82 Theotokopoulou. ℰ **28210/96046.** Admission 2€, combined ticket with Archaeological Museum 3€. Tues–Sun 8:30am–3pm.

Etz Hayyim Synagogue ★★ RELIGIOUS SITE   Beginning in the 17th century, Evraiki, the neighborhood of tall houses and narrow lanes just south of the Firkas, was Chania's sizable Jewish ghetto. German authorities arrested and deported the residents in May 1944; tragically, all but a few drowned when the ship carrying them to Athens for transport to Auschwitz was torpedoed by the British. The Chania community was the last bastion of a Jewish population that had lived in Crete for more than 2,500 years—they are mentioned in the Bible—intermingling successfully over the millennia with the various cultures that occupied the island. Under Venetian rule, many emigrated to Venice and from there to other parts of Europe. This rich legacy is captured in Chania's one remaining synagogue, formerly the Venetian Church of St. Catherine, beautifully restored and reopened in 2000 for the first time since it was destroyed during World War II.

Parodos Kondylaki. ℰ **28210/96046.** Free admission. Mon–Fri 10am–6pm (shorter hours some winter days).

Folklore Museum ★ MUSEUM   Crete's rich folk traditions are captured here in artifact-filled re-creations of farm and domestic scenes. You'll find more orderly presentations of folk heritage elsewhere on Crete, but the casual, overstuffed feel of this cramped space—filled to bursting with furniture, farm implements, looms, and traditional clothing—imparts a strong appreciation for a way of life quickly disappearing.

46 Halidon. ℰ **28210/90816.** Admission 2€. Mon–Sat 9am–3pm and 6–9pm.

Historical Museum ★★ MUSEUM   A walk through the elegant turn-of-the-20th-century residential enclave south of the public gardens is in itself a pleasure, culminating in this town house filled with mementos of the island's 19th- and 20th-century history. These were not peaceful times in Crete, as you'll learn, with exhibits about the freedom fighters who finally won independence from the Turks and grisly photographs documenting the armed resistance against the German occupation during World War II. More peaceful times are evoked in charming rooms furnished with beautiful island textiles and domestic belongings. One room is devoted to Eleftherios Venizelos, born near Chania in 1864, who was instrumental in gaining independence for Crete, and twice served as prime minister of Greece. His influence during the nation's formative years has earned him the moniker "maker of modern Greece." He and his son, Sophocles, prime minister in the early 1950s, are buried on a hilltop just east of the city.

20 Sfakianaki. ℰ **28210/52606.** Admission 3€. Tues–Sun 8:30am–3pm.

Maritime Museum ★★ MUSEUM   The Firkas—the waterside fortress the Venetians built to keep a watchful eye on the sea lanes and their harbor—is the setting for models of prehistoric and Minoan boats and riveting renderings of the great naval battles of the Persian and Peloponnesian wars. The quirky and intriguing collections veer beyond the long history of Cretan and Greek shipping: Attention is paid to Crete's struggle for independence and unification with Greece, celebrated here when King Constantine hoisted the Greek flag above the Firkas on December 1, 1913. Photographs and artifacts also chronicle the Battle of Crete during World War II. A scale model re-creates the 17th-century Venetian city, and a step outside onto the ramparts reveals that palaces, sea walls, churches, and other landmarks remain remarkably intact.

Akti Kountourioti. ⓒ**28210/26437.** Admission 2€. Apr–Oct daily 9am–2pm; Nov–Mar daily 9am–4pm.

Market ★★ MARKET   Chania's handsome, cross-shaped covered market opened in 1913 as part of the celebrations surrounding the island's unification with Greece. Dozens of stalls are enticingly packed with typically Cretan products—olive oil, raki, honey, wild herbs and teas, gravouria and other mountain cheeses. Several small cafes serve spinach pie and other snacks. Just outside the west entrance is an outdoor extension of the market along Odos Skirdlof, where dozens of jam-packed little shops sell Cretan leather goods.

Southeastern edge of Old Town, behind harbor. Mon–Sat 8am–1:30pm; Tues, Thurs, Fri also 5–8pm.

Venetian Harbor ★★★ LANDMARK   The Venetians, accustomed to the beauty of their native city, lavished considerable care when they set about rebuilding the Byzantine town of Chania—renamed *Canea*—to their needs and tastes. First and foremost, they fortified the outer and inner harbors, enclosing the natural inlet with thick **walls** that could be entered only through one well-protected, narrow slip at the foot of a sturdy **lighthouse.** Around the outer harbor rose the palaces of well-to-do officials who reaped considerable profits from the timber for shipbuilding and other raw materials the island supplied, as well as from the lucrative trade routes to which Crete provided easy access. The inner harbor, lined with wharves, was a place of business where goods were stored and ships outfitted in massive *arsenali* (warehouses). The Turks added their own impossibly picturesque element to the east side of the harbor—a **mosque** with a large central dome surrounded by 12 smaller domes. It was intended as a place of worship for the Janissaries, an elite corps of 277 young Christian men whom the Ottoman Turks conscripted from throughout their holdings, converted to Islam, and trained as soldiers (it's open occasionally for temporary exhibitions). **Kastelli Hill** rises above the mosque; excavations at the top of the hill (closed but observable through the fence) reveal the remains of the Minoan city that early Greeks called Kydonia, for quince. Wharves along the harbor at the northern foot of the hill are lined with Venetian *arsenali.* One has been converted to a dramatic exhibition space, and another houses a replica of a Minoan ship.

Shopping in Chania

Among Chania's endless parade of shops, two stand out, and they happen to be side by side. At **Carmela,** 7 Anghelou (ⓒ **28210/90487**), owner-artist

Fitchburg

Fitchburg Public Library
South Central Library System

Items that you checked out

Title: Athens day by day /
ID. 39078075070008
Due: Wednesday, September 14, 2022

Title:
 Frommer's Athens and the Greek Islands.
ID: 39078089959820
Due: Wednesday, September 14, 2022

Title: Greece [2020] :
ID: 39078089817143
Due: Wednesday, September 14, 2022

Title: Greek islands.
ID: 39078082655920
Due: Wednesday, September 14, 2022

Title: Rick Steves Greece.
ID: 39078082559114
Due: Wednesday, September 14, 2022

Total items: 5
8/17/2022 11:57 AM
Checked out: 5
Ready for pickup: 0

Connect ❖ Discover ❖ Enjoy

At the northern tip of the Akrotiri Peninsula, which juts into the Cretan Sea east and north of Chania, stand three adjacent monasteries. Only a half-hour's drive from Chania, they preserve an aura of sanctity amid huge swaths of olive groves next to the sea. Admission is free, and they're open daily 7:30am to 7pm, with a midday break from noon to 3pm. A cypress-lined drive leads to the beautiful Venetian Gate of **Agia Triada,** beyond which are flower-filled courtyards and cloisters, a church, and a small museum of icons. A shop sells the monastery's excellent olive oil, some of Crete's best. The Venetian Renaissance **Moni Gouverneto** monastery at the northern tip of the peninsula is near the even more remarkable 11th-century **Monastery of Katholiko,** the oldest in Crete. The primitive complex was founded by John the Hermit, one of the island's most popular saints. Tradition has it John fled Muslim persecution in Asia Minor by sailing across the Aegean on his cloak and came ashore on these lands, where he and 98 followers lived in the caves that riddle a wild, rocky ravine. These caves, accessible via a 30-minute walk on a path from the Gouverneto courtyard, have long been associated with worship. The **Cave of the Bear,** named for the ursine shape of a stalagmite in the cavern, is believed to have been a place of ritual for the Minoans and a sanctuary of Artemis for the ancient Greeks. John spent his last days in a cave-hermitage farther along the path, near the old Katholiko monastery he founded, partially cut out of the rock face and embellished with a Venetian facade. The steep path ends at the sea, where you can end your pilgrimage with a swim from the rocks surrounding a paradisiacal little cove.

Carmela Latropoulou shows the work of jewelers and sculptors from throughout Greece. The pieces are extraordinary, often inspired by ancient works and made according to traditional techniques. Carmela is often on hand to discuss her wares and Greek craftsmanship. **Cretan Rugs and Blankets,** 3 Anghelou (© **28210/98571**), is enticingly filled with fine examples of top-quality local textile work, much of it antique and hand-woven.

Day Trips from Chania

The broad Akrotiri Peninsula, east of Chania, encloses the deep waters of Souda Bay, one of the finest natural harbors in the Mediterranean. This fact was lost on neither the ancient Greek residents of Aptera (p. 215), who built a port on the shores of the bay as early as the 7th century B. C., nor on the waves of invaders and pirates who followed them. NATO now operates a large naval base on the peninsula, and Chania's airport is there. At the base of the peninsula, Souda—Chania's port—draws visitors to the **Allied War Cemetery,** where some 1,500 of the 2,000 Commonwealth soldiers who died in the Battle of Crete are buried.

Aptera ★ ANCIENT SITE Walking through the hilltop ruins of this ancient city, in the foothills of the mountains just west of the Akrotiri Peninsula, is a head-spinning voyage through Crete's long history. Aptera was founded around 1200 B.C., at the end of the Minoan civilization. It became an important Cretan settlement for 7th- to 4th-century-B.C. Greeks; under them, Aptera had some 20,000 inhabitants and sent soldiers to aid the Spartans in their war against Athens. Aptera then became an important outpost for the Romans, for whom the city was a trading center that minted more than 75 different denominations of coins. You can still see traces of the Romans' elaborate vaulted cisterns and a theater, and a small chapel left by the Byzantines who followed them. Aptera fell into permanent ruin sometime after the 15th century, while the Turks built the 19th-century fortress of Izzedin on a promontory at the far northeastern tip of the site.

5km (3 miles) SE of Souda. Free admission. Daily 9am–5pm.

Stavros ★ TOWN The sandy beach at this scrappy little village on the north coast of the Akrotiri Peninsula is a pleasant place for a swim before heading back to Chania. Even more memorably, it was the setting for an iconic scene in the film *Zorba the Greek*—on this beach, backed by a barren promontory, Zorba teaches the young intellectual, Basil, to dance.

5km (3 miles) W of Gouverneto.

Vrisses and the Gorges ★★ TOWN/NATURAL WONDER This pretty village just off the north coast 35km (21 miles) southeast of Chania rests its fame on thick, creamy yogurt, topped with local honey and savored at a cafe table beneath the shade of plane trees alongside a rushing stream. Two of Crete's most beautiful churches are in the countryside just outside of Vrisses. The 11th-century, honey-colored church at **Samonas** rests atop a knoll in a green valley, with some well-preserved frescoes of the Virgin and Child inside; the **Church of the Panayia** in Alikambos, surrounded by orange groves, houses one of the finest fresco cycles in Crete, a vivid telling of the Bible story from Adam and Eve to the Crucifixion, painted in 1315. Both churches are usually open daily 8am to 5pm and admission is free, though donations are welcome. From Vrisses, a road heads south across the White Mountains to the fishing village of Hora Sfakion, following the fertile Kare Gorge into the rugged landscapes of the Imbros Gorge. The road follows the cliffs atop the gorges, providing some hair-raising views, and you can hike into the narrow canyon from the village of Imbros. On even a short scramble, you can experience the drama of the gorges, flanked by steep cliffs and forested with oak and cypress. Or, you can traverse the 11km (7-mile) length of the gorges, emerging on the south coast at Hora Sfakion after a few hours of fairly easy walking.

Exploring West & South of Chania

The most efficient way to hop from town to town along the southwest coast is often the daily ferry that stops at Loutro, Paleochora, Sougia, and other ports.

Ancient Polyrinia ★ ANCIENT SITE One of the most important Greek city-states of western Crete tops a remote hillside, a half-hour walk from the modern village of Polyrinia through meadows ablaze with wildflowers in spring. Legend has it that Agamemnon stopped at Polyrinia on his way back to Mycenae from Troy. He entered the city to make a sacrifice at the city's famous Temple to Artemis, but the proceedings were cut short when the king saw that his prisoners of war had set fire to his ships, anchored far below. The city still commands a view of much of the northwestern coastline; stone from the temple was used to construct the sturdy 19th-century Church of the Holy Fathers, incongruously still standing amid the ruins.

Take national hwy. from Chania 40km (25 miles) W to Kastelli, then 5km (3 miles) S toward modern Polyrinia. Take path from village to ancient Polyrinia. Free admission. Daily dawn-dusk; site is unattended.

Elafonisi ★★ BEACH A remote location at the southwestern tip of the island does not deter summertime beachgoers. This string of little inlets, lined with tamarisk-shaded sands and washed by shallow turquoise waters, rewards the long overland journey or the boat trip from Paleochora (p. 218). A sandbar, sometimes submerged, links the shoreline to a narrow islet, where another, less frequented, tree-shaded beach faces the open seas.

80km (50 miles) SW of Chania on west coast rd., then 5km (3 miles) S of Moni Chrysos-kalitissa.

Falasarna ★★ TOWN/BEACH Travelers who make it to the far western edges of Crete discover a long white-sand beach, washed by crystal-clear waters and interspersed with boulders. Just behind the beach are the scant remains of an ancient Greek harbor, once protected within thick walls. Due to shifts in sea levels over the past 2,500 years, the old stones are now scattered across a dry, rugged landscape several hundred feet from the shore.

60km (37 miles) W of Chania, after end of national hwy.

Hora Sfakion and Frangokastello ★ TOWNS Hora Sfakion is a rather forlorn-looking little fishing village that's enlivened by summertime hikers, who emerge here from the Imbros Gorge or pass through as they come and go from the Samaria Gorge (p. 219) on the ferries that ply the south coast. Take a moment to ponder the fact that the little port was the stage for a massive evacuation of Allied troops after Germans took the island in the Battle of Crete. **Frangokastello,** 10 km (6 miles) east of Hora Sfakion on a narrow road, surrounds a mighty Venetian fortress, erected on the flat coastal plain in

Crete's Rebel Hero

Frangokastello is most famously associated with one of Crete's favorite folk heroes, **Ioannis Daskalogiannis.** He is largely credited as the father of the movement to free Crete from the Turks, leading an uprising against the island's Ottoman administrators in 1770. Turkish troops suppressed the insurrection in fairly short order, and Daskalogiannis gave himself up outside the Frangokastello fortress, saving the lives of most of his 1,300 followers. He was taken to Iraklion and skinned alive, suffering the ordeal in dignified silence.

1371 as a defense against pirate raids and the rebellious local populace. Admission is 2€ and the fortress is usually open daily 9am to 4pm (hours vary). The surrounding landscape has not been altered much in the intervening centuries; the sandy beach and shallow waters in front of the fortress are especially popular with families.

Hora Sfakion is 60km (37 miles) S of Chania on a well-marked road off the national road.

Loutro ★★ TOWN   One of the most scenic, and remote, villages in Crete sits above a perfect semicircle of a bay and is accessible only on foot or by boat. A blessing for travelers in search of a getaway, its isolation was hardly a hindrance to the Romans, Venetians, and 19th-century Cretan freedom fighters who made use of Loutro's well-protected anchorage. The village's shady taverna terraces and clear waters are its biggest draws, but it's also the starting point for some rewarding hikes. A half-hour coastal walk leads east to **Sweetwater Beach,** named for the springs that bubble forth from the rocks. A more strenuous half-day excursion leads from Marmara Beach, east of Loutro, into the Aradena Gorge, a deep, oleander-scented cleft in the White Mountains. The walk ends at the abandoned village of **Aradena,** where half-ruined houses surround a sturdy 14th-century Byzantine chapel.

On south coast, 24km (15 miles) W of Hora Sfakion.

Moni Chrysoskalitissa ★ RELIGIOUS SITE   The name of this beautiful whitewashed monastery, appearing like a mirage atop an outcropping above the rugged coast, means "golden stair." Legend has it that one of the 90 stairs ascending to the monastery from the sea below is made of gold, but only those without sin can see it—which may explain why the stair has never been sighted in the 600 or so years since the hermitage was established. As many as 200 monks and nuns once lived at Chrysoskalitissa, but today only two remain.

On west coast rd. 35km (21 miles) S of Falasarna. Free admission. Daily 9am–7pm.

Paleochora ★★ TOWN/BEACH   It's been a long time since hippies wandering through southern Europe discovered this once-isolated fishing village, but Paleochora's setting is as appealing as ever—a rambling collection of whitewashed houses tucked into the end of a stubby peninsula, with a pebbly beach on one flank, a carpet of soft sand on the other, and a picturesquely ruined 13th-century Venetian fortress at the end. A quiet, out-of-the-way atmosphere still prevails, and some of Greece's most beautiful and unspoiled coastline scenery can be easily explored from Paleochora by foot and ferry boat. A pleasant walk of about 5km (3 miles) into the hills north of Paleochora ends at **Anidri,** where the simple little chapel is beautifully frescoed with images of St. George. From there, you can scramble down the steep hillside for a swim in one of several idyllic coves.

75km (47 miles) S of Chania.

Sougia ★★ TOWN/BEACH   The ancient Greeks erected a temple at Lissos to the west of Sougia, and the Romans established the port of Elyros, the ruins of which lie just to the east. Today, though, Sougia is a quiet and

HIKING THE samaria gorge ★★★

Although it's tucked away on the remote southwestern coast, the longest gorge in Europe is one of the most traveled places in Crete. Every morning from spring through fall, eager trekkers get off the bus at the head of the gorge on the Omalos Plateau and descend the Xyloskaka, the wooden steps, to begin a 15km (9-mile) walk to the sea at Agia Roumeli. While other gorges on the southern coast offer more solitude, none can match the Samaria for spectacle—the canyon is only 3m (10 ft.) wide at the narrowest passage, the so-called Iron Gates, and the sheer walls reach as high as 600m (1,969 ft.). Copses of pine and cedar and a profusion of springtime wildflowers carpet the canyon floor, where a river courses through a rocky bed, fed by little streams and springs. Kri-kri, the shy endangered Cretan wild goat, can sometimes be sighted on the flanks of the gorge, and eagles and other raptors soar overhead. Samaria has been a national park since 1962, and the only sign of habitation is the now-deserted village of Samaria and a church dedicated to its namesake, St. Maria. You will, of course, be partaking of this natural paradise with hundreds of other enthusiasts, but the experience will be no less memorable.

Many trekkers set off on organized gorge tours from Chania and Rethymnon. Most tour operators provide a bus trip to the drop-off at the Xyloskaka entrance; transfer by boat at the end of the hike from Agia Roumeli to **Hora Sfakion, Paleochora,** or **Sougia;** and a return trip from there by bus. Fees begin at about 30€, though at that price you'll be part of a large group. Out of Chania, **Diktynna Travel** (6 Archontaki St.; www.diktynna-travel.gr; ✆ **28210/43930**) is notable for its small groups and knowledgeable, personable guides; tours start at about 45€.

If you decide to hike the gorge on your own, you can take the morning bus from Chania or Rethymnon to Xyloskala or from Paleochora to Xyloskala. From the mouth of the gorge at Agia Roumeli, boats will take you to Hora Sfakion, Sougia, or Paleochora, and from there you can catch a bus back to Chania or Rethymnon, with connections to other towns on the island.

The gorge is open from mid-April through mid-October, depending on weather conditions; rains raise the risk of flash floods, and winds have been known to send rocks careening from great heights toward hikers. Entry is allowed from 6am to 4pm, and the entrance fee is 6€; you will be asked to show your ticket as you leave the gorge. (This way, park personnel can keep track of numbers entering and leaving and launch a search for errant hikers if necessary.) The trek takes 5 or 6 hours; boulders can make for some rough going in places. Mandatory gear includes sturdy hiking shoes, sunscreen, and a hat, plus a bathing suit for a well-deserved swim in the sea at the end of the hike. You'll want to bring a snack, but don't load yourself down with too much water—you'll come upon several freshwater springs along the way. Any tourist office on Crete can provide additional information on this phenomenal attraction.

unassuming place, where it seems unlikely that anything of too much import ever transpired. Home to no more than a few dozen families, the attractive little village is best known for its long, wide beach backed by cave-etched cliffs. Sougia is a popular outing from Chania, especially with hikers trekking through the Samaria Gorge. The temple at **Lissos,** a 3km (2-mile) walk along a spectacular seaside path, was dedicated to Asklepios, god of healing; a spring that bubbled forth into a fountain was reputedly therapeutic. Romans sought cures from the waters as well, and their small settlement, of which a few ruined houses remain, catered to ill legionnaires and colonists who made the sea journey to Lissos from throughout Crete.

75km (47 miles) S of Chania.

AGIOS NIKOLAOS ★

69km (43 miles) E of Iraklion

Attractive and animated, this busy resort town climbs steep hills above a natural curiosity, small but deep Lake Voulismeni. Just outside of town on the Elounda Peninsula, the shores are lined with some of Greece's most luxurious hotels.

ARRIVING Agios Nikolaos can be reached in about 1 hour by taxi or bus (1½ hr.) from the Iraklion airport. Bus service almost every half-hour of the day (in high season) links Agios Nikolaos to Iraklion; almost as many buses go to and from Sitia, and buses serves other towns in eastern Crete as well. The **KTEL** bus line (© **28410/22-234**) has its terminal in the Lagos neighborhood (behind the city hospital, which is up past the Archaeological Museum).

VISITOR INFORMATION The **municipal information office** in the heart of town at 34 Kondogianni (© **28410/22-357**) is one of the most helpful in all of Greece, perhaps because it's staffed by young seasonal employees with energy and enthusiasm; it's open mid-April to October daily, 8am to 10pm. In addition to providing maps and brochures, the staff can help arrange accommodations and excursions. Among the many travel agencies in town is **Nostos Tours,** 30 R. Koundourou, along the right arm of the harbor (www. nostoscruises.com; © **28410/26-383**); Nostos and other agencies in town arrange boat tours to the island of Spinalonga (p. 225).

Free parking is available along the sea, but observe parking signs carefully. A safe bet is to use one of the private parking lots (about 5€ for a day), including one at the corner of Kyprou and Koziri, just off the square (signed) at the top of Koundourou, the main street leading up from the harbor.

Where to Stay in & Around Agios Nikolaos

Agios Nikolaos is surrounded by some of the most luxurious resorts in the world, along the shores of the Elounda Peninsula. Many guests never leave the grounds of their privileged hideaways.

EXPENSIVE

Elounda Beach ★★★ The most famous and best of the large Greek resorts is a legend, an icon of the good life for generations of international travelers. After 45 years, somehow it keeps finding new ways to pamper guests. Accommodations come in dozens of variations, from standard-but-luxurious doubles to garden villas with private pools to contemporary-chic bungalows with high-tech gadgetry that would make James Bond feel at home. Some of the islands' most memorable lodgings are the terraced units hanging over the water off to one side of the property. The many amenities include water sports, spa treatments, and a variety of dining experiences, even a fake Greek village, and service that is never less than top-notch.

3km (2 miles) S of Elounda village. www.eloundabeach.gr. © **28410/63000.** 240 units. 400€–700€ double. Rates include buffet breakfast. **Amenities:** 5 restaurants; 4 bars; 2 beaches; multiple swimming pools; tennis courts; watersports; spa; Wi-Fi (free). Closed Nov–Mar.

Elounda Mare ★★★   Most of the guests at this idyllic retreat, one of Europe's truly great getaways, come back year after year, and it is easy to see why. Bungalows are tucked into verdant seaside gardens, and rooms and suites furnished elegantly in traditional Cretan style afford expansive views over the Gulf of Elounda. A sandy beach and all sorts of shady seaside nooks are among the many, many amenities. What most sets this luxurious lair apart is a sense of intimacy and a staff that make guests feel they're on a private seaside estate.

3km (2 miles) S of Elounda village. www.eloundamare.com. © **28410/68200.** 88 units. 400€–700€ double. Rates include buffet breakfast. **Amenities:** 3 restaurants; 2 bars; beach; swimming pool; tennis courts; watersports; spa; Wi-Fi (free).

St. Nicolas Bay ★★★   Within walking distance of Agios Nikolaos, this wonderful resort is a world removed, tucked away in gardens above a sandy beach. On hand are many of the same amenities for which the resorts farther out on the Elounda Peninsula are famed. The marble-floored rooms and suites, all with balconies or terraces, are awash in comfort, and low-key Cretan-style hospitality prevails. The final word in luxury here is a seafront bungalow with private pool, but you certainly won't feel deprived in any of these soothing accommodations.

Thessi Nissi. www.stnicolasbay.gr. © **28410/25041.** 90 units. 500€–700€ double. Rates include buffet breakfast. **Amenities:** 2 restaurants; 2 bars; beach; swimming pool; watersports; spa; Wi-Fi (free).

MODERATE/INEXPENSIVE

Akti Olous ★★   A sandy beach and rooftop pool make this affordable waterfront spot near the sunken city of Olus just outside Elounda village (p. 220) an pleasant alternative to the luxurious resorts nearby. All of the small but bright and well-furnished rooms are decorated in soothing aqua blues and greens, most overlook the sea, and all open to balconies. A restaurant and bar are on a waterside terrace just above the beach, a perfect spot for a sunset cocktail.

Waterfront, Elounda. www.eloundaaktiolous.gr. © **28410/41270.** 70 units. 55€–80€ double. Rates include breakfast. **Amenities:** Restaurant; bar; pool; beach; Wi-Fi (free).

Hotel du Lac ★   Though the name conjures up luxury hotels on the Italian Lakes, this hotel in Agios Nikolaos is typically Cretan, offering clean, airy, no-frills accommodations, half of which hang right over Lake Voulismeni. All of the crisply contemporary units have balconies; some are double-size studio suites with kitchenettes. A dining room terrace is tucked right onto the lakeshore.

28 Octobriou. www.dulachotel.gr. ℰ **28410/22711.** 18 units. 60€–80€ double. Rates include breakfast. **Amenities:** Restaurant; bar; Wi-Fi (free).

Where to Eat in & Around Agios Nikolaos

Itanos ★ GREEK   A big room decorated in what can only be called "no-nonsense" style and a good-weather rooftop terrace provide a welcome break from the harbor scene. The dishes served are old taverna favorites—grilled meats; chicken, lamb, or beef in tasty sauces; and hearty helpings of vegetables. The house wine comes from barrels. The old-fashioned approach applies to credit cards, too—they're not accepted, so bring cash.

1 Kyprou, Agios Nikolaos (just off Plateia Venizelos, at top of Koundourou). ℰ **28410/25-340.** Main courses 6€–12€. Daily 10am–midnight.

Marilena ★★ GREEK/MIDDLE EASTERN   The Elounda waterfront is a cluster of garish restaurants, none of which match the excellent cuisine and attentive service offered in this large room and even larger back garden. Grilled fish is a specialty, but you can dine very well on one of the house appetizer platters, a delicious array of spreads and small portions of meat and seafood.

Elounda Harbor. ℰ **28410/41322.** Main courses 6€–20€. Daily noon–midnight. Closed Nov–Feb.

Migomis ★★ GREEK/MEDITERRANEAN   Put on your best resort togs for a meal in the most romantic spot in town. The brick arches and wood-beamed ceilings in the open-air dining room will remind you of Italy, as will the many pastas and grilled Tuscan steaks. Views over the lake, town, and harbor are decidedly Greek, however, as are many of the seafood creations and Cretan salads. The gentle tinkling of ivories in the background, along with polished service, put even more shine on a meal here. A cafe next door serves coffee and light meals throughout the day.

20 Nikou, Agios Nikolaos. migomis.gr. ℰ **28410/24353.** Main courses 10€–25€. Daily noon–1am. Closed Nov–Mar.

Pelagos ★★ SEAFOOD   What many locals consider the freshest fish in town is served in the handsome, simply furnished rooms and garden of this neoclassical mansion near the sea in the heart of town. A good selection of Cretan wines lends another flourish to the reliably memorable meals here.

10 Ketahaki (at corner of Koraka, 1 block from waterfront), Agios Nikolaos. ℰ **28410/25737.** Main courses 6€–20€; some fish by the kilo. Daily noon–1am. Closed Nov–Feb.

Sarris ★ GREEK   It's worth wandering through the back streets of town to find this simple little taverna, where only a few dishes are prepared daily. Offerings often include rich stews of game and seafood. In warm months, service is across the street under a shady arbor overlooking a small church.

15 Kyprou, Agios Nikolaos. ℰ **28410/28059.** Main courses 5€–8€. No credit cards. Daily noon–11pm. Closed Nov–Mar.

Stavrakakis Rakadiko ★★ GREEK   When visiting Krista (p. 225), do yourself a favor and drive the few extra miles to this delightful little village taverna. Many of the ingredients that find their way into salads, *dolmades,* and other dishes are homegrown, served in memorably friendly surroundings.

Exo Laconia, 8km (5 miles) W of Agios Nikolaos.© **28410/22478.** Main courses 4€–8€. Daily noon–11pm.

Exploring Agios Nikolaos

Wedged between the Gulf of Mirabella and the Sitia Mountains, Agios Nikolaos picturesquely climbs the hills that surround **Lake Voulismeni.** There's a cheerful, holiday mood to the crowded waterfront and little lanes of this town, which is small enough that you can walk anywhere you want to go. In high season the streets around the port vibrate with visitors; the main street up from the harbor, **Koundourou,** is a good orientation point. You can swim right in town, from crowded but pleasant strips of sand at **Kitroplatia** and **Ammos.**

Archaeological Museum ★ MUSEUM   Among this museum's finds from the early civilizations of eastern Crete, you'll see one of the great masterpieces of early Greek art, the so-called **Goddess of Myrtos,** from around 2500 B.C. Playful and eerily modern, it's a rython—a libation vessel—in the shape of a long-necked woman cradling a jug in her arms. Artifacts from the many Minoan settlements on Crete's southeast coast include gold hairpins and a clay statue of a woman with a touchingly primitive face, her arms folded in worship. The skull of a Greco-Roman athlete from the 1st century B.C. was unearthed intact, as prepared for burial, with a laurel wreath petrified on his skull; next to it is a coin that was placed in his teeth as payment to Charon for rowing him across the River Styx into the underworld.

74 Paleologou.© **28410/24-943.** Admission 4€. Tues–Sun 8:30am–3pm.

Folklore Museum ★ MUSEUM   Colorful everyday items and local crafts pieces, from carved walking sticks to musical instruments, are displayed here alongside Cretan textiles and embroidery. A re-creation of a typical village house, furnished with traditional wooden pieces and kitchen equipment, is especially appealing.

2 Kondalaki.© **28410/25093.** Admission 2€. Tues–Sun 10am–1pm.

Lake Voulismeni ★ NATURAL SIGHT   Agios Nikolaos sprang up around this tiny, deep lake, lying just inland next to the harbor. Legend has it that the lake was a favorite bathing spot for the goddess Athena, and that the waters are bottomless (in fact the depth has been definitively measured at 65m/213 ft.).

Agios Nikolaos Shopping

At **Ceramica,** 28 Paleologou (© **28410/24-075**) you have a chance to visit the workshop of one of the masters of this art, Nikolaos Gabriel, who creates authentic and vivid vases. He also carries a line of fine jewelry, made by others to his designs. Across the street, at no. 1A, **Xeiropoito** sells handmade rugs. **Pegasus,** 5 Sfakianakis, on the corner of Koundourou (© **28410/24-347**),

Byzantine Art on Crete

Byzantine art flourished on Crete in the 15th century, as artists fled to the island just before and after the fall of Constantinople in 1453. Crete became the center of the Byzantine art world, and hundreds of artists studied and worked in Iraklion (then known as Candia) and elsewhere around the island. As a Venetian possession, Crete met the Republic's need for a steady stream of Byzantine-influenced paintings and icons, but Cretan art was shipped throughout Greece and other parts of Europe as well. Cretan artists also painted frescoes on the walls of churches and monasteries across the island; it's estimated that more than 800 of these beautiful wall paintings remain in place. Some of the most elaborate and best-preserved are those in the **Panagia Kera** in Krista (p. 225). The art of icon painting is kept alive at **Petrakis Workshop for Icons** in Elounda (see below), which supplies churches throughout Europe and North America.

offers a selection of jewelry, knives, icons, and trinkets—some old, some not. **Elixir,** Koundourou 15 (© **28410/82593**) is piled high with Cretan olive oil, spices, wines and other local products. The icon tradition is kept alive in Elounda at the studio/store **Petrakis Workshop for Icons,** 22 A. Papendreou, on the left as you come down the incline from Agios Nikolaos, just before the town square (www.greek-icons.com; © **28410/41669**). Georgia and Ioannis Petrakis work seriously at maintaining this art. Orthodox churches in North America as well as in Greece buy icons from them.

Day Trips from Agios Nikolaos

From Agios Nikolaos, the coast road leads north onto the Elounda Peninsula. Elounda village is 11km (7 miles) north of Agios Nikolaos. Follow the road east another 100 km (62 miles) and you'll end up at one of Greece's most famous beaches, the palm-backed swath of golden sand at **Vai.**

Elounda ★ TOWN   A dramatic hillside road follows the Gulf of Mirabello along the flanks of the Elounda Peninsula to this once quiet fishing village. Some of Greece's most sybaritic resorts now surround Elounda, providing the world-weary with many luxuries—none of which can top the views of the crystal-clear waters of the gulf and the stark beauty of the landscape. Ancient Greeks established the city of Olus on these shores, though a noted temple to the mountain goddess Britomartis and other structures were submerged more than 2,000 years ago. Scant remains are now visible beneath the waves off a causeway just east of the village; the waters above the ruins are popular with snorkelers.

Gournia ★★ ANCIENT SITE   This small town is often called the Minoan Pompeii, because the well-preserved ruins surrounding a small governor's palace so richly evoke everyday life in ancient times. Harriet Boyd-Hawes, an American archaeologist, began to excavate the site in 1901, and her work unearthed olive presses, carpenter's tools, a coppersmith's forge, and other artifacts that yield clues to the enterprises that once kept its 4,000 inhabitants busy. Stepped streets climb hilly terrain and cross two major avenues, running at right angles to each other, that are lined by stone houses with workrooms or shops open to the street. Ladders inside lead to storage rooms below and living quarters above ground level. Gournia is near a narrow neck where the island is only 12km (7 miles) wide, so the fishermen-trader inhabitants could either embark from the town's harbor or make their way to the south shore and set sail from there.

Just off the national hwy. odysseus.culture.gr. ℭ **28410/22462.** Admission 2€. May–Oct daily 8am–7:30pm; Nov–Apr daily 8:30am–3pm.

Krista ★ TOWN Beautiful woven goods are strung in front of shops surrounding the beautiful plateia of this mountain village. More artistry fills the small 14th-century **Panagia Kera,** where some of Crete's most accomplished Byzantine frescoes cover the walls of the three naves: Scenes depict the life of Christ, the Second Coming, some fearsome views of damnation, and several lesser known biblical tales, including the prayer of Saint Anna. The childless Anna prayed fervently, promising to bring a child up in God's ways, and she gave birth to Mary, mother of Christ. Accordingly, the colorful little church is popular with women seeking to bear children. The church is in countryside about 1km (less than a mile) north of the town center and is open Monday through Saturday 9am to 3pm, Sunday 9am to 2pm; admission is 3€.

Krista is 9km (6 miles) SW of Agios Nikolaos.

Palace of Malia ★ ANCIENT SITE Another palace, outside the atrociously overdeveloped resort town of the same name, was once a beachhead of Minoan administration on the eastern end of the island. The ruins of this third-largest Minoan palace on Crete are not as overwhelming as those at Knossos or Phaestos, yet they richly evoke a Minoan settlement. As you walk through the ruins, you'll get a good sense of how the Minoans were both practical and highly ceremonial, placing storage, administrative, religious, and living facilities side by side throughout the palace complex. Granaries and storerooms surround large courtyards that were probably used for public gatherings and religious ceremonies. A limestone *kernos,* a large table etched with hollows in which seeds and other offerings were placed, stands near the central court, once lined with porticos; from there a large staircase, a hallmark of most Minoan palaces, ascends to terraces and more ceremonial spaces. Domestic apartments were located off the northern court. The sea laps against the northern side of the settlement, and the brooding Lasithi Mountains loom just a mile or so to the south—a natural setting that lends Malia a sense of timelessness despite the clutter of nearby resorts.

30km (19 miles) W of Agios Nikolaos on the national hwy. 3km (2 miles) east of Malia. odysseus.culture.gr. ℭ **2897/31597.** Admission 4€. July–Oct Tues–Sun 8am–7:30pm; Nov–June Tues–Sun 8:30am–3pm.

Spinalonga ★★ HISTORIC SITE When the ancient Greeks inhabited nearby Olus, this island in the Gulf of Mirabello was still a peninsula, and its seaward flanks were fortified to protect the busy shipping channels. These bastions did not thwart Arabic pirates, however, who laid waste to the gulf shores around the 7th century. The region was not inhabited again until the 15th century, when the Venetians came to mine salt in the shallows of the gulf. They cut a channel to create an island, which they named Spina Longa (Long Thorn) and turned into a virtually impregnable fortress. Over the centuries, this barren outcropping became a refuge time and again. When the Turks overran the rest of Crete in the late 17th century, Spinalonga was one of the last spots to be conquered, remaining in Venetian hands until 1715; it became a place of refuge for Christians fearing persecution from the Ottoman occupiers. In turn, 200 years later it sheltered Turkish families after the Ottomans were overthrown in the war for Greek Independence in 1866. Another wave of refugees arrived in 1903, this time under force, when Spinalonga became a leper colony, used as such until 1952. One of the entrances to the island, the one used by arriving lepers, is known as Dante's Gate, so fearsome was its reputation. Once there, the ill received decent treatment, though they were condemned to isolation.

Today the island's spooky ruins and pebbly beaches are popular with day-trippers. Tour boats sail from Agios Nikolaos, Elounda, and Plaka (a fishing village just north of Elounda); the trip from Agios Nikolaos takes an hour and costs about 15€ a person, from Elounda or Plaka it's 15 minutes and 7€. Simply walk along the docks in any of these towns and you'll practically be pulled aboard one of the excursion boats. As boats approach the island, they cruise slowly past the tiny, uninhabited nearby islet of Agioi Pantes to catch a glimpse of the *agrimi,* also known as the *kri-kri,* a species of long-horned wild goat endemic to Crete and now endangered; this little island and the Samaria Gorge (p. 219) are among the last refuges for the shy animals. Try to go early in the morning, leaving no later than 10am, to avoid the midday sun and the crowds that converge on the otherwise deserted island. Back on shore, stop by a newsstand to pick up a copy of *The Island,* a novel by Victoria Hislop set in Plaka and Spinalonga.

THE DODECANESE

H ugging the coast of Asia Minor, in the eastern Aegean far from the Greek mainland, the Dodecanese islands are frontier lands, lying at the crossroads of East and West. Over the ages, they have been conquered and settled time and again—by Romans, medieval knights, Ottomans, Venetians, and early-20th-century Italians—who left behind them such landmarks as the ruins of the Askepleion on Kos and the Street of the Knights in Rhodes. These days the islands are invaded every summer by sun worshippers, drawn by beaches that in many cases are among the most spectacular in Greece.

The name means the Twelve Islands (although the archipelago actually consists of 32 islands); each island has its own personality and its own natural beauty. Patmos and Symi are dry and arid in summer, while the interiors of Rhodes and Kos remain fertile and forested. Likewise, Patmos and Symi are relatively quiet, relaxed getaway-from-it-all islands, while Rhodes and Kos are the more popular and brasher siblings.

RHODES (RODOS) ★★

250km (135 nautical miles) E of Piraeus

Selecting a divine patron was serious business for an ancient city. Most Greek cities played it safe and chose a mainstream god or goddess, a ranking Olympian—someone such as Athena or Apollo or Artemis, or Zeus himself. It's revealing that the people of Rhodes chose Helios, the sun, as their signature god.

The islanders made a wise choice, and Helios continues to bestow good fortune on the island. More than two millennia later, this island that receives on average more than 300 days of sunshine a year can still attribute its good fortune to sun-starved travelers from colder, darker, wetter lands around the globe. A strategic location at the intersection of the East and West has been both a blessing and a curse for Rhodes. Floating between Europe, Asia Minor, and North Africa, the island has been a draw for Persians, Hellenistic Greeks, Romans, Byzantines, Crusader Knights, Venetians, Ottomans, and Italians.

Rhodes is also beautiful, though the modern era has always not been gentle with much of the coastal strip. With a selective eye you can still see an island ringed with clean golden beaches, rising across fertile plains to a mountainous interior.

Essentials

ARRIVING **Olympic Airways** (www.olympicairlines.com; ✆ 210/926-9111) offers year-round service between Rhodes and Athens and Thessaloniki, and summer service between Rhodes and Iraklion (Crete), Karpathos, and Santorini. **Aegean Airlines** (www.aegeanair.com; ✆ 801/112-0000 in Greece) has flights to Rhodes and Athens, and in summer adds service between Rhodes and Thessaloniki and Iraklion, Crete. Flights fill quickly, so reserve in advance. The Rhodes **Paradissi Airport** (✆ 22410/83-214) is 13km (8 miles) southwest of the city. Bus service from the airport runs from 6am to 10:30pm; fare to the city center (Plateia Rimini) is 6€. A taxi costs 22€.

Rhodes is a major port with sea links to Athens, Crete, and the islands of the Aegean, as well as to Cyprus, Turkey, and Israel. Service and schedules are always changing; check with the tourist office or a travel agency for the latest information. For detailed information about the most active ship line, **Dodekanisos Seaways,** (www.12ne.gr). In late spring and throughout the summer, there are daily sailings—some with high-speed hydrofoils or catamarans—between Rhodes and many of the Dodecanese and other islands in the eastern Aegean: Kos, Kalimnos, Kastellorizo, Leros, Nissiros, Patmos, Samos, Symi, and Tilos. Ferry, hydrofoil, catamaran, or excursion boat schedules and tickets are available from **Triton Holidays** (tritondmc.gr; ✆ 22410/21690).

VISITOR INFORMATION During the high season only, you'll find a helpful **Rhodes Municipal Tourist Office** at Plateia Rimini, facing the port taxi stand (✆ 22410/35-945). It dispenses information on local excursions, buses, ferries, and accommodations, and offers currency exchange as well. Its hours are Monday through Saturday from about 9am to 9pm, Sunday from 9am to 2pm. **Triton Holidays** (see above) is also willing to answer any traveler's question, free of obligation, and is sometimes open when the tourist offices are closed.

GETTING AROUND Walking is the easiest way of getting around Rhodes Town, and in most of the Old Town it's the only way—taxis are not allowed within the walls unless you have luggage and are arriving or leaving. (Even then, you might have to ask your hotel to meet you at one of the gates and escort you down the narrow lanes.) The largest of many **taxi** stands is on the harbor front in Plateia Rimini. Set fares for one-way trips throughout the island are clearly posted. (A sample fare to Lindos is 40€ one way; add at least another 20€ if the taxi waits for you.)

The rest of the island is well served by **bus;** the tourist office can give you a schedule of routes and times. Buses to points east (except for the eastern

The Dodecanese

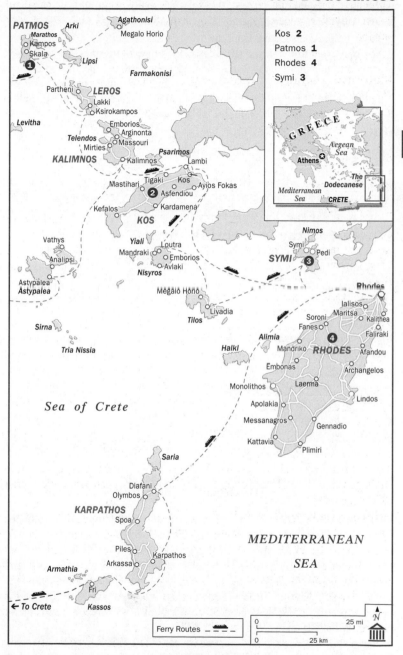

Kos **2**
Patmos **1**
Rhodes **4**
Symi **3**

PATMOS · Arki · Agathonisi
Marathos · Megalo Horio
Kampos
Skala · **1**
Lipsi
Partheni · LEROS · Farmakonisi
Lakki
Levitha · Ksirokampos
Emborios
Telendos · Arginonta
Mirties · Massouri
KALIMNOS · Kalimnos · Psarimos
Lambi
Tigaki · Kos
Mastihari · **2** · Ayios Fokas
Asfendiou
Kefalos · Kardamena
KOS
Vathys · Yiali
Mandraki · Loutra
Analipsi · Emborios
Avlaki
Astypalea · Nisyros
Astypalea
Megalo Horio
Sirna · Livadia
Tilos
Tria Nissia

Nimos
Symi · Pedi
SYMI · **3**

Rhodes
Ialisos · Maritsa
Soroni · Kalithea
Fanes · Faliraki
Alimia · Mandriko · RHODES · **4** · Afandou
Halki · Embonas · Archangelos
Monolithos · Laerma
Apolakia · Lindos
Sea of Crete · Messanagros · Gennadio
Kattavia · Plimiri

Saria
MEDITERRANEAN
Diafani
Olymbos · SEA
KARPATHOS
Spoa
Piles · Karpathos
Armathia · Arkassa
Fri
← To Crete · Kassos

GREECE
Aegean Sea
Athens
Mediterranean Sea · The Dodecanese
CRETE

Ferry Routes

0 · 25 mi
0 · 25 km

N

229

coastal road as far as Falilraki) leave from the **East Side Bus Station** on Plateia Rimini, whereas buses to points west, including the airport, leave from the nearby **West Side Bus Station** on Averof. Buses for the eastern coastal road as far as Falilraki also leave from the West Side Bus Station.

You may want to rent a **car** for a day or two to explore some of the remote beaches and inland villages. Prices begin at about 35€ per day, depending on the season and demand. Keep in mind that some of the more remote roads on Rhodes require all-terrain vehicles, and Rhodian rental-car companies usually stipulate that their standard vehicles be driven only on fully paved roads.

TOURS   Several operators lead nature, archaeology, shopping, and beach tours around the island. **Triton Holidays** (p. 228) offers day and evening cruises, hiking jaunts, and full-day guided tours to Lindos and small villages, churches, and monasteries. Along Mandraki Harbor, you can find excursion boats that leave for Lindos at 9am and return around 6pm, costing about 50€, as well as daily excursions to Symi for 64€ round-trip.

Where to Stay in Rhodes Town

The lanes of Old Town are lined with atmospheric places to stay. Many can be reached only on foot; hosts usually arrange to meet guests at the gates and escort them to the hotel. While you'll forgo a beachfront and sea views, it's hard to imagine more evocative surroundings than history-soaked Old Town.

EXPENSIVE

Kokkini Porta Rossa ★★   Rhodes' long tradition of extending hospitality to travelers comes to the fore in this beautifully restored mansion just inside the St. John Gate (aka Porta Roassa). Fireplaces, enclosed wooden balconies, high wooden ceilings, and treasure-filled nooks and crannies are the legacy of a long succession of Turkish and Greek families, whose former quarters still exude the aura of a private home. Tasteful modern design enhances the rough stone walls and old wood and tile floors, while modern bathrooms are large and sumptuous, and a beautiful garden lies just beyond gracious guest lounges.

Kokkini Porta. www.kokkiniporta.com. ✆ **22410/75111.** 5 units. 195€–340€ double. Rates include buffet breakfast. **Amenities:** Bar; garden; room service; Wi-Fi (free).

Spirit of the Knights ★★★   Five luxurious suites and a cozily medieval chamber are tucked away in a beautifully restored Ottoman house in the quietest part of the Old Town. Hand-painted ceilings, original beams, Ottoman stained glass, marble baths, rich carpets and textiles, and other exquisite details embellish the meticulously maintained surroundings. A courtyard is cooled by a fountain where you're quite welcome to soak your cobble-weary feet. The family members who lovingly created this intimate retreat are just as devoted to making their guests feel welcome.

14 Alexandridou. www.rhodesluxuryhotel.com. ✆ **22410/39765.** 6 units. 200€–350€ double. Rates include buffet breakfast. **Amenities:** Bar; garden; room service; Wi-Fi (free).

ATTRACTIONS ●
Archaeological Museum **2**
City walls **13**
Hospice of St. Catherine **6**
Jewish Quarter **7**
Monte Smith **15**
Street of the Knights **1**

HOTELS ■
Kokkini Porta Rossa **12**
Marco Polo Mansion **8**
Medieval Inn **11**
S. Nikolis Hotel
  and Apartments **10**
Spirit of the Knights **9**

RESTAURANTS ◆
Alexis 4 Seasons **5**
Manolis Dinoris Fish
  Taverna **3**
Marco Polo Mansion **8**
Palia Historia
  (The Old Story) **14**
Pita Fan **4**

MODERATE

Marco Polo Mansion ★★★   A 15th-century Ottoman mansion set in a lush garden is now a positively transcending hotel. Each room is distinctive—one was a harem, another a *hamam,* another is lined with kilims; smaller garden rooms are nestled amid fragrant greenery. All are decorated in deep hues that look like they've been squeezed from a tube, and furnished with low-lying couches and stunning antiques—little wonder style and fashion magazines love to photograph this exotically beautiful place. Excellent meals are served in the garden, where non-guests are welcome to share in one of the island's nicest dining experiences.

Aghiou Fanouriou 40–42. www.marcopolomansion.gr. ⓒ **22410/25562.** 17 units. 120€–180€ double. Rates include breakfast. **Amenities:** Restaurant; bar; garden; Wi-Fi (free). Closed Nov–Apr.

S. Nikolis Hotel and Apartments ★★   You'd be hard-pressed to find a better place to soak in the medieval ambiance of Old Town than this charming and atmospheric cluster of houses from 1300 that surround a flower-filled courtyard. Proprietor and host Sotiris Nikolis and his family have lovingly restored the original structures down to the last stone and beam, unearthing such treasures as a 10-ton marble pediment dating from the 2nd century lodged beneath the medieval foundations. They've filled rooms with antiques and personal flair, and embellished some with sleeping lofts, kitchenettes, balconies, and Jacuzzis. A roof terrace overlooks the Old Town, and a pleasant bar is tucked into the rear of the garden.

61 Ippodamou. www.s-nikolis.gr. ℂ **22410/34-561.** 16 units. 60€–120€ double. **Amenities:** Restaurant (rooftop); bar; garden; Wi-Fi (free). Call ahead Nov–Mar to see if hotel is open.

INEXPENSIVE

Medieval Inn ★★   No medieval gloom and doom here: this whitewashed old house surrounding a shady courtyard is full of bright colors and enhanced with the warmth of hosts Manis and Lily. Rooms are small and fairly basic, and in some the bathrooms are private but not en suite. Still, they're an excellent value given the comfort and ambiance. A courtyard and sunny roof terrace invite long hours of lounging, while the sights of Old Town are just beyond the front gate.

8 Timachida St. www.medievalinn.com. ℂ **22410/22469.** 12 units. 55€–65€ double. Rates include breakfast. **Amenities:** Bar; garden; Wi-Fi (free). Closed Nov–Mar.

Where to Eat in Rhodes Town

EXPENSIVE

Manolis Dinoris Fish Taverna ★ GREEK/SEAFOOD   The former stables of the 13th-century Knights of St. John's provides an atmospheric backdrop to some of the island's best seafood creations. *Psarokeftedaka* (fish balls), made from the kitchen's secret recipe, can be followed by the house's sea urchin salad, one of many shrimp and mussel dishes, or grilled prawns and fresh fish. Meals are served in a quiet side garden in summer and a handsome stone and wood room in winter, next to a blazing fire. Well-priced set menus are available, as is a very reasonable lunch buffet.

14A Museum Sq. www.dinoris.com. ℂ **22410/25-824.** Main courses 30€–65€. Daily noon–midnight.

MODERATE

Alexis 4 Seasons ★★ GREEK/SEAFOOD   The Karapanos family is a Rhodes legend, famed beyond the island for the seafood creations they've served at Alexis Taverna for more 70 years. Now a younger generation continues the tradition, offering a slightly less formal, less expensive, but no less memorable experience in a multilevel rose-and-bougainvillea-scented garden and a stone-walled parlor in colder weather. The emphasis here is also on seafood, from flavorful shrimp risotto to sea bass and other fish plucked from local seas and chargrilled to perfection. Salads and vegetables come from the restaurant's own garden. Any meal should end over an after-dinner drink on the roof terrace, with harbor lights and a canopy of stars adding to the enchantment.

33 Aristoltelous. www.alexis4seasons.com. ℰ **22410/70522.** Main courses 12€–22€. Daily noon–midnight.

Marco Polo Mansion ★★★ GREEK   The danger of dining here is that few other places come close to being as exotic and welcoming as the garden of the home of a 16th-century Ottoman official. Hosts Efi and Spiros encourage their guests, most of whom have dined here many, many times, to settle back and enjoy a meal beneath the banana trees and hibiscus trellises. The kitchen comes up with a few special dishes each evening—grilled lamb, roasted pork filet, a bounty of seafood—made with the freshest ingredients and accompanied by excellent mezes and salads.

Aghiou Fanouriou 40–42. www.marcopolomansion.gr. ℰ **22410/25562.** Main courses 10€–18€. Daily 7:30–11pm. Closed Nov–Apr.

Palia Historia (The Old Story) ★ GREEK   A rustic house in the New Town is the setting for some of the best meals to be had on the island. This doesn't mean exotic, just the freshest local ingredients and time-honored recipes for classic dishes as slow-cookcd pork with mushrooms or shrimp saganaki. Their roasted goat is tender and flavorful enough to dispel any reservations you might have had about this island staple.

108 Mitropoleos (in New Town, below modern stadium). ℰ **22410/32 421.** Main courses 12€–28€. Daily 7pm–midnight.

INEXPENSIVE

Pita Fan ★ GREEK/FAST FOOD   A surprisingly atmospheric spot for a quick lunch or snack—or for that matter, a submission to a late-night craving—is this busy corner with outdoor tables near the Jewish Quarter. From the grill and spit come delicious gyros and souvlaki, served with cold draft beer. These fast-food standards taste all the better when the surroundings are atmospheric Turkish houses with wooden balconies and a splashing seahorse fountain.

Ermou 60. ℰ **2241/073670.** About 5€. Daily noon–6am.

Where to Stay & Eat in Lindos

Mavrikos ★ GREEK/FRENCH   For 70 years, this Rhodes favorite has been a draw for the rich and famous as well as legions of travelers who happen to be famished after the climb to the Acropolis in Lindos. Brothers Michalis and Dimitri Mavrikos carry on the family legacy on a rustic, sea-facing terrace off the main square. It feels like other homey Greek tavernas—until the Greek and French dishes start coming out of the kitchen: oven-baked lamb, beef in a casserole with bergamot, tuna with fenugreek, and perfectly grilled beef filets or seasoned fresh red snapper. The brothers Mavrikos also run an ice-cream parlor **Geloblu,** serving homemade frozen concoctions and cakes. It's in the Old Town, near the church.

Main square, Lindos. ℰ **22440/31-232.** Main courses 10€–30€. Daily noon–midnight.

Melenos Lindos Hotel ★★★   An authentically Lindian-style villa is a work of art, where hand-painted tiles, local antiques, handcrafted lamps, and weavings provide the backdrop for an almost otherworldly experience on a pine-scented hillside at the edge of the Old Town. Huge Lydian beds are multilevel affairs that make anyone feel like a reclining pasha, while all rooms open to large, nicely furnished terraces embellished with statuary and architectural fragments, plus views out to the sea that washes against the shores of an adjacent cove. This distinctive retreat is the work of Michalis Melenos, who is on hand to ensure his guests are well-cared for. His hospitality extends to excellent Mediterranean-influenced dinners served on a roof terrace, and most helpfully, sending a staff member to meet you at the entrance to town and escort you to his gate.

Lindos Town. www.melenoslindos.com. ℂ **22440/32-222.** 12 units. 210€–310€ double. Rates include buffet breakfast. **Amenities:** Restaurant; bar; room service; Wi-Fi (free).

Exploring Rhodes Town ★★★

Rhodes Town (pop. 50,000) is a town divided—between the walled Old Town, a remarkable evocation of the Middle Ages, and the New Town that spreads outside those massive walls. Actually, the so-called New Town is not new at all; it was settled in the 16th century, and its waterfront is lined with the distinctive arcaded New Market and other art deco landmarks erected by the Italians who laid claim to the island in the early 20th century.

Best to know one thing from the start about **Old Town:** It's not laid out on a grid—not even close. There are roughly 200 streets or lanes that have no name. Getting lost here, however, is an opportunity to explore. Whenever you feel the need to find your bearings, ask for **Sokratous,** the closest Old Town comes to having a main street.

When you approach the walls of Old Town, you are about to enter what is arguably the most impressive continuously inhabited medieval town in Europe, a thrill to explore and a character-infused place to stay (p. 230). Of the 11 gates, the best way to enter is through **Eleftheria (Liberty) Gate** into **Plateia Symi.** Ruins of the **Temple of Venus,** which date from the 3rd century B.C., are somewhat diminished by the adjacent parking lot, but the few stones and columns still standing are reminders of the great Greek and Roman city that once stood here. The population of Ancient Rhodes is thought to have equaled that of the entire island today, roughly 100,000.

Archaeological Museum ★ MUSEUM   The stone halls where the knights once fed the poor and tended to the infirm now house finds from around the island. The most elegant and acclaimed presence is *Aphrodite of Rhodes,* fashioned in creamy marble from the island of Paros 2,000 years ago; the plump beauty is pushing her long tresses back as she prepares to step into her bath. Underfoot in the courtyard are some paving stones of the ancient road that led to the harbor, and some touching Roman-era tombstones (steles) line the walls. Among the deceased so honored is Ploutos, aged 3, who died "loosening the support of a cart which had upon it a heavy load of stakes."

The Knights of St. John

The great walls of Rhodes Town's Old Town and its impressive medieval landmarks are the work of the Knights of the Order of St. John (aka Hospitallers), a mixed lot of western European Catholic crusaders who functioned as occupation army and charity foundation wherever they settled. Forced by the Muslims to abandon the Holy Land in 1309, they retreated to Rhodes, where they built castles and fortifications using the forced labor of the native Rhodians. The knights remained on Rhodes until 1522, when, after a 6-month siege, the Muslims forced them to surrender again and retreat to Malta.

Museum Sq. odysseus.culture.gr. ⓒ **22410/31048** or 25500. Admission 3€. April–Oct Mon 1:30–8pm, Tues–Sun 8am–8pm; winter reduced hours.

City Walls ★★★ LANDMARK   Among the knights' most formidable achievements was the circuit of walls that still enclose the Old Town. It's awe-inspiring to imagine the engineering skill and brute labor that went into constructing the 4km (2½ miles) of masonry, up to 40 feet thick in places. With fortified gates, bastions, and such innovations as curvatures to deflect cannon balls, the walls repelled attacks by Egyptians and Ottomans and were compromised only when an earthquake rocked the island in 1481. You can walk around the walls in their entirety by following a path in the dry moat between the inner and outer walls, or by walking the ramparts that top part of the circuit, entered through the Palace of the Grand Masters. Admission to the ramparts is 4€ for adults, 2€ for students.

Jewish Quarter ★ HISTORIC SITE   The Old Town was home to a Jewish community whose origins date back to the days of the ancient Greeks. Little survives other than a few homes with Hebrew inscriptions, a Jewish cemetery, and the **Plateia ton Martiron Evreon (Square of the Jewish Martyrs),** embellished with a seahorse fountain and dedicated to the 1,604 Rhodian Jews who were rounded up here and sent to their deaths at Auschwitz. On Dosiadou, leading off just below the square, is a synagogue (www. jewishrhodes.org). Services are held on Friday nights, and the synagogue and a small museum are usually open daily from 10am to 3pm; admission is free.

Hospice of St. Catherine ★ HISTORIC SITE   At the eastern end of the main street of the Jewish Quarter (see below), this inn was built in the late 14th century by the Knights of St. John to house and entertain guests, much like the inns on the Street of the Knights (p. 236). One such guest, the traveler Niccole de Martoni, described the hospice in the 1390s as "beautiful and splendid, with many handsome rooms, containing many and good beds." The description still fits, though only one "good bed" remains amid the magnificent sea-pebble and mosaic floors, carved and intricately painted wooden ceilings, grand hall, lavish bedchamber, and engaging exhibits.

Plateia ton Martiron Evreon. Free admission. Mon–Fri 8am–2pm.

Monte Smith ★ NATURAL LANDMARK   The ancient Greeks, ever mindful of a great location, chose this 100m (328-ft.) hill to build their 3rd-century-B.C. Temple of Apollo. A few columns remain, next to a little theater that the Italians restored a century ago. The summit, named for a British admiral who fought Napoleon and American revolutionaries, is best known for its far-reaching views over the island and sea.

3km (2 miles) W from center of Rhodes Town. Free admission to ruins.

Street of the Knights ★★★ HISTORIC SITE   One of the best-preserved and most evocative medieval relics in the world is this 600m-long (1,968-ft.) stretch of cobbles, following an ancient pathway that once led from the Acropolis of Rhodes to the port. By the early 16th century the street was the address of the inns of knights of various nations who belonged to the Order of St. John. The inns were eating clubs and temporary residences for visiting dignitaries, and their facades reflect the architectural details of their respective countries. While most of the inns now house offices or private residences, the **Inn of France,** constructed in 1492 and the most ornate of the inns, is open to the public, Monday to Friday, 8am to noon. The ground floor houses the Institut Français, but you can step in to see the garden. At the top of the street stands the massive **Palace of the Knights** ★ (also known as Palace of the Grand Masters). Amid all the turrets and crenellations, it's easy to imagine knights in armor and maidens in cone-shaped hats exiting one of the entrances, but this is actually a 1930s fantasy built to flatter Mussolini on a state visit. (The original palace was destroyed in an accidental explosion of a nearby ammunition storehouse in 1856.) Its vast halls house mosaics stolen from Kos by the Italian military as well as a collection of antique furniture. Hours vary, but, in summer, the galleries are usually open Tuesday through Sunday 8am to 7pm, Monday 12:30 to 7pm. Admission is 6€.

Excursion to Lindos ★★

47km (28 miles) S of Rhodes Town

The most picturesque town on the island outside of Rhodes Old Town is a collection of white-stucco houses tucked between the sea and a towering **ancient acropolis.** Those glistening white ruins exert an almost irresistible pull—and you need only follow the signs (and the crowds) to reach them. Should a steep climb in the summer heat seem like too much, you'll pass a stand where, for 8€, you can climb aboard a donkey (also known as a "Lindian taxi") for a slow plod all the way to the top.

GETTING THERE   Be warned that Lindos is often deluged with tourists, and your first visit may be unforgettable for the wrong reasons. Public buses leave for Lindos from Plateia Rimini in Rhodes Town frequently, and the fare is 8€; a taxi will cost 40€ one-way. In the busy square near the entrance to town, you'll find the **Tourist Information Kiosk** (© **22440/31-900;** Apr–Oct daily 9am–10pm).

EXPLORING LINDOS

As you climb through town toward the acropolis, you'll notice that the lanes are strewn with embroidery and lace for sale, some of which may be the handiwork of local women (beware, though, because much of what's sold in Lindos today is from Asia). Embroidery from Rhodes was highly coveted in the ancient world; it's claimed Alexander the Great wore a grand Rhodian robe into battle. In Renaissance Europe, French ladies used to yearn for a bit of Lindos lace.

Acropolis of Lindos ★★★ ANCIENT SITE   Before you start the final ascent up a flight of stone steps to the acropolis, stop to inspect the relief carving of a Lindian ship, dating from the 2nd century B.C. The path then passes a medieval castle built by the Knights of St. John; the ruins of a Roman temple; and finally, an upper terrace planned by the ancient Greeks in the 4th century B.C. Upon this airy balcony stand the remains of a great assembly hall, a stoa, with a grand portico once supported by 42 columns. The glorious views from this perch now extend over medieval Lindos to the sea. To the south you can see the beach at St. Paul's Bay—legend claims St. Paul put ashore here. To the southwest rises Mount Krana, where caves served as ancient tombs and are thought to have sheltered cults to Athena well into the Christian period. At the very top of the Acropolis is a small temple to Athena, still fronted by four columns and still a statement of elegant grace.

odysseus.culture.gr. ⓒ **22440/31258.** Admission 6€. Apr–Oct Mon 1:30–7:40pm, Tues–Sun 8am–7:40pm; Nov–Mar Tues–Sun 8am–2:40pm.

Church of the Panagia ★ CHURCH   More than 200 frescoes, covering every inch of the walls and arched ceilings here, are the work of an 18th-century master, Gregory of Symi. With a close look, you can pick out scenes of the Creation, the Nativity, and the Last Judgment. To soothe your stiff neck, look down at the extraordinary floor, made of sea pebbles.

Old Town, Lindos. Free admission. May–Oct, daily 9am–2pm and 5–9pm.

Exploring the Rest of Rhodes

Ruins and beaches lure visitors out of Rhodes Town. The best beaches are along the island's east coast, while the west coast is wilder, heavily forested, and littered with crusader castles and ancient ruins.

Ancient Kamiros ★ ANCIENT RUINS   Much of this once extensive hillside city has yet to be unearthed (the Italians began excavations in 1928) but enough has been brought to light and is well enough preserved to suggest what life in this ancient Greek city was like more than 2,000 years ago. In a small valley are ruins of houses and shops along gridlike streets, as well as the foundations of a large temple. On a slope above are the remains of two aqueducts, assuring residents of a year-round supply of water. Bring a bathing suit, because across from the site is a good stretch of beach.

Kamiros, 34km (21 miles) SW of Rhodes Town, with regular bus service. ⓒ **22410/40037.** Admission 4€. Apr–Oct Mon 1–7pm, Tues–Sun 8am–7:30pm; Nov–Mar Tues–Sun 8:30am–2:40pm.

Epta Piges (Seven Springs) ★ NATURAL LANDSCAPE   You won't come out to this wooded glen from Rhodes Town to get away from it all, as the resident peacocks put on a show for an almost steady stream of visitors. Even so, the seven springs of the name surface quite charmingly as bubbling streams that feed a small lake. Shaded walks and a swim can be a refreshing break from more sun-parched parts of the island. A waterside tavern, established by a far-sighted farmer 70 years ago, does a brisk business throughout the day.

Archangelos, 30km (18 miles) SW of Rhodes Town. Open site, free admission.

Filerimos and Ancient Ialyssos ★★ ANCIENT RUIN   One of the island's three founding city-states was once home to the Phoenicians, whom the Dorians ousted in the 10th century B.C. An oracle had predicted that white ravens and fish swimming in wine would be the final signs before the Phoenicians were annihilated—so the cunning Dorians painted enough birds, and threw enough fish into wine jugs, that the Phoenicians left without raising their arms. When the Knights of St. John invaded the island, they, too, made their first base at Ialisos, a minor town in Byzantine times. Their small, whitewashed church, decorated with frescoes of Jesus and heroic knights, was built right into the hillside above the ruins of a Dorian temple to Athena and Zeus Polios from the 3rd to 2nd centuries B.C. Nearby the knights later established the Monastery of Filerimos to house an icon of the Virgin, believed to have been painted by St. Luke and brought to Rhodes from Jerusalem around the year 1000. The knights attributed the icon with the miraculous power of repelling the Turks during a 15th-century attack. Later, however, the icon did not prevent the Turks under Suleiman the Magnificent from overrunning the island with his army of 100,000 men. Basing themselves in Ialisos, they destroyed the monastery. It was reconstructed, with beautiful cloisters, by the Italians in the 1920s, while the icon eventually found its way to Italy, then Russia (it's now in Montenegro).

14km (8½ miles) from Rhodes Town; 6km (3½ miles) inland from Trianda, on the island's NW coast. Admission 3€. Summer: Mon–Sat 8am–7pm; hours irregular rest of year.

Kallithea Spa ★★ SPA   The curative springs at Thermi Kallithea were praised for their therapeutic qualities by Hippocrates and attracted visitors through the Middle Ages. The place had been forgotten and abandoned until the 1920s, when the Italians restored the site as a classic curative spa, erecting an exotic complex of buildings in what is best described in an Arabic/Art Deco style. After World War II Kallithea was once again abandoned until the late 1990s, when work began on a complete restoration of the site and its structures. You can't soak these days, but a small bay is ideal for swimming and snorkeling; you can sit in the cafe or walk along garden paths and contemplate the history of such an unexpected place.

Off Kallithea Ave., 9km (6 miles) SE of Rhodes Town; 5km (3 miles) NE of Faliraki. www.kallithea springs.gr. ℂ **22410/65691**. Admission 2.50€. May–Oct 8am–8pm; Nov–Apr 8am–5pm.

Petaloudes ★ NATURAL WONDER   The Valley of the Butterflies is one of the world's few natural habitats for resin-seeking Jersey Tiger moths (*panaxia*

A Driving Tour of Rhodes' West Coast

The west coast of Rhodes is particularly scenic, with deep green forests rising from the rugged coast toward mountain peaks. Above the coast 2.5km (1½ miles) southwest of Kamiros (p. 237) is the late 15th-century knights' castle of **Kastellos (Kritinias Castle),** a romantic ruin perched high above the sea; visitors are free to wander around this open site.

From there a winding road leads inland 13km (8 miles) up the stony flanks of the island's highest mountain, **Attaviros** (1,196m/3,923 ft.) to **Embonas,** the island's wine capital. Surrounded by vineyards, the village is bucolic but very busy in summer, when it's a stop on the tour-group circuit. Tavernas accommodate visitors with meat-heavy barbecues accompanied by live music and folklore performances. A 15km (9-mile) drive

southwest takes you to another picturesque village, **Siana,** nestled on the mountain's southern slopes above a verdant valley. Stands along the road sell the village's famously fragrant honey (p. 240) and a sweet wine that goes down all too easily and can make the most robust drinker tipsy after just a few sips—if you're doing the driving, sample the wares gingerly.

Drive southwest another 6.6km (4 miles) to **Monolithos,** a spectacularly sited crusader castle perched atop a rocky outcropping on a coastal mountain. A steep path leads up to the stony ruins, where the ramparts provide an eagle's-eye view of the coast and sea lanes below. At the foot of the mountain (5km/3 miles southeast), you can end your drive by relaxing on a nice beach at **Fourni.**

quadripunctaria). The moths overtake this verdant valley in July and August to reproduce, drawn by the scent of sweet gum trees and storax plants. They feed at night but by day rest quietly on plants or leaves, well-camouflaged, until you realize that an entire branch is filled with the sleeping creatures. If you're in search of serious nature viewing, this might not the place for you: The parklike setting, with its many ponds, bamboo bridges, and rock displays, is artificial, and it's hard not to feel that you're intruding upon the fragile creatures.

25km (16 miles) S of Rhodes Town and inland. Admission 5€ mid-June to late September, 3€ rest of year. Daily 8:30am–6:30pm.

The Best Beaches on Rhodes

The east coast beaches south of Lindos, from Lardos Bay to Plimmiri (26km/16 miles in all), are the best on Rhodes, especially the long line of sand between Lahania and Plimmiri. Some stretches at **Lahania** ★★★ are relatively deserted and backed by dunes. **Plimmiri** ★★★ is especially picturesque, as the soft sands skirt a bay that's ideal for swimming. At the southernmost tip of the island, for those who seek off-the-beaten-track places, is **Prasonisi (Green Island)** ★★, connected to the main island by a narrow sandy isthmus, with waves and world-class windsurfing on one side and calm waters on the other.

In Rhodes Town, the place for a dip is **Elli beach** ★, where the waves almost lap up against the walls surrounding the Old Town. The shoreline is pebbly and almost always crowded, but that doesn't deter hordes of eager beachgoers from enjoying the chance to get into the sea so close to town. **Faliraki beach ★★,** 9km (6 miles) south of Rhodes Town with frequent bus service, is the island's most popular and developed beach resort, offering every possible vacation distraction imaginable—from bungee jumping to laser clay shooting. For families with kids in tow, there is a **water park** and a sort of Disneyland-type amusement park, the **Magic Castle.** The southern end of the beach is less crowded and frequented by nude bathers. To the south are a number of sandy, sheltered beaches with relatively little development.

Shopping on Rhodes

In Old Town, Sokratous was once the Turkish bazaar, and it still seems to be one, with many shops selling Turkish leather goods. (*But note:* Most of these shops close at the end of Nov and don't reopen until Mar.) Antiquity buffs should drop by the **Ministry of Culture Museum Reproduction Shop,** on Plateia Simi, which has an enticing selection of well-made reproductions of ancient sculptures, friezes, and tiles. True **antiques**—furniture, carpets, porcelain, and paintings—can be found at **Kalogirou Art,** 30 Panetiou, in a wonderful old building with a pebble-mosaic floor and an exotic banana-tree garden, opposite the entrance to the Knights Palace.

Several products for sale around the island bear a special Rhodian mark. **Rhodian wine** has a fine reputation, and, on weekdays, you can visit two distinguished island wineries: **Cair,** 2km (1¼ miles) outside of Rhodes Town, on the way to Lindos (www.cair.gr); and **Emery** (www.emery.gr) in the village of Embonas (p. 239). Another distinctive product of Rhodes is a rare form of **honey,** made by bees who feed exclusively on *thimati* (like oregano). To get this you may have to drive to the village of Siana (p. 239); it's mostly sold out of private homes and at roadside stands.

Rhodes is also famed for handmade **carpets** and **kilims,** an enduring legacy from centuries of Ottoman occupation. Some 40 women around the island currently make carpets in their homes; some monasteries are also involved. There's a local carpet factory, known as **Kleopatra,** at Ayios Anthonias, on the main road to Lindos, near Afandou. In the Old Town, these and other Rhodian handmade carpets and kilims are sold at **Royal Carpet,** at 46 Aristotelos.

Nightlife in Rhodes Town

Many cafes and bars stay open late, or even all night. In the Old Town bars are clustered around Arionos Squre and in the New Town along Orfanidou Street. It's hard for even non-gamblers to walk by **Casino Rodos,** in the Grande Albergo Delle Rose Hotel on Papanikolaou Street, without stepping in (www.casinorodos.gr; ℂ **22410/97500**). The plush gaming space is housed in an Arab-Byzantine fantasy palace built by the Italians in the early 20th century. Games include American roulette, blackjack, casino stud poker, and, of course, slot machines. The casino is open around the clock, and admission 15€, valid for 24 hours. Patrons must be 23 years old.

SYMI ★★

Tiny, rugged Symi is often called "the jewel of the Dodecanese." Many other places are called "jewels" of this or that, yet as you sail into beautiful **Yialos harbor,** the claim really does seem to apply. Pastel-colored houses and gracious mansions line the broad horseshoe-shaped harbor, reminders of the island's shipbuilding and sponge-fishing heydays.

Outside of this picturesque port, and the similarly scenic old capital on a ridge above, this small island has very little settlement. There's a welcome absence of any buildings that aren't traditional (most are neoclassical), and a near-dearth of car traffic on the island; a tiny road network means the only way to get around is by boat or on foot. Sights are few and far between, too—aside from churches, that is. Amid rugged landscapes where sparkling blue waters wash against a rocky coast backed by pine forests, you'll find so many little chapels and remote monasteries, including the famous one at Panormitis, that islanders claim you can worship in a different sanctuary every day of the year.

It's a credit to the island's allure that many descendants of Symoites who once emigrated have returned, and the island's picture-perfect houses have become cherished retreats for Athenians and other Europeans. Symi provides a welcome tonic from the crowds on Rhodes and is popular with summertime day trippers. The island is also a favorite spot for travelers who want to get away from it all—that is, without leaving all the sophisticated comforts behind.

Visitors should be aware that Symi has no natural source of water; all water must be transported by boat from nearby islands. Conservation is key. Symi is also one of the hottest places in Greece during the summer, so come prepared with a hat, sunscreen, and a willingness to settle into a long siesta in the heat of the day.

Essentials

ARRIVING A car ferry runs daily in season to Symi from Athens' port, Piraeus. However, many (if not most) visitors to Symi arrive by boat from Rhodes. From late spring to summer, **hydrofoils** operated by **Dodekanisos Seaways** (www.12ne.gr) skim the waters daily from Rhodes to Symi, usually making both morning and afternoon runs in less than an hour. Several **excursion boats** arrive daily from Rhodes. Schedules and itineraries vary, but all boats leave in the morning from Rhodes Town's Mandraki Harbor (where touts will explain the details) and stop at Yialos, the main port of Symi—some with an additional stop at Panormitis Monastery or the beach at Pedi—before returning to Rhodes later in the day.

VISITOR INFORMATION Symi does not have an official tourist information office. For information, check out Symi's delightful independent monthly, The **Symi Visitor** (www.symivisitor.com; ✆ **22460/71-785**), with free copies available at tourist spots. The long-established agency **Kalodoukas Holidays** (www.kalodoukas.gr; ✆ **22410/71-077**) can help with everything from booking accommodations to chartering a boat. The office, at the base of the stairway to Horio, is open Monday through Saturday 9am to 1pm and 5 to 9pm. The agency offers many excursions during the summer.

GETTING AROUND   Symi's main, and just about only, road leads to Pedi, a little beach village one cove east of Yialos. A road also goes up to Horio, the old capital. In season, **buses** leave hourly from Yilaos for Pedi from 8am until 11pm, making the short trip via Horio (1€). **Taxis** at the center of the harbor charge a set fee of 8€ to Horio and 10€ to Pedi. **Mopeds** are also available, but due to the limited network of roads, you'll do better relying on public transportation and your own two feet. Many of the island's 4,000 daily visitors rely on **excursion boats** that stop at Panormitis Monastery or at Pedi beach. **Caiques** (converted fishing boats) shuttle people to various beaches, with prices ranging from 15€ to 25€, depending on distance. You can rent sun beds at these beaches.

Where to Stay & Eat on Symi

Giorgios and Maria Taverna ★ GREEK   A simple whitewashed room opening to a vine-shaded terrace is the mainstay of social life in Horio, Meals are as traditional as the surroundings, often accompanied by impromptu music provided by one of the villagers. A big selection of *mezedes* can furnish a meal in themselves, though fish fresh and delicious kebabs come off the grill.

Horio. ⓒ **22460/71984.** Main courses 8€–15€. Daily noon–3pm and 7–11pm.

Hotel Aliki ★   A grand Italianate sea captain's mansion from 1895 whisks guests back to Symi's booming heydays, with charming, high-ceilinged lounges and homey guest rooms where antiques sit on slightly creaky but highly polished floors. The waters of the port practically wash up against the front door, and many of the character-filled rooms and suites have sea views—as does a panoramic terrace above the rooftop garden. The Aliki is a popular overnight getaway from bustling Rhodes, so reservations are a must.

Akti Gennimata, Yialos. www.symi-hotel-aliki.gr. ⓒ **22460/71665.** 15 units. 120€–150€ double. Rates include buffet breakfast. **Amenities:** Bar; restaurant; Wi-Fi (free). Closed mid-Nov. to Mar.

Hotel Nireus ★   A shaded cafe terrace, sunning dock, and swimming area compensate for pleasant but blandly contemporary-style rooms behind a Symiot-style facade on the waterfront. If you get one of the sea-facing, view-filled rooms, especially one with a balcony, you can set your sights on island life unfolding along the harbor and you won't really care about the decor anyway. The prime location and many amenities make this a favorite on Symi for many vacationing Greeks, so reserve well in advance.

Akti Gennimata, Yialos. www.nireus-hotel.gr. ⓒ **22460/72-400.** 35 units. 90€ double. Rates include buffet breakfast. **Amenities:** Restaurant; bar; Wi-Fi (free). Closed Nov–Easter.

Hotel Nirides ★★   For a bit of tranquil seclusion with many conveniences, this small cluster of apartments, surrounded by pine trees and flowers

The spartan accommodations at **Taxixarchis Mihailis Panormitis Monastery** (p. 244) are especially with popular with Athenians and other urbanites looking to get away from it all and spend a few days with nothing to do but swim and take long walks. Some basic units share outdoor toilets, while others have indoor plumbing and kitchenettes. Prices range from 20€ to 75€. Call the guest office (*①* **22410/72-414**) to book accommodations; it's open daily 9am to 2:30pm from April to October, when the guest houses are often fully booked. In winter, the office is irregularly tended, but you can usually find a room here if you just show up. The exception is the much-attended Feast of Archangel Mihaili on November 8.

on a rise overlooking Nimborios Bay, is a perfect spot. The one-taverna village of Nimborios, with a pristine beach, is just down the road, and it's a pleasant 20-minute walk to Yialos along the coast (with many swimming coves below). Commodious apartments have kitchenettes and separate bedrooms and surround a pleasant terrace where drinks and informal meals are served; most units have their own terrace or balcony. Bikes are available for a quick trip into Yialos, or you can take a taxi or boat. Keep in mind, though, that many taxi drivers on the island refuse to drive on the rough road out to Nimborios; if you arrive at the port and need a lift, one of the staff will pick you up.

Nimborios Bay. www.niriideshotel.com. *①* **22460/71784.** 11 units. 65€–90€ double. Rates include breakfast. **Amenities:** Cafe/bar; bikes; Wi-Fi (free). Closed Nov–Mar.

The Old Markets ★★   The island's 19th-century sponge-trading halls and a captain's mansion across the road provide some of the island's most comfortable and atmospheric lodgings. Stone walls, arches, mosaic floors, and handsome woodwork show off the landmark's provenance, while modern touches include sumptuous bathrooms and a small swimming pool. Drinks, and meals on request, are served on the waterside terrace overlooking the harbor.

Yialos harbor. www.theoldmarkets.com. *①* **22460/71440.** 175€–320€ double. Rates include buffet breakfast. **Amenities:** Restaurant; bar; pool; Wi-Fi (free). Closed late Oct–Apr.

Vasilis ★ GREEK/MEDITERRANEAN   If you've begun to think that Greek island fare is predictable, you need to spend time on this lively terrace just off the town square in Yialos. Fresh Symi shrimps are served in many different ways (best when broiled with tomatoes, feta, and herbs), and fresh fish is simply grilled or appears alongside other seafood in pastas. Breaking the rule that a kitchen can't master both seafood and meat, anything that comes off the grill (even the vegetables) is delicious.

Yialos. *①* **22460/71753.** Main courses 9€–18€. Daily 10am–2am. Closed Nov–Apr.

Exploring Symi

In Yialos, the ground floors of colorful waterside mansions are occupied by cafes, with shady terraces for some lazy lingering while watching the boats bob in the harbor. Just behind the quay, 375 or so wide stone steps—known as the **Kali Strata (the Good Steps)**—ascend to whitewashed **Horio,** the old town and erstwhile island capital. (One recent innovation is a paved road, along which taxis, cars, motorbikes, and a bus chug up to Horio, much to the relief of villagers who have counted those stone steps one too many times.) By the late 19th century, Horio had been eclipsed by the picturesque port below. Day-to-day business on little lanes and shady squares still goes on as it has for centuries, providing a glimpse of island life that is long departed in other parts of Greece. Old women sweep the stone paths outside their homes, and occasionally a young boy or very old man can be seen retouching the neon-blue trim over doorways and shutters. At the top, donkey is still the means of transport for carting goods around the village.

Archaeological and Folklore Museum ★ MUSEUM Two neoclassical houses on the narrow lanes of Horio are the repository for some fairly routine ancient sculpture that doesn't do justice to the island's ancient distinction. (Even Homer talks about Symi, as home to the beautiful King Nireus, the second most handsome man among the Greeks—after Achilles—who sailed from Symi with three ships to assist the Greeks in the Trojan War.) Most engaging are island weavings and other handicraft, and a replica of an old Symiot house—all the more revealing since the living and kitchen arrangements are still typical of the surrounding dwellings. The English-speaking staff is usually eager to tell visitors about the past of the island, which as recently as a century ago had as many as 20,000 inhabitants, compared to about 2,500 today.

Horio. © **22460/71114.** Admission 2€. Tues–Sun 8am–2:30pm.

Maritime Museum ★ MUSEUM An ochre-blue-and-white mansion on the main square of Yialos is filled to the rafters with dusty navigation equipment and sponge-diving paraphernalia. Though some in-depth English descriptions would be welcome, the displays speak volumes about the island's maritime past, when a good natural harbor and vast holdings of forested tracts in Asia Minor assured islanders a major role in shipbuilding and trade. Symiots who stayed closer to home prospered from sponges; divers brought up a bountiful harvest to satisfy demand from Western Europe and North America markets before the introduction of synthetic sponges. One prominent display celebrates Stathis Hatzis (1878–1936), a revered local seafarer who set a world record in 1913 by diving without equipment to a depth of 84m (276 ft.) to free a ship's anchor.

Main Sq., Yialos. © **22460/72363.** Admission 2€. Daily 10am–3pm. Hours vary off season.

Taxixarchis Mihailis Panormitis Monastery ★★★ CHURCH
Tucked away on Symi's hilly, green southwestern corner is this unexpectedly

grand whitewashed compound dedicated to the patron saint of seafaring Greeks. The monastery, with a tall bell tower visible from miles away at sea, is still popular with Greeks as a place of pilgrimage and a refuge from modern life. A storied past of providing solace for sailors comes to light in the charming **museum,** where wooden ship models line the shelves next to bottles of thick, centuries-old glass stuffed with bank notes, all left to beseech the patron for deliverance from the perils of the sea. Legend has it that many of the bottles miraculously washed up on the beach at the foot of the monastery, just as the faithful intended. Opening off a courtyard paved in black-and-white pebbles, a heavily frescoed church and chapels are filled with icons, including one of Michael and the archangel Gabriel adorned in silver and jewels. Entrance fees go to support the almshouse in the surrounding settlement, which provides shelter for the elderly. A tiny settlement of houses, a few shops, and a tavern just outside the monastery gates comes alive during the November 8 **Feast of Archangel Mihaili.** Panormitis is a popular summer destination; visitors arrive by excursion boat, twice-a-day buses from Yialos and Horio, or a fairly strenuous 6-hour hike across the countryside. If you walk, time your excursion to avoid the heat of the day and follow it up with a refreshing swim in Panormitis Bay.

Panormitis www.imsymis.org. ⓒ **22460/71501.** Admission 2€. Monastery: daily 7am–8pm. Museum: Apr–Oct daily 8:30am–1pm and 3–4pm.

Beaches on Symi

Beaches are not the main draw on Symi, yet there are many good places to get into the water. Closest to Yialos is **Nos** ★, a 15m-long (50 ft.) rocky stretch, and **Nimborios** ★, a 10-minute walk along the shoreline past the clock tower. A bus to **Pedi,** followed by a short walk, takes you to **St. Nikolaos beach** ★, with shady trees, or to **St. Marina** ★, a small beach with little shade but turquoise waters. In season, boat taxis leave Yialos for several beaches hourly and return in the evening. Boat is the only way to reach the beautiful and isolated beaches at **Nanou Bay** ★★ and **Marathounda** ★★.

KOS ★

98km (61 miles) NW of Rhodes; 370km (230 miles) E of Piraeus

In many ways, Kos is paradise. Miles and miles of golden sand rings the coastline. Oleander and scented pines carpet landscapes that climb from a fertile plain into rugged mountains. A formidable 14th-century knight's castle overlooks the pretty waterfront capital, where ancient ruins seem to be laid out at your feet wherever you stroll. The most evocative ancient remnants are those outside town at the Asklepieion, the great healing center of antiquity that carried on the tradition of Hippocrates, who was born on Kos in the 5th century B.C. and taught here.

None of this history and beauty, of course, has gone unnoticed. While Kos is rich in sights, fine beaches, and plenty of sea-and-mountain scenery, the coastal plain has been zealously overbuilt. You won't find much of authentic Greek island life on Kos, unless you go way off the beaten path in the mountains, but the islanders are warm and welcoming and justifiably proud of Kos.

Essentials

ARRIVING   Hippocrates International Airport (www.kosairportguide.com; ℭ 22420/51-229) is served by **Olympic Airways** (www.olympicairlines.com; ℭ 210/926-9111) and **Aegean Airlines** (www.aegeanair.com; ℭ 22420/51-654), with several flights a day to and from Athens in season, as well as seasonal service to and from Crete. In summer, British Airways, Swiss Air, Air Berlin, and many other European carriers fly in and out of Kos from cities across the Continent. From the airport a public bus will take you the 26km (16 miles) to Kos Town for 8€, or you can take a taxi for about 25€.

Ferries link Kos with Piraeus and Rhodes, as well Bodrum, Turkey, with most boats operated by **Blue Star Ferries** (bluestarferries.gr; ℭ 210/8919800). Kos is also linked to other islands in the Dodecanese by high-speed boats, with fairly frequent service in the summer season; the major operator is **Dodekanisos Seaways** (www.12ne.gr). Kos harbor is strewn with travel agents, who can assist you with tickets and current schedules.

VISITOR INFORMATION   Facing the harbor near the hydrofoil pier, the **Municipal Tourism Office** on Vas. Yioryiou (www.kosinfo.gr; ℭ 22420/24460) is your one-stop source of information in Kos. It's open May through October Monday to Friday 8am to 2:30pm and 5 to 8pm, Saturday and Sunday 9am to 2pm; November through April, hours are Monday to Friday 8am to 2:30pm. Hotel and pension owners keep the office informed of what rooms are available in the town and environs; however, you must book your room directly with the hotel. Across from the castle, the **tourist police** (ℭ 22420/22-444) are available 24 hours to address any outstanding need or emergency, even trouble finding a room.

GETTING AROUND   Kos town **DEAS buses** offer service within roughly 6.5km (4 miles) of the town center, and the Kos island **KTEL buses** will get you nearly everywhere else. For the latest schedules, consult the **town bus office** on the harbor at 7 Akti Kountourioti (ℭ 22420/26-276), or the **island bus station** at 7 Kleopatras (ℭ 22420/22-292). The majority of DEAS town buses leave from the central bus stop on the south side of the harbor.

This is a congenial island for **cyclists.** Much of the coastal plain of Kos is quite flat, and aside from the main road from Kos town to Kefalos, roads are generally lightly traveled and well-suited to safe cycling. Bike trails wind through Kos town and its surroundings. Rentals are available throughout Kos town and can be arranged through your hotel. Prices range from 10€ to 25€ per day.

It's easy to rent a **car, moped, or all-terrain vehicle** through your hotel or any of the many agencies around the harbor. Car rentals are about 50€ a day in high season and rentals for mopeds and all-terrain vehicles range from 25€ to 40€.

For a **taxi,** drop by or call the **harbor taxi stand** beneath the minaret and across from the castle (② **22420/23-333** or 22420/27-777). All Kos drivers are required to know English.

Where to Stay on Kos
EXPENSIVE
Aqua Blu ★★★   On Lambi Beach just outside Kos Town, the best hotel on Kos combines chic contemporary design with comfort, intimacy, and elegance. A sensational pool terrace merges seamlessly with handsome lounges, while guest rooms are design statements set up to pamper guests with sea views and terraces. You'll find fireplaces and private pools in some, and a wealth of built-ins and sleek bathrooms in all. Somehow the design-magazine-worthy surroundings don't dampen the staff's down-to-earth hospitality and close eye to every detail. Amenities include a hedonistic spa and a strip of private beachfront across the road.

Lambi Beach. www.aquabluhotel.gr. ② **22420/22277.** 51 units. 200€–300€ double. **Amenities:** 2 restaurants; 2 bars; pool; spa; bikes; Wi-Fi (free). Closed mid-Oct to late Apr.

Grecotel Kos Imperial Thalasso ★★   Kos has many all-inclusive resorts, geared mostly to visitors who fly in from Northern Europe, plunk themselves down in a beach chair, and never leave the grounds. This sprawling, attractive resort on a garden-filled hillside above Psalidi Beach just east of Kos Town is the island's best-equipped hideaway, with a long list of amenities that includes dozens of swimming pools and artificial lagoons laced around the grounds; for good measure, some of the waters are said to be therapeutic. Guest rooms are large and gracious, and most have indoor/outdoor living rooms that open to shady lawns. When swimming and lounging aren't enough, the beach is a launching pad for waterskiing, snorkeling, jet-skiing, and every other watersport imaginable.

Psalidi. www.kosimperial.com. ② **22420/58000.** 330 units. 200€–250€ double. Rates include buffet breakfast; all-meals-inclusive rates available. **Amenities:** 3 restaurants; 2 bars; room service; many swimming pools; beach; watersports; Wi-Fi (free). Closed mid-Oct to late Apr.

MODERATE
Kos Aktis Art Hotel ★★   A pool is one of very few amenities lacking at this lovely harborside spot at the edge of Old Town, though that doesn't mean you'll be aquatically deprived. Sea views fill each of the chic, contemporary rooms that hang over the water from glass-fronted balconies; even the bathrooms seem to be floating in the blue Aegean, as sliding panels open to minimalist bedrooms enlivened with colorful sea murals that mimic the blue waters beyond. If you can't resist diving in, a nice pebble beach fronts the property. The sleek, contemporary restaurant downstairs is built around a reflecting pool and is appropriately called H2O.

7 Vas. Georgiou St. www.kosaktis.gr. ② **22420/47200.** 42 units. 100€–195€ double. Rates include buffet breakfast. **Amenities:** Restaurant; bar; beach; Wi-Fi (free).

INEXPENSIVE

Hotel Afendoulis ★ Nowhere in Kos do you receive so much for so little as you do in these sparkling, bright rooms nestled in a gracious residential neighborhood, a few hundred yards from the water and less than 10 minutes on foot from the center of Kos Town. Nearly all rooms have private balconies, most have views of the sea, and downstairs is a jasmine-scented garden shaded by arbors. If you are coming to Kos to bask in luxury, go elsewhere, but that would mean missing out on the hospitality of the Zikas, who are in vigilant attendance. The family also owns the Pension Alexis several blocks away and can usually accommodate you there when the Afendoulis is full.

1 Evrepilou, Kos Town. ⓒ **22420/25-321.** 23 units. 30€–50€ double. **Amenities:** Bar; laundry; Wi-Fi (free). Closed mid-Oct to mid-Apr.

Where to Eat on Kos

Petrino ★ GREEK A 150-year-old, two-story stone *(petrino)* house is a longtime Kos favorite, with food to match, plus gracious and friendly service extended by three brothers and their well trained staff. Summertime visitors sit outside on a three-level terrace filled with extravagant plantings and statuary, overlooking the ancient agora. In winter service moves to the cozy parlors. Many diners see no need to venture beyond the huge menu of mezedes—stuffed peppers and figs, grilled octopus, shrimps in ouzo, *beki meze* (marinated pork), and other favorites—but those who do will be treated to moussaka and other Greek taverna specialties, as well as what's said to be the island's best filet mignon and other cuts of beef. More than 50 carefully selected wines, all Greek, line the cellar—the dry red kalliga from Kefalonia is exceptional.

1 Plateia Theologou (abutting east end of agora). www.petrino-kos.gr. ⓒ **22420/27-251.** Main courses 10€–55 €. Mid-Dec to Nov daily 5pm–midnight.

Platanos Restaurant ★ GREEK/INTERNATIONAL A former Italian officers' club on a square overlooking the Hippocrates Tree warrants a bit of pomp, but you'll find these to be hospitable surroundings as well. The main dining room is suited to a feast for a king, or at least visiting dignitaries, with arches and original tile work, while a candlelit balcony and a terrace overlooking the square are choice warm-weather spots. Service is professional yet graciously personable, and the menu sticks to well-prepared classics. Among the house specialties are an appetizer of chicken stuffed with dates in a spicy sauce, a heaping main course serving of souvlaki, and a grilled combo of chicken, lamb, and beef.

Plateia Platanos. www.platanoskos.gr. ⓒ **22420/28-991.** Main courses 12€–32€. Apr–Oct daily noon–11:30pm.

Taverna Ampavris ★ GREEK One of the best tavernas on Kos is just outside the bustling town center, in a 130-year-old house down a quiet village lane in Platani. The rustic courtyard is the setting for meals based on local dishes from Kos and the surrounding islands. The *salamura,* from Kefalos, is

Hippocrates Under the Plane Tree

Hippocrates, the father of modern medicine, was born on Kos to a physician around 460 B.C., Inducted into the cult or teachings of the Asclepiads (physicians) at an early age, he also studied philosophy, rhetoric, and the sciences and learned the theories of Pythagoras. He traveled to Asia Minor, Egypt, Libya, Thrace, and Macedonia in pursuit of knowledge, and became renowned when he is said to have delivered Athens from a cholera epidemic. An ardent teacher and practitioner, he attracted the ill and infirm to Kos from throughout the ancient world. Under the shade of a plane tree in **Platanou Square** he allegedly expounded upon the arts of empirical medicine and its attending moral responsibilities. (Among his prolific writings is the Hippocratic oath, still a code of conduct for doctors today.) Little matter that the tree is a best a few centuries old, and that Hippocrates—who allegedly lived to the ripe old age of 104—is recorded as teaching at ancient Astypalatia on the far western end of the island. The legendary tree presents a romance-infused scene.

mouthwatering pork stewed with onions and coriander; the *lahano dolmades* (stuffed cabbage with rice, minced meat, and herbs) is delicate, light, and not at all oily; and the *faskebab* (veal stew on rice) is tender and lean. Fresh-from-the-garden vegetable dishes, such as the broad string beans cooked and served cold in garlic and olive-oil dressing, are out of this world.

Ampavris. www.ampavris.gr. *©* **22420/25-696.** Main courses 8€–18€. Apr–Oct daily 5:30pm–1am.

Taverna Mavromatis ★ GREEK   A meal like the one you'll enjoy in the Mavromati brothers' 40-year-old vine- and geranium-covered beachside taverna just outside Kos Town is probably what brought you to Greece: melt-in-your-mouth *saganaki* (grilled halloumi cheese), mint- and garlic-spiced *sousoutakia* (meatballs in red sauce), tender grilled lamb chops, moist beef souvlaki, and perfectly grilled fresh fish. The setting is as satisfying as the food—in summer seating spills out to the beach, where you'll sit only feet from the water watching the sunset and gazing at the nearby Turkish coast. A dinner here can be quite magical, something locals know very well, so arrive early to ensure a spot by the water. It's a 20-minute walk southeast of the ferry port, or you can get there on the local Psalidi Beach bus.

Psalidi beach. mavromatisrestaurant.gr.kbpe. *©* **22420/22-433.** Main courses 6€–20€. Wed–Sun 11am–11pm.

Exploring Kos Town

Looming over the harbor, the **Castle of the Knights** was constructed by the Knights of St. John (p. 235) in the 15th century and fell to the Turks in 1522. What you see today, however, is merely a hollow shell—it's best just to stand back and admire from a distance this massive reminder of the vigilance that has been a part of life in Kos from prehistory to the present.

Nearby, **Platanou Square** is the site of the Hippocrates Plane Tree (see box, p. 249) as well as the Ottoman-era **Loggia Mosque of Hassan Pasha.**

Kos town is strewn with archaeological sites, scattered amid the streets. Intermittently, steps lead into the excavations, where the curious can wander freely (and for free) amid scattered columns and building blocks. The ruins of the ancient Greek **agora** and some section of the **walls** of the classical city lie across a bridge from Platanou Square. To the southwest, in the so-called **West Excavations,** an ancient road leads past some 3rd-century-A.D. mosaics, including a depiction of the rape of Europa by Jupiter, and columns marking the portico of a 2nd-century-B.C, gymnasium. The senate met in the nearby **Odeon,** a small 2nd-century-A.D. theater, with 18 remaining rows of seats. It was once thought that the **Nymphaion** was a sanctuary to the nymphs, though the elaborate arches enclose what now appears to have been a public lavatory.

Asklepeion ★★ ANCIENT SITE   The mecca of modern Western medicine occupies an elevated site with grand views of Kos town, the sea, and the Turkish coastline. This first medical school of the western world—named for Asclepius, the Greek god of healing—was established here shortly after the death of Hippocrates (see box, p. 249); healing continued here until the end of the Roman Empire. Temples to Asclepius stand on the middle and topmost of the three terraces, while an allegedly curative spring still gushes forth on the lower terrace below, A grand central staircase ascends from the lower terrace, also the venue for the **Asklepieion Festivals,** where games, dancing, and sacrifices paid homage to the god. Clearly, physicians were consulted and higher powers invoked in equal measure. About half a mile down the road from the ruins, the **International Hippocratic Foundation** (www.ihfk.gr; ✆ 22420/22131) has planted a medicinal herb garden containing 158 of the 254 healing species cited by Hippocrates; open the door into the front garden and follow the signs. It's usually open Monday through Friday from 10am to 1pm and admission is 3€.

Located 4km (2½ miles) SW of Kos town (take bus no. 8 from Aktaion sq. in Kos Town). odysseus.culture.gr. ✆ **22420/28763.** Admission 4€ adults, free for children 16 and under. Late June–Sept Tues–Fri 8:30am–7pm and Sat 8:30am–3pm; Oct to mid-June Tues–Sun 8:30am–3pm.

Casa Romana ★ ANCIENT SITE   The largest Roman villa in Greece, with 37 rooms surrounding three atria, was built and rebuilt over the centuries. What you see today is from the 3rd century A.D. Enough of the lavish mosaics, frescoes, marble paving, and fountains remain to suggest the high-flying lifestyle of the elite of the time in this city where the arts, science, and commerce flourished for many centuries.

Leoforos Grigoriou. ✆ **22420/23234.** Admission 3€. Tues–Sun 8:30am–3pm.

Kos Archaeological Museum ★ MUSEUM   The Italians established this collection of Greek and Roman sculptures and mosaics in the 1930s to display their finds from around the island. The 1935 fascist-era surroundings are as much an attraction as the ancient bits and pieces, the most intriguing of which are from the Asklepeion (p. 250). Among these is a 3rd-century Roman mosaic showing Hippocrates and Pan welcoming Asclepius, the god of healing, to Kos, the birthplace of Western medicine.

Plateia Eleftherias (across from the municipal market). ✆ **22420/28-326.** Admission 3€ adults, 2€ seniors and students, free for children 16 and under. Tues–Sun 8:30am–3pm.

Around Kos

Verdant, aromatic forests and mountains stretch from outlying Platani all the way south to Plaka. The highest point is **Mount Dikeos**, reaching nearly 900m (3,000 ft.). From **Zipari**, 9km (5 miles) southwest of Kos Town, the road climbs through stands of cypress and pines to several white-washed mountain villages. The most appealing and animated is **Zia** ★★, with farm stands selling honey and embroidery and wide-ranging views across the fertile coastal plains to the sea. A 5km (3-mile) walk from Zia to Pili passes the ruins of **old Pili** ★, a mountaintop castle growing so organically out of the rock that you might miss it. If you don't have a car, you can take a bus from Kos to Zia, make the walk from Zia to Pili, then return from Pili to Kos Town by bus.

From Pili, the road twists and turns another 10km (6 miles) to the **Castle of Antimachia** ★★, a well-preserved 13th-century fortress that was another stronghold of the Knights of St. John (p. 235). Not much remains within the thick walls, though the sight of the formidable castle against a backdrop of stark mountains and the views across Kos to the sea and Turkey are transporting.

Beaches on Kos

Every foot of the 290km (180 miles) of Kos' mostly sandy coastline has been plotted and claimed, though with a little effort you may find a quiet spot. The beaches 3 to 5km (2–3 miles) east of Kos town are among the least congested, probably because they're pebbled rather than sandy.

One of the island's most relaxing beach experiences can be had at **Bros Therma** ★★, at the eastern tip of the island, 12km (7½ miles) southeast of Kos Town on the coast west of **Agios Fokas.** Sulfurous water bubbles to the surface of a natural, boulder-enclosed pool on the beach. You can soak up therapeutic benefits—treatment of rheumatism and arthritis, among other ailments—then plunge into the cooler sea.

On the north coast, a long strip of sandy beach begins at **Tigaki** ★★, 13km (8 miles) west of Kos Town. The 10km (6 miles) of sand extends into adjacent **Marmari** ★★, and behind them are dunes, scrubby pines, and, at the south end of Tigaki, extensive salt marshes that attract migrating flamingos and other birds. If you walk beyond the resorts and umbrellas, you'll find some relatively open patches. The north side of the island is popular for **windsurfing;** try Tigaki and Marmara, where everything you need can be rented on the beach.

The island's most acclaimed beaches are on the southwest coast, where long rows of sunbeds and concessions face calm seas at many spots between

Kardamena ★ and Kefalos ★. Many watersports outfitters are geared to beachgoers who don't just want to lie in the sun. **Kardamena Watersports Center,** at the port in Kardamena (www.koswatersports.gr; ✆ **22420/91444**), is especially well equipped. Amid all the fray down here are some quieter coves, such as on one below Agios Theologos, where the Vavithis family, including some repatriated from North America, operate **Sunset Wave Beach** ★★ concession and restaurant, a most enjoyable place to relax and enjoy a meal. Northeast of Kefalos, a swim at **Agios Stefanos** ★★ comes with water-level views of two early Christian basilicas, and **Poulemi** ★★★, 10km (6 miles) north of Kefalos, is backed by dunes and miraculously undeveloped—perhaps why it's also called Magic Beach.

Nightlife on Kos

Blessa Street, Kos Town's bar strip, starts at the harbor front. For live music and dancing in a former Turkish bath, try **Hamam Club** at 1 Nafklirou St. (✆ **22420/24938**), next to the taxi station. Happy hour runs nightly from 9pm until midnight.

PATMOS ★★★

81km (50 miles) NW of Kos; 302km (187 miles) E of Piraeus

Tiny Patmos—only 12km (7 miles) north to south—is where St. John the Divine (aka the Theologian) spent several years in exile, dwelling in a cave and composing the Book of Revelation. From that time on, the island has been regarded as hallowed ground, and a place of pilgrimage. A magnificent monastery was established in 1088, and the island has more than 300 churches, one for every 10 residents.

Not that the people of Patmos necessarily spend their days in prayer or expect you to. The rocky, rugged island is also a sanctuary for Athenians and many European visitors, who enjoy the island's relaxed yet sophisticated atmosphere. Most Patmians live in Skala, a pleasant port town strung out along the seaside in the middle of the island.

Essentials

ARRIVING   Patmos has no airport; most visitors fly to Kos and take the boat to Patmos from there (especially by hydrofoil and catamaran in spring and summer). Patmos, the northernmost of the Dodecanese Islands, is on the ferry line operated by **Blue Star Line** (www.bluestarferries.com) from Piraeus to Rhodes, though boats do not run daily. On days when boats are not running, you may be able to take a ferry to Kos and transfer there. The island is well connected to Rhodes, Kos, and other islands of the Dodecanese, as well as with the islands of the northeast Aegean, with most boats operated by **Dodekanisos Seaways** (www.12ne.gr).

VISITOR INFORMATION   The **tourism office** (✆ **22470/31-666**) in the port town of Skala is directly in front of you as you disembark from your ship;

it's open June through August daily from 9am to 10pm. It shares the Italianate "municipal palace" with the post office and the **tourist police** (℃ **22470/31-303**), who take over when the tourism office is closed. The **port police** (℃ **22470/31-231**), in the first building on your left on the main ferry pier, are very helpful for boat schedules.

Apollon Travel, on the harbor near the central square (www.travelling.gr; ℃ **22470/31-724**), can book excursion boats and hydrofoils and arrange lodging in hotels, rental houses, and apartments throughout the island. It's open year-round from 8am to noon and 4 to 6pm, with extended summer hours.

GETTING AROUND **Mopeds** are definitely the vehicle of choice on Patmos. At the shops that line the harbor, 1-day rentals start at around 25€ and go up to 50€. Daily **car** rentals in high season start about 50€. The island does not have many gas stations, so be sure you watch your gas tank gauge. As the island is quite small, however, it's much cheaper to hire a **taxi** than to rent a car; the island's main taxi stand is on the pier in Skala Harbor, right before your eyes as you get off the boat. The entire island has a single **bus,** whose current schedule is available at the tourist office and is posted at locations around the island. Needless to say, service is limited to Skala, Hora, Grikos, and Kambos.

Where to Slay & Eat on Patmos

On the main square in Skala, **Koumanis Bakery** (℃ **22470/32894**) is the island's favorite stop for bread, cookies, and cakes, serving cheese pies that are ideal as a light lunch.

Benetos Restaurant ★★★ MEDITERRANEAN Benetos Matthaiou and his American wife, Susan, make it their business to deliver one of the island's nicest dining experiences, on the terrace of a Tuscan-style villa at the edge of the sea, between Skala and Grikos. Fresh ingredients come from gardens on the property and nearby waters, and show up in such dishes such as shrimp in phyllo and fresh fish baked in a citrus sauce, or a simple arugula salad with shaved Parmesan. The couple spends winters in Miami, so a bit of international flair infuses the menu as well—the filet mignon, a rarity on a Greek island, is delicious. Carefully chosen wines accompany the meals, served at just 12 tables, so reservations are a must in summer season.

Sapsila. benetosrestaurant.com. ℃ **22470/33-089.** Main courses 9€–26€. June–Sept Tues–Sun 7:30pm–1am.

Petra Hotel and Apartments ★★★ The Stergiou family has created a luxurious haven on a hillside above Grikos Bay, lavishing personal attention on their guests in spacious, beautifully appointed rooms and one- and two-bedroom suites that exude island style. Most quarters have balconies or open to terraces furnished with pillowed divans for some Greek-island-style lounging. The main veranda is another gracious living space, where snacks and excellent, causal meals are served. A pool sparkles off to one side, while sandy Grikos beach is just at the bottom of the lane. The Stergious are devoted to making sure their guests enjoy the best of the island and also offer a four-bedroom villa in Horio.

Grikos. www.petrahotel-patmos.com. ✆ **22470/34-020**. 13 units. 175€–275€ double. Rates include buffet breakfast. **Amenities:** Restaurant; bar; room service; pool; Wi-Fi (free). Closed Oct–May.

Porto Scoutari ★★ Elina Scoutari has created her version of paradise on a hillside above the sea just outside Skala, where she attentively hosts guests in spacious, sparkling white, tile-floored accommodations embellished with nautical prints and antiques. Guest rooms, a beautifully furnished lounge filled with fine art and bibelots, and a casual dining area all face the large, deep swimming pool, surrounded by well-tended grounds. There's also a gym and small spa, as well as a wedding chapel, in keeping with the romantic aura of this choice spot.

Outside Skala center. www.portoscoutari.com. ✆ **22470/33123**. 30 units. 140€–240€ double. **Amenities:** Restaurant; bar; pool; spa; Wi-Fi (free). Closed Nov–Apr.

Vegghera Restaurant ★★ GREEK/MEDITERRANEAN With its veranda overlooking the marina, this restaurant draws a lot of repeat customers. Proprietor and chef George Grillis combines traditional Greek fare with French-influenced Mediterranean cuisine in creations like salmon smoked with rose sticks or lobster with tagliatelle, the house favorite. Fish and seafood have all just been plucked from the sea, and George raises the vegetables, pork, and rabbit himself. The wine list is equally selective.

Nea Marina, Skala. ✆ **22470/32-988**. Main courses 9€–34€. Daily 7:30pm–1am. Closed Nov–Easter.

Exploring Patmos

The island's two most extraordinary sights are perched on a hillside above town: the **Cave of the Apocalypse** and the **Monastery of St. John.** Surrounding the monastery, medieval **Hora** is a labyrinthine maze of whitewashed stone homes, shops, and churches, in which getting lost is the whole point.

Off season, the opening days and times for the cave and the monastery are unpredictable. It's best to consult the tourist office or a travel agency for the open hours on the day of your visit (the times given below are for the peak season, May–Aug). Appropriate attire is required: women must wear full-length skirts or dresses and have covered shoulders, and men must wear long pants.

Cave of the Apocalypse ★★ RELIGIOUS SITE Through a cleft in an overhang in this small cave, St. John the Divine (see box, p. 256) is said to have received divine visions, hearing "a great voice, as of a trumpet." He dictated what he heard to his disciple Prochoros, who wrote the messages down, using a slope of the cave wall as his desk. These words have come down to us as the Book of the Apocalypse, or Revelation, the last book of the New Testament of the Christian Bible. The cave is now encased within a sanctuary, which, in turn, is encircled by chapels and a 17th-century monastic school. You can take a seat on a stool in the cave and, surrounded by numerous icons and the very stone that served as John's pillow, experience the spiritual aura of the surroundings. An excellent way to prepare for the experience is to bone up on the Book of Revelation.

On the road to Hora. © **22470/31-234.** Free admission. May–Aug Sun 8am–1pm and 2–6pm, Mon 8am–1:30pm, Tues–Wed 8am–1:30pm and 2–6pm, Thurs–Sat 8am–1:30pm. Otherwise, hours vary.

Monastery of St. John the Theologian ★★ RELIGIOUS SITE Towering over the southern part of the island is this formidably fortified medieval monastery. Bristling with towers and buttresses, it looks far more like a fortress than a house of prayer. Within the thick walls the monks have lived a quiet life for a millennia, repelling pirate attacks, surviving successive waves of occupiers—Normans, Franks, Knights of St. John, Venetians, Turks, Italians, all the way to the Germans during World War II. Built to withstand pirates, the complex seems up to the task of deterring any onslaught of tourism that could spoil the island's charm—especially since the monastery owns much of the south end of the island. In 1088, with a hand-signed document from the Byzantine emperor Alexis I Comnenus ceding the entire island, Blessed Hostos Christodoulos arrived on Patmos to establish what was to become an independent monastic state and a great center of learning through many dark centuries. The monastery soon had a fleet of trading ships and vast holdings as far away as Crete and Asia Minor. The skull of Christodoulos rests in a silver case in the main church, while the adjoining **Chapel of the Theotokos** is covered with some of the monastery's earliest artworks, frescoes from the 12th century. The treasury shows off only a fraction of the monastery's exquisite Byzantine icons, including one said to be by El Greco, as well as vestments and rare codices and books.

One of the many footpaths that crisscross Patmos connects the monastery with the Cave of the Apocalypse. The downhill walk from the monastery to the cave is easy and rewarding, with views to the sea and the fresh island air fragrant with herbs. The stones are rough, so wear thick-soled shoes.

Hora. © **22470/31-234.** Free admission to monastery; 4€ to treasury. May–Aug Sun 8am–1pm and 2–6pm, Mon–Sat 8am–1:30pm, Tues–Wed also 2–6pm.

Patmos Beaches

In the north, the nicest beaches lie along the eastern coastline. **Meloï** ★, just 2km (1 mile) north of Skala and **Kambos Bay** ★ about 6km (4 miles) north of Skala, offer a much-desired commodity—shade—along with umbrellas and other amenities. At **Livada** ★, 8km (5 miles) northeast, it's possible to swim or sometimes to walk across to **Ayiou Yioryiou Isle;** be sure to bring shoes or sandals, or the rocks will do a number on your feet.

The island's south end has two beaches, one at Grikou Bay and the other at Psili Ammos. **Grikou Bay** ★, only 4km (2½ miles) south from Skala, is the busiest beach on Patmos, while on the southwest end of the island, **Psili Ammos** ★★★ is another story, an isolated fine-sand cove bordered by cliffs.

The Star Saint of Patmos

St. John the Divine, also known as John the Apostle and John the Evangelist, is said to have been exiled to Patmos in 95 A.D, when he was close to 90, for preaching Christianity. He made his home in a small cave, now known as the **Cave of the Apocalypse** (p. 254), where he remained for 2 years. His life on the island was not entirely hermitlike—he sometimes walked around the countryside, preaching and talking with those he met. John lived to a ripe old age, 94, and is the only one of the 12 apostles who did not die a violent death—10 were martyred and Judas committed suicide—yet he outlived his brother, the apostle James, by 50 years. Some scholars question whether the John who lived on Patmos and received the revelations was indeed the same man as John the Apostle. Despite the doubts, John is a powerful presence on the island. He not only continues to attract the faithful by the boatload but over the centuries he and his mystical revelations have inspired masterpiece paintings by artists as diverse as Hieronymus Bosch, Titian, and Nicolas Poussin.

It's possible to walk to Psili Ammos from the little settlement of Diakofti, about a 30-minute trek on goat paths (wear real shoes). Most people arrive by one of the caiques leaving Skala harbor in the morning and returning around 4 to 5pm. Round-trip fare is about 30€ and 20€ one-way.

Shopping on Patmos

Parousia, just behind the main square in Skala (© **22470/32-549**), is the best single stop for hand-painted icons and a wide range of books on Byzantine subjects. The proprietor, Mr. Alafakis, is quite learned in the history and craft of icon painting and can tell you a great deal about the icons in his shop and the diverse traditions they represent.

The most fascinating shop on Patmos may be **Selene** (© **22470/31-742**), across from the port authority office. The highly selective array of Greek handmade art and crafts here is extraordinary, from ceramics to hand-painted Russian and Greek icons to marionettes, some as tall as 1m (3 ft.). The 1835 building is also a work of art, once a storage space for sails and later a boat-building workshop. The shop's extraordinary floor, made of handmade stamped and scored bricks, a traditional art on Patmos.

THE SPORADES

As everyone knows, this archipelago of 24 islands came to be when a god threw stones randomly in the sea. (You did know that, didn't you?) True or not, it's a poetical way to describe these widely scattered little outcroppings across the Aegean Sea, off the northeast coast of the mainland. While most of the islets are uninhabited, four islands have captured attention since ancient times: Skiathos, Skopelos, Alonissos, and Skyros. Skiathos has the bounty of beaches—among them Lalaria, where sea cliffs amplify a soft incessant rumble of white marble stones rolling in the surf, and Koukounaries, where a perfect crescent is backed by sandy-floored pine groves. Skopelos has so many churches it's said that islanders count churches, not sheep, to induce sleep, and its capital, Skopelos Town, is one of the most appealing towns in Greece. You'll want to wake up early to explore its rugged coastline and mountainous interior. Forested Alonissos, surrounded by pristine waters, is not only a pleasant place to get away from it all but is also the gateway to the National Marine Park of Alonissos Northern Sporades. On Skyros, hilltop Hora, clinging to a rock high above the coastal plain, is so spectacular that it alone makes the effort to reach the remote island worthwhile. Indeed, all of this rugged island seems like something out of this world, adrift on its own away from the other Sporades and the rest of Greece.

SKIATHOS ★

108km (58 nautical miles) from Ayios Konstandinos on the Greek mainland

Philip of Macedonia, Persian king Xerxes, and many occupiers over the centuries probably made less of an impact on this island than sun-seeking travelers have made in the past 30 years or so. Yet Skiathos doesn't entirely lose its identity in the presence of 50,000 visitors a year. Outside Skiathos Town and the resort-and-sand-lined south coast, the small island retains much of its rugged, pine-clad beauty.

Essentials

GETTING THERE   The fastest and easiest way to reach Skiathos is on a short flight from Athens. **Olympic Air** (www.olympicair.com; ✆ **210/966-6666**) has service daily (twice daily Apr–May, five times daily June–Sept) from Athens. Public bus service to and from the airport is so infrequent that everyone takes a taxi; expect to pay about 10€ depending on your destination. The airport also handles many flights to and from European cities, usually filled with eager northern Europeans desperately seeking some sun.

By **boat,** the options are ferry (3 hr.) or hydrofoil (1 hr.) from the mainland ports of **Volos** or **Agios Konstantinos** (respectively 4 hr. and 3 hr. from Athens by bus). In season, Skiathos is also served by hydrofoil (1 hr.) or ferryboat service (4 hr.) from **Kymi,** on the island of Evvia, which is closer to Athens (2 hr. by bus). Hydrofoils and ferries also link Skiathos to neighboring Skopelos (30–45 min.) and Alonissos (60–75 min.); high-season-only hydrofoils make the crossing to and from Skyros (2⅓ hr.). For hydrofoil (Flying Dolphins) tickets and information, contact **Hellenic Seaways** (www.hellenicseaways.gr; ✆ **210/419-9000**) and for ferryboat information contact the **G.A. Ferries** (www.ferries.gr/gaferries; ✆ **210/458-2640**).

VISITOR INFORMATION   The town maintains an **information booth** at the western corner of the harbor; in summer, at least, it's open daily from about 9am to 8pm. Meanwhile, private travel agencies abound and can help with boat tickets, hotel bookings, and other needs.

GETTING AROUND   Skiathos has excellent **public bus** service along the south coast of the island, running from the bus station on the harbor to Koukounaries (5€), with 25 well-marked stops at the beaches in between. A conductor will ask for your destination and assess the fare. Buses run at least six times daily April through November, with increasing frequency as the season sets in: every hour 9am to 9pm in May and October; every half-hour from 8:30am to 10pm in June and September; and, July through August, every 20 minutes from 8:30am to 2:30pm and 3:30pm to midnight. It's a handy and efficient system, with a dash of island life thrown in—on some trips you might find yourself sitting next to a dog, more often than not belonging to the driver.

Dozens of reliable **car** and **moped** agencies are located on and just off the *paralia* (shore road). In high season, expect to pay as much as 60€ per day for a small car with manual transmission; weekly and off-season rates are significantly cheaper. Mopeds start at about 35€ per day. Parking around Skiathos Town is tight, but be sure to find a space in a legal zone—police ticket readily and eagerly.

The north coast beaches, adjacent islands, and historic Kastro are most easily reached by **caique;** these smaller vessels, which post their beach and island tour schedules on signs, sail frequently from the fishing harbor west of the Bourtzi fortress. An around-the-island tour that includes stops at Lalaria Beach and the Kastro will cost about 50€.

The Sporades

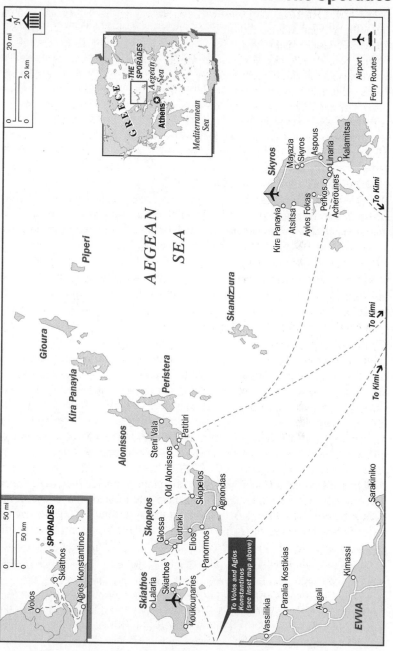

Where to Stay on Skiathos

EXPENSIVE

Atrium Villas ★★★   Your dreams of a luxurious island hideaway will come true in this gorgeous grouping of three hillside villas, tucked into scented pine forests high above the sea on the rugged north coast. In each beautifully designed glass-and-stone villa, four bedrooms and airy living spaces surround a seaview terrace with an outdoor dining area and, in a garden below, a private pool. Kastro, hidden beaches, and some of the island's most stunning scenery surround this remarkable getaway, while Skiathos Town is just 8km (5 miles) away.

North coast. www.atriumhotel.gr. ✆ **0030/697-044-0025.** 3 units. From 300€ a day. **Amenities:** Private pools; kitchens; extensive grounds; Wi-Fi (free). Closed mid-Oct to Apr.

MODERATE

Astoria Hotel ★★   Just steps away from a sandy beach along Troulos Bay, this low-key retreat is nicely tucked away in a shady garden. Lots of glass and stone lend a contemporary design flair to the airy lounges and large rooms, all with balconies that face pine groves or a handsome, tree-filled pool terrace. The relaxed beach town of Troulos is just down the road; the beautiful beaches at the west end of the island are near at hand in one direction and Skiathos Town in the other, all accessible by bus.

Troulos. www.astoriahotel.gr. ✆ **24270/49361.** 45 units. 110€–120€ double. Rates include buffet breakfast. **Amenities:** Cafe; bar; pool; nearby beach; Wi-Fi (free). Closed Nov–Apr.

Atrium Hotel ★★★   Beautiful and comfortable accommodations that range from doubles to lavish maisonettes tumble down a pine-clad hillside above one of the island's nicest beaches, commanding endless sea views from the many terraces and outdoor living spaces. Wood and warm stone are accented with antiques and island-style furnishings, all carefully chosen by the architect-family that built and still runs this stunning retreat, now meticulously overseen by the gracious Elektra Chatzimciahli. The beach is a short walk down the road, and two restaurants, a cocktail lounge, and a beautiful pool help make Atrium an ideal refuge.

Agia Paraskevi. www.atriumhotel.gr. ✆ **24270/49345.** 75 units. 120€–160€ double. Rates include buffet breakfast. **Amenities:** 2 restaurants; bar; pool; private pools in some units; nearby beach; Wi-Fi (free). Closed Oct to mid-May.

Bourtzi ★★   It only stands to reason that sophisticated Skiathos should have accommodations as chic as this contemporary oasis in the center of Skiathos Town. Commodious guest rooms all open to private balconies facing a courtyard or the streets of the old quarter, and sleek furnishings sit atop cool marble floors beneath color-rich murals. The pool will tide you over between trips to the beach, and the inviting indoor/outdoor cocktail lounge may provide all the nightlife you need.

8 Moraitou. www.hotelbourtzi.gr. ✆ **24270/21304.** 38 units. 135€–150€ double. Rates include buffet breakfast. **Amenities:** Bar/lounge; pool; Wi-Fi (free). Closed Oct–Apr.

INEXPENSIVE

Architectonika Design Hotel ★ For convenience and a surplus of good-value comfort, it's hard to beat this in-town spot that makes "basic" into a pleasing design statement of concrete floors and spartan low-slung furnishings. The longer the climb up a tight staircase, the better the rewards: top-floor rooms have views over tile rooftops to the sea, and above them is a breezy roof deck. All rooms open to nice terraces. Just outside, intriguing little alleys lead to the nearby waterfront or into the quieter sections of the mazelike old town.

Mitropolitou Ananiou 20. hotelarchitectonika.gr. © **24270/23633.** 9 units. 60€–80€ double. **Amenities:** Roof terrace/bar; Wi-Fi (free).

Where to Dine on Skiathos

The Borzoi ★★ GREEK/MEDITERRANENAN You'll still find a few patrons here—often looking a little the worse for wear after decades of the good life—who remember this hidey-hole from the 1970s, when it was THE place on the island to see and be seen. You can't really use the term "wholesome" to describe any place that serves a drink as stiff as the excellent house cocktails, but these days this restaurant/bar/club at the end of an alley is certainly tamer than it once was (despite the adjoining late-hours club). Meals are served in one of the island's most delightful dining rooms, a huge interior garden that's whitewashed to a soothing sheen and littered with colorful flowers and bright cushions. A thoughtful, Mediterranean menu includes some delicious seafood risottos, fresh fish, and heaping salads, served with down-to-earth hospitality.

Polytexneiou 27, Skiathos Town. theborzoi-skiathos.com. © **694/424-7349.** Main courses 12€–20€. Daily 6pm–midnight. Closed mid-Oct to Apr

Ergon ★ GREEK/DELI In an attractive, brightly lit space that spills onto a terrace, Ergon is part grocery shop, part cafe, and part *ouzeri*. The emphasis is on organic, small-production foods from throughout Greece, with vegetables from the island, tuna from Alonissos, fava beans from the mainland, and on and on and on it goes, showing up in a tempting assortment of small plates and main courses. You can mix and match in creative ways—maybe some gruyere from Naxos, served in fruit syrup, or grilled chicken breast served on a bed of Cretan pilaf. Excellent breakfasts are served as well.

Papadiamandis, Skiathos Town. www.ergonfoods.com. © **24270/21441.** Starters from 6€, main courses 12€–14€. Noon–midnight.

Taverna Alexandros ★★ GREEK This beloved Skiathos institution serves traditional taverna fare on a tree-shaded terrace and in a stone-walled room just off the harbor. Best bets are the standards—lamb chops and other meats grilled over an open fire, and huge fresh salads of beets and other island-grown vegetables, varying according to the freshest market offerings. Live bouzouki music adds a festive note to dinners on most nights. In high season you'll have to wait for a table (no reservations), and payment is in cash only.

Kapodistríou, behind the old port, Skiathos Town. © **24270/22431.** Main courses 8€ to 12€. Noon–3pm and 7–11pm. Closed Oct–Apr.

Taverna Sklithiri ★★★ SEAFOOD   If you're not swept away by the setting—a flowery terrace right on a golden beach with a turquoise sea almost lapping up against the tables—you really don't belong on a Greek island. Off the grill comes, of course, the freshest fish, along with simply prepared vegetables and all manner of other seafood, including plump mussels roasted in white wine. Service is as welcoming as the transporting surroundings. Though the restaurant is about 8km (5 miles) west of Skiathos Town, it's easy to reach by bus, halfway between stops 11 and 12.

Tzaneria Beach. ℂ **694/693-2869.** Main courses 9€–18€. Daily noon–midnight. Closed Oct–Apr.

Exploring Skiathos Town

No matter where you stay on the island, you'll spend some time in Skiathos Town. All roads converge there, and the port is the departure point not only for ferries but also for excursion boats to the relatively remote north coast and islets just off shore. The attractive town is relatively new, mostly built in the 1930s then reconstructed after heavy German bombardment in World War II. Outdoor cafes, postcard stands, and souvenir shops are as profuse as the bougainvillea that climbs whitewashed houses clustered on two low hills above the harbor.

Among the picturesque remnants of old Skiathos are the 13th-century fort that knights of Venice erected on a pine-clad peninsula known as **Bourtzi.** Connected to the mainland by a causeway, it's now a cultural center. Ferries and hydrofoils stop at the port on the east side of the fortress, while fishing boats and excursion caiques dock to the west. An old quarter of cobblestone and stepped lanes surrounds the **Church of Trion Ierarchon (Three Archbishops)** to the west of the port.

Far more popular than any relic of erstwhile island life, however, are the bars, clubs, and *ouzeries* stretching cheek-by-jowl along the waterfront all the way to the yacht harbor—confirming that most visitors come to Skiathos in search of sun and fun.

Around Skiathos

The island's top attractions are the famed beaches ringing the coves and bays that etch the south coast. All are sandy and protected from the northerly *meltemi* winds; a welcome barrier of pine trees also shields them from an almost unbroken line of resorts, shops, and restaurants.

If you can tear yourself away from the beaches, however, the island's rugged, mountainous interior is a world removed, with enough sights to make it worthwhile to rent a car for a day of exploring. You can easily see both of the sights listed below and still have time to hit the beach in the late afternoon: Moni Evangelistrias is only a 10-to-15-minute drive north of Skiathos town, and Kastro another 20 minutes beyond that. If you enjoy hiking, there's an easy-to-follow footpath through the brush to Moni Evangelistrias; ask at the tourist information office for directions.

The Skiathos Man of Letters

Writer **Alexandros Papadiamandis** (1851–1911) was born and raised on Skiathos. After a career as a journalist in Athens, he returned to the island in 1908 and lived until his death in this humble dwelling now known as the **Papadiamandis House**, off an alley to the right of Papadiamandis, near the harbor (ⓒ **24270/23-843**); admission 3€; Tues–Sun 9:30am–1pm and 5–8pm). The simply furnished rooms are now filled with the writer's personal possessions and tools of his trade and are well worth a visit for the light they shed on a style of island life that has all but disappeared in the past century. Papadiamandis is not widely translated or known outside of Greece, though his nearly 200 short stories and novellas, mostly about Greek island life, assured him a major reputation at home. His *Tales from a Greek Island,* set on Skiathos, is good reading before a visit. Although the tales are rife with superstition, hardship, and the insularity of island life, they are not without beauty and even some juicy sensuality (as in "The swelling flesh beneath the thin camisole hinted that here was a store of pale lilies, dewy and freshly cut, with veins the color of a white rose"). You'll find a statue of Papadiamandis standing in front of the Bourtzi fortress.

Kastro ▲▲ RUIN   By the 16th century, repeated pirate raids had forced Skiathos islanders to take refuge in a fortified compound on high ground. A drawbridge, moat, and high, thick walls deterred invaders approaching by land, while steep cliffs dropping into the water thwarted any raid by sea. The settlement thrived for years, with a village of 300 houses and 22 churches eventually taking root within the walls. It lasted until the 1820s, when piracy ended under the newly created Greek state, making seaside settlement safe once again. Kastro was abandoned for Skiathos Town, and the elements began to take their toll on the wind-swept headland. Today, all but a few houses and churches have crumbled into the Aegean. A short but steep path leads uphill from the road to the ruins, where you can walk around, peering in at the faded frescoes in the church of Yeni Nisi tou Khristou. Most impressive, however, are the views across the sea to the islet of Kastronisia. Another steep path drops from the ruins to a pebbly beach beneath the headland.

8.5km (5 miles) NE of Skiathos Town. From Moni Evangelistrias (see below), drive W then N (3km/2 miles).

Moni Evangelistrias ★★ RELIGIOUS SITE   A setting atop a deep ravine amid pines and cypresses lends this large monastery of golden stone an especially ethereal quality. Founded by monks who left Mount Athos after a dispute in 1794, like many monasteries around Greece the compound was soon sheltering revolutionaries fighting for freedom from the Turkish occupation. It's claimed that the first Greek flag was woven here and raised above the high walls in 1807. The icon-filled church has been restored, and monks' cells, a kitchen, and a refectory surround the shady courtyard.

5km (3 miles) N of Skiathos Town (take airport rd). Free admission. Daily 10am–7pm. Bus from Skiathos Town.

The Best of Skiathos Beaches

More than 50 beaches ring Skiathos, and 50,000 summertime visitors set their sights on them. In July and August, you'll be hard pressed to find an unoccupied patch of sand anywhere on the island, but if you don't mind company, you'll enjoy some of Greece's most beautiful shores. You'll be able to rent beach chairs and umbrellas on most beaches, even on the more remote north coast strands that are accessible only by boat.

You'll also find plenty of ways to stay active, especially on the south coast beaches. Activities abound on Kanapitsa Beach, where the **Kanapitsa Water Sports Center** (✆ **24270/21298**) will equip you to water-ski, jet-ski, and windsurf, and the **Dolphin Diving Center** (✆ **24270/21599**), organizes dives and offers certification. On Vassilias Beach, **Stefanos Ski School** (✆ **24270/21487**) rents boats and runs water-skiing and wakeboard lessons.

SOUTH COAST BEACHES   Some of Greece's most beautiful beaches are along this stretch of coast, but they are just too idyllic to have remained undiscovered and are now perhaps a bit too appreciated. A shuttle bus plies the south coast as often as every 20 minutes in the summer, making 25 stops between Skiathos Town and Koukounaries. At the far western end of the island, the bus chugs along an inland waterway, Lake Strofilias, making stops at the edge of a fragrant pine forest, beyond which are long ribbons of sand. **Koukounaries ★★★**, 12km (7 miles) west of Skiathos Town, is widely touted as the most beautiful strand on the island. No one can deny the loveliness of this golden crescent, stretching for 1km (½ mile) with crystalline waters backed by fragrant pine groves (*Koukounaries* means "pine cones" in Greek), but you'll be sharing paradise with thousands of other beachgoers. Those in search of relative quiet can stroll from Koukounaries for about 2km (1 mile) through shady groves to **Limonki Xerxes** and **Elias,** two lovely beaches on the **Mandraki Peninsula ★★★** at the far northwestern tip of the island. (Rough dirt roads lead to all these beaches.) Limonki Xerxes is named for the Persian king, who moored his fleet here before his ill-fated attempt to conquer the Greek mainland during the Persian wars in the 5th century B.C. A few piles of stones on the peninsula are believed to be some of the world's first lighthouses, erected by the Persians to guide their triremes safely across the reefs at night. Nudists usually find their way to **Little Banana ★★** (a non-anatomical reference to the shape and color of the beach), also known as Krasa.

NORTH COAST BEACHES   The top contender for the island's most scenic spot is **Lalaria ★★★**, a stretch of marble pebbles nestled beneath limestone cliffs. The Tripia Petra—natural arches sculpted from the rock by wind and waves—frame the beach, and the marble seabed gives the turquoise waters a nearly supernatural translucence. Caves are etched into the base of the cliffs, and just to the east are three spectacular sea grottoes—Spilia Skotini (Dark Cave), Spilia Galazia (Azure Cave), and Spilia Halkini (Copper Cave). Boats squeeze through the narrow channel into Spilia Skotini and shine a light to transform the 6m-high (20-ft.) cavern into a neon-blue water world. Boat excursions to Lalaria leave from the port in Skiathos Town about 10am every day and usually include a stop on the beach beneath Kastro (p. 263), from which a steep trail climbs the cliffs to the ruins. Lalaria and the grottoes can be reached only by boat excursions. You can also hire a water taxi, but it's costly and you'll share the beach and grottoes with excursion boat tours anyway.

Skiathos After Dark

You can count on Skiathos Town for a lively nightclub scene, just as you can be assured of finding a bar or club to your taste on the narrow lanes off Papdiamandis Street in the center of town and on the quays of the old port. **Polytechniou** is especially lively and also known as "Bar Street." What you can't rely on is a club surviving much longer than a season or two. A reliable year-in, year-out island institution is the **Aegean Festival,** staged from late June through early October in the outdoor theater of the Bourtzi, the pine-clad fortress that Venetians erected in the harbor in the 13th century. Events range from classical Greek drama to modern dance and experimental music; most begin at 9:30pm and cost 15€. Movie fans might enjoy the open-air showings at **Attikon** (on Papadiamandis, opposite Marc Nostum Holidays). A perennial favorite is *Mama Mia!,* filmed on neighboring Skopelos and screened to boisterous audience participation.

SKOPELOS ★

13 km (8 miles) east of Skiathos

Just to the east of Skiathos, its neighbor island Skopelos is larger and greener, and, for the most part, carpeted by pine groves and orchards rather than by resorts. Not that Skopelos shuns visitors—a still-lingering surge in popularity was inspired by the film *Mamma Mia!,* shot in large part on the island. (Bar owners and even bus drivers proudly blast the soundtrack to show off their fame.) Yet you'll still encounter relatively undisturbed island life in the empty countryside, on the cove-etched coast, and in two of the most beautiful small island towns in Greece, Skopelos Town and Glossa. Skopelos Town is especially appealing, a dazzling display of white houses, with a ruined Venetian fortress overlooking terracotta roofs, the sea, and the blue domes of dozens of chapels.

All in all, Skopelos has 360 churches, many built by grateful islanders who survived the mass slaughter wreaked by Barbarossa, the Ottoman pirate. The sight of so many white churches glistening on the hillsides inspired the novelist Lawrence Durrell to remark that Skopelos islanders count churches, not sheep, when they can't sleep. Visiting churches and monasteries is one of the great appeals of Skopelos, along with seeking out beaches in secluded coves and visiting the mountainous interior and remote villages.

Essentials

GETTING THERE   Most boats from the mainland ports of **Agios Konstantinos** and **Volos** first stop at Skiathos, where you sometimes have to change boats. Total travel time from the mainland ports to Skopelos is a little less than 4 hours by ferry, about 2 hours by hydrofoil. From Skiathos, about eight hydrofoils make the 45-minute crossing to Skopelos Town daily; most also serve Glossa. While Skopelos does not have an airport, many visitors fly to Skiathos and continue by boat from there. For more information, see Skiathos Essentials, p. 258.

VISITOR INFORMATION The **Municipal Tourist Office** of Skopelos is on the waterfront, to the left of the pier as you disembark (✆ **24240/23-231**). Open daily from 9:30am to 10pm in high season, it's handy for maps and information on beaches and hikes, and will also help you find a room if you arrive without a reservation. Of the many private agencies on the waterfront, **Madro Travel,** opposite the ferry dock (www.madrotravel.com; ✆ **24240/22-300**) is open all year and is a handy place to purchase boat tickets.

GETTING AROUND You can get around Skopelos fairly easily by **bus,** with service every half-hour in the high season beginning in Skopelos and making stops at Stafilos, Agnondas, Panormos, Milia, Elios, Klima, Glossa, and Loutraki. You can buy tickets on the bus. Fares vary depending on distance; the ride from Skopelos to Glossa costs 3€. **Taxis** will take you to almost any place on the island; the taxi stand is at the far end of the waterfront (left off the dock). Taxis are not metered—negotiate the fare before you get in. A typical fare, from Skopelos to Glossa, runs 40€. The easiest way to see the island is by **car** or **moped,** rented at one of the many shops on the port. In season, car rentals begin at about 50€ a day, while mopeds rent for about 20€ a day, Excursion boats to Glisteri, Gliphoneri, and other beaches operate from the port in peak season.

Where to Stay & Eat on Skopelos

While Skopelos is fairly well endowed with comfortable hotels, if you arrive in high season without a reservation, your only option may be to rent one of the many rooms available in private homes. You'll find rooms to let signs all over the island, especially in Skopelos Town and Glossa (in Glossa, shops and tavernas often advertise rooms).

Adrina Beach Hotel and Resort & Spa ★ With a romantic namesake (the female pirate Adrina) and a perch above a beautiful cove, this pleasant little resort is a true island getaway. Guest rooms are large and tastefully done in whites and pastels with sleek contemporary furnishings, and each has its own sea-view balcony or veranda, surrounded by greenery. Large, simply furnished two-floor maisonettes are ideal for families. More luxurious villa units sleep up to six and are raked down the steep slope toward the hotel's private beach. A big saltwater pool is one of many amenities.

About 500m (¼ mile) from Panormos. www.adrina.gr. ✆ **24240/23373.** 52 units. 75€–145€ double; villas 150€–250€. Rates include buffet breakfast. **Amenities:** 2 restaurants; bar; children's playground; Jacuzzi; minimarket; pool; beach; spa; Wi-Fi (free). Closed Oct–Apr.

Hotel Denise ★★   One of the most pleasant lodgings in town sits on a hillside just above the port, affording views of the town, sea, and surrounding mountains. All the large, bright rooms open to balconies. The pool is a perfect retreat after a day spent on the beach or sightseeing. Credit cards are accepted only as a deposit on a reservation, and it's best to make a reservation. When you do, also arrange for a lift up the hillside from the port upon arrival.

Skopelos Town. www.denise.gr. ℂ **24240/22-678.** 25 units. 50€ double. Rates include Continental breakfast. **Amenities:** Restaurant; bar; pool; Wi-Fi (free). Closed Oct–May.

Skopelos Village ★   This low-key resort is just a short walk from the port, yet it seems to be in a world of its own. Extremely spacious, bungalow-like accommodations have crisp, attractive furnishings, fully equipped kitchens, and one or two bedrooms. The units are scattered amid fragrant gardens and around two inviting swimming pools. A beach is just beyond the entrance, and there's daily transport to other island beaches.

About 1km (½ mile) SE of Skopelos Town center. www.skopelosvillage.gr. ℂ **24240/22-517.** 36 units. 175€–195€ double; 210€ bungalow for up to 6. Rates include buffet breakfast. **Amenities:** 2 restaurants; babysitting; pool; room service; beach adjacent; Wi-Fi (free).

Taverna Agnanti ★ TRADITIONAL SKOPELITIAN   Despite considerable acclaim, and the occasional celebrity sighting, this informal Glossa favorite remains unfussy, focusing on serving the freshest seafood and other island fare. A long menu ranges from herb fritters or smoked cheese in grape leaves to succulent pork roasted with prunes or chicken breast with sun-dried tomatoes. Seafood is just caught and prepared to perfection. The terrace is by far the choice place to be on an evening in Glossa, all the better when musicians are on hand to provide *rembetika*, the Greek version of American blues.

Glossa, near Town Hall. agnanti.com.gr. ℂ **24240/33-076.** Main courses 6€–22€. Daily 11am–midnight.

Taverna Alexander ★★ GREEK   Islanders tend to call this place the Garden, and an al fresco meal in this stone-walled courtyard in the upper reaches of Skopelos Town is an ever-popular occasion. The taverna fare is traditional, served around a well that supplies fresh spring water. That water, along with a palatable island wine, accompanies such standards as mushrooms with garlic, calamari stuffed with cheese, and some excellent fish and pork dishes.

Manolaki St., Skopelos Town. ℂ **24240/22324.** Main courses 7€–15€. Daily 7–11pm. Closed Nov–Mar.

Exploring Skopelos Town

The island capital and the administrative center for the Sporades is one of the most appealing island towns in Greece, holding its own against an onslaught of visitors. White houses and blue-domed churches climb a hillside above the bay, and brightly painted shutters and balconies complement a colorful array of climbing vines. The hilly quarters above the waterfront reward casual strollers with views back to the sea over rooftops of rough-hewn slate.

Folklore Museum ★ MUSEUM   A couple of minutes' walk up from the waterfront, this museum focuses on domestic furnishings and the embroidery for which island women are known throughout Greece. Just as interesting is the old mansion in which the costumes, ceramics, and other handiwork are displayed.

Hatzistamatis St. ⓒ **24240/23494.** Admission 3€. May–Sept daily 10am–10pm.

Kastro ★ HISTORIC RUIN   Keep walking up and up from the waterfront, and you'll eventually reach the 13th-century Kastro, erected by the Venetian lords who were awarded the Sporades after the sack of Constantinople. They built this stronghold on the foundations of an ancient acropolis from the 5th century B.C.; amid the ancient masonry you may spot the ruins of fortress walls built by Philip of Macedonia when he took the island in 340 B.C. The highest and oldest of the town's 123 churches, 11th-century **Agios Athanasios,** rises from within the Kastro walls.

Free admission. Open site.

The Mount Poulouki Monasteries ★★ RELIGIOUS SITES   The slopes of Mount Poulouki, topping a peninsula to the east of Skopelos Town, cradle a clutch of the island's 40 monasteries amid olive groves and prune and almond orchards that give way to deeply green pine forests. **Moni Evangelismou,** about 4km (2½ miles) east of Skopelos Town, was founded in 1712 by a Skopelitan noble who imported monks from Mount Athos to establish a center of learning. Today the all-but-deserted compound is best appreciated for its remote location and spectacular views toward Skopelos Town and the sea, as well as a beautiful, 11th-century icon of the Virgin Mary. **Agia Barbara,** about 6km (4 miles) east of Skopelos Town, is heavily fortified and surrounded by a high wall; its church is decorated with frescoes that colorfully depict the main feasts in the Orthodox calendar. **St. John the Baptist** (also known as Prodromos, or Forerunner) is only 300m (984 ft.) away, housing some especially beautiful icons. Just beyond the pair is **Metamorphosis,** the oldest monastery on the island, founded in the 16th century (hours for the last three vary considerably). You can visit them on foot along a well-marked path; the tourist office can give you a map. Some can also be reached by car, though the roads are rough; follow signs toward Moni Evangelismou from Skopelos Town.

Free admission (donations are welcomed). In season, open daily 8am–1pm and 4–7pm.

Around Skopelos

A single highway curves around the island, with short spurs at each significant settlement. It runs south from Skopelos town, then swings northwest to skirt the west coast, eventually arriving at Glossa and Loutraki.

South of Skopelos Town, the rugged terrain drops down to seaside promontories surrounded by small, sparkling bays along the **Drachondoschisma Peninsula.** This is where St. Reginos is believed to have slain a dragon that was devouring islanders in the 4th century. **Agnonda,** a small fishing port on the west side of the peninsula (5km/3 miles south of Skopelos Town), is

Pirates of the Aegean

Greece has a long tradition of piracy that dates back to ancient times. Hundreds of islands, most of them uninhabited, once provided hidden anchorages from which to launch attacks on merchandise-laden ships crisscrossing the Aegean on the way to and from the Near East, North Africa, and Western Europe. The Sporades, floating in the lucrative sea routes to and from Thessaloniki, were pirate lairs well into the 19th century. An infamous female pirate, Adrina, operated out of the Sporades until islanders slaughtered her marauders and she plunged to her death from a rock above the bay at Panormos, on **Skopelos**—but not, or so the story goes, before burying a horde of gold somewhere along the shoreline. On **Skyros,** islanders cashed in on the marauding business by alerting pirates to merchant ships that were especially ripe for plunder (receiving, of course, a cut of the profits in return). Skyrian workshops still turn out ceramics and hand-carved chests and chairs based on exotic designs that pirates brought to the island from afar.

named for an island youth who sailed into the cove after his victory in the 546 B.C. Olympic games. **Stafylos,** 2 km (1 mile) east across the peninsula, is also steeped in ancient legend. It's named for the son of Ariadne—daughter of Crete's King Minos—and Dionysos, the god who rescued her when she was abandoned on Naxos (p. 171). Whatever the real parentage of Stafylos may have been, he is believed to have been a Minoan who found his way this far north. A 3,500-year-old tomb thought to be his was unearthed in 1935, filled with gold and weapons. Stafylos is these days a popular but low-key beach, while **Velania,** a short trek across a headland, is more isolated and quieter; bathing suits are optional.

Panormos Bay ★★ NATURAL SIGHT   Beach life on Skopelos centers on Milia, Adrina, and other strands lining this broad, sheltered bay, once a lair for pirates (see box, above). A few stony remnants of an 8th-century-B.C. settlement are hidden amid the pine woods above the sparkling waters. Inland are the orchards where farmers grow plums and apricots, for which Skopelos is famous throughout Greece—plums and prunes appear frequently in stews and other dishes served on the island.

About 11km (7 miles) W of Skopelos Town.

Klima ★ TOWN   An earthquake dislodged all the residents of one of the island's most prosperous towns in 1965, but Klima is slowly being reclaimed. Some trim houses, newly whitewashed and roofed with red tiles, are taking shape amid the rubble in Ano Klima, the upper town, and Kato Klima, the lower town. Even so, the place still has the atmospheric feel of a ghost town. Looking through paneless windows and open doorways, you'll catch glimpses of abandoned bakery ovens and *kalliagres,* hand-operated olive presses, remnants of life the way it was when the village came to a standstill. **Elios,** just 3km (2 miles) south, hurriedly assembled in the wake of the 1960s earthquake, is far less colorful than Klima, whose residents were resettled here.

Carnival Madness

The 12 days of pre-Lenten Carnival celebrations are especially festive on Skopelos, with two idiosyncratic traditions. The **Trata** is a raucous celebration of seagoing life, stemming from the islanders' history as master shipbuilders until well into the early 20th century. Men gather in the morning to construct makeshift boats, then put on masks and costumes and carry the craft through the streets, singing, dancing, and goading onlookers as they go. Once at the seaside, they burn and sink the boats in a final burst of revelry. **Valch's Wedding** is a women-only event, in which costumed bridal parties dance their way through the streets and squares of Skopelos Town to the accompaniment of folk music, stopping along the way for sweets and wine. Valch's Wedding isn't the only time women call the shots; Skopelos is a matrilineal society, and property is passed to women and held in a woman's name even after marriage.

Next to town, though, is cliff-backed **Hovolo,** one of the island's most scenic beaches. **Kastani,** about 2km (1 mile) south of Elios, is one of the few sandy beaches on the island.

13km (10 miles) N of Panormos Bay; 17km (10 miles) NW of Skopelos Town.

Glossa ★★ TOWN The island's second settlement after Skiathos Town is much more bucolic and also beautiful, rising from the sea on terraced hillsides. Steep streets wind past gardens where residents grow prunes and almonds, just as they do in the surrounding orchards, and most of the houses have sturdy balconies looking out to sea. The most popular landmark these days is just to the east of town, **Agios Ioannis** church. On a rocky outcropping above the sea, the little chapel is so incredibly picturesque, it steals the show in the film *Mamma Mia!*

3.5km (2 miles) N of Klima on the coast rd.; 20km (12 miles) NW of Skopelos Town.

Skopelos After Dark

The nightlife scene on Skopelos isn't nearly as active as on neighboring Skiathos, but there are still plenty of bars and late-night cafes. Most of the coolest bars are on the far (east) side of Skopelos Town, but you can wander the scene around **Platanos Square,** beyond and along the paralia. Skopelos is known for keeping alive *rembetika* music, the Greek version of American blues, that can be heard in many tavernas late in the evening. In Skopelos Town, you can often hear *rembetika* at **Ouzerie Anatoli** (*©* **24240/22851**), above the Kastro, and in Glossa at **Taverna Agnanti** (*©* **24240/33076**).

ALONISSOS ★★★

10km (6 miles) east of Skopelos

Cloaked in green and surrounded by pristine waters, little Alonissos is an especially pleasant place to get away from it all. Adding to the allure is the **National Marine Park of Alonissos Northern Sporades** (p. 273). Alonissos is the only inhabited island within the boundaries of the park, founded in 1992 to protect the waters and islands of the eastern Sporades and the myriad creatures who thrive there. These include dolphins, falcons, seabirds, and, most notably, the highly endangered monk seal (see box, p. 274). By land, Alonissos is a treasure, too, with its rugged landscapes of pine and cedar forests, rockbound coasts, and an ambience that is far more low-key than that of Skiathos or Skopelos. You can easily visit Alonissos on a day trip from one of those busier places, but the island is a great place to settle in and relax for a few days or a week.

Essentials

GETTING THERE   Alonissos is on the same hydrofoil and ferry routes that serve Skiathos and Skopelos. It's about 4½ hours by ferry and 2 hours by hydrofoil from the mainland ports of **Volos** or **Agios Konstantinos.** In summer there is also once-a-week ferryboat service (2½ hr.) from **Kymi,** on the island of Evvia. Since these boats connect all three islands, it's easy to get from Alonissos to Skopelos (about ½ hr. by ferry, 25 minutes by hydrofoil) and Skiathos (about 1½ hr. by ferry, ½ hr by hydrofoil). For more information, see Skiathos Essentials, p. 258.

VISITOR INFORMATION   Any of the many agencies near the waterfront in the island's main town, Patitiri, can provide information about enjoying the island and surrounding national park. Two of the best-established agencies are **Albedo Travel** (www.alonissosholidays.com; © **24240/65804**) and **Alonissos Travel** (www.alonnisostravel.gr; © **24240/66000**).

GETTING AROUND   You can do most of your touring on foot and by taxi, boat, and seasonal bus. Alonissos has limited **bus** service, but it's handy for getting from Patitiri to Hora and some of the beaches around the fishing port of Steni Vala, the end of the route. It runs only from June 1 to the end of September, and even then, not too frequently. Fare is 1.70€, payable on the bus. If you take the bus up to Hora, you can walk back down to Patitiri via a centuries-old stepped path; the 3 km (2-mile) hike takes less than an hour.

You might want to rent a **car** for a day to explore the island's hinterlands and beaches. Many agencies in Patitiri rent cars and bikes, from about 30€ a day for a small car with manual transmission, including both Albedo Travel and Alonissos (see above).

Where to Stay & Eat on Alonissos

Archipelagos ★ GREEK/SEAFOOD   Many islanders claim that the fish and seafood at this waterfront favorite is the freshest and best prepared on Alonissos. Even something as basic and often poorly done as fried calamari is excellent, as is the fresh fish of your choice grilled to perfection and often infused with mountain herbs. While fish is the star of the show, a huge selection of spreads and mezes are available, as are some excellent meat standards, including lamb cooked with tomatoes and artichokes.

Patitiri. © **24240/65031.** Main courses 9€–18€. Daily 6pm–midnight. Closed Oct–Apr.

Atrium Hotel ★   Some of the island's most stylish and comfortable accommodations are on a pine-clad hillside behind Patitiri. The beach is a short walk away, and all the bright, nicely equipped rooms face the sea from balconies. A large pool gleams in the garden, surrounded by a terrace and cocktail bar.

Patitiri. www.atriumalonnissos.gr. ✆ **24240/65750.** 80€–160€ double. Rates include buffet breakfast. **Amenities:** Bar; pool bar; Wi-Fi (free).

Ostria ★★★ GREEK/SEAFOOD   A standout in a line of eateries along the Patitiri waterfront takes traditional cooking up a notch or two, with such innovations as sea bream stuffed with mountain herbs and ouzo, or pork fillet baked in a ginger-orange sauce. These preparations, along with a long list of standards like mussels saganaki and grilled sardines, bring many island visitors back night after night to try yet another dish. Friendly service is on a covered terrace facing the port.

Patitiri. www.ostria-restaurant.gr. ✆ **24240/65243.** Main courses 9€–18€. Daily 6pm–midnight. Closed Oct–Apr.

Paradise Hotel ★★   This laid-back little retreat looks out to sea from one of the forested hillsides around the port—from the entrance, handy staircases and a path lead right into the heart of Patitiri. Rooms are simple and fairly basic, though polished stone floors, paneled ceilings, and loads of informal hospitality add character. Most rooms overlook the nice pool and terraced gardens to the sea; terraces in ground-floor units are surrounded by scented greenery, while others have sunny balconies. The property drops through a series of terraces to a beautiful cove, where a swim in the pristine waters can be the highlight of a stay on the island.

Above Patitiri. www.paradise-hotel.gr. ✆ **24240/65160.** 45€–90€ double. Rates include buffet breakfast. **Amenities:** Bar; pool; Wi-Fi (free). Closed Oct to mid-May.

Exploring Alonissos

This long, narrow island, 23km (14 miles) from north to south and 3km (2 miles) at its widest point, is covered with pine, oak, and scrub in the north and olive groves and fruit orchards in the south. Beaches are pebbly and less spectacular than those on Skiathos and Skopelos, but the waters, protected as they are by the national park, are some of the purest in the Mediterranean.

The island's only two sizable settlements are in the south. Beautiful hilltop **Hora** ★★★, or Old Town Alonissos, was largely toppled by an earthquake in 1965 and abandoned. Residents were relocated to the hastily expanded, yet quite pleasant, port town, **Patitiri**—which takes its name from the dockside wine presses that were much in demand until the 1950s, when a phylloxera infestation laid waste to the island's vines.

Now populated mostly by Northern Europeans, Hora is slowly being restored and is more pretty than authentic. On a clear day, the views extend all the way to Mount Athos on the northern mainland. A road, with bus service in season, connects the two towns, just 3km (2 miles) apart; you can also take an old, stepped mule track on which you can make the ascent in less than an hour.

Most beaches are on the east coast, accessible off the island's only north–south road; several cluster around **Kokkinokastro,** about 3km (2 miles) north of Patitiri, and can also be reached by bus. The walls of the ancient city of Ikos are visible beneath the waves.

THE NATIONAL MARINE PARK OF ALONISSOS NORTHERN SPORADES

The marine park was established in 1992 chiefly to protect the endangered Mediterranean monk seal (see box, p. 274), whose numbers in Greek seas are now estimated to be less than 200. The park covers 2,200 sq. km (849 sq. miles), making it the largest marine protected area in the Mediterranean. Within the park are eight islands (of which only Alonissos is inhabited), 22 rocky outcroppings, and the marine habitats that surround them. In addition to the shy seals, who rarely make an appearance, falcons, dolphins, and wild goats also call the island home, along with many less showy but nonetheless invaluable species of sponges, algae, and land-lubbing flora, including the wild olive.

In summer, you can tour the park on **excursion boats** from Alonissos, including trips arranged through Albedo Travel (p. 271); you'll see signs advertising trips along the dock in Patitiri, where the park also runs an information booth (summer only, hours vary). On the day-long outings (about 45€, with lunch), tour boats chug past the scattered island refuges, though sightings of the seals and wild goats they protect is almost as rare as a glimpse of the Cyclops, who in Homer's *Odyssey* inhabited a cave on one of the islands, cliff-ringed **Gioura.** Dolphins often escort the boats, however. Boats keep a safe distance from **Piperi,** the major habitat for the monk seal and rare Eleonora's falcon. Stops often include **Kyra Panagia,** for swimming, snorkeling, and a walk to the island's one outpost of civilization, the all-but-abandoned **Megistis Lavras** monastery; **Psathoura,** where the tallest lighthouse in the Aegean rises above a white-sand beach and the remains of an ancient city is visible on the seabed; and **Peristera,** opposite Alonissos and alluring for its remote beaches.

Conservationists applaud the park's preservation efforts, while many locals claim the park impinges on resort development, fishing, and other economic opportunities. Make it a point to let restaurateurs and hoteliers know that you have come to the Sporades in part to enjoy the park—that the park enhances tourism rather than hindering it.

HIKING THE INTERIOR

Alonissos is laced with a network of 14 trails that traverse the length of the island, crossing olive groves, pine forests, and rocky gorges and dropping down to secluded coves. Walking tours and route maps are available through Albedo Travel on the waterfront in Patitiri (www.alonissosholidays.com; © **24240/65804**). If you plan to do some serious walking on Alonissos, pick up a copy of *Alonissos Through the Souls of Your Feet,* available at Albedo and elsewhere on the island, as well as one of the good hiking maps available at shops along the Patitiri waterfront.

The Mediterranean monk seal is one of the world's most endangered marine mammals—only an estimated 600 exist worldwide. Hunting probably pushed the numbers close to extinction as early as Roman and medieval times, and even until recently fishermen routinely killed off the seals to cut down on competition—these huge creatures (on average 2.5m long, or more than 8 ft., and weighing up to 300kg/661 lb.) devour 3kg (7 lb.) of fish, octopus, squid, and other sea creatures a day. Since development has sullied once pristine shorelines, the seals no longer lounge and whelp on open beaches and instead seek out sea caves with submerged entrances far from human intrusion. Battered by waves, the caves are less than ideal nurseries, and infant mortality is high. For ancient Greeks, sighting a monk seal was an omen of good fortune. The creature's survival would bode equally well for the Sporades.

WRECK DIVING OFF OF ALONISSOS

These seas also harbor a number of ancient shipwrecks as well as some sunken vessels from the days of Byzantine and Venetian occupation. Diving and snorkeling tours, along with instruction and gear, is available from **Alonissos Triton Dive Center,** in Patitiri (bestdivingingreece.com; ☎ **24240/65804**).

SKYROS ★★

47km (25 nautical miles) NE from Kymi; 182km (113 miles) NE from Athens

Adrift by itself in the Aegean, far from the other major Sporades, Skyros is a land apart. You will discover that there is something different about this island as soon as you set eyes on **Skyros Town,** a cliff-hugging, white mirage that seems to float above the surrounding plain. The impression won't wane as you explore the rest of this most distinctive Greek island.

Essentials

GETTING THERE The challenge of getting to Skyros can deter even the most determined traveler. From Athens, the trip is easiest by air. In summer, **Olympic Air** (www.olympicair.com; ☎ **210/966-6666**) has about three flights a week between Athens and Skyros, as well as between Thessaloniki and Skyros. A bus meets most flights and goes to Skyros town, Magazia, and sometimes Molos; the fare is 6€. A taxi from the airport is about 18€, but expect to share a cab.

　Skyros Shipping Company (www.sne.gr; ☎ **22220/91-780**) offers the only ferry service to Skyros; stockholders are all citizens of the island. Service runs from **Kymi,** on the east coast of the island of Evvia, which is about 2 hours from Athens by bus. In summer, service runs at least twice daily (usually early afternoon and early evening) from Kymi to Skyros, and twice daily (usually early morning and mid-afternoon) from Skyros to Kymi; the trip takes a little over 2 hours, making this by far the quickest boat connection to Skyros. Off season, there's one ferry each way, leaving Skyros early in the morning and Kymi in late afternoon. Skyros Shipping and the many agencies that sell tickets for the boat service also sell bus tickets to and between Athens and Kymi. In the summer only, the company's boats also link Skyros to the other Sporades and to **Volos** on the mainland, about a 4-hour bus trip from Athens. It's a long trip through the Sporades, though, 5 hours from Alonissos to Skyros, 6 hours from Skopelos to Skyros, 7½ hours from Skiathos to Skyros, and 10 hours from Volos to Skyros. The best way to see if and how you might be able to travel between Skyros and one of the other Sporades is to go to the company's website, **www.sne.gr**, or to the ferries section of the website **www.gtp.gr**.

VISITOR INFORMATION   The largest tourist office on the island is **Skyros Travel and Tourism** (www.skyrostravel.com; ✆ **22220/91-123**), next to Skyros Pizza Restaurant in the main market. The English-speaking staff offers assistance with accommodations, tickets, car and bike rentals, and tours.

GETTING AROUND   On Skyros, the ferries and hydrofoils dock at **Linaria,** on the opposite side of the island from Skyros town. The island's only **public bus** will meet the boat and take you over winding, curving roads to Skyros town for 2€. In high season, Skyros Travel (see above) offers a twice-daily **excursion bus** to the beaches, as well as a daylong island excursion in a small bus with an English-speaking guide. For many, this may be the best way to get an overview of the island. A small **car** rents from about 30€ per day. **Mopeds** and **motorcycles** are available near the police station or the taxi station for about 25€ per day. The island has a relatively well-developed network of roads.

Where to Stay & Eat on Skyros

Skyros has relatively few hotels, but finding a room is generally very easy—an eager throng, mostly women, meets passengers disembarking from boats with signs and cries of room to let. You will also encounter room-letters near the main bus stop in Skyros Town. These accommodations are in private homes and immaculately kept. You'll save yourself and a potential host time and trouble if you arrive with some idea of where you want to stay on the island. Set your sights on the upper part of Skyros Town—the narrow lanes are delightful, the views are sweeping, and the beach is a pleasant walk away.

A Holistic Getaway

Skyros Centre is a well-established "holistic" vacation resort with beachside units near Atsitsa and accommodations in traditional houses in Skyros Town. This is not a hotel: Guests don't just stay but participate in programs that last a week or two and include sessions in dance, yoga, handicrafts, sailing, meditation, writing, and more. All are a very nice way to experience the island. For more information, check out the center at **www.skyros.com**.

Hotel Angela ★   This lovely little whitewashed compound run by a young couple surrounds a swimming pool. The location is well-suited for guests without their own transport, as it's just below Skyros Town and steps from the beach at Molos. Rooms are simple but perfectly kept and comfortable. All have balconies with glimpses of the sea and the white town on the bluff above.

Molos. ☏ **22220/91-764.** 14 units. 90€–100€ double. Rates include breakfast. **Amenities:** Pool; Wi-Fi (free).

Hotel Nefeli ★★   Suites, apartments with kitchenettes, and hotel-style rooms are spread through three buildings, and many have sea views. All are distinctly decorated and furnished in traditional Skyrian style, with lots of carved wood pieces. The center of Skyros Town and the beach are a short walk away, and the pool is surrounded by a welcoming terrace. Reserve in advance, as this is one of the favorite choices on Skyros and it's often booked.

Skyros town center. www.skyros-nefeli.gr. ☏ **22220/91-964.** 16 units. From 100€ double. Breakfast 6€ extra. **Amenities:** Restaurant; bar; children's play area; 2 pools (1 children's); Wi-Fi (free).

Maryetes ★★ GREEK   This longtime favorite restaurant is known for fish and grilled meats, served in a simple-as-can-be but always crowded dining room in the center of Skyros Town. Scenes spied from the warm-weather terrace, on the town's main street, add a great deal of entertainment value to a meal. You can eat very well during your stay on Skyros by alternating meals between Maryetes and O Pappous ki Ego (below), just up the street.

Main st., Skyros Town. ☏ **22220/91311.** Main courses 6€–10€. Daily 1–3pm and 6pm–midnight.

O Pappous ki Ego ★★ GREEK   The name translates as "My grandfather and I," and the appealing room, a former pharmacy in Skyros Town, is now under the watchful eye of the grandson. The *dolmades* and other *meze* are delicious, as are some of the meat and fish dishes; cuttlefish in anise sauce is a specialty. Live music is sometimes performed on weekend evenings.

Main st., Skyros Town. ☏ **22220/93200.** Main courses 6€–10€. Daily 1–3pm and 6pm–midnight.

Skiros Palace Hotel ★   One of the few real resorts on the island is low-key and comfortably simple, set in well-tended gardens. You will not find much in the way of world-class luxuries, but furnishings are comfortable, and terraces and balconies face a large saltwater pool. A long, sandy beach is just across the road; Skyros Town is 3km (2 miles) away, but a minibus makes the run several times a day. Among the many amenities are a sailboat for excursions, a basketball court, and the island's most sophisticated disco (so well sound-proofed that you will not even know it's there, unless you choose to seek it out).

Girismata Kampos. www.skiros-palace.gr. ☏ **22220/91994.** 80 units. 110€ double. Rates include buffet breakfast. **Amenities:** 2 restaurants; bar; minibus to town; pool; tennis; Wi-Fi (free).

Exploring Skyros Town

The island's only sizable town and home to most of the 3,000 Skyrians inspires many flattering comparisons—to a mirage, a magical kingdom, or, most accurately and prosaically, to a village on one of the islands in the Cyclades. It's only fitting that this stunning collection of white, flat-roofed houses clinging to a high rocky bluff has figured in myth since ancient times. The sea nymph Thetis sent her son, Achilles, to the island disguised as a young woman to outwit the oracle's prediction that he would die in the Trojan War; the ruse worked until Odysseus unmasked the boy's true identity and sent him off to battle on a Skyrian pony. In another legendary episode, Theseus—founder-king of Athens and son of Poseidon and Aegeus—fled to Skyros when he fell out of favor; Lycomedes, king of the island, eventually pushed him over a cliff.

Even the town's main street is known as Sisyphus, and the reason soon becomes abundantly clear once you start hiking up the steep incline. At the top is the Venetian-era **Kastro** and, within its walls, the **monastery of Agios Yeoryios.** The monastery was founded in 962 and contains a famous black-faced icon of St. George brought from Constantinople. From one side of the citadel, the view is over the rooftops of the town; from the other, the cliff drops precipitously to the sea (this, according to myth, is where King Lycomides pushed Theseus to his death).

Farther down the slope on **Plateia Rupert Brooke,** a statue memorializes the British poet, who in 1915 died on a hospital ship just off Skyros and is buried on the southern end of the island (p. 278). The flatteringly virile bronze nude is not a likeness—it was intended as an immortalization of poetry—and it caused a public outcry when it was unveiled in the 1930s. The **Folklore Museum** (see below) is on Plateia Rupert Brooke, as is the **Archaeological Museum** (© **22220/91327**), which displays small stone vessels and other primitive finds from Palamari (p. 278). It's open Tuesday through Sunday, 8:30am to 3pm; admission is 2€.

As you wander the steep lanes of Skyros Town, you'll notice women in long scarves sitting in doorways, bent over vibrantly colored embroidery with fanciful flower and bird designs. Some older men on the island still wear their traditional baggy trousers and black caps. Many Skyrian homes are museum-like repositories for colorful plates, embroidery, copperware, and carved furniture—a point of pride and a throwback to the days of Byzantine occupation, when families made fortunes from the lucrative Near East sea lanes. The merchant ships were soon followed by pirates, with whom the Skyrian ruling families went into business. The families knew what boats were expected and what they were carrying, and the pirates had the ships and bravado to steal the cargo—and then share with their informants.

The Manos Faltaits Historical and Folklore Museum ★★

MUSEUM/HISTORIC HOME The private collection of islander Manos Faltaits, lodged in the family home, contains a large and varied selection of plates, embroidery, weaving, woodworking, and clothing, as well as many rare books and photographs. Seeing the fascinating collection is all the more satisfying once you begin to witness how many of these collectibles are still part of everyday island life. Attached to the museum is a workshop where young artisans make lovely objects using traditional patterns and materials. The proceeds from the sale of workshop items go to the upkeep of the museum. The museum also has a shop, **Argo,** on the main street of town (② **22220/92-158**). It's open daily from 10am to 1pm and 6:30 to 11pm.

Plateia Rupert Brooke. www.faltaits.gr. ② **22220/92158.** Admission 2€. May–Oct Tues–Sun 8:30am–3pm. Hours vary rest of year.

Around Skyros

You can drive around the north half of this cinch-waisted island in a counter-clockwise circuit from Skyros Town; the entire circuit on a well-marked road is less than 30km (19 miles).

THE NORTH

Skyros' fertile, forested north varies so much from the arid, rugged south that it has been conjectured, wrongly, that the island was at one time two separate land masses. Two seaside villages lie side by side, just below Skyros Town. **Magazia,** at the bottom of a stairway from Plateia Rupert Brooke, fronts a sandy beach that extends north into **Molos,** a fishing village. **Pouria,** just to the north of there, is surrounded by weirdly shaped rock formations that were shaped not by wind and waves but by Romans, who quarried the stone. **Pala-mari,** near the airport at the northern tip of the island, was settled around 2000 B.C. by traders and sailors for whom, judging by the trenches and thick stone walls, life on the island must have been a tenuous business. A sandy beach skirts the harbor where the inhabitants once beached their vessels. **Ats-itsa,** directly west of Molos but on the west coast's Bay of Petros, is surrounded by several beaches along the pine- and cedar-clad northwest coast; one of the most appealing, **Kyra Panagia ★★**, is a 15-minute walk north of Atsitsa. **Agios Fokas ★★**, a short drive south of Atsitsa, is usually touted as the island's most beautiful beach, though it's actually a triplet of little bays edged with white pebbles. From here, the road swings east and then north back up to Skyros Town.

THE SOUTH

From Aspous, a short drive south of Skyros Town, a single road leads south through a rocky landscape that is desolate, yet hauntingly beautiful. As you head south, the rocky coast gives way to beaches at **Kalamitsa,** about 10 minutes' drive southwest of Aspous across the island's narrow waist, and just south of there, **Kolymbada.** The scrappy collections of houses that surround both are some of the few signs of human habitation on this end of the island. The road ends on the shores of **Tris Boukes Bay,** a half-hour's drive south of Kolymbada. The British poet Rupert Brooke is buried here, amid an olive grove, in a simple grave inscribed with words from his own poem "The

Large herds of the diminutive Skyrian pony once scampered across the rocky interior of Skyros, though now they number less than 150. It's believed that these beautiful little beasts are the horses that frolic on the Parthenon frieze; Achilles allegedly rode one into battle during the Trojan War. Since the ponies were isolated on Skyros, their bloodlines have changed little over the millennia.

Time was, Skyros farmers put the ponies to work for the harvest, then released them to graze on upland plateaus in the winter. Farm machinery has curtailed the ponies' careers as beasts of burden, and they vie for terrain with sheep and goats. The ponies are now protected, however, and efforts are afoot to preserve and restore the remaining herds. While you are unlikely to catch a glimpse of a Skyrian pony in the wild, at the **Skyrian Horse Project** in Molos (© **22220/92918**) you can get as close as you wish—and, if you are under the age of 15, climb onto one.

Admission is free, though donations are accepted; the center is open daily 11am to 1pm and 6:30 to 8pm.

Another age-old tradition in Skyros is the pre-Lenten (*apokriatika*) festival, famous throughout Greece. On each of the four Sundays before Clean Monday (the first Monday of Lent), men and a few large women don goat-hair jackets and goat masks and drape themselves in goat bells. Other men, dressed in traditional wedding garb, and women and children, in their Sunday Western-style dress, surround them. The ensembles proceed through the streets of Skyros Town, singing, brandishing shepherds' crooks, and reciting bawdy verses. When two groups meet, they try to outdo each other with bell clanking, ribald gestures, and shouting. Scholars trace this traditional event tradition to pagan Dionysian revels and Achilles-style cross-dressing (p. 277). Many spectators make it a point to visit the island for the goings-on. If you plan to attend, book a room months in advance.

Soldier": "If I should die think only this of me/ That there's some corner of a foreign field/ That is forever England." Brooke spent only a few days on the island in 1915—long enough to incur a mosquito bite that led to blood poisoning. He died on a hospital ship in the bay.

Shopping

Skyros is a good place to buy local crafts, especially embroidery and ceramics. **Ergastiri,** on the main street of Hora, is noted for its wood furniture. **Yiannis Nicholau,** whose studio is next to the Xenia Hotel, is known for his handmade plates. You can find good hand-carved wooden chests and chairs made from beech (in the old days it was blackberry wood) from **Lefteris Avgoklouris;** his studio (© **22220/91-106**) is on Konthili, around the corner from the post office in Skyros Town. Another fine carver is **Manolios,** in the main market.

PLANNING YOUR TRIP TO GREECE

News and images coming out of Greece over the past few years have been unsettling, at best. The country's finances, economy, government, and society all appear to be in turmoil. And yet, you'll notice that tourism numbers remain high—in fact, there's been a significant increase—and for a very good reason. A visit to Greece should be an occasion for sheer enjoyment, even exultation. All it takes is a bit of planning to make the visit all the smoother and more pleasant.

10

This chapter provides planning tools and other resources to help you get around and get the most out of your time in Greece. First and foremost, it's important to keep in mind that while Athens goes full-tilt 12 months a year, the time slot for enjoying island life is relatively short, from May to mid-October. Obviously, you can visit the islands outside of those times. Crete, especially, with its big cities of Iraklion and Chania, gets some wintertime visitors. But for the most part, islands are geared to warm weather, and most hotels and restaurants close up tight from fall to late spring.

Whenever you visit, and wherever you go, you'll enjoy Greece the most if you get into Greek time. That has nothing to do with a clock or season, just a rhythm. Slow down to take notice of life swirling around you. Take a siesta in the heat of the day. Eat late, and dine outdoors under the stars. The Greek economy might be in tatters, but in many ways the Greek way of life is as rich as ever.

GETTING THERE
By Plane

The majority of travelers reach Greece by plane, and most arrive at the Athens airport—officially **Eleftherios Venizelos International Airport** (ATH), sometimes referred to by its new location as "the Spata airport."

Airlines currently offering direct flights from North America to Athens are American, Continental, Delta, Olympic Air, and United.

The greatest threats to your well-laid Greek vacation plans may well be the strikes that can close museums and archaeological sites, shut down the metro, keep ferries in port, and stop buses, taxis, and even flights. Strikes are commonplace and often deliberately planned to have the maximum inconvenience on commuters and tourists. The good news is, strikes are usually short-lived and announced in advance. Many websites post strike updates, among them www.ekathimerini.com and www.livinlovin.gr. Your hotel will probably have its own sources and can check to see if buses will be running when you want to get to the airport or if ferries are operating when you're headed to the islands. One way to protect yourself is to leave time to adjust to last-minute changes—for instance, plan to arrive back in Athens the day before your out-bound flight, just in case you need extra time to get to the airport.

Many airlines these days belong to an "alliance" or code-sharing group so you might be able to use or earn frequent-flyer miles with one of the other members. On many other airlines you can make connections at most major European airports. Nearly all the major European airlines fly to Greece, and Greece's own **Olympic Airlines** (www.olympicair.com) and **Aegean** (www.aegeanair.com) also fly to and from European cities. **Ryanair** (www.ryanair.com), **EasyJet** (www.easyjet.com), and **Air Berlin** (www.airberlin.com) are among the many low-cost carriers that fly between European hubs and Greece. Some island airports also handle a good number of flights from European countries, especially those on Rhodes and Crete (both Iraklion and Chania), and to a lesser degree, on Skiathos and Kos. Summertime flights increase considerably and expand to such smaller islands as Mykonos, Paros, and Santorini.

By Car

Many Europeans drive to Greece, and some North Americans may also wish to bring in rented cars if they're traveling from another European country. (Make sure a car rented in another country is allowed to be taken to Greece, including into the countries you may have to drive through en route.) Drivers often come from Italy via ferry, usually disembarking at Patras; the drive to Athens from there is about 210km (130 miles). Others enter from the Former Yugoslavian Republic of Macedonia, or FYROM. (The road from Albania, although pass-able, doesn't attract many tourists.) There are no particular problems or delays at the border crossings, providing all your papers are in order. These include valid registration papers, an international third-party insurance certificate, and a driver's license. In any case, arm yourself with a good up-to-date map such as the ones published by Baedeker, Hallwag, Michelin, or Freytag & Berndt.

By Train

There is train service to Greece from virtually all major points in Europe, although the trains tend to be slow and uncomfortable—almost 24 hours from

Venice, for example. A **Eurailpass** is valid for connections all the way to Athens or Istanbul and includes the ferry service from Italy. North Americans must purchase their Eurailpasses before arriving in Europe. For information, see **www.raileurope.com**.

By Ship

Probably most people traveling to Greece from foreign ports these days are on cruise ships, but there are still many who come on other ships—mainly from Italy. There is also occasional service from Cyprus, Egypt, Israel, and Turkey. The most common ferry crossing is from Brindisi, Italy, to Patras, Greece—about a 10-hour voyage, with as many as seven departures a day in summer. There is also regular service, twice a day in summer, from the Italian cities of Ancona and Bari, once daily from Otranto, and two or three times a week from Trieste or Venice. Passage is often included in Eurailpass, though holders should consult **www.raileurope.com** to see which operators will honor their passes.

Because of the number of shipping lines involved and the variations in schedules, consult a travel agent about the possibilities. The best website is Paleologos Agency's www.ferries.gr; another good source for up-to-date routing and schedules is www.gtp.gr. Book well ahead of time in summer, and reconfirm with the shipping line on the day of departure.

GETTING AROUND

By Plane

Olympic Air (www.olympicair.com) and **Aegean Airlines** (www.aegeanair.com) offer intra-Greece flights that can be a convenient alternative to boat travel, and depending on the time of travel, not much more expensive. Among the many airports served are those in Iraklion, Chania, and Sitia, Crete; Kos; Mykonos; Naxos; Paros; Santorini (aka Thira); Skiathos; and Skyros. **Sky Express** (www.skyexpress.gr) also offers limited service between Athens and various major cites and islands.

By Car

Driving in Greece is a bit of an adventure, but there's no denying that it's the best way to see the country at your own pace. Renting a car is the most convenient way to make a circuit of the ancient sites in the Peloponnese, and you'll probably want to rent a car for at least a day or two of exploring when visiting the islands. The Peloponnese and other regions are now linked to Athens by modern toll roads that are extremely well maintained. The posted speed limit is 120km per hour (75mph), 50km (31mph) in built-up areas, and 80km (50mph) on rural roads.

However, it's important to keep alert and drive defensively. Greece has an unenviable road-fatality record, and a very high accident rate. Drivers can be aggressive and erratic, often exceeding the limit, tail-gating (if they're flashing their headlights, move to a slower lane), and using the shoulder as an extra lane for slower traffic. Drivers often pass on the right, crowd you onto the shoulder in order to pass, ignore stop signs and red lights, and fail to give the right of way. Police are increasingly vigilant, especially about driving under the influence of alcohol; offenses result in stiff fines and jail sentences.

Signs are in Greek and English, but some are easy to miss, obscured by branches, poorly placed, or neglected. Buy a good map. Observe highway signs for how far away the next gas (petrol) station is if you need to fill up (full service), and note that in towns gas stations close in the evenings and on Sundays (though one is always open on a rotation system). Fuel is quite expensive by American standards, close to $6 a gallon.

CAR RENTALS You will find no end of car-rental agencies throughout Greece, both the familiar international ones and many Greek firms. There is considerable variation in prices, although rates in high season generally begin at about 65€ a day and 240€ for a week. Prices will be lower on some islands, depending on the competition, and are definitely lower outside of high season. Shop around and don't be shy about bargaining. Most cars have a **standard shift;** if you must have an automatic, make sure in advance that one is available (and be prepared to pay extra). Always ask if the quoted price includes insurance; many credit cards make the collision-damage waiver unnecessary, but you will find that most rental agencies automatically include this in their rates, usually with a deductible of about 500€. Most companies require that the renter be at least 21 years old (25 for some car models). You must also have a major credit card (or be prepared to leave a *very* large cash deposit).

PARKING Parking is a serious challenge in the cities and towns of Greece. The better hotels provide parking, either on their premises or by arrangement with a nearby lot. Most city streets have restricted parking of one kind or another. Observe signs carefully, as police are quick to ticket and fines can be steep. Police often remove license plates, necessitating a visit to the police station and payment on the spot to retrieve them. If you lock the car and remove valuables from sight, you should not have to worry about a break-in.

By Boat

Ferries are the most common, cheapest, and generally most "authentic" way to visit the islands. A wide variety of vessels sail Greek waters—many, especially those making longer trips, are huge, sleek, and new, with TV lounges, discos, and good restaurants.

Ferry service (often accommodating vehicles) is available between Athens (Piraeus) and other Greek ports. There's regular service from **Piraeus** to Aegina and to Poros in the Saronic Gulf; to most of the Cyclades; to Chania and Iraklion on Crete; Kos; to Rhodes; and to the Dodecanese island of Patmos.

For the Cyclades, crossing is shorter and less expensive from **Rafina,** an hour east of Athens. The Sporades are served by boats from Agios Konstantinos, **Kymi,** and **Volos** (with connecting bus service from Athens). There's also, of course, service between many of the islands. So-called "Flying Catamarans" and hydrofoils dubbed "Flying Dolphins" serve many of the major islands, though their schedules are often interrupted by weather conditions. Drinks and snacks are almost always sold on board ferries and hydrofoils.

For schedules maintained by the dozens of shipping companies, search online at **www.gtp.gr** or **www.ferries.gr**. You can usually depend on purchasing a ticket from a dockside agent or aboard the ship itself, though this is often more expensive. Different travel agencies sell tickets to different lines—this is usually the policy of the line itself—and one agent might not know or bother to find out what else is offered. However, reputable agencies will present you with all the options. At the height of the summer, when boats can be crowded, it's best to buy tickets well in advance of the planned day of travel.

First-class accommodations are usually in roomy air-conditioned cabins. Second-class cabins are smaller and you may share with strangers. Tourist-class fare entitles you to a seat on the deck or in a lounge. (Tourists usually head for the deck, while Greeks stay inside and watch TV.) Hold onto your ticket; crews conduct ticket-control sweeps. While the cost of an overnight cabin can seem steep, remember this: You're saving on hotel accommodations for a night.

BY HYDROFOIL Hydrofoils (often referred to as Flying Dolphins, or by Greeks as to *flying*) are faster than ferries and their stops are much shorter. They have comfortable airline-style seats but are noisy and provide little or no view of the passing scenery. Though fares are higher than those in ferries, they can save quite a bit of time.

Flying Dolphins are operated by **Hellenic Seaways,** 6 Astiggos, Karaiskaki Square, Piraeus (www.hellenicseaways.gr; © **210/419-9000**). The service from Zea Marina in Piraeus to the Saronic Gulf islands and throughout the Sporades is recommended for its speed and regularity. There is also service from Rafina, on the east coast of Attika, and Piraeus to several of the Cyclades islands.

By Train

Greek trains are generally slow but inexpensive and fairly pleasant. For information and tickets in Athens, visit the **OSE office** at 1–3 Karolou (© **210/**

522-4563), or at 6 Sina (© **210/362-4402**), both near Omonia Square. Note that OSE does not have an online presence to supply timetables or ticketing.

Purchase your ticket and reserve a seat ahead of time, as a 50% surcharge is added to tickets purchased on the train, and some lines are packed, especially in summer. A first-class ticket may be worth the extra cost, as seats are more comfortable and less crowded. **Trains** leave from the Larissa station (Stathmos Larissis); to get there, take trolley no. 1 or 5 from Syntagma Square.

By Bus

Greece has an extensive **long-distance bus service (KTEL),** an association of regional operators with green-and-yellow buses that leave from convenient central stations. For information about the long-distance-bus offices, contact the KTEL office in Athens (© **210/512-4910**). Note that KTEL does not have a unified online presence to supply timetables or ticketing.

In Athens, most buses heading to destinations within **Attica** leave from the Mavromateon terminal, north of the National Archaeological Museum. Most buses to **Central Greece** leave from 260 Liossion, 5km (3 miles) north of Omonia Square (take local bus no. 024 from Leoforos Amalias in front of the entrance to the National Garden and tell the driver your destination). Most buses to the **Peloponnese,** and to **western** and **northern Greece,** leave from the long-distance bus terminal at 100 Kifissou, 4km (2½ miles) northeast of Omonia Square. To get to the long-distance bus terminal, take local bus no. 051 from a stop 2 blocks west of Omonia, near the big church of Ayios Konstandinos, at Zinonos and Menandrou.

Express buses between major cities, usually air-conditioned, can be booked through travel agencies. Even many express buses take tortuous routes and make frequent stops (including meal and toilet breaks). NO SMOKING signs are generally disregarded by drivers and conductors, as well as by many older male passengers.

Organized and guided **bus tours** are widely available from Athens. Some of them will pick you up at your hotel; ask the hotel staff or any travel agent in Athens. **CHAT Tours** is the oldest and probably most experienced provider of a wide selection of bus tours led by highly articulate guides. Almost any travel agent can book a CHAT tour, but if you want to deal with the company directly, contact them through their website, www.chatours.gr. In Athens, the CHAT office is at 9 Xenofontos, 10557 Athens (© **210/323-0827**).

TIPS ON ACCOMMODATIONS

Greece offers a full spectrum of accommodations, ranging from the extravagant to the basic, from massive, all-inclusive hotel complexes at beach resorts to an extra room in a private house. Classes are indicated by a star system, from 1 to 5, but these are based more on facilities such as public areas, pools, and in-room amenities than on comfort, charm, or service.

Many major chains operate in Greece, alongside some Greek-owned groups, but most Greek hotels are independent lodgings run by hands-on owners. Greece has some of the most luxurious lodgings in the world, setting the gold standard with such amenities as private pools, in-suite gyms, and marble-clad bathrooms. At the other end of the scale are perfectly acceptable but modest lodgings. Especially in the countryside and on the islands, you will often encounter bathrooms that, while decently equipped, lack enclosed showers (a hose and a drain suffice). Whatever the level of luxury, however, standards of cleanliness are generally very high. Most rooms, even modest ones, offer air-conditioning in the hot season and heating in the colder months, as well as TVs and, often, small refrigerators. Private bathrooms are the norm, although these are sometimes accessed from a hallway or courtyard outside the room.

Note that a **double room** in Greece does not always mean a room with a double bed, but *might* be a room with twin beds. Double beds in Greece are called "matrimonial beds," and rooms with such beds are often designated "honeymoon rooms." Also note that a **passport** or other form of identification is usually required when registering in a hotel.

Hotels in Athens, Santorini, and Mykonos tend to be expensive, but in the countryside and on many islands, hotel rates in general are a relative bargain when compared to those elsewhere in Europe. Which leads to the subject of bargaining—don't be shy about doing so, whether it's in an email, on the phone, or in person. Many hotels offer discounted rates for longer stays, for Internet bookings, advance payment, or payment in cash.

ACCOMMODATION SOURCES You probably won't get too far off an arriving ferry or bus before encountering someone offering a "room to rent." This might be in a private home, a full-blown hotel dredging up clients, or in a purpose-built or refitted "room to rent" structure. The price is almost always on the low side. Accommodations are rarely luxurious, but they are often extremely comfortable and full of character and usually have private bathrooms and other amenities. The tout often comes equipped with photos or a printed pamphlet; aside from price, you should ask about location up front, before following a stranger through the back streets. Inquire about terms of payment (usually cash only) and any amenities you require—terrace, view, inclusive breakfast, pool, whatever. Soliciting clients is honorable in Greece, and not a sign of desperation; in fact, finding a room in this way can ensure a nice bond with the proprietor.

Apartment and house rentals are common in Greece, with a wide-range of offerings from such sources as **Airbnb** (www.airbnb.com) and **VRBO** (www.vrbo.com). **Yades Historic Hotels** (www.yadeshotels.gr) represents stylish and distinctive hotels throughout Greece, with many excellent properties in the Peloponnese and on Santorini and Crete. **True Greece** (www.truegreece.com) also represents some especially distinctive hotels in Athens and on the islands.

MINDING YOUR LOCAL MANNERS

DRESS CODES   Most Greeks wear bathing suits only on the beach and do not go into restaurants, cafes, or shops without putting something over their swimsuits. Also, most Greeks consider bare feet off the beach seriously odd and quite rude. Almost no Greek man would go into a church in shorts, and virtually no Greek woman would go into church in a sleeveless top or shorts. Slacks for women are now acceptable almost everywhere, however, except in the most traditional churches and monasteries.

SAYING HELLO & GOODBYE   Few Greeks go into a bakery and say "Loaf of bread, please," and then pay and leave. Almost all encounters begin with a greeting: *"Kali mera"* (Good day) is always acceptable, but on Monday, you'll hear *"Kali ebdomada"* (Good week) and on the first of the month *"Kalo mena"* (Good month). Sprinkle your requests on how to find the Acropolis or where to buy a bus ticket with *"Sas para kalo"* (Excuse me, please) and *"Eucharisto"* (Thanks), and you'll help make Greeks reconsider all those things they've come to believe about rude tourists. And on that topic, although most Greeks don't mind having their photo taken, always ask first.

TOURS/SPECIAL-INTEREST TRIPS

You can find a wide variety of tours, special-interest trips, classes, and workshops available when you travel to Greece, focusing on everything from antiquities to wine tasting. In addition, there are a number of organized possibilities for volunteerism, whether on excavations or on farms. Here are some suggestions.

Educational Trips

Archaeological Tours, 271 Madison Ave., Suite 904, New York, NY 10016 (www.archaeologicaltrs.com; © **866/740-5130**), offers tours led by expert guides; typical tours might be to classical Greek sites or to Cyprus, Crete, and Santorini. **The Aegean Center for the Fine Arts** (www.aegeancenter.org), based on the island of Paros, offers courses in painting, photography, music, creative writing, and modern Greek. Most of the students are college-age Americans.

The American-run **Island Center for the Arts** conducts classes in painting, photography, and Greek culture on the island of Skopelos between June and September (www.islandcenter.org; © **617/623-6538**). As the school is affiliated with the Massachusetts College of Art, some educational institutions grant credits for its courses.

The popular **Road Scholar** program (formerly Elderhostel; www.roadscholar.org; © **800/454-5768**) is a learning experience for adults (with some intergenerational programs) that offers a couple dozen trips to Greece and the surrounding area each year, ranging from cruises on smaller ships that explore the history and culture of the Aegean Islands, to overland road trips where participants explore the art, architecture, and archeology of the region.

The **Dartmouth College Rassias Center** (www.rassias.dartmouth.edu) language program in modern Greek is a very popular 10-day total-immersion session that should have you arriving ready to amaze and delight Greeks with your command of their glorious and tricky language. This is the same method used to train Peace Corps volunteers. Classes are held in totally un-Greek surroundings, on the Dartmouth campus in Hanover, New Hampshire. In Greece, the **Athens Centre,** 48 Archimidou, Athens (athens centre.gr), which has been around since 1969, offers modern Greek classes year-round, with 3-week language immersion courses. During the summer, the center also hosts 2-week workshops in painting, photography, poetry, and theater.

Adventure & Wellness Trips

Trekking Hellas (www.trekking.gr) offers white-water rafting excursions in the Peloponnese and northern Greece. Although plenty of beginners go on these trips, most foreign participants have had some rafting experience. Trekking Hellas also organizes hiking tours (see "Walking Tours," p. 289). **Backroads** (www.backroads.com; © 800/462-2848) leads cycling tours in Crete, open to avid cyclists and easygoing riders alike.

Eumelia (www.eumelia.com), in the Peloponnese south of Sparta, has five rental houses, a staff of three, and never more than 25 guests on its organic farm outside the hamlet of Gouves. Eumelia (the name means "melody") focuses on agrotourism and the manufacture and sale of organic produce (olive oil, herbs, and so on). There are frequent workshops and seminars; Eumelia aims for "100% self-sufficiency" and all its buildings are built with great attention to environmental issues—while still offering TV and Internet access.

Limnisa (Creative Holidays by the Sea; www.limnisa.com) offers silent retreats, writing retreats, and workshops by the sea near Methana, in the east Peloponnese, near the island of Poros. **Skyros Center** (www.skyros.com) offers yoga and holistic holidays (as well as writing holidays and singles holidays) on the island of Skyros.

Food & Wine Trips

If you're heading for Santorini and want to learn about Greek cuisine, the island's best restaurant, **Selene** (www.selene.gr), offers cooking classes with the most varied and fresh local ingredients each summer. **Diane Kochilas** (www.dianekochilas.com), a Greek-American expert on Greek foods, offers a variety of activities, including cooking classes in Athens and culinary tours in Athens or throughout Greece. **Nikki Rose** (www.cookingincrete.com), a Cretan-American professional chef, operates seminars on Crete that combine some travel with cooking lessons and investigations of Crete's diet.

Want to mix seeing where the Olympic games began with some cooking, creative writing, or painting? Check out the website of the **Hotel Pelops** (www.hotelpelops.gr), where co-owner Susanna Spiliopoulou offers 3- and 4-day workshops a short walk from the pine groves of ancient Olympia.

Guided Tours

Organized and guided **bus tours** focusing on the glories of ancient Greece are widely available. Escorted tours are structured group tours, with a group leader. The price usually includes hotels, meals, tours, admission costs, and local transportation. Single travelers are usually hit with a "single supplement" to the base price for package vacations and cruises, while the price of a single room is almost always well over half that for a double.

CHAT Tours (www.chattours.gr), founded in 1953, is the oldest and most experienced provider of a wide selection of bus tours led by highly articulate guides. Its main office is at 9 Xenofontos St., Athens 10557 (✆ **210/323-0827**). Be sure to ask how many will be on your tour, as a large group usually results in a more regimented and much less personal tour.

Fantasy Travel, 19 Filelinon (www.fantasytravel.gr; ✆ **210/ 331-0530**), is another solid travel agency in Athens that offers tours. Two other long-standing Greek tour organizers are **Homeric Tours** (www.homerictours.com; ✆ **800/223-5570**) and **Tourlite International** (www.tourlite.com; ✆ **800/272-7600**). Such tours fall into the "moderate" category in pricing and accommodations. They're especially handy for a quick visit to some of the archaeological sites around Athens (see chapter 5).

A more upscale agency is **TrueGreece** (www.truegreece.com; ✆ **800/817-7098** in North America or 210/612-0656 in Greece), which escorts individuals and small groups on customized and more intimate tours to selected destinations.

If you'd like to take a day tour of Athens, or a week-long tour of Greece, that focuses on Greece's **Jewish heritage,** check out **www.jewishtours.gr**.

Walking Tours

Trekking Hellas (www.trekkinghellas.gr), based in Athens at 10 Rethimnou (✆ **210/331-0323**), is the best-known outfit offering guided hiking tours of the Greek mainland, Crete, and several Cycladic islands. If you don't want to be with a group, but do want some pointers, Trekking Hellas will help you plan an itinerary and book you places to stay along the way. The Crete-based **Happy Walker,** Tombazi 56 in Rethymnon (www.happywalker.com; ✆ **28310/52920**) leads day hikes into the mountains and gorges of Western Crete, as well as multiday hikes on Crete and elsewhere in Greece.

[Fast FACTS] GREECE

Area Codes All phone numbers in Greece are 10 digits long. Area codes range from three digits in Athens **(210)** to as many as five digits in less populated locales; the phone numbers themselves range from five digits to eight but all must add up to a total of ten including the area code. All numbers provided in the text start with the proper area code. Also see "Telephones," later in this section.

ATMs In commercial centers, airports, all cities and larger towns, and most tourist centers, you will find at least a couple of machines accepting a wide range of cards. Smaller towns will often have only one

ATM—and it may not accept your card. **Commercial Bank (Emboriki Trapeza)** services Plus and Visa; **Credit Bank (Trapeza Pisteos)** and **AlphaBank** accept Visa and American Express; **National Bank (Ethiniki Trapeza)** takes Cirrus and MasterCard/Access.

But for all the prevalence of ATMs, you should keep at least some actual cash on you for those occasions when all the ATMs you can locate are out of order or out of cash. Keep enough euros or your own currency to get you through at least 24 hours.

Note: Greek ATMs accept only a four-digit PIN—you must change yours before you go. And since Greek ATMs use only numeric PINs (personal identification numbers), before you set off for Greece be sure you know how to convert letters to numerals as the alphabet will be in Greek.

Business Hours Greek business and office hours take some getting used to, especially in the afternoon, when most English-speaking people are accustomed to getting things done in high gear. Compounding the problem is that it is nearly impossible to pin down the precise hours of opening. We can start by saying that almost all stores and services are **closed on Sunday**—except, of course, tourist-oriented shops and services. **Supermarkets, department stores,** and **chain stores** are usually open 9am to 9pm, Monday through Saturday. On Monday, Wednesday, and Saturday, smaller **retail shops'** hours are usually 9am to 3pm; Tuesday, Thursday, and Friday, it's 9am to 2pm and 5 to 7pm. The **afternoon siesta** is generally observed from 3 to 5pm, though many tourist-oriented businesses have a minimal crew on duty during naptime, and they may keep extended hours, often from 8am to 10pm. (In fact, in tourist centers, shops may be open at all kinds of hours.) Call ahead to check the hours of businesses you must deal with, and try not to disturb Greek friends during siesta hours.

Most **government offices** are open Monday through Friday only, from 8am to 3pm. **Banks** are open to the public Monday through Thursday from 8am to 2:30pm, Friday from 8am to 2pm. Banks at a few locations may be open for some services such as foreign currency exchange into the evening and on Saturday. All banks are closed on the long list of Greek holidays. (See p. 29.)

Final advice: Anything you really need to accomplish in a government office, business, or store should be done on weekdays between about 9am and 1pm.

Credit Cards In Greece, Visa and MasterCard are the most widely accepted cards. Diners Club is less widely accepted; American Express is even less frequently accepted, because it charges a higher commission and is more protective of the cardholder in disagreements. Credit cards are accepted throughout Greece in the better hotels and at most shops, but even many of the better restaurants in major cities do *not* accept credit cards. Certainly most restaurants and many smaller hotels in Greece do not. Some hotels that require a credit card number when you make advance reservations will demand payment in cash; inquire beforehand if this will be the case. Many establishments will offer you a discount if you pay in cash.

Customs What you can bring into Greece: Passengers from North America arriving in Athens aboard international flights are generally not searched, and if you have nothing to declare, continue through the green lane. (Because of the continuing threat of terrorism, baggage is X-rayed before boarding domestic flights.) Citizens of the United States, Canada, Australia, New Zealand, and other non-E.U. countries do face a few commonsensical restrictions. Clearly, no narcotics: Greece is *very* tough on drug users. No explosives or weapons—although upon application, a sportsman might be able to bring in a legitimate hunting weapon. Only medications for amounts properly prescribed for your own use are allowed. Plants with soil are not. Dogs and cats can be brought in, but they must

THREE warnings ABOUT DEBIT & CREDIT CARDS

As part of banks' and credit card companies' increasing concern about fraud, it is our experience that they are apt to deny your cards if you try to use them too far out of your normal circuit. It's a wise idea to contact your cards' customer service department by phone and tell them in advance which countries you plan to travel to.

Meanwhile, **Chip-and-PIN** (aka "Smart Cards") credit cards are now being introduced throughout much of the world. Unlike the long-standard credit cards that have only a magnetic strip, these have a small chip embedded in them and then require the user to enter a PIN. The European Union has required all its member nations to introduce these, but many American issuers of credit cards have not adopted them widely. This means that Americans abroad may face a problem when presenting their standard magnetic strip cards: some places may claim that they are no longer acceptable. In fact, they are: If the individual rejecting your card doesn't know this, he must punch in your card number manually—and you must provide them with that card's PIN. So, if you do not know your card's PIN, call your card issuer before you leave home to obtain one (for **MasterCard,** call ℂ **800/622-7747;** for **Visa,** ℂ **800/857-2911**). Allow some time for this, as it may involve sending mail from and back to the issuer. *Note:* This problem does not arise if you are using a card as a debit card, which already requires its PIN.

Beware of **hidden credit card fees** while traveling. Check with your credit or debit card issuer to see what fees, if any, will be charged for overseas transactions. Recent reform legislation in the U.S., for example, has curbed some exploitative lending practices. But many banks have responded by increasing fees in other areas, including fees for customers who use their cards while out of the country. Fees can amount to 3% or more of the purchase price. Check with your bank to avoid any surprise charges on your statement.

have proof of recent rabies and other health shots.

What You Can Take Out of Greece:

(All Nationalities): Exportation of Greek antiquities is strictly protected by law. No antiquities may be taken out of Greece without prior special permission from the **Archaeological Service,** 3 Polignotou, Athens. Also, you must be able to explain how you acquired your purchase—in particular, icons or religious articles. A dealer or shopkeeper must provide you with an export certificate for any object dating from before 1830. In general, **keep all receipts** for major purchases in order to clear Customs on your return home.

For further information on what you're allowed to bring into your country of residence, contact one of the following agencies:

U.S. Citizens: U.S. Customs & Border Protection (CBP), 1300 Pennsylvania Ave. NW, Washington, DC 20229 (www.cbp.gov; ℂ **877/227-5511**).

Canadian Citizens: Canada Border Services Agency (www.cbsa-asfc.gc.ca; ℂ **800/461-9999** in Canada, or **204/983-3500**).

U.K. Citizens: HM Revenue & Customs (www.hmce.gov.uk; ℂ **0845/010-9000;** from outside the U.K., 020/8929-0152).

Australian Citizens: Australian Customs Service (www.customs.gov.au; ℂ **1300/363-263**).

New Zealand Citizens: New Zealand Customs, the Customhouse, 17–21 Whitmore St., Box 2218, Wellington (www.customs.govt. nz; ℂ **0800/428-786**).

Doctors Any foreign embassy or consulate can

provide a list of area doctors who speak English. If in a town without these offices, ask your hotel management to recommend a local doctor—even his or her own.

Drinking Laws The minimum age for being served alcohol in public is 18. Wine and beer are generally available in eating places, but not in all coffeehouses or dessert cafes. Alcoholic beverages are sold in food stores as well as liquor stores. Although a certain amount of high spirits is appreciated, Greeks do not appreciate public drunkenness. The resort centers where mobs of young foreigners party every night are tolerated as necessary for the tourist trade, but such behavior wins no respect for foreigners. Do not carry open containers of alcohol in your car and don't even think about driving while intoxicated—offenders are often jailed and almost always fined heavily.

Electricity Electric current in Greece is 220 volts AC, alternating at 50 cycles. (Some larger hotels have 110-volt low-wattage outlets for electric shavers, but they aren't good for hair dryers and most other appliances.) Electrical outlets require Continental-type plugs with two round prongs. U.S. travelers will need an adapter plug. Laptop computer users will want to check their requirements; a transformer may be necessary, though many laptops function at 220 volts.

Embassies & Consulates **Australia,** Level 6, Thon Building, corner Kiffisias & Alexandras, Ambelokipi (www.greece.embassy.gov.au; ✆ **210/870-4000;** **Canada,** 48 Ethnikis Antistaseos St. (www.greece.gc.ca; ✆ **210/727-3400); Ireland,** 7 Vas. Konstantinou (✆ **210/723-2771); New Zealand,** 76 Kifissias Ave, Ambelokipi (✆ **210/692-4136); South Africa,** 60 Kifissias, Maroussi (✆ **210/680-6645); United Kingdom,** 1 Ploutarchou (www.ukingreece.fco.gov.uk; ✆ **210/727-2600); United States,** 91 Leoforos Vas, Sofias (athens.usembassy.gov; ✆ **210/721-2951).** Be sure to phone ahead before you go to any embassy; most keep limited hours and are usually closed on their own holidays as well as Greek ones.

Emergencies Contact the local police at ✆ **100.** For fire, call ✆ **199.** For medical emergencies and/or first aid and/or an ambulance, call ✆ **166.** For hospitals, call ✆ **106.** For automobile emergencies, put out a triangular danger sign and call ✆ **10400.** Embassies, consulates, and many hotels can recommend an English-speaking doctor.

Health If you suffer from a chronic illness, consult your doctor about your travel plans before your departure. If you have special concerns, before heading abroad you might check out the United States **Centers for Disease Control**

and Prevention (www.cdc.gov/travel; ✆ **800/232-4636).**

Travelers should check their health plans to see if they provide appropriate coverage; you may want to buy **travel medical insurance.** Bring your insurance ID card with you when you travel.

Drugstores/Chemists: These are called *pharmikon* in Greek; aside from the obvious indications in windows and interiors, they are identified by a green cross. For minor medical problems, go first to the nearest pharmacy. Pharmacists usually speak English, and many medications can be dispensed without prescription. In the larger cities, a sign in the window of a closed pharmacy will direct you to the nearest open one.

Common Ailments: Diarrhea is no more of a problem in Greece than it might be anytime you change diet and water supplies, but occasionally visitors do experience it. Common over-the-counter preventatives and cures are available in Greek pharmacies, but if you are concerned, bring your own. If you expect to be taking sea trips and are inclined to get **seasick,** bring a preventative.

Allergy sufferers should carry antihistamines, especially in the spring.

Sun Exposure: Between mid-June and September, too much exposure to the sun during midday could well lead to sunstroke or heatstroke. High-SPF

sunscreen and a hat are strongly advised. Stock up on sunscreen before setting out to the islands, where these products tend to be more expensive and choices are limited.

Hospitals In Greece, modern hospitals, clinics, and pharmacies are found everywhere, and personnel, equipment, and supplies ensure excellent treatment. Dental care is also widely available. Most doctors in Greece can speak English (many having trained in North America or the U.K.).

You can also try the emergency room at a local hospital. Many hospitals also have walk-in clinics for emergency cases that are not life threatening; you may not get immediate attention, but you won't pay the high price of an emergency room visit. In an emergency, call a **first-aid center** (✆ **166**), the nearest **hospital** (✆ **106**), or the **tourist police** (✆ **171**).

Emergency treatment is usually given free in state hospitals, but be warned that only basic needs are met. The care in outpatient clinics, which are usually open mornings (8am–noon), is often somewhat better; you can find them next to most major hospitals, on some islands, and occasionally in rural areas, usually indicated by prominent signs.

Internet & Wi-Fi Internet connection with or without Wi-Fi is now available virtually anywhere a visitor is apt to be. Most bars have Wi-Fi, as do hotels and many public places.

Language Language is usually not a problem for English speakers in Greece, as so many Greeks have studied it and find it necessary to use in their work worlds—most particularly, in the tourist realm that visitors encounter. Many Greeks have also lived abroad where English is the primary language. Young people learn it in school, from Anglo American–dominated pop culture, and in special classes meant to prepare them for the contemporary world of business. Several television programs are broadcast in their original languages, and American prime-time soaps are very popular, nearly inescapable. Even advertisements have an increasingly high English content. Don't let all this keep you from trying to pick up at least a few words of Greek; your effort will be rewarded by your hosts, who realize how difficult their language is for foreigners and will patiently help you improve your pronunciation and usage. Meanwhile, see the "Useful Words & Phrases" at the end of this chapter.

Legal Aid If you need legal assistance, contact your own or another English-speaking embassy or consulate. If these institutions cannot themselves be of help, they can direct you to local lawyers who speak English and are willing to help.

LGBT Travelers
Greece—or at least parts of it—has a long tradition of being tolerant of gay men, and in recent years these locales have extended this tolerance to lesbians. Bars, clubs, and hotels that are especially open to and frequented by LBGT travelers are identified in the relevant locales. However, although Greeks in Athens, Piraeus, and perhaps a few other major cities may not care one way or the other, Greeks in small towns and villages—indeed, most Greeks—do not appreciate flagrant displays of dress or behavior.

Among the best-known hangouts for gays and lesbians are Mykonos and Chania, Crete, but gays and lesbians travel all over Greece without any particular issues. The age of consent for sexual relations with homosexuals is 17, and this can be strictly enforced against foreigners.

Mail The mail service of Greece is reliable—but slow. (Postcards usually arrive after you have returned.) You can receive mail addressed to you c/o Poste *Restante*, General Post Office, City (or Town), Island (or Province), Greece. You will need your passport to collect this mail. Many hotels will accept, hold, and even forward mail for you; ask first. For the fastest service, try FedEx or one of the other major private carriers; travel agencies can direct you to these.

Postage rates have been going up in Greece, as they are elsewhere. At press time, a postcard or a letter under 20 grams (about .7 oz.) to foreign countries costs .75€; 20 to 50 grams (up to 1.75 oz.), 1.30€; 50 to 100 grams (3.5 oz.), 1.75€. Rates for packages depend on size as well as weight, but are reasonable. *Note:* Do not wrap or seal any package—you must be prepared to show the contents to a postal clerk. If you are concerned about some particular item, you might consider using one of the well-known international commercial delivery services. Your hotel or any travel agency can direct you to the nearest local office.

Medical Requirements   There are no immunization requirements for getting into Greece, though it's always a good idea to have polio, tetanus, and typhoid covered when traveling anywhere. See "Health," p. 292.

Mobile Phones   The three letters that define much of the world's wireless capabilities are **GSM (Global System for Mobile Communications),** a big, seamless network that makes for easy cross-border cellphone use throughout Europe—including Greece—and indeed most countries around the world. In the United States, T-Mobile and AT&T Wireless use this quasi-universal system; in Canada, Microcell and some Rogers customers are GSM. Most Australians use GSM.

GSM phones function with a removable plastic SIM card, encoded with your phone number and account information. But some phones are "locked" and must be unlocked; go to your phone's website and get information as to how to unlock your phone. If your cellphone is on a GSM system, and you have a world-capable multiband phone such as many Sony Ericsson, Motorola, or Samsung models, you can make and receive calls around much of the globe. Just call your wireless operator and ask for "international roaming" to be activated on your account. Unfortunately, per-minute charges can be high—usually $1 to $1.50 in Greece. But the reassuring point is that cellphone services are generally available wherever you go in Greece.

An alternative way if you intend to make many phone calls in Greece is to bring your unlocked cellphone to Greece and buy a SIM card in the national telephone office (OTE) center in major cities or a commercial phone store. These cards—actually a tiny chip inserted into your phone—cost about 20€ and include a Greek phone number and a number of prepaid minutes; when you have used up these minutes, you can purchase a phone card at a kiosk that gives you more minutes. But it must be said that any calls outside of Greece by this system are very expensive.

For many, **renting** a phone in Greece is a good idea. You can rent a phone from any number of places in Greece—including kiosks at major airports, OTE offices, and cellphone stores.

If you expect to be abroad for more than a brief time, however, and/or to be visiting more than one country, **buying a phone** can make economic sense. Numerous companies now sell phones with a SIM card included and with a U.S. or U.K. phone number assigned to it—so-called global roaming services that offer relatively cheap per minute rates for both outgoing and incoming calls: Google "global roaming SIM card" to compare various services and charges or look into **www.cellular abroad.com.** You can buy a phone in Greece in either the national telephone office (OTE) in any decent-size city or a retail electronics store. If you take the cheapest package; you'll probably pay less than $100 for a phone and a starter calling card. Local calls may be as low as 10¢ per minute, and in many countries incoming calls are free.

Money   The currency in Greece is the **euro** (pronounced *evro* in Greek), abbreviated "eu" and symbolized by €. (If you still own the old drachmas, it is no longer possible to exchange them.) The euro comes in seven paper notes and eight coins. The **notes** are in different sizes and colors, and come in the following denominations: 5, 10, 20, 50, 100, 200, and 500. (Considering that each euro is worth over $1, those last bills are quite pricey!) Six of the **coins** are officially denominated in "cents"—e.g., one-hundredths of a euro—but in Greece the name for this is *lepta,* the old Greek name for sums smaller than the drachma. These smaller coins, which come in different sizes, are valued at 1, 2, 5, 10, 20, or 50 *lepta.* There are also 1€ and 2€ coins. Although one side of the coins differs in each of the member E.U. nations, all coins and bills are legal tender in all countries using the euro.

Warning: The 1€ and 2€ coins look similar to a 1 lira Turkish coin—worth less than half the 1€, so count your change carefully.

It's a good idea to exchange at least some money—enough to cover airport incidentals and transportation to your hotel—before you leave, so you can avoid lines at airport ATMs.

You can exchange money at your local American Express or Thomas Cook office or at some banks.

Frommer's lists exact prices in the local currency (the euro). The conversion rate provided was correct at press time. However, rates fluctuate, so before you leave, check a website like **www.oanda.com/currency/converter** online for the latest rates.

THE VALUE OF THE EURO VS. OTHER POPULAR CURRENCIES

Euro€	Aus$	Can$	NZ$	UK£	US$
1	A$1.47	C$1.46	NZ$1.55	£.84	$1.12

Costs   Greece is no longer the bargain it once was, though it is still not in the category of London or New York or Paris or Tokyo. Even so, in Athens and on Santorini and Mykonos, prices at many hotels and upscale restaurants are comparable to those in most other developed countries. Admission to major museums and archaeological sites is comparable to fees in major European cities. But it is still possible to have a reasonably modest holiday in Greece. You can start by visiting outside the high season—July and August. Pick mid-price hotels and restaurants—and make sure breakfast is included in your hotel price. Look for deals on car rentals. Fly at off-peak times, and avoid expensive services such as spas or purchases such as jewelry.

WHAT THINGS COST IN ATHENS

	€
Taxi from the airport to downtown Athens	35–50
Double room, moderate	101–150
Double room, inexpensive	80–100
Three-course dinner for one without wine, moderate	12–20
Bottle of beer	2.50–4
Cup of coffee	1.50–3.50
1 gallon/1 liter of gas	5.50/1.45
Admission to museums and archaeological sites	2–12

Newspapers & Magazines   All cities, large towns, and major tourist centers have at least one shop or kiosk that carries a selection of foreign-language publications; most of these are flown or shipped in on the very day of publication. English-language readers have a wide selection, including most of the British papers (*Daily Telegraph, Financial Times, Guardian, Independent, Times*), the *International Herald Tribune* (with its English-language insert of the well-known

Athens newspaper, *Kathime-rini*), and *USA Today*. *Kathi-merini*, by the way, has an online English edition that is quite adequate for keeping up with Greek news (**www. ekathimerini.com**).

Packing   As most visitors to Greece tend to be there between the first of May and the end of September, light jackets and sweaters should suffice for any over-cast days or cool eve-nings—unless, of course, you are planning to spend time in the mountains. Except for the really high-class hotels and resorts, casual dress is accepted in almost all restaurants and facilities. But Greeks remain uncomfortable with beach-wear or too-casual garb in villages and cities. And females are expected—indeed, often required—to cover their arms and upper legs before entering monas-teries and churches. Some priests and monks are stricter than others and may flatly bar men as well as women if they feel that the men are not dressed suitably.

Passports   For entry into Greece, citizens of Australia, Canada, New Zealand, South Africa, the United Kingdom, the United States, and almost all other non-E.U. countries are required to have a **valid passport,** which is stamped upon entry and exit, for stays up to 90 days.

Citizens of other mem-bers of the European Union are required to present a valid ID (driving licenses do

not qualify) for entry into Greece; you may stay an unlimited period (although you should inquire about this at a Greek consulate or at your embassy in Greece). Children under 16 from E.U. countries may travel without an ID if accompanied by either parent. All E.U. citi-zens are reminded that they should check the require-ments for non-E.U. coun-tries through which you might travel to get to Greece.

For stays longer than 90 days, all non-E.U. citizens will require visas from the Greek embassies or consuls in their home countries. If already in Greece, arrange-ments must be made with the **Bureau of Aliens,** 173 Leoforos Alexandras, 11522 Athens (© **210/770-5711**).

For Residents of Aus-tralia   Contact the **Austra-lian Passport Information Service** at © **131-232,** or visit the government web-site at www.passports.gov. au.

For Residents of Can-ada   Contact the central **Passport Office,** Depart-ment of Foreign Affairs and International Trade, Ottawa, ON K1A 0G3 (www.ppt. gc.ca; © **800/567-6868**).

For Residents of Ire-land   Contact the **Passport Office,** Setanta Centre, Molesworth Street, Dublin 2 (www.irlgov.ie/iveagh; © **01/671-1633**).

For Residents of New Zealand   Contact the **Pass-ports Office** at www.pass-ports.govt.nz or call © **0800/225-050** in New

Zealand, or 04/474-8100 elsewhere.

For Residents of the United Kingdom   Visit your nearest passport office, major post office, or travel agency or contact the **United Kingdom Passport Service** at www.ukpa.gov. uk, © **0870/521-0410,** or search its website at.

For Residents of the United States   To find your regional passport office, either check the U.S. State Department website or call the **National Pass-port Information Center** toll-free number (© **877/ 487-2778**) for automated information.

Police   To report a crime or medical emergency, or for information or other assistance, first contact the tourist police (© **171**), where an English-speaking officer is more likely to be found. If there is no tourist police officer available, con-tact the local police at © **100.** Tourists who report petty thievery to the local police will probably feel that they are not being taken all that seriously, but it is more likely that the Greek police have realized there is little they can do without solid identification of the culprits.

Note: The Greek authori-ties and laws are extremely tough when it comes to for-eigners with drugs—starting with marijuana. Do *not* attempt to bring any illicit drug into or out of Greece.

Safety   Crime directed at tourists was traditionally unheard of in Greece, but in more recent years there are occasional reports of cars broken into, pickpockets, purse snatchers, and the like. Normal precautions are called for. For instance, if you have hand luggage containing expensive items, whether jewelry or cameras, never give it to an individual unless you are absolutely sure it will be safe with him or her. Lock the car and don't leave cameras or other such gear visible. Don't leave your luggage unattended when entering or leaving hotels. Also, it is probably safer not to leave valuables unattended at beaches. Young women should observe the obvious precautions in dealing with men in isolated locales.

High among potential dangers are automobile accidents: Greece has one of the worst vehicle accident rates in Europe. You should exercise great caution when driving over unfamiliar, often winding, and often poorly maintained roads. This holds true especially when you're driving at night. As for those who insist on renting motorbikes or similar vehicles, at the very least wear a helmet.

Senior Travel Greece does not offer too many discounts for seniors. Some museums and archaeological sites offer discounts for those 60 and over, but the practice is unpredictable, and in almost all instances the discount is restricted to citizens of an E.U. nation.

Many reliable agencies and organizations target the 50-plus market. **Road Scholar** (formerly

Elderhostel; www.road scholar.org; ℂ **800/454-5768**) arranges study programs for those ages 55 and over (and a spouse or companion of any age) in the U.S. and in more than 80 countries around the world. Most courses last 5 to 7 days in the U.S., or 2 to 4 weeks abroad; many include airfare, accommodations in university dormitories or modest inns, meals, and tuition. In Greece, groups typically settle in one area for a week or so, with excursions that focus on getting to know the history and culture. Canada-based **ElderTreks** (www.eldertreks.com; ℂ **800/741-7956**) offers small-group tours to off-the-beaten-path or adventure-travel locations, restricted to travelers 50 and older. Britons might prefer to deal with **Saga Holidays** (Saga Building, Folkestone, Kent CT20 1AZ; www.saga.co.uk; ℂ **800/096-0084** in the U.S. and Canada, or 0808/234-1714 in the U.K.), which offers all-inclusive tours in Greece for those ages 50 and older.

Single Travelers Single travelers are usually hit with a "single supplement" to the base price for package vacations and cruises, while the price of a single room is almost always well over half of that for a double. Many reputable tour companies offer singles-only trips, however. **Singles Travel International** (www.singles travelintl.com; ℂ **877/765-6874**) offers escorted tours to places like the Greek

Islands. **Backroads** (www.backroads.com; ℂ **800/462-2848**) offers "Singles + Solos" active-travel trips to destinations worldwide.

Smoking In recent years the Greeks have imposed no-smoking regulations on airplanes, on areas of ships, and all public locations (banks, post offices, and so on). Small restaurants, tavernas, and cafes must declare whether they allow smoking or not; larger such establishments are supposed to set aside smoking areas. But Greeks continue to be among the world's most persistent smokers and, except on airplanes, many Greeks—and some foreigners—feel free to puff away at will. Hotels are only beginning to claim that they have set aside rooms or even floors for nonsmokers, so ask about them, if it matters to you. If you are really bothered by smoke while eating, about all you can do is position yourself as best as possible—and then be prepared to leave if it gets really bad.

Student Travel In Greece, students with proper identification (ISIC and IYC cards) are given reduced entrance fees to archaeological sites and museums, as well as discounts on admission to most artistic events, theatrical performances, and festivals. So if you're eligible, you'd be wise to arm yourself with an **International Student Identity Card (ISIC),** which offers substantial savings on rail passes, plane tickets, and entrance fees. It also provides you with basic health and life insurance and a 24-hour help line. The card is available for $25 from **STA Travel** (www.statravel.com; ✆ **800/781-4040**), the biggest student travel agency in the world.

The **International Student Travel Confederation** (**ISTC;** www.istc.org) was formed in 1949 to make travel around the world more affordable for students. Check out its website for comprehensive travel services information for students.

If you're no longer a student but are still under 26, you can get an **International Youth Travel Card (IYTC)** from ISTC which entitles you to some discounts. **Travel CUTS** (www.travelcuts.com; ✆ **800/592-2887**) offers similar services for both Canadians and U.S. residents. Irish students may prefer to turn to **USIT** (www.usit.ie; ✆ **01/602-1906**), an Ireland-based specialist in student, youth, and independent travel.

A **Hostelling International** membership can save students money in some 5,000 HI hostels in 70 countries (including Greece), where sex-segregated, dormitory-style sleeping quarters cost about $15 to $35 per night. In Greece, an International Guest Card can be obtained at the **Greek Association of Youth Hostels (OESE),** in Athens at 75 Dhamereos, Athens 11633 (www.

athens-yhostel.com; ✆ **210/751-9530**).

Taxes & Service Charges   The **Value Added Tax** (VAT) has in response to Greece's economic crisis been greatly increased—it now stands at 23% for many purchases and services, including restaurants and car rentals; food and medicine and certain other "vital goods" tend to have a VAT of 11% while books and newspapers have 5.5%. You may sometimes be given a printed receipt that shows these percentages, but the point to realize is that the taxes have already been included in the price quoted and charged. In addition to the VAT, hotel prices usually include a **service charge** of up to 12% and a "community tax," about 4% to 5%. (By the way, don't confuse any of these charges with many restaurants' "cover charge" that may be .50€–2€ per place setting.) Also see "Tipping," p. 300.

If you have purchased an item that costs 100€ or more and are a citizen of a non–European Union nation, you can get most of the VAT refunded (provided you export it within 90 days of purchase). It's easiest to shop at stores that display the sign **"Tax-Free for Tourists."** However, any store should be able to provide you with a Tax-Free Check Form, which you complete in the store. If you use your charge card, the receipt will list the VAT separately from the cost of the item. As you are leaving the country,

present a copy of this form to the refund desk (usually at the Customs office). Be prepared to show both the goods and the receipt as proof of purchase. Also be prepared to wait a fair amount of time before you get the refund. (In fact, the process at the airport seems designed to discourage you from trying to obtain the refund.)

Telephones   Public phones take prepaid phone cards, available at OTE offices or at most kiosks. The cards come in various denominations, from 3€ to 25€. The more costly the card, the cheaper the units. The cost of a call with a phone card varies greatly depending on local, domestic, and international rates. A local call of up to 3 minutes to a fixed phone costs about .10€, which is three units from a phone card; for each minute beyond that, it costs another .06€, or two units off the card (so that a 10-min. local call costs 17 units, or .52€). All calls, even to the house next door, cost Greeks something, so if you use someone's telephone even for a local call, offer to pay the charges.

In larger cities and larger towns, kiosks have telephones from which you can make local calls for .10€ for 3 minutes. (In remote areas, you can make long-distance calls from these phones.) A few of the older public pay phones that required coins are still around, but it's better to buy a phone card. If you must use an older pay phone, deposit the required coin and listen for a dial tone, an irregular beep. A regular beep indicates that the line is busy.

Note: All phone numbers in Greece are 10 digits long, including the area code; the area code may range from 3 to 5 digits, and the number itself may range from 5 to 8 digits, but the total will always be 10. All (except for cellphones—see below) also precede the city/area code with a 2 and end that with a 0. For example, since the Athens city code was originally 1, it is now 210, followed by a seven-digit number. Most other numbers in Greece are six digits with a four-digit area code. In all cases, even if you are calling someone in the same building, you must dial all 10 digits.

Calling a **cellphone** (mobile) in Greece requires substituting a 6 for the 2 that precedes the area code.

Long-distance calls, both domestic and international, can be quite expensive in Greece, especially at hotels, which may add a surcharge of up to 100%, unless you have a telephone credit card from a major long-distance provider such as AT&T, MCI, or Sprint. But if possible, avoid making long-distance calls from a hotel; use your cellphone instead (see **Mobile Phones**, p. 294).

You can also make your long-distance call from an OTE office; these are centrally located in all decent-sized cities. At OTE offices,

a clerk will assign you a booth with a metered phone. You can pay with a phone card, international credit card, or cash. Collect calls take much longer.

To Call Greece from the United States, Canada, U.K., Australia, or New Zealand:

1. Dial the international access code: 011 from the U.S or Canada.; 00 from the U.K., Ireland, or New Zealand; or 0011 from Australia
2. Dial the country code: 30
3. Dial the city code (three to five digits) and then the number. *Note:* All numbers in Greece must have 10 digits, including the city code.

To Make International Calls from Within Greece

The easiest and cheapest way is to call your long-distance service provider before leaving home to determine the access number that you must dial in Greece. The principal access codes in Greece are: AT&T, ✆ **00800-1311;** MCI, ✆ **00800-1211;** and Sprint, ✆ **00800-1411.**

If you use the Greek phone system to make a direct call abroad—whether using an OTE office, a phone that takes cards, or a phone that takes coins—dial the country code plus the area code (omitting the initial zero, if any), then dial the number. Some country codes are: Australia, 0061; Canada, 001; Ireland, 00353; New Zealand, 0064; United Kingdom, 0044; and

United States, 001. Thus, if you wanted to call the British Embassy in Washington, D.C., you would dial 001-202-588-7800.

Note that if you are going to put all the charges on your phone card (that is, not on your long-distance provider), you will be charged at a high rate per minute (at least 3€ to North America), so you should not make a call unless your phone card's remaining value can cover it.

For Operator Assistance: If you need operator assistance in making a call, dial ✆ **139** if you're trying to make an international call and ✆ **169** if you want to call a number in Greece.

Toll-Free Numbers: Numbers beginning with **080** within Greece are toll-free, but calling an 800 number in the States from Greece is not toll-free. In fact, it costs the same as any overseas call.

Rechargeable Phone Cards: One of the newest, easiest, and cheapest ways to make calls while abroad is to sign on for a phone card that can be used in most countries and can be recharged (that is, money and therefore minutes added from your charge card account). To learn more about this card and its various other features, see **www.ekit.com**.

Time The European 24-hour clock is used to measure time, so on schedules you'll see noon as 1200, 3:30pm as 1530, and 11pm as 2300. In informal conversation, however,

Greeks express time much as we do—though noon may mean anywhere from noon to 3pm, afternoon is 3 to 7pm, and evening is 7pm to midnight.

Greece is 2 hours ahead of Greenwich Mean Time. In reference to North American time zones, it's 7 hours ahead of Eastern Standard Time, 8 hours ahead of Central Standard Time, 9 hours ahead of Mountain Standard Time, and 10 hours ahead of Pacific Standard Time. Note that Greece does observe daylight saving time, although it may not start and stop on the same days as in North America.

Tipping Restaurant bills include a service charge, yet it is customary to leave a tip. Good service merits a tip of 5% to 10%, or round up, so 17€, say, becomes 20€. Greeks rarely tip taxi drivers, but tourists are expected to, at least by rounding cents up to a full euro figure. Hotel chambermaids should be left about 2€ per night per couple. Bellhops and doormen should be tipped 1€ to 5€, depending on the services they provide.

Toilets Most Greek establishments—hotels, restaurants, museums, and so on—provide clean and well-equipped facilities, but often in Athens and almost always on the islands, you may still be asked to deposit toilet paper in a container beside the toilet. In cheaper and more remote restaurants,

however, you may find that there is no water at the hand bowl or a shortage of toilet paper; you might consider carrying some tissues with you.

Public restrooms are generally available in any good-size Greek town, and though they are sometimes rather crude, they usually do work. (Old-fashioned stand-up/squat facilities are still found.) If there is an attendant, you are expected to leave a small tip. In an emergency, you can ask to use the facilities of a restaurant or shop; however, near major attractions, the facilities are denied to all but customers, because traffic is too heavy. If you use any such facilities, respect its sponsor and give an attendant a tip.

Travelers with Disabilities Few concessions exist for travelers with disabilities in Greece. Steep steps, uneven pavements, almost no cuts at curbstones, few ramps, narrow walks, slick stone, and traffic congestion create obstacles. The stepped streets of Santorini and other islands are especially difficult to navigate, as are archaeological sites, by their very nature. An elevator takes individuals in wheelchairs to the top of the Acropolis; but even this requires that the wheelchair be pushed up a lengthy path.

The new airport and the Athens Metro system are wheelchair accessible, however, and more modern and private facilities are beginning to provide ramps.

Increasingly, hotels are setting aside rooms that they advertise as "disability-friendly" or "handicap accessible," although that may mean nothing more than handrails in the bathtub. Nonetheless, foreigners in wheelchairs—accompanied by companions—are becoming a more common sight in Greece. Several travel agencies now offer customized tours and itineraries for travelers with disabilities; one is the British-based **Makin' Tracks** (www.makintracks.eu). A number of agencies offer customized tours and itineraries for travelers with disabilities. Among them are **Flying Wheels Travel** (www.flyingwheelstravel.com; ✆ **877/451-5006**) and **Accessible Journeys** (www.disabilitytravel.com; ✆ **800/846-4537**).

Visitor Information The **Greek National Tourism Organization** (**GNTO** or **EOT** in Greece—and increasingly referred to as the Hellenic Tourism Organization) has offices throughout the world that can provide you with information concerning all aspects of travel to and in Greece. Look for them at **www.gnto.gr** or contact one of the following GNTO offices:

United States Olympic Tower, 645 Fifth Ave., 5th Floor, New York, NY 10022 (✆ **212/421-5777**).

Australia & New Zealand 37–49 Pitt St., Sydney, NSW 2000 (✆ **29/241-1663**).

Canada 1500 Donmills Rd., Toronto, ON M3B 3K4 (☎ 416/968-2220).

United Kingdom & Ireland 4 Conduit St., London W1S 2DJ (☎ 207/495-9300).

Among the sites we've used for broad-based searches on Greece are:

o **www.mfa.gr** (official Greek matters)

o **www.gtp.gr** (ship and air travel in Greece)

o **www.phantis.com** (current news about Greece)

o **www.culture.gr** (official site for Greek's cultural attractions)

o **www.perseus.tufts. edu** (classical Greek texts)

Water The public drinking water in Greece is safe to drink, although it can be slightly brackish in some locales near the sea. For that reason, many people prefer the bottled water available at restaurants, hotels, cafes, food stores, and kiosks. If you do order bottled water, you will have to choose between natural or carbonated (*metalliko*), and domestic or imported.

Women Travelers
Young women—especially singles or small groups—may well find Greek males coming on to them, especially at beaches, clubs, and other tourist locales, in a rather forward manner. But our informants tell us that, in general, Greek males (a) do not attempt any physical contact; and (b) sooner or later respect "No." One tactic said to work for women is to say, "I'm a Greek-American." The other advice is not to leave well-attended locales with someone you don't really know. Women should also be aware that some cafes and even restaurants are effectively male-only haunts; men will not appreciate attempts by foreign women to enter these places.

USEFUL WORDS & PHRASES

When you're asking for or about something and have to rely on single words or short phrases, it's an excellent idea to use *"sas parakaló,"* meaning "please" or "you're welcome" to introduce or conclude almost anything you say.

Airport	Aerothrómio
Automobile	Aftokínito
Avenue	Leofóros
Bad	Kakós, -kí, -kó*
Bank	Trápeza
Breakfast	Proinó
Bus	Leoforío
Can you tell me?	Boríte ná moú píte?
Cheap	Ft(h)inó
Church	Ekklissía
Closed	Klistós, stí, stó*
Coffeehouse	Kafenío
Cold	Kríos, -a, -o*
Dinner	Vrathinó
Do you speak English?	Miláte Angliká?
Excuse me.	Signómi(n).
Expensive	Akrivós, -í, -ó*
Farewell!	Stóka-ló! (*to person leaving*)

Glad to meet you.	Chéro polí.**
Good	Kalós, lí, ló*
Goodbye.	Adío or chérete.**
Good evening.	Kalispéra.
Good health (cheers)!	Stín (i)yá sas or Yá-mas!
Good morning or Good day.	Kaliméra.
Good night.	Kaliníchta.**
Hello!	Yássas or chérete!**
Here	Ethó
Hot	Zestós, -stí, -stó*
Hotel	Xenothochío**
How are you?	Tí kánete or Pós íst(h)e?
How far?	Pósso makriá?
How long?	Póssi óra or Pósso(n) keró?
How much does it cost?	Póso káni?
I am a vegetarian.	Íme hortophágos.
I am from New York.	Íme apótí(n) Néa(n) lórki.
I am lost or I have lost the way.	Écho chathí or Écho chási tón drómo(n).**
I'm sorry.	Singnómi.
I'm sorry, but I don't speak Greek (well).	Lipoúme, allá thén miláo elliniká (kalá).
I don't understand.	Thén katalavéno.
I don't understand, please repeat it.	Thén katalavéno, péste to páli, sás parakaló.
It's (not) all right.	(Dén) íne en dáxi.
I want a glass of beer.	Thélo éna potíri bíra.
I want to go to the airport.	Thélo ná páo stóaerothrómio.
I would like a room.	Tha íthela ena thomátio.
Left (direction)	Aristerá
Lunch	Messimerianó
Map	Chártis**
Market (place)	Agorá
Mr.	Kírios
Mrs.	Kiría
My name is . . .	Onomázome . . .
New	Kenoúryos, -ya, -yo*
No	Óchi**
Old	Paleós, -leá, -leó* (pronounce palyós, -lyá, -lyó)
Open	Anichtós, -chtí, -chtó*
Patisserie	Zacharoplastío**
Pharmacy	Pharmakío
Please or You're welcome.	Parakaló.
Please call a taxi (for me).	Parakaló, fonáxte éna taxi (yá ména).
Point out to me, please . . .	Thíkste mou, sas parakaló . . .
Post office	Tachidromío**
Restaurant	Estiatório

Restroom	Tóméros or I toualétta
Right (direction)	Dexiá
Saint	Áyios, ayía, (plural) áyi-i (abbreviated ay)
Show me on the map.	Díxte mou stó(n) chárti**
Square	Plateia
Station (bus, train)	Stathmos (leoforíou, trénou)
Stop (bus)	Stási(s) (leoforíou)
Street	Odós
Thank you (very much).	Efcharistó(polí).**
Today	Símera
Tomorrow	Ávrio
Very nice	Polí oréos, -a, -o*
Very well	Polí kalá or En dáxi
What?	Tí?
What's your name?	Pós onomázest(h)e?
What time is it?	Tí ôra íne?
Where am I?	Pou íme?
Where is . . . ?	Poú íne . . . ?
Why?	Yatí?

*Masculine ending -os, feminine ending -a or -i, neuter ending -o.

**Remember, *ch* should be pronounced as in Scottish *loch* or German *ich,* not as in the word *church.*

Numbers

0	Midén
1	Éna
2	Dío
3	Tría
4	Téssera
5	Pénde
6	Éxi
7	Eftá
8	Októ
9	Enyá
10	Déka
11	Éndeka
12	Dódeka
13	Dekatría
14	Dekatéssera
15	Dekapénde
16	Dekaéxi
17	Dekaeftá
18	Dekaoktó
19	Dekaenyá

20	Íkossi
21	Íkossi éna
22	Íkossi dío
30	Triánda
40	Saránda
50	Penínda
60	Exínda
70	Evdomínda
80	Ogdónda
90	Enenínda
100	Ekató(n)
101	Ekatón éna
102	Ekatón dío
150	Ekatón penínda
151	Ekatón penínda éna
152	Ekatón penínda dío
200	Diakóssya
300	Triakóssya
400	Tetrakóssya
500	Pendakóssya
600	Exakóssya
700	Eftakóssya
800	Oktakóssya
900	Enyakóssya
1,000	Chílya*
2,000	Dío chilyádes*
3,000	Trís chilyádes*
4,000	Tésseris chilyádes*
5,000	Pénde chilyádes*

*Remember, *ch* should be pronounced as in Scottish *loch* or German *ich*, not as in the word *church*.

Days of the Week

Monday	Deftéra
Tuesday	Tríti
Wednesday	Tetárti
Thursday	Pémpti
Friday	Paraskeví
Saturday	Sávvato
Sunday	Kiriakí

SOME COMMON MENU ITEMS

Below are translations of several words you'll see while ordering from Greek menus. *Kali orexi*—bon appétit!

Arní	**Lamb**
Brizóla	**Steak**
Gigandes	**Giant beans**
Horiátiki	**Greek salad**
Kafe	**Coffee**
Keftedes	**Meatballs**
Kotópoulo	**Chicken**
Meli	**Honey**
Mezedes	**Appetizers or small dishes, like tapas**
Moussaka	**Eggplant casserole with béchamel sauce**
Nehro	**Water**
Octapódi	**Octopus**
Spanakopita	**Spinach pie**
Stifad	**A stew of meat, tomatoes, onions, and herbs**
Tsáee	**Tea**
Tzatziki	**A sauce of yogurt, cucumbers, and garlic**
Yiaoúrti	**Yogurt**

Index

Restaurants

Photo Credits

Map List

Published by
FROMMER MEDIA LLC

ISBN 978-1-62887-286-6 (paper), 978-1-62887-287-3 (e-book)

Editorial Director: Pauline Frommer
Editor: Holly Hughes
Production Editor: Donna Wright
Cartographer: Roberta Stockwell
Photo Editor: Helen Stallion
Indexer: Maro Riofrancos
Cover Designer: Howard Grossman

For information on our other products or services, see www.frommers.com. Frommer Media LLC also publishes its books in a variety of electronic formats.

Manufactured in the United States of America

5 4 3 2 1

HOW TO CONTACT US

In researching this book, we discovered many wonderful places—hotels, restaurants, shops, and more. We're sure you'll find others. Please tell us about them, so we can share the information with your fellow travelers in upcoming editions. If you were disappointed with a recommendation, we'd love to know that, too. Please write to: Support@FrommerMedia.com

ABOUT THE AUTHOR

Stephen Brewer is a book and magazine writer who spent a summer discovering Crete 30 years ago and has been returning ever since. While he's partial to Sivas, a tiny Cretan village on the south coast, he's never stepped foot on another Greek island he didn't like. He's also spent much time hiking around Olympia and Nafplion and exploring other parts of the Peloponnese as well as Athens. From home bases in New York and Italy, he also writes about England, Scotland, Germany, and Italy for *Frommer's Travel Guides*.

ABOUT THE FROMMER'S TRAVEL GUIDES

For most of the past 50 years, Frommer's has been the leading series of travel guides in North America, accounting for as many as 24% of all guidebooks sold. I think I know why. Although we hope our books are entertaining, we nevertheless deal with travel in a serious fashion. Our guidebooks have never looked on such journeys as a mere recreation, but as a far more important human function, a time of learning and introspection, an essential part of a civilized life. We stress the culture, lifestyle, history, and beliefs of the destinations we cover and urge our readers to seek out people and new ideas as the chief rewards of travel.

We have never shied from controversy. We have, from the beginning, encouraged our authors to be intensely judgmental, critical—both pro and con—in their comments, and wholly independent. Our only clients are our readers, and we have triggered the ire of countless prominent sorts, from a tourist newspaper we called "practically worthless" (it unsuccessfully sued us) to the many rip-offs we've condemned.

And because we believe that travel should be available to everyone regardless of their incomes, we have always been cost-conscious at every level of expenditure. Although we have broadened our recommendations beyond the budget category, we insist that every lodging we include be sensibly priced. We use every form of media to assist our readers and are particularly proud of our feisty daily website, the award-winning Frommers.com.

I have high hopes for the future of Frommer's. May these guidebooks, in all the years ahead, continue to reflect the joy of travel and the freedom that travel represents. May they always pursue a cost-conscious path, so that people of all incomes can enjoy the rewards of travel. And may they create, for both the traveler and the persons among whom we travel, a community of friends, where all human beings live in harmony and peace.

Arthur Frommer